The
Greatest
Disaster Stories
Ever Told

The
Greatest
Disaster Stories
Ever Told

EDITED BY

LAMAR UNDERWOOD

THE LYONS PRESS
Guilford, Connecticut
An imprint of The Globe Pequot Press

The Lyons Press is an imprint of the Globe Pequot Press.

Printed in The United States of America

10 9 8 7 6 5 4 3 2 1

ISBN 1–58574–615–0
The Library of Congress Cataloging-in-Publication Data is available on file.

Contents

Introduction

Although I have no credentials whatsoever for speaking in phrases like a psychologist or psychiatrist or philosopher, I suspect that I am safe in saying that my reactions to great disasters are fairly ordinary. Certainly I am not alone when newspaper headlines and radio and television voices and images pull me into news of tragedy and suffering. I do not look away. On the contrary, I am eager to learn what happened, to know the details of the catastrophe that has suddenly befallen innocent people just like myself, even small children and babies. "There but for the grace of God . . . " The words are old, and I know they are true.

The sheer randomness of natural disasters and the seemingly inevitable breakdowns of man's complex technological dependencies are disturbing to contemplate and downright heart wrenching to witness. We cannot merely shrug and say, "Those folks were in the wrong place at the wrong time. Bad luck." Out of the turmoil and pain must come some answers to the great question, "Why?"—and some courses of action that will hopefully prevent such events from occurring again. Scientists and meteorologists study terrain and weather in an attempt to create warnings that will save lives when Mother Nature runs amok with hurricanes, tornadoes, and earthquakes. Investigators probe the ruins left by man-caused disasters—the plane crashes, shipwrecks, great fires, chemical and nuclear catastrophes. Life moves on, but the mirror to the past is replete with images of horrific events that have been burned into remembrance. They are reminders that the price of carelessness, recklessness, or ignorance can reap a deadly toll.

Wherever, whenever great disasters strike, most of us feel something of the horror of the victims' plights. Our hearts go out to them and their families, no matter how far away the events took place. At the time I am writing these words a jet filled with Russian schoolchildren on their way to summer vacation has crashed in Europe in a terrible mid-air collision. The photographs of the shocked and grieving parents are still in my mind, days after the event. The world seems a small place at such times.

A disaster that occurs close to where we live and work is obviously the ultimate shocker. Our neighbors have been struck down. The very world we live in seems torn asunder. I personally have seen and felt that happen. I work in New York City, and I was there on 9/11. Like millions of other New Yorkers, I was unharmed and safe but within plain sight of the slaughter of our fellow citizens in the World Trade Center buildings. For those of us standing on the streets or looking out windows, gazing into the holocaust we were powerless to stop, the experience was excruciating. The anguish was just as strong, I am sure, for television viewers all over the world, staring at the images that instantly transported them to the scene.

A characteristic shared by most great disasters is that they draw writers like moths to lights. First come the reporters. Later, when the events have long since departed the front pages and nightly network news reports, other writers will be engrossed with the work of telling the full story of what happened. Sometimes these scribes have personal connections to the event, and their sensibilities are stirred to the ultimate. In other cases, we see the inquisitive mind of the professional journalist at work, probing to bring the truth to public attention. With the event long past, everybody knows *what* happened. But the stories and books that appear months, even years, after the disaster took place will reveal *why* it happened, and the plight and suffering of the victims. The drama of narrow escapes will be documented, the bravery of heroes, the cowardice of the weak and panicked. These are the writers who have been so touched by the events of the disaster, that they feel duty-bound to make sure the story is fully told, down to the smallest details. The disaster stories selected for this book have been chosen with such writers in mind.

Here you will find such eminent authors as David McCullough, Dan Kurzman, and Walter Lord, all of whom have produced bestsellers on many subjects. In addition, you will see the names of many distinguished and talented writers whose bylines and prose may not be familiar to you but whose interest in certain great disasters has inspired them to write books that are absolutely riveting.

In addition to choosing good writers and storytellers, I have tried to bring together a variety of disaster stories related more to the drama of the situation than to numbers of lives lost or damaged inflicted. The Challenger Space Shuttle disaster only took eight lives, for instance, but the event was significant and deeply sad. Selecting stories on the basis of body counts was never something I had in mind. Instead, I have sought disaster stories that are the most dramatic and illuminating I could find. I have focused on good reading instead of scientific explanations. I have looked for prose with the feeling of putting me on the scene of the disaster as it took place. I have tried to learn the answer to the question, "What was it like?"

The disaster stories you will find here range through events as recent as the World Trade Center attacks to the Johnstown Flood of 1889. The stories focus on tragedies that shocked the world, including the eruption of Mount St. Helens; the sinking of the Titanic, the Lusitania, and the U.S.S. Indianapolis; the Hartford, Connecticut circus fire; the Bhopal catastrophe, and many others too numerous to mention without repeating the contents page. Obviously, it was not possible in the pages of a single book to include stories of every single natural and man-made disaster throughout history, or even of every event of the most recent century. Instead, my goal as editor has been to concentrate on finding and presenting the most readable stories of great disasters that were terrifying to behold and tore hearts and souls loose from the moorings of safety and contentment. Many of the events described led to landmark changes in safety procedures, laws, and technology—changes paid for by human lives lost. An example is the Chicago My Lady of Angels catholic school fire of 1958, in which 92 children and three nuns burned to death despite the fact that the school was only two blocks from the fire station. [See "To Sleep With Angels," by David Cowan and John Kuenster.] The tragedy led to sweeping changes nationwide in school evacuation procedures and safety regulations. The same thing occurred after many of the other disasters described in this book.

As your editor, I can honestly say I will be surprised if there are not times when reading these stories that you will find yourself blinking through misty eyes. The events seem poignant with deep sorrow at times, inspirational with courage and dedication at others. Everything that follows really happened. As you will see, those who perished, and those who somehow survived, have not been forgotten.

—Lamar Underwood
July, 2002

The
Greatest
Disaster Stories
Ever Told

PART ONE

Terrorist Attacks: Evil At Its Ultimate

9/11: Tower One

BY MICHAEL WRIGHT

Interviewed for Esquire Magazine by Cal Fussman

So many memorable personal accounts of survivors, firefighters and police concerning the attacks of 9/11 have been published in books, magazines and on the internet, that singling out one for its impact is a somewhat daunting enterprise. For this reader, however, one story seems so meaningful and strong that it cries out to reach as large an audience as possible.

When *Esquire* Magazine presented Michael Wright's account of the 9/11 tragedy in the January, 2002, issue, the editors prefaced the piece with the following blurb:

"At 8:48 on the morning of September 11, Michael Wright was a thirty-year-old account executive working on the eighty-first floor of the Word Trade Center. Two hours later, he was something else. The story of his escape is the fastest 3,863 words you will ever read."

The editors were right.

✳   ✳   ✳   ✳   ✳

Up to that day, I'd had a *Brady Bunch,* cookie-cutter, beautiful life. I now know what it's like to have a 110-story building that's been hit by a 767 come down on my head. For better or for worse, it's part of my life. There are things I never thought I'd know that I now know.

It was as mundane a morning as you can imagine. Tuesdays are usually the days I go out to see clients and make sales calls. I get to my office at a quarter to eight, eat a bran muffin, drink a cup of coffee, and get my head straight for the day.

I was actually in a good mood. A couple of us were yukking it up in the men's room. We'd just started sharing the eighty-first floor of 1 World Trade

Center with Bank of America, and they'd put up a sign telling everyone to keep the bathroom clean. "Look at this," one of us said. "They move in and now they're giving us shit." It was about quarter to nine.

All of a sudden, there was the shift of an earthquake. People ask, "Did you hear a boom?" No. The way I can best describe it is that every joint in the building jolted. You ever been in a big old house when a gust of wind comes through and you hear all the posts creak? Picture that creaking being not a matter of inches but of feet. We all got knocked off balance. One guy burst out of a stall buttoning up his pants, saying, "What the *fuck*?" The flex caused the marble walls in the bathroom to crack.

You're thinking, gas main. It was so percussive, so close. I opened the bathroom door, looked outside, and saw fire.

There was screaming. One of my coworkers, Alicia, was trapped in the women's room next door. The doorjamb had folded in on itself and sealed the door shut. This guy Art and another guy started kicking the shit out of the door, and they finally got her out.

There was a huge crack in the floor of the hallway that was about half a football field long, and the elevator bank by my office was completely blown out. If I'd walked over, I could've looked all the way down. Chunks of material that had been part of the wall were in flames all over the floor. Smoke was everywhere.

I knew where the stairs were because a couple of guys from my office used to smoke butts there. I started screaming, "Out! Out! Out!" The managers were trying to keep people calm and orderly, and here I was screaming, "The stairs! The stairs!"

We got to the stairwell, and people were in various states. Some were in shock; some were crying. We started filing down in two rows, fire-drill style. I'd left my cell phone at my desk, but my coworkers had theirs. I tried my wife twenty times but couldn't get through. Jenny had gone up to Boston with her mother and grandmother and was staying with my family. Our son was with her. Ben's six months old. It was impossible to reach them.

The thing that kept us calm on the stairs was the thought that what happened couldn't possibly happen. The building could not come down. After a while, as we made our way down, we started to lighten up. Yeah, we knew something bad had happened, but a fire doesn't worry you as much when you're thirty floors below it. I even made an off-color joke to my buddy Ryan. The intent was for only Ryan to hear, but things quieted down just as I said it, so everyone heard. I said, "Ryan, *hold* me."

He said, "Mike . . . I didn't know."

I said, "Well, we're all going to die, might as well tell you."

Some people were laughing, but not the guy in front of me. "I really think you should keep that humor down!" he said. I felt lousy. In hindsight, he may have known more than I did. Even though I'd seen physical damage, what I can't stress enough is how naïve I was at that point.

Some floors we'd cruise down; others we'd wait for ten minutes. People were speculating, "Was it a bomb?" But we were all getting out. I didn't think I was going to die.

At the fortieth floor, we started coming in contact with firemen. They were saying, "C'mon, down you go! Don't worry, it's safe below." Most of them were stone-faced. Looking back, there were some frightened firemen.

When we got below the thirtieth floor, they started to bring down injured people from flights above. There was a guy with the back of his shirt burned off, a little burn on his shoulder. One woman had severe burns on her face.

We got down to the twentieth floor and a fireman said, "Does anyone know CPR?" I'm no longer certified, but I know it from college. That was ten years ago. You wouldn't want me on an EMT team, but if it comes down to saving somebody, I know how.

So me and this other guy volunteer. We helped this one heavy, older man who came down huffing and puffing, and we kept our eyes out for anyone else. "Do you need help? Do you need help?" Nobody needed help. The stairway became wide-open. It was time to go. The other guy took off in front of me. We were going pretty fast.

Have you ever been to the World Trade Center? There's a mezzanine level, then you go downstairs, which is subterranean, into this big mall. Our stairwell exited out onto that mezzanine level. At that point, I could look out across the plaza at 2 World Trade Center. That's when I realized the gravity of what had happened. I saw dead bodies everywhere, and none that I saw were intact. It was hard to tell how many. Fifty maybe? I scanned for a second and then focused on the head of a young woman with some meat on it. I remember my hand coming up in front of my face to block the sight. Then I took off. As I ran, people were coming out of another stairwell. I stopped and said, "Don't look outside! Don't look outside!" The windows were stained with blood. Someone who'd jumped had fallen very close to the building.

It felt like my head was going to blow up.

I made it to the stairwell and got down. The mall was in bad shape. It must have been from chunks of the plane coming down. Windows were smashed. Sprinklers were on.

I saw Alicia, the coworker who'd been trapped in the bathroom. She'd seen what I'd seen in the plaza and was traumatized. She was crying and moving slowly. I put my arm around her. Then there was another woman—same thing. I put my arm around the two of them, saying, "C'mon. We gotta go. We gotta go."

We were moving through the mall toward the escalator that would take us back up to street level and out to Church Street. There were some emergency workers giving us the "head this way" sign. I think they were trying to get us as far away from the fire as possible and out toward Church Street and the Millenium Hilton hotel.

I got to the bottom of the escalator, and that's when I heard what sounded like a *crack*. That was the beginning of it. I ran to the top of the escalator as fast as I could and looked east, out toward Church Street at the Millenium hotel. The windows of the hotel are like a mirror, and in the reflection I saw Tower Two coming down.

How do you describe the sound of a 110-story building coming down directly above you? It sounded like what it was: a deafening tidal wave of building material coming down on my head. It appeared to be falling on the street directly where I was headed.

I turned to run back into the building. It was the instinctual thing to do. You're thinking, If you stay outside, you're running *into* it. If you go inside, it might not land there. So I turned and ran into the building, down into the mall, and that's when it hit. I dove to the ground, screaming at the top of my lungs, "Oh, no! Oh, no! Jenny and Ben! Jenny and Ben!" It wasn't a very creative response, but it was the only thing I could say. I was gonna die.

The explosion was extreme, the noise impossible to describe. I started crying. It's hard for me to imagine now that when I was on the ground awaiting my doom, hearing that noise, thousands of people were dying. That noise is a noise thousands of people heard when they died.

When it hit, everything went instantly black. You know how a little kid packs a pail of sand at the beach? That's what it was like in my mouth, my nose, my ears, my eyes—everything packed with debris. I spat it out. I puked, mostly out of horror. I felt myself: Am I intact? Can I move? I was all there. There was moaning. People were hurt and crying all around me.

Then I had my second reckoning with death. I'm alive, yeah. But I'm trapped beneath whatever fell on top of me and this place is filled with smoke and dust. This is how I'm gonna die—and this was worse. Because I was going to be cognizant of my death. I was going to be trapped in a hole and it was going to fill with smoke and they were going to find me like one of those guys buried in Pompeii.

I sat there thinking of my wife and son again. It wasn't like seeing the photos of Jenny and Ben that I had on my desk, though. The images I had were of them *without* me. Images of knowing that I'd never touch them again. As I sat there, thinking of them, I suddenly got this presence of mind: *I gotta try to survive.*

I tore off my shirt and wrapped it around my mouth and nose to keep some of the smoke out. I started crawling. It was absolutely pitch-black. I had no idea where I was crawling to, but I had to keep trying. It's haunting to think about it now.

I saw a light go on. I can't say I was happy, because I was horrified, but that light was hope.

Luckily, I was buried with a fireman. I got over to him and stuck to this guy like a sticky burr on a bear's ass. He was frazzled, but he had it a lot more together than I did. I was like, "What are we gonna *do?*" You can't imagine the ability to have rational thought at that point. I was purely in survival mode. It wasn't like, The smoke is traveling this way, so I'll go that way to the fresh air. It's whatever presents itself.

The fireman looked like a big Irish guy. Big, bushy mustache. He had an axe. He was looking at a wall, and it looked solid, but when he wiped his hand on it, it was glass, a glass wall looking into a Borders bookstore. There was a door right next to it. He smashed the door and it spread open.

Everyone gravitated to the light. Now there was a bunch of us. People were screaming. We got into Borders, went upstairs, and got through the doors heading outside. The dust was so thick, there was barely any light.

At this point, I still had no idea what was going on. I didn't know if we were being bombed or what. I didn't know if this was over or if it was just beginning.

I took off into the cloud. I crossed Church Street, and some light started coming in, and I could see a little bit. I saw a woman standing there, horrified, crying, lost. I stopped and said, "Are you okay? Are you okay?" She couldn't speak. I kept going.

I went along Vesey Street, using it as a guide. It started clearing up more and more, and I got to an intersection that was completely empty. That's where I saw one of the weirdest things—a cameraman near a van with the NBC peacock on it, doubled over with his camera, crying.

I was all disoriented. I saw a turned-over bagel cart, and I grabbed a couple of Snapples. I used one to rinse out my mouth and wash my face. I drank some of the other. Then I started running again. It was chaos.

Even though I'd been around these streets a million times, I was completely lost. I looked up and saw my building, 1 World Trade Center, in flames.

I looked for the other tower because I always use the two buildings as my North Star. I couldn't see it. I stood there thinking, *It doesn't make sense.* At that angle, it was apparent how devastating it all was. I looked up and said, "Hundreds of people died today." I was trying to come to terms with it—to intellectualize it. My wife's family is Jewish, and her grandparents talk about the Holocaust and the ability of humans to be cruel and kill one another. This is a part of a pattern of human behavior, I told myself. And I just happen to be very close to this one.

Maybe it seems an odd reaction in hindsight. But I was just trying to grab on to something, some sort of logic or justification, rather than let it all overwhelm me. I was raised Irish-Catholic, and I consider myself a spiritual person. I did thank God for getting me out of there for my kid. But I also tend to be a pretty logical thinker. I'm alive because I managed to find a space that had enough support structure that it didn't collapse on me. I'm alive because the psycho in the plane decided to hit at *this* angle as opposed to *that* angle. I'm alive because I went down *this* stairwell instead of *that* stairwell. I can say that now. But at that moment, I was just trying to give myself some sanity.

I was still running when I heard another huge sound. I didn't know it at the time, but it was the other tower—*my* tower—coming down. A cop on the street saw me and said, "Buddy, are you okay?" It was obvious that he was spooked by looking at me. Aside from being caked with dust, I had blood all over me that wasn't mine. He was trying to help, but I could tell he was shocked by what he was seeing.

I was looking for a pay phone to call my wife, but every one I passed was packed. My wife never entertained for a minute that I could be alive. She had turned on the TV and said, "Eighty-first floor. Both buildings collapsed. There's not a prayer." It was difficult for her to look at Ben because she was having all these feelings. "Should I be grateful that I have him? Is he going to be a reminder of Mike every time I look at him?" At the time, these thoughts just go through your head.

Finally, I got to a pay phone where there was a woman just kind of looking up. I shoved her out of the way. I guess it was kind of harsh, but I had to get in touch with my family. I dialed Boston and a recording said, "Six dollars and twenty-five cents, please." So I pulled out a quarter and called my brother at NYU. I got his voice mail. "I'm alive! I'm alive! Call Jenny! Let everyone know I'm alive!" It was 10:34.

I started running toward where my brother Chris worked at NYU. I'm the last of six in my family. The two oldest are girls, the four youngest, boys. Chris is the second oldest above me. The classic older brother. The one who'd put you down and give you noogies. He probably would have had the best view of the whole thing going on. But he'd left his office, thinking, My brother is dead. He walked home to Brooklyn across the Manhattan Bridge, unable to look back.

On my way to NYU, I met this guy—a stranger named Gary—who had a cell phone. He tried and tried and couldn't get through to Boston. I said, "I gotta get to NYU" and left him. But he kept calling Boston and eventually got through to my family. At that point, four of my five siblings were at the house. My wife's father was on his way from New York with a black suit in the car.

The people at NYU took me in. They were great. I said, "I don't need anything. Just call my family." They kept on trying to get through. They couldn't, they couldn't. Finally, they got through.

I said, "Jenny, it's me." And there was a moan. It was this voice I'd never heard before in my life. And I was saying, "I'm alive. I'm alive. I love you. I love you. I love you." We cried and cried. Then the phone went dead.

At that point, I went into the bathroom to clean myself off, and suddenly I couldn't open my eyes anymore. They were swollen. I knew I wasn't blind, but if I opened my eyes toward any amount of light there was intense, intense pain. I didn't feel this while I was running. It seemed to happen as soon as I was safe and the adrenaline came out of me.

At the NYU health center, the doctors said, "Yeah, your eyes are scratched to shit." They put drops in them, but they needed more sophisticated equipment to see what was going on. I wound up having 147 fiberglass splinters taken out of my eyes.

Chris came back from Brooklyn to pick me up, and I held on to him and hugged him. Later, he said, "You know, Michael, this is why I stuffed you in sleeping bags and beat on you all those years as a kid. Just to toughen you up for something like this."

When we got back to my place, I collapsed and it all hit me. I cried like I've never cried in my life. I finally let loose, and it felt better. My brother helped me pack, and we got to Westchester, where my wife and family had gone. Jenny came running to the door. I can remember hearing the *dum, dum, dum, dum, dum* of her footsteps.

My mother was there. My dad. My father-in-law. They all hugged me. Then they gave me my son. I could tell by the noises he was making that he was happy. I hugged him and sort of started the healing process there.

Later, I went to Maine to sit by the ocean for a few days and get my head together. I saw all of my old friends. It was amazing. Everyone I know in my life has called me to tell me they love me. It's like having your funeral without having to die.

For a while right after, I wondered, How the hell am I going to work again? How am I going to give a damn about selling someone a T-1 line? I had a list of people who were going to be my business for the next year, hundreds of people, all on my desk—blown up. For the life of me, I can't dredge up those names. That will cost me a quarter of my income, maybe more. You know what? Who cares? I'm alive and I'm here. A *big deal* has gone to big deal.

I lost a friend in 2 World Trade Center. He was one of those guys you liked as soon as you met him. Howard Boulton. Beautiful person. His baby was born three months ahead of mine. He was on the eighty-fourth floor and I was on the eighty-first. The last conversation he had with his wife was by telephone. He told her, "Something happened to 1 World Trade Center. It's very bad. I don't think Michael Wright is okay. I'm coming home." I like to think Howard wasn't scared like I wasn't scared in the stairwell. I like to think that he heard a rumble like I heard a rumble and then he was gone.

I went to his funeral. To see his wife and his baby—it would have made you sad even if you didn't know him. But it was much more loaded for me. Here was a perfect reflection of what could've been.

One of the hardest things I had to deal with up to this point—and still do—is that my brother Brian, who's one year older than me, has cancer. He and I are practically twins. He has germ-cell cancer in his chest. He recently told me that the good news is they can go in and get it. But the bad news is they might have to take a lung with it. Before September 11, maybe the fact that he was going to lose a lung might have thrown me for a loop. But I found out I love my brother for my brother. I don't love him to run up mountains at a brisk pace with me. My reaction was: Thank God they can get it.

Luckily, I've been well equipped to deal with this. I have a family that's unbelievably close and supportive and a lot of friends. I've been to therapy, and I can do the whole checklist: Do you have a sense of fear and not know where it's coming from? Yup. Can you no longer take pleasure in things you once took pleasure in? Yup. Claustrophobic? Yup. I have nightmares. I jump when I hear a siren. But it's the smell that haunts me. Talk to anyone who was within ten blocks of it and they'll tell you that. I had vaporized people packed up my nose, in my mouth and ears. For weeks, I was picking stuff out of my ears.

I've been giving myself the space to be a little freaky for a while. I don't think this is going to turn me into Rambo or motivate me to go out and sleep with nineteen-year-old girls. Yeah, it's gonna bug me for a while. I'm gonna have some scars on my brain. But I don't think it's going to affect me long term.

I don't wonder, Why me? Some people say, "You made it out; you're destined for great things." Great, I tell them. I made it out, now why not put a little pressure on me while you're at it.

9/11: The 102 Minutes

REPORTED AND WRITTEN FOR THE *NEW YORK TIMES*
BY JIM DWYER, ERIC LIPTON, KEVIN FLYNN, JAMES
GLANZ, AND FORD FESSENDEN

(Published in the Sunday New York Times, May 26, 2002)

The agony of the victims must never be forgotten. Nor their fights to live as the Towers died around them.

*   *   *   *   *

They began as calls for help, information, guidance. They quickly turned into soundings of desperation, and anger, and love. Now they are the remembered voices of the men and women who were trapped on the high floors of the twin towers.

From their last words, a haunting chronicle of the final 102 minutes at the World Trade Center has emerged, built on scores of phone conversations and e-mail and voice messages. These accounts, along with the testimony of the handful of people who escaped, provide the first sweeping views from the floors directly hit by the airplanes and above.

Collected by reporters for The New York Times, these last words give human form to an all but invisible strand of this stark, public catastrophe: the advancing destruction across the top 19 floors of the north tower and the top 33 of the south, where loss of life was most severe on Sept. 11. Of the 2,823 believed dead in the attack on New York, at least 1,946, or 69 percent, were killed on those upper floors, an analysis by The Times has found.

Rescue workers did not get near them. Photographers could not record their faces. If they were seen at all, it was in glimpses at windows, nearly a quarter-mile up.

Yet like messages in an electronic bottle from people marooned in some distant sky, their last words narrate a world that was coming undone. A man sends an e-mail message asking, "Any news from the outside?" before perching on a ledge at Windows on the World. A woman reports a colleague is smacking useless sprinkler heads with his shoe. A husband calmly reminds his wife about their insurance policies, then says that the floor is groaning beneath him, and tells her that she and their children meant the world to him.

No single call can describe scenes that were unfolding at terrible velocities in many places. Taken together though, the words from the upper floors offer not only a broad and chilling view of the devastated zones, but the only window onto acts of bravery, decency, and grace at a brutal time.

Eight months after the attacks, many survivors and friends and relatives of those lost are pooling their recollections, tapes, and phone records, and 157 have shared accounts of their contacts for this article. At least 353 of those lost were able to reach people outside the towers. Spoken or written at the hour of death, these are intimate, lasting words. The steep emotional cost of making them public is worth paying, their families say, for a clearer picture of those final minutes.

Many also hope the history of the day is enlarged beyond memorials to the unquestioned valor of 343 firefighters and 78 other uniformed rescuers. It is time, they say, to account for the experiences of the 2,400 civilians who also died that day. Iliana McGinnis, whose husband, Tom, called her from the 92nd floor of the north tower, said, "If they can uncover even one more piece of information about what happened during those last minutes, I want it."

Some details remain unknowable. Working phones were scarce. The physical evidence was destroyed. Conversations were held under grave stress, and are recalled through grief, time, and longing. Even so, as one fragile bit of information elaborates on the next, they illuminate conditions on the top floors.

The evidence strongly suggests that 1,100 or more people in or above the impact zones survived the initial crashes, roughly 300 in the south tower and 800 in the north. Many of those lived until their building collapsed.

Even after the second airplane struck, an open staircase connected the upper reaches of the south tower to the street. The Times has identified 18 men and women who used it to escape from the impact zone or above. At the same time they were evacuating, at least 200 other people were climbing toward the roof in that tower, unaware that a passable stairway down was available, and assuming—incorrectly—that they could open the roof door. "The belief that they had a rooftop option cost them their lives," said Beverly Eckert, whose husband, Sean Rooney, called after his futile trek up.

Hundreds were trapped on floors untouched by the airplanes. Even though the buildings survived the initial impacts, the twisting and bending of the towers caused fatal havoc. Stairwells were plugged by broken wallboard. Doors were jammed in twisted frames. With more time and simple tools like crowbars, rescue workers might have freed people who simply could not get to stairways. In the north tower, at least 28 people were freed on the 86th and 89th floors by a small group of Port Authority office workers who pried open jammed doors. Those self-assigned rescuers died.

In both towers, scores of people lost chances to escape. Some paused to make one more phone call; others, to pick up a forgotten purse; still others, to perform tasks like freeing people from elevators, tending the injured, or comforting the distraught.

The crises had identical beginnings and endings in each tower, but ran different courses. At least 37 people, and probably well over 50, can be seen jumping or falling from the north tower, while no one is visible falling from the south tower, in a collection of 20 videotapes shot by amateurs and professionals from nearby streets and buildings. Both towers had similar volumes of smoke and heat, but in the north tower, about three times as many people were trapped in roughly half the space. Scores were driven to the windows of the north tower in search of relief. In the south tower, people had more opportunities to move between floors.

The impact zones formed pitiless boundaries between those who were spared and those who were doomed. Even at the margins, the collisions were devastating: the wingtip of the second plane grazed the 78th floor sky lobby in the south tower, instantly killing dozens of people waiting for elevators. In all, about 600 civilians died in the south tower at or above the plane's impact. In the north tower, every person believed to be above the 91st floor died: 1,344.

The farther from the impact, the more calls people made. In the north tower, pockets of near-silence extended four floors above and one floor below the impact zone. Yet remarkably, in both towers, even on floors squarely hit by the jets, a few people lived long enough to make calls.

To place these fragmentary messages in context, The Times interviewed family members, friends, and colleagues of those who died, obtained times of calls from cellphone bills and 911 records, analyzed 20 videotapes and listened to 15 hours of police and fire radio tapes.

The Times also interviewed 25 people who saw firsthand the destruction wreaked by the planes, because they escaped from the impact zone or above it in the south tower, or from just below it in the north.

8:00 North Tower, 107th Floor, Windows on the World, 2 hours 28 minutes to collapse

"Good morning, Ms. Thompson."

Doris Eng's greeting was particularly sunny, like the day, as Liz Thompson arrived for breakfast atop the tallest building in the city, Ms. Thompson remembers thinking. Perhaps Ms. Eng had matched her mood to the glorious weather, the rich blue September sky that filled every window. Or perhaps it was the company.

Familiar faces occupied many of the tables in Wild Blue, the intimate aerie to Windows that Ms. Eng helped manage, according to two people who ate there that morning. As much as any one place, that single room captured the sweep of humanity who worked and played at the trade center.

Ms. Thompson, executive director of the Lower Manhattan Cultural Council, was eating with Geoffrey Wharton, an executive with Silverstein Properties, which had just leased the towers. At the next table sat Michael Nestor, the deputy inspector general of the Port Authority of New York and New Jersey, and one of his investigators, Richard Tierney.

At a third table were six stockbrokers, several of whom came every Tuesday. Ms. Eng had a treat for one of them, Emeric Harvey. The night before, one of the restaurant's managers, Jules Roinnel, gave Ms. Eng two impossibly-hard-to-get tickets to "The Producers." Mr. Roinnel says he asked Ms. Eng to give them to Mr. Harvey.

Sitting by himself at a window table overlooking the Statue of Liberty was a relative newcomer, Neil D. Levin, the executive director of the Port Authority. He had never joined them for breakfast before. But his secretary requested a table days earlier and now he sat waiting for a banker friend, said Mr. Levin's wife, Christy Ferer.

Every other minute or so, a waiter, Jan Maciejewski, swept through the room, refilling coffee cups and taking orders, Mr. Nestor recalls. Mr. Maciejewski was one of several restaurant workers on the 107th floor. Most of the 72 Windows employees were on the 106th floor, where Risk Waters Group was holding a conference on information technology.

Already 87 people had arrived, including top executives from Merrill Lynch and UBS Warburg, according to the conference sponsors. Many were enjoying coffee and sliced smoked salmon in the restaurant's ballroom. Some exhibitors were already tending to their booths, set up in the Horizon Suite just across the hallway.

A picture taken that morning showed two exhibitors, Peter Alderman and William Kelly, salesmen for Bloomberg L.P., chatting with a colleague beside a table filled with a multi-screened computer display. Stuart Lee and Garth Feeney, two vice presidents of Data Synapse, ran displays of their company's software.

Down in the lobby, 107 floors below, an assistant to Mr. Levin waited for his breakfast guest. But when the guest arrived, he and Mr. Levin's aide luckily boarded the wrong elevator, Ms. Ferer would learn, and so they had to return to the lobby to wait for another one.

Upstairs, Mr. Levin read his newspaper, Mr. Nestor recalled. He and Mr. Tierney were a little curious to see whom Mr. Levin, their boss, was meeting for breakfast. But Mr. Nestor had a meeting downstairs, so they headed for the elevators, stopping at Mr. Levin's table to say goodbye. Behind them came Ms. Thompson and Mr. Wharton. Mr. Nestor held the elevator, so they hopped in quickly, Ms. Thompson recalled.

Then the doors closed and the last people ever to leave Windows on the World began their descent. It was 8:44 a.m.

8:46 North Tower, 91st Floor, American Bureau of Shipping, 1 hour 42 minutes to collapse

The impact came at 8:46:26 a.m. American Airlines Flight 11, a Boeing 767 measuring 156 feet from wingtip to wingtip and carrying 10,000 gallons of fuel, was moving at 470 miles an hour, federal investigators estimated. At that speed, it covered the final two blocks to the north tower in 1.2 seconds.

The plane ripped a path across floors 94 to 98, directly into the office of Marsh & McLennan Companies, shredding steel columns, wallboard, filing cabinets, and computer-laden desks. Its fuel ignited and incinerated everything in its way. The plane's landing gear hurtled through the south side of the building, winding up on Rector Street, five blocks away.

Just three floors below the impact zone, not a thing budged in Steve McIntyre's office. Not the family snapshots propped up on a bookcase. Mr. McIntyre found himself in front of a computer that was still on.

Then came the whiplash.

A powerful shock wave quickly radiated up and down from the impact zone. The wave bounced from the top to the bottom of the tower, three or four seconds one way and then back, rocking the building like a huge boat in a storm.

"We got to get the hell out of here," yelled Greg Shark, an American Bureau of Shipping engineer and architect, who was bracing himself in the swaying while he stood outside Mr. McIntyre's office.

Somehow, they were alive. Only later would the two men realize the slender margin of their escape. In their accounts of hunting for a way out, they provide a survey of a border territory, an impregnable zone through which the people imprisoned above would never pass.

Mr. McIntyre, Mr. Shark, and nine other employees, all uninjured, hustled out of the A.B.S. reception area in the northwest corner and turned left toward the elevators and stairways in the tower's core.

Mr. McIntyre recalls peering into a dim, shattered stairwell, billowing with smoke. He heard nothing but water cascading down the stairs, as if he had encountered a babbling brook on a mountain hike. The water almost certainly came from severed sprinkler pipes. Seeing and hearing no one else in the stinking gloom, he looked up.

The stairwell was blocked from above—not by fire or structural steel, but by huge pieces of the light gypsum drywall, often called Sheetrock, that had enclosed the stairwell to protect it. In huge hunks, the Sheetrock formed a great plug in the stairwell, sealing the passage from 92, the floor above. Going down the stairs, it made a slightly less formidable obstruction.

"This is no good," Mr. McIntyre would remember saying.

Mr. McIntyre could hardly have known it, but he stood at a critical boundary. Above him, across 19 floors, were 1,344 people, many of them alive, stunned, unhurt, calling for help. No one would survive.

Below, across 90 floors, thousands of others were also alive, stunned, unhurt, calling for help. Nearly all of them lived.

Bad as this staircase was, the two other emergency exits were worse, Mr. McIntyre later said. So he went back to that first staircase, northwest of the building's center. He stepped inside and immediately slipped down two flights of grimy gypsum. Unhurt, he stood and noticed lights below. He remembers calling: "This way!" His A.B.S. colleagues joined the exodus from 91.

One floor above them, on the 92nd floor, employees of Carr Futures were doing exactly what the A.B.S. people had done: hunting for a way out.

They did not realize they were on the wrong side of the rubble.

On the 92nd floor, Damian Meehan scrambled to a phone at Carr Futures and dialed his brother Eugene, a firefighter in the Bronx. "It's really bad here—the elevators are gone," Mr. Meehan told him.

"Get to the front door, see if there's smoke there," Eugene Meehan recalled urging him. He heard his brother put the phone down, then followed the sounds drifting into his ear. Yelling. Commotion, but not panic.

A few minutes later, Damian Meehan returned and reported that the front entrance was filled with smoke.

"Get to the stairs," Eugene remembered advising him. "See where the smoke is coming from. Go the other way."

Then he heard Damian for the last time.

"He said, 'We've got to go.' Or he said, 'We're going,'" Eugene Meehan said. "I've been racking my brains to remember.

"I know he said, 'We.'"

9:00 North Tower, 106th Floor, Windows on the World, 1 hour 28 minutes to collapse

"What do we do? What do we do?"

Doris Eng, the restaurant manager, called the Fire Command Center in the lobby repeatedly with that question, according to officials and co-workers. Just minutes after the plane hit, the restaurant was filling with smoke and she was struggling to direct the 170 people in her charge.

Many in the crowd made their living providing information or the equipment that carried it, communications experts taking part in the morning's conference in the ballroom. But with thickening smoke, no power and little sense of what was going on, the restaurant was fast becoming an isolation zone, where people scrambled for bits of news.

"Watch CNN," Stephen Tompsett, a computer scientist at the conference, e-mailed his wife, Dorry, using his BlackBerry communicator. "Need updates."

Videos from two amateur photographers show that the smoke built with terrifying speed at the top of the building, cascading thicker from seams in windows there than from floors closer to the plane. Early on, Rajesh Mirpuri called his company, Data Synapse, coughing, and said he could not see more than 10 feet, his boss, Peter Lee, would remember. Peter Alderman, the Bloomberg salesman, also told his sister about the smoke, using his BlackBerry to send an e-mail message: "I'm scared."

Ms. Eng and the Windows staff, following their emergency training, herded people from the 107th floor down to a corridor on the 106th near the stairs, where they used a special phone to call the Fire Command Center. The building's policy was to immediately evacuate the floor on fire and the one above it. People farther away, like those in Windows on the World, were to leave only when directed by the command center "or when conditions dictate such actions."

Conditions were quickly deteriorating, though. Glenn Vogt, the restaurant's general manager, said that 20 minutes after the plane hit, his assistant, Christine Olender, called him at home. She got his wife instead, Mr. Vogt said, because he was on the street outside the trade center. Ms. Olender told Mrs. Vogt that they had heard nothing on how to leave. "The ceilings are falling," she said. "The floors are buckling."

Within 20 minutes of the crash, a police helicopter reported to its base that it could not land on the roof. Still, many put their hopes on a rescue by someone, some way.

"I can't go anywhere because they told us not to move," Ivhan Carpio, a Windows worker, said in a message he left on his cousin's answering machine. "I have to wait for the firefighters."

The firefighters, however, were struggling to respond. No one in New York had ever seen a fire of this size—four and five floors blazing within seconds. Commanders in the lobby had no way of knowing if any stairwells were passable. With most elevators ruined, firefighters were toting heavy gear up stairwells against a tide of evacuees. An hour after the plane crash, they would still be 50 floors below Windows.

Downstairs, the authorities fielded calls from the upper floors. "There's not much you could do other than tell them to go wet a towel and keep it over your face," said Alan Reiss, the former director of the world trade department of the Port Authority. But the plane had severed the water line to the upper floors. Mr. Maciejewski, the waiter, told his wife in a cellphone call that he could not find enough to wet a rag, she recalled. He said he would check the flower vases.

The room had almost no water and not much air, but there was no shortage of cellphones or BlackBerries. Using them and a few intact phone lines, at least 41 people in the restaurant reached someone outside the building. Peter Mardikian of Imagine Software told his wife, Corine, that he was headed for the roof and that he could not talk long, she recalled. Others were waiting for one of the few working phones.

Garth Feeney called his mother, Judy, in Florida. She began with a breezy hello, she later recalled.

"Mom," Mr. Feeney responded, "I'm not calling to chat. I'm in the World Trade Center and it's been hit by a plane."

The calm manner of the staff could not contain the strain. Laurie Kane, whose husband, Howard, was the restaurant's comptroller, said she could hear someone screaming, "We're trapped," as they finished their final conversation. Gabriela Waisman, a conference attendee, phoned her sister 10 times in

11 minutes, frantic to keep the connection. Veronique Bowers, the restaurant's credit collections manager, kept telling her grandmother, Carrie Tillman, that the building had been hit by an ambulance.

"She was so confused," Mrs. Tillman said.

9:01 North Tower, 104th Floor, Cantor Fitzgerald, 1 hour 27 minutes to collapse

Just two floors below Windows, the disaster marched at an eerily deliberate pace, the sense of emergency muted. The northwest conference room on the 104th floor held just one of many large knots of people in the five floors occupied by Cantor Fitzgerald. There, the smoke did not become overwhelming as quickly as at Windows. And the crash and fires were not as immediately devastating as they had been a few floors below, at Marsh & McLennan.

In fact, Andrew Rosenblum, a Cantor stock trader, thought it would be a good idea to reassure the families. With his wife, Jill, listening on the phone from their home in Rockville Centre, N.Y., he announced to the room: "Give me your home numbers," his wife recounted.

"Tim Betterly," Mr. Rosenblum said into his cellphone, reeling off a phone number. "James Ladley." Another number.

As the list grew, Mr. Rosenblum realized that 40 or 50 colleagues were in the room, having fled the smoke. "Please call their spouses, tell them we're in this conference room and we're fine," he said to his wife. She remembers scribbling the names and numbers on a yellow legal pad in her kitchen, as the burning towers played on a 13-inch television in a cubby-hole near the back door.

Mrs. Rosenblum handed pieces of paper with the numbers to friends who had shown up. They went either to the leafy, fenced-in backyard, where the dog wandered among them, or to the front lawn, calling the families on cellphones.

Mr. Rosenblum's group, including Jimmy Smith, John Salamone, and John Schwartz, sat on the eastern side of the bond trading area, in one of the open areas, according to John Sanacore, one of the group who was not at work that day. The spot offered expansive views of the Empire State Building.

On the opposite end of the bond area, overlooking the Hudson River, other traders were gathered. John Gaudioso, who normally worked in that section but was on a golf outing that morning, recalled that Ian Schneider sat at the head of a string of desks where he led a global finance group. Michael Wittenstein, John Casazza, and Michael DeRienzo were all in that area, and, like Mr. Schneider, were using land lines at their desks to take calls from concerned customers and loved ones, according to six people who spoke with them. "The building rocked like it never has before," said Mr. Schneider, who was there for the 1993 bombing, in a phone call with his wife, Cheryl.

In the equities trading area in the southern part of the 104th floor, looking toward the Statue of Liberty, there was a third group. Here, Stephen Cherry and Marc Zeplin pushed a button at their desk to activate the squawk box, a nationwide intercom to other Cantor offices around the country. "Can anybody hear us?" Mr. Cherry asked. A trader in Chicago who was listening in later said that she managed to reach a firehouse near the trade center. "They know you're there," the trader told them.

Mike Pelletier, a commodities broker in a Cantor office on the 105th floor, reached his wife, Sophie Pelletier, and was then in touch with a friend who told him that the airplane crash had been a terrorist attack. Mr. Pelletier swore and shouted the information to the people around him, Mrs. Pelletier said.

In Rockville Centre, on the front lawn of the Rosenblums' house, Debbie Cohen dialed the numbers on the yellow pieces of paper she had been handed by Jill Rosenblum.

"Hello? You don't know me, but I was given your number by someone who is in the World Trade Center," she said. "About 50 of them are in a corner conference room, and they say they're O.K. right now."

9:02 South Tower, 98th Floor, Aon Corp., 57 minutes to collapse

Those in the south tower were still spectators, if wary ones. "Hey Beverly, this is Sean, in case you get this message," Sean Rooney said on a voice mail message left for his wife, Beverly Eckert. "There has been an explosion in World Trade One—that's the other building. It looks like a plane struck it. It's on fire at about the 90th floor. And it's, it's—it's horrible. Bye."

Even in Mr. Rooney's tower, people could feel the heat from the fires raging in the other building, and they could see bodies falling from the high floors. Many soon began to leave. The building's staff, however, announced that they should stay—judging that it was safer for the tenants to stay inside an undamaged building than to walk ont a street where fiery debris was falling.

That instruction would change at the very moment that Mr. Rooney, who worked for the insurance company Aon, was leaving a second message for his wife, at 9:02 a.m.

"Honey, this is Sean again," he said. "Looks like we'll be in this tower for a while." He paused, as a public announcement in the background could be heard.

"It's secure here," Mr. Rooney continued. "But—" He stopped again to listen: *"if the conditions warrant on your floor you may wish to start an orderly evacuation."*

"I'll talk to you later," Mr. Rooney said. "Bye."

As Mr. Rooney spoke, United Flight 175 was screaming across New York Harbor.

9:02 South Tower, 81st Floor, Fuji Bank, 57 minutes to collapse

Yes, Stanley Praimnath told the caller from Chicago, he was fine. He had actually evacuated to the lobby of the south tower, but a security guard told him to go back. Now, he was again at his desk at Fuji Bank. "I'm fine," he repeated.

As he would later tell his story, those were his final words before he spotted it.

A gray shape on the horizon. An airplane, flying past the Statue of Liberty. The body of the United Airlines jet grew larger until he could see a red stripe on the fuselage. Then it banked and headed directly toward him.

Another one.

"Lord, you take over!" he remembers yelling, dropping under his metal desk.

At 9:02:54, the nose of the jetliner smashed directly into Mr. Praimnath's floor, about 130 feet from his desk. A fireball ignited. Steel furnishings and aluminum plane parts were torn into white-hot shrapnel. A blast wave hurled computers and desks through windows, and ripped out bundles of arcing electrical cables. Then the south tower seemed to stoop, swinging gradually toward the Hudson River, ferociously testing the steel skeleton before snapping back.

Through most of both towers, the staircases were tightly clustered, and in the north tower, they were all immediately severed or blocked by the blast. Along the impact zone of the south tower, floors 78 to 84, however, the stairs had to divert around heavy elevator machinery. So instead of running close to the building core, two of the stairways serving those floors were built closer to the perimeter. One of them, on the northwest side, survived. A report in USA Today this month also suggested that the surviving stairway might have been shielded by the machinery.

However the stairway survived, it made all the difference to Stanley Praimnath, who, huddled under his desk, could see a shiny aluminum piece of the plane, lodged in the remains of his door.

The plane, entering at a tilt, raked across six floors. Three flights up was the office of Euro Brokers, on the 84th floor. Most of the company's trading floor there was annihilated. Yet even there—at the bull's-eye of the airplane's impact—other people were alive: Robert Coll, Dave Vera, Ronald DiFrancesco and Kevin York, among others. Within minutes, they headed to the closest stairwell, led by Brian Clark, a fire warden on the 84th floor, who had his flashlight and whistle.

A fine powder mixed with light smoke floated through the stairwell. As they approached the 81st floor, Mr. Clark would recall, they met a slim man and a heavyset woman. "You can't go down," the woman screamed. "You got to go up. There is too much smoke and flame below."

This assessment changed everything. Hundreds of people came to a similar conclusion, but the smoke and the debris in the stairwell proved less of an obstacle than the fear of it. This very stairwell was the sole route out of the building, running from the top to the bottom of the south tower. Anyone who found this stairwell early enough could have walked to freedom.

This plain opportunity hardly read that way to the band of survivors who stood on the 81st floor landing, moments after the plane crash. They argued the alternatives, with Mr. Clark shining his flashlight into his colleagues' faces, asking each, "Up or down?" The debate was interrupted by shouts on the 81st floor.

"Help me! Help me!" Mr. Praimnath yelled. "I'm trapped. Don't leave me here!"

With no further discussion, the group in the stairs turned in different directions. As Mr. Clark recalls it, Mr. Coll, Mr. York, and Mr. Vera headed up the stairs, along with the heavyset woman, the slim man and two others he knew from Euro Brokers but could not identify. Mr. York and Mr. Coll hooked arms to support the woman, Mr. Clark recalled. One of them said: "Come on, you can do it. We're in this together."

Mr. Clark and Mr. DiFrancesco headed toward the man yelling for help. Mr. Praimnath saw the flashlight beam and crawled toward it, over toppled desks and across fallen ceiling tiles. Minutes earlier, this had been Fuji Bank's loan department, employee lounge, and computer room. Finally, he reached a damaged wall that separated him from the man with the flashlight.

From both sides, they ripped at the wall. A nail penetrated Mr. Praimnath's hand. He knocked it out against a hard surface in the darkness. Finally, the two men could see each other, but were still separated.

"You must jump," Mr. Clark told Mr. Praimnath, whose hand and left leg were now bleeding. "There is no other choice."

As Mr. Praimnath hopped up, Mr. Clark helped boost him over the obstacle. They ran to the stairwell and headed down. The steps were strewn with shattered wallboard. Flames licked in through cracks in the stairwell walls. Water from severed pipes poured down, forming a treacherous slurry.

They moved past the spot with the heavy smoke that the woman had warned Mr. Clark against. Perhaps the draft had shifted; maybe the smoke had not been all that bad to begin with. In any case, the stairs were clear and would be clear as late as 30 minutes after the south tower was hit.

Meanwhile, Mr. DiFrancesco took a detour in search of air, climbing about 10 floors, where he found the first group to go upstairs. They could not leave the stairwell; the doors would not open. Exhausted, in heavy smoke, people were lying down, Mr. DiFrancesco included. "Everyone else was starting to go to sleep," he said. Then, he recalled, he sat up, thinking, "I've got to see my wife and kids again." He ran down.

9:05 South Tower, 78th Floor, Elevator Sky Lobby, 54 minutes to collapse

Mary Jos cannot say for sure how long she was lying there, unconscious, on the floor of the sky lobby, outside the express elevator. Her first recollection of stirring is when she felt searing heat on her back and face. Maybe, she remembers thinking, she was on fire. Instinctively, she rolled over to smother the flames. She saw a blaze in the center of the room, and in the elevator shafts.

That was terrifying enough. Then, below the thick black smoke and through clouds of pulverized plaster, she gradually noticed something worse. The 78th floor sky lobby, which minutes before had been bustling with office workers unsure whether to leave the building or go back to work, was now filled with motionless bodies.

The ceilings, the walls, the windows, the sky lobby information kiosk, even the marble that graced the elevator banks—everything was smashed as the second hijacked plane dipped its left wingtip into the 78th floor.

In an instant, the witnesses say, they encountered a brilliant light, a blast of hot air, and a shock wave that knocked over everything. Lying amid the deathly silence, burned and bleeding, Mary Jos had a single thought: her husband. "I am not going to die," she said, remembering her words.

In the 16 minutes between attacks, those in the south tower scarcely had time to absorb the horrors they could see across the plaza and decide what to do. To map their choices about movements is to see the geography of life and death.

Before the second plane hit, survivors said, the mood in the sky lobby was awkward: relief at the announcements that their building was safer than walking on the street, and fear that it really wasn't. In these critical moments, people milled about, trying to decide. Be at trading desks for the opening of the market, or grab a cup of coffee downstairs? At Keefe, Bruyette & Woods, nearly the entire investment banking department left and survived. Nearly all the equities traders stayed and died.

One of them, Stephen Mulderry, spoke to his brother Peter, and described the blaze in the north tower he could see from a window. Still, the word had come from the building management that his tower was "secure"—and his soundless phone was blinking for his attention. "He said, 'I got to go—the lights are ringing and the market is going to open,'" Peter Mulderry recalled.

In the moments before the second impact, everyone in the 78th floor sky lobby was poised between going up or down. Kelly Reyher, who worked on the 100th floor at Aon Corporation, stepped into a local elevator headed up. He wanted to get his Palm Pilot, figuring it might be a while before he could return to his office. Judy Wein and Gigi Singer, also both of Aon, debated whether to go back and get their pocketbooks from their 103rd floor office. But Howard L. Kestenbaum, their colleague, told them to forget about it. He would give them carfare home.

As some office workers spoke nervously of the loved ones they were rushing to rejoin, there was even a bit of humor.

"I have a horse and two cats," Karen E. Hagerty, 34, joked, as she was squeezed out of an elevator spot.

At the instant of impact, a busy lobby of people—witness estimates range from 50 to 200—was struck silent, dark, all but lifeless. For a few, survival came from having leaned into an alcove. Death could come from having stepped back from a crowded elevator door.

As Ms. Wein came to, she had her own battered body to deal with: her right arm was broken, three ribs were cracked, and her right leg had been punctured. In other words, she was lucky. All around her were people with horrific injuries, dead or close to it. Ms. Wein yelled out for her boss, Mr. Kestenbaum. When she found him, she said, he was expressionless, motionless, silent. Ms. Hagerty, who had joked about the cats at home, showed no signs of life when a colleague, Ed Nicholls, saw her. And Richard Gabrielle, another Aon colleague, was pinned to the ground, his legs apparently broken by marble that had fallen on them.

Ms. Wein tried to move the stone. Mr. Gabrielle cried out from pain, she said, and told her to stop.

Gradually, those who could move, did. Ms. Wein found Vijayashanker Paramsothy and Ms. Singer, neither of whom had life-threatening injuries.

Kelly Reyher, who had been on his way to get his Palm Pilot, managed to pry open the elevator doors with his arms and his briefcase. He crawled out of the burning car and found Donna Spira 50 feet away. Her arm fractured, her hair burned, Mrs. Spira could still walk.

A mysterious man appeared at one point, his mouth and nose covered with a red handkerchief. He was looking for a fire extinguisher. As Judy Wein recalls, he pointed to the stairs and made an announcement that saved lives: Anyone who can walk, get up and walk now. Anyone who can perhaps help others, find someone who needs help and then head down.

In groups of two and three, the survivors struggled to the stairs. A few flights down, they propped up debris blocking their way, leaving a small passageway to slip through.

A few minutes behind this group was Ling Young, who also survived the impact in the sky lobby. She, too, said she had been steered by the man in the red bandanna, hearing him call out: "This way to the stairs." He trailed her down the stairs. Ms. Young said she soon noticed that he was carrying a woman on his back. Once they reached clearer air, he put her down and went back up.

Others never left.

The people who escaped said Mr. Paramsothy, who had only been scraped, remained behind. Ms. Young said that Sankara Velamuri and Diane Urban, colleagues of Mrs. Jos from the State Department of Taxation and Finance, tried to help two more seriously injured friends, Dianne Gladstone and Yeshavant Tembe, both also state employees.

All five of these people would die.

Of the dozens of people waiting in the sky lobby when the second plane struck, 12 are known to have made it out alive.

9:35 North Tower, 104th Floor, Cantor Fitzgerald; 106th Floor, Windows on the World; 53 minutes to collapse

So urgent was the need for air that people piled four and five high in window after window, their upper bodies hanging out, 1,300 feet above the ground.

They were in an unforgiving place.

Elsewhere, two men, one of them shirtless, stood on the windowsills, leaning their bodies so far outside that they could peer around a big intervening column and see each other, an analysis of photographs and videos reveals.

On the 103rd floor, a man stared straight out a broken window toward the northwest, bracing himself against a window frame with one hand. He wrapped his other arm around a woman, seemingly to keep her from tumbling to the ground.

Behind the unbroken windows, the desperate had assembled. "About five floors from the top you have about 50 people with their faces pressed against the window trying to breathe," a police officer in a helicopter reported.

Now it was unmistakable. The office of Cantor Fitzgerald, and just above it, Windows on the World, would become the landmark for this doomed moment. Nearly 900 would die on floors 101 through 107.

In the restaurant, at least 70 people crowded near office windows at the northwest corner of the 106th floor, according to accounts they gave relatives and co-workers. "Everywhere else is smoked out," Stuart Lee, a Data Synapse vice president, e-mailed his office in Greenwich Village. "Currently an argument going on as whether we should break a window," Mr. Lee continued a few moments later. "Consensus is no for the time being."

Soon, though, a dozen people appeared through broken windows along the west face of the restaurant. Mr. Vogt, the general manager of Windows, said he could see them from the ground, silhouetted against the gray smoke that billowed out from his own office and others.

By now, the videotapes show, fires were rampaging through the impact floors, darting across the north face of the tower. Coils of smoke lashed the people braced around the broken windows.

In the northwest conference room on the 104th floor, Andrew Rosenblum and 50 other people temporarily managed to ward off the smoke and heat by plugging vents with jackets. "We smashed the computers into the windows to get some air," Mr. Rosenblum reported by cellphone to his golf partner, Barry Kornblum.

But there was no hiding.

As people began falling from above the conference room, Mr. Rosenblum broke his preternatural calm, his wife, Jill, recalled. In the midst of speaking to her, he suddenly interjected, without elaboration, "Oh my God."

9:38 South Tower, 97th Floor, Fiduciary Trust; 93rd Floor, Aon Corp.; 21 minutes to collapse

"Ed, be careful!" shouted Alayne Gentul, the director of human resources at Fiduciary Trust, as Edgar Emery slipped off the desk he had been standing on within the increasingly hot and smoky 97th floor of the south tower.

Mr. Emery, one of her office colleagues, had been trying to use his blazer to seal a ventilation duct that was belching smoke. To evacuate Fiduciary employees who worked on this floor, Mr. Emery and Mrs. Gentul had climbed seven floors from their own offices.

Now the two of them, and the six or so they were trying to save, were all in serious trouble.

As Mrs. Gentul spoke to her husband on the phone—he could overhear what was happening—Mr. Emery got up and spread the coat over the vent. Next, he swung a shoe at a sprinkler head, hoping to start the flow of water.

"The sprinklers aren't going on," Mrs. Gentul said to her husband, Jack Gentul, who listened in his office at the New Jersey Institute of Technology in Newark, where he is a dean. No one knew the plane had cut the water pipes.

"We don't know whether to stay or go," Mrs. Gentul told her husband. "I don't want to go down into a fire," she said.

Among the doomed, the phone calls, messages, and witnesses make clear, were many people who had put themselves in harm's way by stopping to offer a hand to colleagues or strangers. Others acted with great tenderness when all else was lost.

Mrs. Gentul and Mr. Emery of Fiduciary, whose offices stretched from the 90th to the 97th floors, had made their own fateful decisions to help others.

When the first plane hit across the plaza, the fireball billowed across the western facade of the 90th floor, where Mr. Emery was in his office. "I felt the heat on my face," said Anne Foodim, a member of human resources who worked nearby.

Mr. Emery, known for steadiness, emerged, the lapels on his blue blazer flapping as he waved people out. "Come on, let's go," he said, escorting five employees into a stairwell, including Ms. Foodim, who recounted the events. They walked down 12 floors, reaching the 78th floor and the express elevator, with Mr. Emery giving encouragement.

"If you can finish chemo, then you can get down those steps," Mr. Emery told an exhausted Ms. Foodim, who had just completed a round of chemotherapy. When they finally reached a packed elevator on the 78th floor, Mr. Emery made sure everyone got aboard. He squeezed Ms. Foodim's shoulder and let the door close in front of him. Then he headed back up, joining Alayne Gentul.

Like Mr. Emery, Mrs. Gentul herded a group out before the second plane hit. A receptionist, Mona Dunn, saw her on the 90th floor where workers were debating when or if to leave. Mrs. Gentul instantly settled the question. "Go down and go down orderly," she said, indicating a stairway.

"It was like the teacher saying, 'It's O.K., go,'" Mrs. Dunn recalled.

Together, Mrs. Gentul and Mr. Emery went to evacuate six people on the 97th floor who had been working on a computer back-up operation, Mrs. Gentul told her husband.

Mr. Emery was hunting for a stairwell on the 97th floor when he reached his wife, Elizabeth, by cellphone. The last thing Mrs. Emery heard before she lost the connection was Alayne Gentul screaming from somewhere very near Ed Emery, "Where's the stairs? Where's the stairs?"

Another phone call was under way nearby. Edmund McNally, director of technology for Fiduciary, called his wife, Liz, as the floor began buckling. Mr. McNally hastily recited his life insurance policies and employee bonus programs. "He said that I meant the world to him and he loved me," Mrs. McNally said, and they exchanged what they thought were their last goodbyes.

Then Mrs. McNally's phone rang again. Her husband sheepishly reported that he had booked them on a trip to Rome for her 40th birthday. "He said, 'Liz, you have to cancel that,'" Mrs. McNally said.

On the 93rd floor, Gregory Milanowycz, 25, an insurance broker for Aon, urged others to leave—some of them survived—but went back himself, after hearing the announcement. "Why did I listen to them—I shouldn't have," he moaned after his father, Joseph Milanowycz, called him. Now he was trapped. He asked his father to ask the Fire Department what he and 30 other people should do. His father said he passed word from a dispatcher to his son that they should stay low, and that firefighters were working their way up. Then, he says, he heard his son calling out to the others: "They are coming! My Dad's on the phone with them. They are coming. Everyone's got to get to the ground."

Even when the situation was most hopeless, the trapped people were still watching out for one another. On the 87th floor, a group of about 20 people from Keefe, Bruyette & Woods took refuge in a conference room belonging to the New York State Department of Taxation and Finance. During the final minutes, Eric Thorpe managed to get a call to his wife, Linda Perry Thorpe, who was waiting to hear from him at a neighbor's apartment. No one spoke from the tower. Instead, Ms. Thorpe and the neighbor listened to the ambient noise.

"I hear everything in the background," Mrs. Thorpe recalled, including, she said, gasping. "Someone asks, 'Where is the fire extinguisher?' Someone else says, 'It already got thrown out the window.' I heard a voice asking, 'Is anybody unconscious?' Some of them sounded calm.

"One man went berserk, screaming. I couldn't understand that he was saying anything. He just lost it.

"I heard another person soothing him, saying, 'It's O.K., it'll be O.K.' "

9:45 South Tower, 105th Floor, 14 minutes to collapse

Minutes after the second plane struck the south tower, Roko Camaj called home to report that a throng had gathered near the roof, according to his son, Vinny Camaj. "I'm on the 105th floor," Roko Camaj told his wife. "There's at least 200 people here."

The promise of sanctuary on the roof had seemed so logical, so irresistible, that scores of people chased their fates up the stairs. They were blind alleys.

Mr. Camaj, a window washer who had been featured in a children's book, carried the key to the roof, his son said. That key alone would not open its door: a buzzer also had to be pressed by the security staff in a command post on the 22nd floor. And the post had been damaged and evacuated.

The roof seemed like an obvious choice—and the only one—to people on the upper floors. A police helicopter had evacuated people from the roof of the north tower in February 1993, after a terrorist bomb exploded in the basement. For a variety of reasons, though, the Port Authority, with the agreement of the Fire Department, discouraged helicopters as part of its evacuation plan. Police commanders ruled out a rooftop rescue that morning.

Whatever the wisdom of the policy, it came as a shock to many people trapped in the towers, according to their families and summaries of 911 calls. Only a few realized that Stairway A could take them down to safety, and that information never circled back upstairs from those escaping or from the authorities. Frank Doyle, a trader at Keefe, Bruyette & Woods, called his wife, Kimmy Chedell, to remind her of his love for her and the children. She recalls he also said: "I've gone up to the roof and the rooftop doors are locked. You need to call 911 and tell them we're trapped."

The 105th floor was the last stop for many of those who had climbed toward the roof, a crowd dominated by Aon employees. At 9:27, a man called 911 and said a group was in the north conference room on the 105th floor. At 9:32, a man on the 105th floor called 911 and asked that the roof be opened. At 9:38, Kevin Cosgrove, a fire warden for Aon, called 911, then rang his brother.

Sean Rooney called Beverly Eckert. They had met at a high school dance in Buffalo, when they were both 16. They had just turned 50 together.

He had tried to go down but was stymied, then had climbed 30 floors or so to the locked roof. Now he wanted to plot a way out, so he had his wife describe the fire's location from the TV pictures. He could not fathom why the roof was locked, she said. She urged him to try again while she dialed 911 on another line. He put the phone down, then returned minutes later, saying the roof door would not budge. He had pounded on it.

"He was worried about the flames," Ms. Eckert recalled. "I kept telling him they weren't anywhere near him. He said, but the windows were hot. His breathing was becoming more labored."

Ceilings were caving in. Floors were buckling. Phone calls were being cut off. He was alone in a room filling with smoke. They said goodbye.

"He was telling me he loved me.

"Then you could hear the loud explosion."

10:00 North Tower, 92nd Floor, Carr Futures, 28 minutes to collapse

"Mom," asked Jeffrey Nussbaum, "What was that explosion?"

Twenty miles away in Oceanside, N.Y., Arline Nussbaum could see on television what her son could not from 50 yards away. She recalls their last words:

"The other tower just went down," Mrs. Nussbaum said.

"Oh my God," her son said. "I love you."

Then the phone went dead.

The north tower, which had been hit 16 minutes before the south, was still standing. It was dying, more slowly, but just as surely. The calls were dwindling. The number of people falling from windows accelerated.

That morning, the office of Carr Futures on the 92nd floor was unusually busy. A total of 68 men and women were on the floor that morning, 67 of them associated with Carr.

About two dozen brokers for Carr's parent company had been called to a special 8 a.m. meeting. When the building sprang back and forth like a car antenna, door frames twisted and jammed shut, trapping a number of them in a conference room.

The remaining Carr employees, about 40, migrated to a large, unfinished space along the west side. Jeffrey Nussbaum called his mother, and shared his cellphone with Andy Friedman. In all, the Carr families have counted 31 calls from the people they lost, according to Joan Dincuff, whose son, Christopher, died that morning.

Carr was two floors below the impact, and everyone there had survived it; yet they could not get out. Between 10:05 and 10:25, videos show, fire spread westward across the 92nd floor's north face, bearing down on their western refuge.

At 10:18, Tom McGinnis, one of the traders summoned to the special meeting, reached his wife, Iliana McGinnis. The words are stitched into her memory.

"This looks really, really bad," he said.

"I know," said Mrs. McGinnis, who had been hoping that his meeting had broken up before the airplane hit. "This is bad for the country; it looks like World War III."

Something in the tone of her husband's answer alarmed Mrs. McGinnis.

"Are you O.K., yes or no?" she demanded.

"We're on the 92nd floor in a room we can't get out of," Mr. McGinnis said.

"Who's with you?" she asked. Mr. McGinnis mentioned three old friends—Joey Holland, Brendan Dolan, and Elkin Yuen.

"I love you," Mr. McGinnis said. "Take care of Caitlin." Mrs. McGinnis was not ready to hear a farewell.

"Don't lose your cool," she urged. "You guys are so tough, you're resourceful. You guys are going to get out of there."

"You don't understand," Mr. McGinnis said. "There are people jumping from the floors above us."

It was 10:25. The fire raged along the west side of the 92nd floor. People fell from windows. Mr. McGinnis again told her he loved her and their daughter, Caitlin.

"Don't hang up," Mrs. McGinnis pleaded.

"I got to get down on the floor," Mr. McGinnis said.

With that, the phone connection faded out.

It was 10:26, two minutes before the tower crumbled. The World Trade Center had fallen silent.

PART TWO

The Crucible of Fire: Tragedy, Escape, and Remembrance

To Sleep With the Angels:
The Story of a Fire

BY DAVID COWAN AND JOHN KUENSTER

First published in 1996, the book *To Sleep With the Angels: The Story of a Fire* brought the story of one of America's most tragic and wrenchingly sad disasters into the minds and hearts of thousands of readers who no doubt wondered: How can such horror be possible? What can be done to prevent something like this from happening again?

Critical praise for the book was extraordinary, with such phrases as, "Riveting ... a devastating tale that will not soon be forgotten." "An absorbing account ... a tale of terror." "A harrowing depiction of carnage, hysteria, fear, faith, heroism, and heartbreak."

The jacket copy on the book describes perfectly the storytelling mission of Cowan and Kuenster:

"On a grey winter day in December, 1958, one of the deadliest fires in American history took the lives of ninety-two children and three nuns at a Catholic elementary school on Chicago's West Side. The blaze at Our Lady of the Angels School shocked the nation, tore apart a community, left a mystery unsolved to this day, sowed popular suspicion of the church and city fathers, and prompted nationwide fire safety reform in American schools. In *To Sleep with the Angels*, two veteran journalists tell the moving story of the fire and its consequences. It is a tale of ordinary people caught up in a mind-numbing disaster."

As our excerpt begins, it is Monday morning, December 1, 1958, destined to become one of the most tragic days in Chicago history, indeed, in American history.

*　　　*　　　*　　　*　　　*

The thermometer was sitting at twenty degrees when the bell inside the school began ringing at 8:40 a.m. Outside a morning ritual was already under way. Parents and relatives were arriving with children in tow, seeing their youngsters safely to school. The streets and sidewalks around the old school swelled with pedestrians. Patrol boys set up wooden horses on Iowa Street to keep traffic from clogging the building's front entrance, and a couple of priests were standing outside the rectory, next to the flagpole, talking with mothers and fathers. Priests in the parish always made sure one or two of them were on hand in the mornings to stand watch outside, just in case any boys had ideas of starting a fistfight. More times than not, though, the men were in place simply to greet the children, to give them a wink and say hello. And though the priests didn't know all the kids by name, certainly they knew their faces.

The students were toting books and folders, and those living farthest away carried lunch boxes. They marched dutifully through the school's front doors, headed for classrooms they would occupy until the school day ended at three o'clock. Once out of the cold, the children doffed their caps, scarves, and mittens, and hung up their coats and jackets in closets and on coatracks set in the hallways and narrow corridors.

The youngsters were attired according to Catholic school regulations. Boys wore dress shirts, dark pants, and ties. Girls dressed in blue or white sweaters, white blouses and jumpers, and blue plaid skirts. The school sweaters were embroidered with the letters "OLA," an acronym the kids— when safely out of earshot of their nuns and lay teachers—referred to as "Old Ladies Association."

A number of desks in the classrooms were empty that Monday. Colds, flu, and other childhood ailments had taken their usual toll on the school's attendance record. And because it was the first day after a cold holiday weekend, there seemed to be more absences than usual.

One of the empty desks in Room 212 belonged to Linda Malinski, a ten-year-old fifth-grader with long blond hair and hazel green eyes. Linda and her older brother Gerry, a sixth-grader, awoke that morning with colds, and their mother, Mary, decided the children should stay home from school.

The Malinskis' conversion to Roman Catholicism had come a year and a half earlier when the family was visited by a nun canvassing the neighborhood. The process was hastened when a parish priest, Father Alfred Corbo, persuaded the children's father, Nicholas Malinski, to rejoin the church he had left in his youth. Nicholas and Mary were soon remarried in Our Lady of the Angels Church, and all six of their children were baptized in the Catholic faith.

Nicholas Malinski became a devout Catholic, and he and his wife wanted their children to attend parochial schools. In the fall of 1958 Nicholas Jr., the oldest of the Malinski children, was enrolled at St. Benedict's High School, and Gerry and Linda transferred to Our Lady of the Angels. A younger daughter, Barbara, was denied admission because of overcrowding in the first grade. Instead she was enrolled in Ryerson public elementary school, across the street from the family's home on North Lawndale Avenue.

Linda Malinski was a cheerful, happy girl with a bright disposition. She was a joy to her parents and helpful at home. And though she had acquired many of the playful mannerisms of her older brothers, she fell short of being a tomboy.

During the dark, early morning hours of that same Monday, Mary Malinski awoke in the stillness of the family's home to the sound of someone crying. Outside it was chilly and silent. She listened intently, wondering to herself if she had in fact heard one of her six children cry out.

"Mommy?"

Now certain she had not imagined the muffled sobs, Mary arose and quietly crept past the children's beds. Linda awoke with a start.

"Mommy," Linda cried. "I can't breathe. I can't breathe."

Linda was choking on a nightmare. She dreamed of a fire and imagined that smoke was filling the family's tiny apartment. Mary assured her daughter that everything was all right, that there was no fire. Linda suffered from asthma, and her mother figured the ailment was responsible for the girl's coughs and labored breathing. But what Linda said next would later cause Mary to believe her daughter had had a premonition of the disaster that was to occur later that day.

"Mommy," she cried. "I hear people screaming."

Mary was concerned. She stayed at Linda's bedside and comforted her daughter back to sleep.

Later that morning, after school had already begun, Linda told her mother she felt better and wanted to attend afternoon classes. When Mary took the temperatures of both Linda and Gerry, the readings showed normal, and she told the children they could join their classmates after lunch. The decision would haunt Mary Malinski for years to come.

As Linda prepared for school, she took great pains in fixing her long blond hair, a task usually performed by her mother.

"Mommy," Linda asked, "does my hair look all right?"

Mary looked down at her daughter and smiled. "You look like an angel."

After luncheon recess, the schoolchildren returned to their classrooms for the final two hours of study. Up to now the school day had passed uneventfully; the youngsters sat at their desks and endured the normal routines of reading, writing, and figuring.

Inside Room 206, tucked away in the annex on the second floor between the school's north and south wings, lay teacher Pearl Tristano was readying her fifth-graders for their end-of-day chores. Tristano, a dark-haired twenty-four-year-old, was unmarried and lived at home with her parents in suburban Oak Park; she had been teaching at OLA for some time and was one of nine lay teachers on the school's staff.

Sometime after 2:20 p.m., as the school day drew to a close, Tristano assigned two boys in her room to the daily task of carrying wastebaskets down to the basement boiler room. There they dumped the refuse into large metal bins so the janitor could burn it later in an outside incinerator. Their errand completed, the boys returned to the classroom and took their seats. Earlier Tristano had also excused from the room another boy—a bespectacled, blond-haired youth who asked to use the lavatory. This boy also returned a short time later and, with his classmates, sat down to resume his last-minute studies.

There was nothing unusual about these closing minutes of the school day, and nothing would be made of these temporary absences from Tristano's classroom for some time. In fact, there was much movement in the normally deserted hallways of the school that afternoon: boys leaving their rooms to empty wastebaskets in the basement or stepping outside into the courtway to clean erasers; a girl walking to the convent to attend a music lesson; another girl going into a seventh-grade room to pick up a homework assignment for her sick sister; several boys leaving their room for neighborhood sidewalk patrol.

Unnoticed, something else was occurring that afternoon in an isolated, seldom-used corner of the school basement.

Located in the north wing, at the bottom of the building's northeast stairwell, beyond a door that was only steps from where students were emptying their wastebaskets in the boiler room, a fire in a cardboard trash drum had been burning for several minutes. And though the exact time of the fire's ignition would never be fixed to the precise minute, the date of its occurrence would soon be etched in the dark ledger of the nation's terrible tragedies.

After consuming refuse in the container, the fire smoldered from a lack of oxygen, elevating temperatures in the confined stairwell. Suddenly, when a window in the basement broke from the heat, a fresh supply of air rushed in, and the deserted stairwell turned into a blazing chimney. Without a sprinkler system in place to check their advance, flames, smoke, and heat roared upward, feeding on the old wooden staircase and bannisters, melting asphalt tile covering the stairs.

On the first floor a closed fire door blocked the fire's path. But no door was in place on the second floor. Consequently heavy black smoke and superheated air began pouring into the second-floor corridor. Lurking behind the smoke, flames crept along, feeding off combustible ceiling tile, painted walls, and varnished hardwood flooring.

At the same time hot gases from the fire entered an open pipe shaft in the basement stairwell and flowed upward into the cockloft between the roof and ceiling of the school. Flames erupted as well in this hidden area directly above the six north-wing classrooms packed with 329 students and six nuns. The out-of-control blaze was now raging undetected through the school, devouring everything in its path, cutting off escape for the unsuspecting occupants.

Despite the intensity of the fire, several minutes passed before anyone realized the school was ablaze. Two teachers wondered why the building seemed excessively warm, but they mistakenly assumed the janitor had over-stoked the furnace. Finally a chain of events occurred alerting the entire school to the danger at hand.

The fire in the school was discovered in close sequence by several people, though no one at the time realized that this discovery would turn into a race against death.

School janitor Jim Raymond was one of the first to notice that something was wrong. Sometime before 2:30 p.m., Raymond was walking west on Iowa Street, returning to the school from a job in a nearby parish property on Hamlin Avenue. As was his habit, when he reached the rectory he turned right and walked north through the narrow gangway separating the priests' house and the rear of the school. He was headed for the school's boiler room, and as he approached the building's northeast corner, he noticed a faint wisp of smoke.

Puzzled at what could be burning, Raymond quickened his pace. When he moved toward the corner of the building, he was startled to see a red glow coming from the frosted window pane near the back stairwell. He retreated into the gangway and ran through a door leading down into the boiler room. Once inside, Raymond peered between the two cylindrical boilers and saw that the interior door leading to the stairwell was slightly ajar, and that a fire was raging upward on the other side. The fire appeared to be out of control. It was too big for Raymond to fight himself.

Fifth-graders Ronald Eddington and James Brocato were in the boiler room, emptying waste paper baskets from Room 205, when the janitor appeared. The noisy boilers had masked the sound of the fire in the stairwell, and the boys apparently did not realize that a blaze was burning only a few feet away. They were startled to see Mr. Raymond so excited.

"Go call the Fire Department!" he yelled to them.

The boys looked at each other, puzzled. Then they caught a glimpse of the fire.

"Let's get out of here!" Ronnie shouted.

The janitor left too. He raced back outside to the rectory next door. When he stormed into the residence, Nora Maloney, the silver-haired, thick-brogued housekeeper was standing in the kitchen, preparing a sauce for the evening meal. She jumped when the back door slammed.

"Call the Fire Department! The school's on fire!" Raymond shouted to her.

Nora Maloney was unaware of the situation beginning to unfold only a few yards from where she stood. She set her ladle down on the stove and walked over to a small window above the sink that faced the back of the school. She looked out and saw smoke. When she turned around to respond, Raymond was gone. He had already run back into the burning school; inside were four of his own children.

Elmer Barkhaus, an amiable, sixty-one-year-old part owner of a glue company, turned his black Buick off Augusta Boulevard and drove south on Avers Avenue that afternoon. He spent most of his working hours traveling, selling his wares to local floor-covering contractors, and he had a few more stops to make before starting the long drive to his home on the city's South Side.

As Barkhaus neared Iowa Street, something caught his eye. He slowed his car to a crawl and peered into the alley just north of the maroon-brick building of Our Lady of the Angels School. Smoke was pouring out the rear stairwell door.

Barkhaus thought a second. Stay calm. Don't get excited. He had to be careful. The ulcers in his stomach were fragile. He pulled over to the curb, then looked for a fire alarm box on the corner.

He didn't see one; not all Chicago schools had them. He spotted a small candy store next to the alley directly north of the school. There must be a telephone inside.

Barbara Glowacki, the store's plump, twenty-nine-year-old owner, was sitting in the back kitchen, next to the living room, riffling through the newspaper. Duke, her German shepherd, was barking as Joseph, her three-year-old, pedaled his little blue car around the apartment.

Barbara was waiting for school next door to let out in another twenty minutes, when her store would be invaded by youngsters stopping in to spend their nickels and dimes on the array of candy she had for sale. Helena, her seven-year-old, would be among the kids.

Only two years earlier she and husband Joseph had become naturalized citizens of what she fondly called her "promised land." The couple had met and married in postwar Germany. Being Polish, Joseph had not been well received in Germany, and Barbara, a German, had been unwelcome in Poland. After shifting around, the couple followed thousands of other displaced Europeans, emigrating to Chicago in 1950.

The front door rattled. Barbara looked up from her TV listings, her view blocked partially by a refrigerator. She saw it was a man, someone she had never seen before. He looked worried, nervous. Perhaps he was ill. She went to see.

"Ma'am," he said, "you got a phone?"

There was a phone in the back, but Barbara thought it unwise to let the stranger use it, not when she was home alone. She was leery.

"No," she replied, "I don't have a public telephone."

Barkhaus wheeled around and headed for the door. Before running out he turned back to the woman at the counter. "The school next door is on fire!"

The salesman darted outside and across the street to a two-flat building where he began ringing the doorbells of both apartments, hoping to find a telephone.

Barbara was skeptical. Why would he say such a thing? He must be mad. Still, she was curious. Shoving her hands in the pockets of her sweater, she walked outside, shivering as she stepped into the cold. She took a few steps and turned left into the alley between her store and the school. Everything seemed normal. She took a few more steps. Then she saw it.

A tongue of bright orange flame was curling up over the transom above the back stairwell door. "Oh my God!" she yelled.

Barbara clutched herself, then pictured Helena, whose classroom was on the first floor. She turned around, hoping to see someone, anyone. She looked for the stranger. He was gone. She turned back to the stairwell. Smoke and flames pouring out the doorway were all that met her frantic glances.

For the moment Barbara was alone in the cold, quiet alley. She looked up at the school windows. The building was filled with children, but she heard no fire alarm. Suddenly her fears were realized.

They don't know!

Barbara couldn't move fast enough. She ran back to her building and crashed through the front door, knocking down a candy display in front of the store. Her mind was scattered. Everything was a blur except the black telephone sitting on the kitchen table.

When Barbara reached the kitchen, she picked up the phone. Her hands were shaking and she was out of breath. She thought "Fire Department" but drew a blank; she couldn't remember the seven-digit number. Instead she dialed the operator.

"Give me the firemen, quick!"

After she was connected, a man on the other end responded: "Chicago Fire Department."

"Our Lady of Angels School is on fire. Hurry!"

"Somebody called in already. Help is on the way."

The fire alarm operator's voice was cool and reassuring. For the moment it had a calming effect on Barbara.

Frankie Grimaldi raised his hand.

"Yes?" Miss Tristano asked.

"May I go to the washroom?"

"You may."

Frankie got up from his seat in Room 206 and walked out of the classroom. Something strange caught his attention. There was smoke in the hallway. When he turned, Miss Tristano was right behind him. She too had caught a whiff of the smoke.

"Get back in the room," she ordered the boy.

Following Frankie back inside, Tristano looked to her students. "Stay here," she said. "I'm going next door."

When Tristano returned to the hallway, the smoke had grown darker and hotter. She walked next door to Room 205 to alert Dorothy Coughlan, the lay teacher there.

"What should we do?" Tristano asked, aware of the strict rule that permitted only the mother superior, the school's principal, to ring the fire alarm.

"I'll go to the office," Coughlan said. "You stay here."

When Coughlan reached the principal's second-floor office in the middle of the south wing, she found that the superior, Sister Mary St. Florence Casey, was substituting for a sick teacher in a first-floor classroom. By the time Coughlan returned to her own classroom, the smoke entering the tiny annex corridor had worsened. She and Tristano decided not to wait for an alarm and instead to evacuate their classes.

Tristano reentered her room. "Everybody get up," she announced to her students. "We're leaving the building."

The two teachers lined up their pupils in fire-drill formation, then marched them into the corridor and down a set of stairs in the south wing that led to the first floor. Once downstairs, the two groups filed through doors leading to the Iowa Street sidewalk. When Tristano reached the first floor behind the children, she flipped the switch on the wall-mounted fire alarm located at the bottom of the stairway. Nothing happened. She darted outside. Coughlan was yelling, "Take them to the church. I'm going to the convent. I'm calling the Fire Department."

Obeying her older colleague, Tristano hurried the two classes into the parish church next door. Then she returned to the school and the fire alarm. The alarm on the wall resembled a light switch and was almost six feet off the floor. When Tristano flipped it the second time, the audible buzzer started sounding in the school. But the alarm was merely a local one—it rang only inside the school; it did not transmit a signal to the Fire Department.

It was now 2:42 p.m. Nearly eight minutes had elapsed since Tristano first noticed the smoke.

A mile south of Our Lady of the Angels School, the merchants along Madison Street were looking forward to the holiday shopping season, optimistic that sales would improve over the recession-ridden Christmas of 1957. They were already dressing up their storefronts and the streetlights along the avenue with decorations in green, red, silver, and gold.

Mary Stachura picked up a packet of invoices and looked around the crowded back office of Madigan's department store. She was happy to have this, her first Christmas job, now that both her sons were in school. And the fashionable ladies' store, located in the midst of the area's main shopping hub—Crawford Avenue and Madison Street—was just minutes from home.

Mary loved the family atmosphere in the neighborhood. She and her husband, Max, could reach out and almost touch the bricks of Our Lady of the Angels Church from their two-flat on Hamlin Avenue. They never had an excuse for being late for Sunday Mass.

Max's parents lived upstairs and last year began teaching Polish to Mark Allen and John, both students at Our Lady of the Angels. Proud of their European heritage, the elder Stachuras, like many Chicago Poles, hoped that heritage would be treasured by their grandsons.

Mark was tolerant of his language lessons, but one aspect of his ancestry bothered him: his blond hair. "Why can't I have black hair like all the other kids?" he would grumble.

His schoolmates were mostly dark-haired Italians, and Mark hadn't seen them in a week; he'd been home ill. In his eagerness to get to school that morning, he'd almost forgotten to kiss Mary good-bye.

"Bye, Mom," he had said, planting a kiss on her cheek. Running down the short flight of stairs, the fourth-grader had been singing. His glee may have been due in part to being over his recent minor illness, but for some reason Mary had a feeling of apprehension.

It was going on 3 p.m. when she looked up at the clock and thought of Max. He'd soon be picking up their children, and at five o'clock they would meet her and go to dinner. Later they would take the boys to see Santa Claus.

Mary was fingering through invoices when a dissonant sound began to mingle with the generic, piped-in Christmas music. At first she didn't notice it. But soon the wailing grew closer, louder, demanding to be heard.

"There must be a big fire somewhere," Mary thought.

Instinctively she clutched the gold crucifix around her neck.

It had been only seconds since the calming voice of the fire alarm operator had assured Barbara Glowacki that help was on the way. But when she ran back outside, the scene in the alley had changed dramatically. The single flame she had first seen in the school doorway had grown into a raging inferno. The windows of the second-floor classrooms had been thrown open and were filling with dozens of terrified, familiar faces. Some were screaming, gasping for air. Black smoke was billowing over their heads. The little faces in the windows seemed to be piled on top of one another.

Barbara trembled. "Lord have mercy!"

The kids were screaming to her. "Get me out of here! Catch me!"

Some of them knew her name. "Barb! Help us! Help me!"

Sister Mary Seraphica was leaning out the middle windows of Room 210, hacking and coughing. She spotted Barbara. "Please help, help!" she screamed. "Call the Fire Department!"

Barbara yelled back. "Why don't you get out?"

"We can't. We're trapped."

"Hold on, sister! Help is on the way! The Fire Department is on the way!"

The nun kept on screaming and Barbara wondered why she and the children didn't leave their rooms and run down the stairs. She didn't know the fire and smoke had completely engulfed the upstairs corridor, making escape through the hallway seem impossible. She ran over to the side door near the front of the school to see if it was jammed shut. When she pulled on it, the door opened an inch or two but black smoke inside pushed out and drove her back. The smoke was too much; it was burning her lungs.

Suddenly Barbara was overwhelmed by fear. She remembered her daughter Helena, whose second-grade classroom was on the first floor.

"My child! Where's my child!" she screamed.

She scurried around the corner and ran through the schools' front door on Avers. A nun was leading of group of frightened students out of the building. They were filing out fast, one after the other.

"Oh sister," Barbara cried. "They can't get out. They can't get out."

The nun was calm; she didn't realize what was happening upstairs. "We all got out. We all got out."

Barbara ran back into the alley. All of the windows were open and children were hanging from the sills. They were throwing books and shoes and screaming for rescue. She ran back and forth, yelling up to them. "Help is coming! Help is coming!"

Then . . . children began jumping from the windows, landing on the pavement twenty-five feet below.

Still no firemen. The alley was filling with people. A woman ran up to Barbara.

"Why don't the firemen come?" they asked each other simultaneously.

It had been only a minute since Barbara called the Fire Department, but it seemed like an eternity had passed.

Youngsters were landing all around. Some of them had been burned. Others were bleeding. A few got up and hobbled away. Still more lay motionless and silent. They looked broken up. Barbara began dragging kids out of the way, setting them against the wall of her adjacent store.

Some youngsters clearly had broken bones—arms and legs—and Barbara kept thinking, "Isn't it wrong to move injured people?" But she had no choice; she had to make room or the injured would be struck by other falling bodies. She grabbed one boy whose leg was dangling over the other. He was big and heavy, almost too much for her. Still, she found the strength. She grabbed under his armpits and yanked, dragging him out of the way.

Barbara placed six youngsters against the side of her building. Their faces were blistering and swelling up. On some, their clothing was smoldering. Barbara ran into her store and filled a pot with water. Returning to the alley, she began pouring water over the children.

She walked some of the youngsters into her store, out of the cold, shielding them from the awful sights outside. She put them in the kitchen and bedroom, setting them in chairs and laying them in her bed. She grabbed her rosary and handed it to a girl. "Pray for the children," Barbara told her.

Then, once again, thoughts of her daughter flashed through her mind: "Where is my Helena! She hasn't come out."

Barbara rushed back outside, her eyes searching. She brushed past a nun carrying an injured child. She saw Monsignor Cussen, his face contorted in horror, running through the alley, crying. Finally, she spotted Helena's nun in the street.

"Where is my child? She didn't get out."

"She did get out," the nun screamed. "Someone grabbed her and took her to one of the houses."

Steve Lasker saw the plume of smoke in the distance as he drove along Grand Avenue. He was trying to warm up. The twenty-eight-year-old newspaper photographer had just completed an assignment outdoors at a fire extinguisher company. The firm had conducted a test, dropping an extinguisher from its roof to prove that its product wouldn't explode upon impact. The test was in response to a charge that one of its units had done just that.

The smoke in the sky to the south was growing thicker and blacker.

Looks like a good fire, Lasker thought. He grabbed the microphone on his two-way radio and called the *Chicago American* city desk. "Do you have a fire working somewhere on the West Side?"

The day city editor came back. "Don't know anything about it."

Just then the police radio in Lasker's car started blaring. "Send all the help you can! They're jumping out all over!" It was the excited voice of a lone patrolman, the first to arrive at the school.

"Attention, cars in the 28th District," responded the police operator. "Assistance is needed at Our Lady of the Angels, Avers and Iowa."

Lasker stepped on the gas and headed toward the smoke.

Mario Camerini, a friendly twenty-year-old who had grown up in the neighborhood, emerged from the back door of the church basement carrying a case of empty Pepsi bottles. In his part-time job as assistant janitor, he helped out in the church, and on Mondays he always returned the empties from the week before.

Mario was walking into the alley, on the way to Barbara Glowacki's store, when he heard the commotion. He looked up to the windows of Room 208, next to the back stairwell, and saw dozens of seventh-graders jamming the open spaces. Smoke was pouring from the windows. Only a few years ago Mario had been a student in that same classroom. He recognized some of the faces of the youngsters who were screaming down to him for help. He set the bottles down and ran to the garage behind the rectory. There were ladders stored inside.

Max Stachura was napping on the front-room couch facing the television set when he looked at his watch and saw that it was almost time to pick up the boys at school. As a driver for United Parcel Service, Max worked odd hours. He was catching up on his sleep.

Max arose and stepped into the kitchen, putting water on for coffee. Smoke wafted past the back window. When it cleared for a moment, he was startled to see that it was coming from the school. Like many parents, the Stachuras had been concerned about fire in the old building. Only a few weeks before, a small blaze had erupted in the school's basement, just papers and rags. The family consoled Mark, who had come home that day worried.

"Always listen to your nun, and the Fire Department will help you," Max had told him. And to Mary: "We live so close, if there's any big trouble we'll get them out."

Following his own advice, Max grabbed his jacket and ran out the back porch, down the stairs, and into the alley where he saw Mario struggling with a ladder in the garage.

"C'mon," Max yelled. "I'll help you."

The two men picked up the extension ladder used to put up screens and hurried to the burning school. They heaved it up against the wall, raising it to an open window of Room 208. As soon as the ladder touched the sill, seventh-graders began crowding and pushing in a rush to get on it. They started climbing down.

Max felt a momentary sense of relief. But when he glanced over to the smoke-filled windows of the classroom next door, his heart sank.

"That's Mark's room!" he screamed.

Sickening black smoke was pouring over the little faces of students who fought for every inch of space in the small, dark openings. The fourth-graders' heads barely cleared the sills. Mark's face had to be among them. Kids were climbing over one another. The windows were filling with teetering children. Then the pushing and jumping started.

Max fretted. "Where's Mark?"

Finally he spotted his son's little blond head bobbing up and down in the crowd.

"Daddy!" the youngster shrieked. "Help me!"

"Stay there!" Max yelled. "Don't jump!"

Max looked around. He was surrounded by chaos. The fire alarm was ringing over the shouts and screams. Bodies were dropping and landing all over, hitting the pavement and crushed rock with sickening thuds. One man caught a girl whose hair was on fire. He used his coat to smother the flames. Another man standing nearby was being battered to the ground by more falling bodies. Men and women were dragging limp children away from the burning building. Some were badly injured, screaming. Others were deathly still.

"This is crazy! They're killing themselves," Max thought.

He looked back up. Mark was getting ready to jump too.

"No, son! Wait! I'll get you down!"

He ran to his garage in the adjoining alley. Fumbling for his keys, he unlocked the overhead door, grabbed a paint-spattered ladder, and ran back to his son's window at Room 210. The cloud of black smoke pouring from the school was turning darker and denser by the second. The whole place looked like it was ready to explode.

Mark was still struggling at the windowsill when Max returned with the ladder.

"Hold on son! I'm coming!"

The father's heart was pounding wildly. He was nearly out of breath when he flung the ladder against the wall. His momentary elation turned sour. The ladder was too short.

In fact the north side of the building was now dotted with home ladders perched against the school's outer brick wall. All the ladders were too short; children hanging from the windows couldn't reach them. The screams from above forced Max to refocus his attention on Mark's position in the window.

His son called for him. "Daddy!"

The large man's shoulders slumped, and tears began to fill his eyes. The ladder had been his only chance. What else could he do?

"Mark!" he yelled. "Jump! I'll catch you!"

Mark's eyes never left his father. The little fourth-grader tried one last time to pull himself over the windowsill. But just as his elbows touched the ledge, a whoosh of flames crawled up and pulled him back down into the room. Max watched in horror as his son disappeared in the smoke. He was standing in the alley, arms outstretched, helpless. It was the last time he would see Mark alive. The crushing grief dropped him to his knees. He was too late. Despite the nearness of his home, it wasn't close enough.

Irene Mordarski was seated patiently at her desk in the back of Room 208, listening to Sister Canice's history lesson, watching an electric wall clock above the blackboard tick away the final half-hour of school.

Like many of her classmates, Irene's parents had been born in Europe and survived World War II. Her father had served in the Polish army, had been taken prisoner by the Germans, and had later escaped from a concentration camp. Still, Irene had little liking of history, even though she herself was a naturalized citizen of the United States. "It's my least favorite subject," she would often remind her girlfriends.

Sister Canice had already told her pupils there would be a history quiz later in the week, and Irene knew she would have to study. She was hoping something would happen so they wouldn't have to take the test. Her wishful thinking was suddenly interrupted when the room's two wooden doors started ratting.

"Must be ghosts," whispered one boy, and some of the girls giggled. Another boy sitting near Irene stood up from his desk, curious to see what was causing the strange sound. He walked over to the back door.

"There's smoke in the hallway!" he exclaimed.

Sister Canice walked to the front door and opened it. A cloud of black smoke swirled into the room. She slammed the door shut, but almost immediately more smoke began seeping in through the partially opened glass transoms and cracks around the two doors. Irene and her forty-six classmates stopped giggling. As more smoke poured into the room, they started rising from their seats, looking nervously at their nun.

"Just sit tight," said Sister Canice. "The janitor's probably done something with the furnace."

The nun's speculation, of course, was in error—the coal-burning furnace in the basement was working just fine. The truth of the situation at that moment was much more fearsome. The janitor was running into the rectory, yelling to the housekeeper to call the Fire Department, as flames and smoke roared unchecked up the back stairway adjacent to Room 208.

Within seconds the scene inside the classroom began to change rapidly. Smoke passing through the transoms was turning thicker. The children began coughing, confused by the sudden turn of events.

For the moment everyone was silent. Sister Canice could feel her heart starting to pound as her mind raced for answers. A fire was burning somewhere in the building. But how? The fire alarm had not sounded, even though at that moment it no longer mattered. The hallway outside was already impassable. The only way out now was through the windows. Stay calm. Maintain order. Don't lose control. The Fire Department will come. Everything will be all right.

The room was quickly turning warmer and darker. The children were getting nervous. Sister Canice clutched the silver crucifix hanging from her neck. "We mustn't panic," she said. "Get down on your knees. Say a prayer. The firemen will come."

The nun meant well. It was a natural reaction for her, at first, to have her pupils seek divine help. But as conditions inside the room quickly worsened, prayers were discarded, replaced by the instinct for survival. One boy jumped up from his desk. "I'm not staying here any longer." Impulsively, he and the others rushed to the four windows overlooking the alley. Sister Canice followed. So did Irene. But the girl's approach to the last window on the west end of the room was blocked by a crowd of classmates who had jammed themselves in front of the sill. Those nearest the windows threw up the sashes and leaned out into the fresh, clean air. They began screaming. "The school's on fire! The school's on fire!"

The room was growing hotter with each passing second. The old paint covering its worn, wooden walls was changing color—from white to tan to brown. Irene was gasping for air. She yanked a handkerchief from the breast pocket of her navy blue uniform and pressed it against her face, trying desperately to breathe through it. That day was the first time she had ever worn nylon stockings to school, and in the morning, she had slipped on a pair of bobby socks over the stockings to keep out the cold. Heat in the classroom was becoming unbearable, and she could feel the nylons melting to her legs.

Suddenly the big round globe lights that hung from the ceiling began popping from the intense heat, sending shards of glass crashing to the floor. The students dropped to their knees, terrified. Irene now became aware of the crescendo of screams coming not only from her room but from the other classrooms in the stricken school. The screams were loud, chilling. Irene would remember them for the rest of her life.

Then it happened—a bright orange flash followed by a loud, thunderous boom. The fire exploded into the room. It crashed in the doors and burst through the walls. Flames swarmed unhindered across the flammable ceiling tile, spilling like a molten waterfall down to the floor, devouring everything in their path. They ate away at the old wooden flooring and swallowed up desks, tables, and wall hangings. The fire started grabbing the scrambling figures trying to outrun it.

Irene fell to her hands and knees. She could feel her skin burning. She had only seconds to get out of the room. Thoughts of her parents flashed through her mind. Stanley and Amalia Mordarski, Polish and Austrian by birth, had brought her to the United States in 1952, when she was just six years old. She thought of her little sister, Monica, a first-grader downstairs.

With a sudden surge of energy, the girl sprang up and pushed her way through the pile of children bunched in front of her, stepping over those who had passed out or were already dead. Crawling over desks and chairs, she made her way to the window. Then she felt a tug on her shoulder. It was Sister Canice.

"Quick," the nun beckoned. "Get up here!"

A high radiator sat next to the windowsill, and with the help of her nun Irene managed to climb up and gain access to the ledge. Dense smoke was obscuring her vision. She couldn't see her classmates descending the ladder placed at the room's east window by Mario Camerini and Max Stachura. At least one boy had already jumped from another window near the front of the room, breaking a leg as he landed on the sloping roof of a basement window enclosure that shortened his fall.

Irene looked down at the hard gravel and asphalt surface twenty-five feet below. The drop was daunting. A neighbor had propped another ladder directly beneath the windowsill. But it was a few feet short. That's okay, she thought. I'll use it anyhow. She stood up on the ledge and pivoted her body around. Then, dangling from the sill, she reached down with her toes, attempting to get a foothold on the ladder's top rung. Just then the hot fire gases building inside the room ignited and blew out through the windows. The blast caught Irene square in the face, knocking her unconscious. She dropped off the sill, falling straight down, scraping her face all the way against the building's rough brick wall. She hit the pavement with a crash, shattering her pelvis.

When Irene awoke she was in a daze. She found herself sitting against the north wall of the blazing school, inexplicably clutching a string of white rosary beads. The beads had been in her uniform pocket when she plummeted to the ground; she had no idea how they came to be in her burned hands. Nor did she know how long she'd been lying on the ground—seconds or minutes. She couldn't remember if she had fallen from the window or was pushed out by Sister Canice.

Irene looked down at her feet. Both of her black suede shoes were missing.

"Oh, my new shoes," she murmured. "They're gone."

Her entire body was numb and hot. The fresh, cold air felt good against her skin. She was drifting euphorically into shock and began to feel an overwhelming sense of relief in having escaped the inferno above. Still, she didn't feel right; she knew something was wrong.

Her face was cut and bleeding from rubbing against the wall. Her pelvis was fractured in two places. Both her legs were covered with second- and third-degree burns—from her knees to a point just above her ankles, where her bobby socks had provided some protection against the searing flames. Her face, arms, and hands were burned.

She looked up dazedly at several of her stunned classmates who were gathering around her.

"Somebody, please help me," she cried.

In Room 209, Gerry Andreoli was sitting in the second row of desks, near windows overlooking the U-shaped courtway separating the school's north and south wings. Sister Davidis was teaching a math lesson, charting figures on the blackboard. At full capacity Room 209 held sixty-three students— "wall-to-wall kids," Sister Davidis would say with resigned good humor. But because of absences there were only fifty-five pupils in place that Monday, thirty-four boys and twenty-one girls.

The first sign of trouble came when Danny Patano rose to begin his daily chore of collecting waste paper from his classmates. When he walked over to pick up the metal basket near the back of the room, the basket for some reason felt hot. At the same time Richard Sacco, another student sitting near the back door, raised his hand.

"Yes?" inquired Sister Davidis.

"Sister, I think I smell something burning."

Gerry Andreoli and the other eighth-graders turned to see what was happening. Sister Davidis was standing at the front, or west end, of the room and had not detected the odor herself.

"Let's check it out," she said.

It was a little before 2:30.

Sister Davidis moved toward the front door, Richard Sacco the back door. The boy was closer, and when he grabbed the knob and opened the door, a mass of heavy smoke looking like large bales of black cotton rolled into the room. When the nun reached the front door, she touched the metal knob but withdrew immediately. It felt red-hot. She and the children were becoming aware of the fire tornado gathering force in the ten-foot-wide hallway separating the upper classrooms in the north wing.

Sister Davidis quickly sized up the predicament she and her students were facing. She knew the odds were against trying to escape through the hallway. If she started her kids out that way, chances were they'd get lost in the smoke, maybe even pass out and be trampled to death. She couldn't chance it. Her street-smarts took over. She moved into action.

"All right," she announced. "You boys start gathering up books and start blocking up the cracks at the bottom of the doors. The rest of you stay put."

The boys responded, grabbing books off the desks and stacking them around the doors to keep out the smoke. When the job was finished, Sister Davidis directed her students to the south windows overlooking the twenty-foot-wide cement courtway.

Gerry Andreoli felt the room growing warmer as he and his classmates crowded near the four windows. In his haste to reach the window on the west end of the room, he had climbed over his nun's desk, knocking a stack of papers to the floor. He managed to stake out a small space for himself, and it was only then he realized that the occupants in the classroom across the courtway, in the south wing, were still unaware of the unfolding situation.

"Call to them!" Sister Davidis said.

The eighth-graders began yelling as loud as they could. "The school's on fire! The school's on fire!"

Kathy Meisinger was one of those in the opposite classroom. She was staring out her second-floor window, trying to pay attention to a music lesson, when she noticed students across the courtway in the north wing jumping up and down on their desks, looking like they were having a party. It was then she and her classmates heard the screams. They began evacuating their room just as smoke started drifting into the south wing. The fire alarm had not yet sounded, and the occupants in the room directly below Kathy's remained oblivious to the excited shouts. Sister Davidis told her students to start throwing pencils at the lower windows. When the teacher there heard them bouncing off the glass, she knew something was wrong. Sister Davidis's students were not in the habit of hanging out windows, throwing pencils.

At that moment Sister Davidis heard a loud crack. She turned to see that the glass transoms above the doors were shattering from the intense heat. A wave of flames came pouring into the room, spreading across the acoustical wheat-fiber ceiling tile. A small canopy was located a few feet below the room's back window. Eddie Maggerise turned to his nun. "Sister, it's not far. Can I go?"

Sister Davidis yelled back. "If you can make it, jump."

He could and did. After dropping himself to the canopy, the boy jumped down to the ground. He looked up to his nun in the smoke-filled window. She leaned out to shout him an order. "Go get help!"

Eddie ran to the front of the courtway. He climbed over the high iron picket fence and took off running.

Sister Davidis stayed with her students at the windows. The smoke was getting worse, obscuring her vision. The heat was intensifying. The flames were flowing across the ceiling. The room was growing dark. She feared one of her charges might stray from her sight. She felt herself losing consciousness. She forced her head out the window, gasping for air.

"Smoke's coming through the floor!" yelled one of the boys, more astonished than frightened as he pointed to an opening around a radiator pipe.

"Just keep your heads out," the nun said.

Gerry Andreoli had spent all his grammar school years at Our Lady of the Angels. But behind his shy demeanor was a sense of fierce determination, one that would carry him through his ordeal. He would be one of the last pupils to escape the inferno inside Room 209, and one of the most critically burned students to survive the catastrophe. With time slipping away and flames bearing down, he glanced at the forbidding cement courtway two and a half stories below. It looked awfully far.

Sam Tortorice had just returned home to his two-flat on Hamlin Avenue, directly across the street from Our Lady of the Angels Church. He had spent the day shopping, and he was reaching inside his car to collect his grocery bags when he noticed the pungent odor of burning wood. Tortorice, forty-two, was short, dark-haired, and wore glasses. He looked up in the direction of the smell. It was strong. He took only a few steps before he saw a cloud of black smoke rolling from the top of the parish school. Inside were his two daughters, thirteen-year-old Rose and eleven-year-old Judy.

Tortorice took off running for the burning building. When he reached the front of the school on Avers, he looked up to the smoke-filled windows overlooking the courtway. There was Rose among the frightened faces crowding the far window of Room 209.

"Rose," he screamed, "wait! I'm coming!"

Tortorice ran around to the Iowa Street doors, where he entered the school and, dodging children making their way down, ran up the stairs to the second floor. There he made his way into the annex corridor, then crawled to a set of windows overlooking the courtway and directly adjacent to the windows in Room 209. Tortorice threw up the sash, then swung his left leg over the ledge. Straddling the windowsill, he reached over with his arms and began swinging the panicky eighth-graders into the annex.

"Rose," he yelled, "come closer!"

Try as she might, Rose could not reach the rescuing hands of her father. She was struck behind the others lined up at the window. With smoke pouring over her head, she pleaded for help. "Daddy!" she cried, "come quick!"

Tortorice knew he had to reposition himself. He swung his legs over the window ledge, lowering himself down onto a small canopy roof set over a doorway directly beneath him. Another neighbor had tossed a ladder over the fence into the blocked courtway. Tortorice dropped down to the pavement and grabbed the ladder, using it to climb back up onto the canopy. "Hold on," he shouted to the kids above.

At about the same time Father Joseph Ognibene was driving east on Iowa Street, returning to the rectory after lunch with friends in a neighboring parish. As he neared Avers Avenue, the south wing of the school came into view, and Father Ognibene could see smoke pouring from the building and children being led outside onto the sidewalk.

Tall, dark-skinned, and athletic, "Father Joe" was thirty-two, the senior curate assigned to the parish. He was popular with the students and active in the school's physical education programs. During spring and summer months he could often be found on neighborhood ball diamonds, wearing a T-shirt and old slacks, shagging fly balls with boys from the parish. The older children were especially fond of him; they enjoyed it when he came out to play ball with them, and they were impressed to find that he was pretty good at it too. The girls in the parish liked him as well. They thought he was "cute."

Immediately Father Ognibene screeched his car to a halt, curbing it in front of the convent, then darted across the street and entered the school through the front doors on Iowa Street. It was approximately 2:40 p.m. The first call to the Fire Department had yet to be made.

Bounding up the stairs to the second-floor landing, Father Ognibene was met by a scene of crowded confusion. Some of the students gathering in the hallway were frightened by the thickening smoke. Father Joe didn't fully realize what was happening, but he knew he had to hurry them down.

"Let's get going," he shouted. The priest began shoving the students one by one toward the stairs. One of the children having difficulty was a sixth-grade girl. She had polio, and the heavy metal braces strapped to her legs were causing her to struggle. Father Ognibene scooped the girl into his arms and carried her down the stairs. He didn't care that her braces tumbled off when he did so. After handing the girl off to a nun, he raced back up the stairs to the second floor. It was then Father Ognibene realized that something more terrible than he imagined was unfolding.

Unable to stand up because of the worsening smoke, he dropped to his hands and knees and began crawling through the dark abyss of smoke filling the tiny annex corridor, headed for the doomed classrooms of the north wing. He was able to go as far as the end of the corridor, but that was all. Beyond him in the smoke were raging flames, which cut off further access. On his left were the two corner windows facing the courtway. Father Ognibene looked out and saw Tortorice standing on the ladder, trying to lift children out of Room 209. "Here," the priest yelled, "swing them to me."

Quickly Father Ognibene doffed his black suit coat and clerical vest. Thus unencumbered, he hoisted himself up to the ledge of the corner window adjacent to Room 209. Straddling the window frame, he leaned out, placing himself in a position to help Tortorice by reaching for students hanging from the adjacent window. Together the two men proceeded with their daring joint rescue: Tortorice yanking the children from the burning classroom, Ognibene reaching out and swinging them into the annex.

Gerry Andreoli watched as the two men pulled his classmates from the corner window. Smoke inside the room was getting worse. Unable to breathe, Gerry dropped to the floor and curled up in a ball. He was losing track of time. He noticed his girlfriend, Beverly Burda, lying next to him. Her white sweater was turning color. "I'm getting out of here," he yelled to her.

Gerry got back up and grabbed onto the windowsill, stepping up to the ledge. As he mounted the sill he was being enveloped by flames and smoke shooting around the window frames. Suddenly a whoosh of flames crashed down through the ceiling. Fire was now shooting from the sides of the windows, burning Gerry on the head, arms, and shoulders. His vision became clouded, but he could still see well enough to spot—for the first time—a ladder resting just below the windowsill, short by about two feet.

Gerry wavered on the ledge, feeling dizzy, like he might fall back into the flames or straight down to the concrete below. He somehow managed to maintain his balance, long enough to lower his feet onto the ladder. The flesh on his hands had been peeled back, resembling bloodied pieces of raw meat, and his elbows were burned to the bone. Yet he was able to slide his feet down far enough to reach the top rung. Then, in an awkward, forward fashion, he descended the ladder, hooking his feet around the rungs and working his way down, one step at a time.

Once on the ground he could see only a few feet ahead of him. He felt he was about to collapse but managed to stagger the few feet to the iron fence. Firefighters who had managed to break down its gate were running into the courtway carrying ladders and life nets. Children bunched up at the win-

dows were jumping like crazy, bouncing off the pavement. Firemen were trying to catch them or break their falls.

Gerry thought of walking to his father's clothing store on Chicago
Avenue when his endurance finally gave out. He looked—for the first time—
at his hands and began to realize the seriousness of his injuries. His face had
swelled up and his body felt sunburned. His white shirt was tattered, disintegrated by flames; only the dangling cuffs remained intact.

He stumbled to the front of the courtway.

"Get me some help," he pleaded to a fireman, who directed him to an
ambulance parked on Avers Avenue.

Sister Seraphica could feel her heart skip as the rock came crashing
through the middle window in Room 210. She was busy handing out a homework assignment to her fourth-graders and walked to the window to look
outside. Standing below in the alley was a handful of adults, each pointing and
shouting, trying to get her attention.

"Sister! Sister! The school's on fire!"

The nun looked to her right. "Oh, my God!" she shrieked, raising her
hand to her mouth.

Smoke and flames were licking out the back stairwell enclosure. More
smoke was billowing out the open windows of Room 208 next door, and children inside were climbing out onto the ledges. By the time the startled Sister
Seraphica returned to her desk at the front of the classroom, smoke was already
seeping through cracks around the doors. She tried to catch up with the scene.
Why isn't the fire alarm ringing? There had been no warning. She looked at
her little fourth-graders, then made a decision.

"Listen, everyone," she said, feigning a smile, trying to look calm.
"There's a little fire in the stairway. Everyone say a 'Hail Mary,' and when the
firemen come we can leave."

Vito Muilli didn't understand. The twelve-year-old had arrived in the
United States from his native Italy the previous June, and because he spoke
little English, had been placed in the fourth grade. He turned to a girl sitting
next to him who spoke Italian.

Cosa dice, lei? "What is she saying?" he asked.

La scuola è in fuoco. Bisognamo di pregare. "The school's on fire. We have
to pray."

Vito laughed. Why, he asked himself, does she want us to pray if there's
a fire?

He didn't wait for an answer.

Sister Seraphica was a petite woman whose diminutive size in no way hampered her authoritarian reign in the classroom. But as noxious smoke continued to fill the room, her hold on the students began slipping. Struggling to maintain control, she ordered them to gather in a semicircle around her desk. They began reciting the Rosary, one of the longest prayers in the Catholic church. Vito and another boy got up and lunged for the back door. When they swung it open, a hot blast of smoke crashed through like a hammer, knocking them back.

Unable to enter the hallway and reach the front stairs that led to Avers Avenue, the boys scrambled to the open windows, joining their classmates at the sills. The gasping fourth-graders were several deep. They were stacked on top of each other, fighting for space. Pandemonium reigned as an ocean of smoke, followed by raging flames, poured inside the room through the open door.

Conditions in Room 210 deteriorated rapidly as flames swarmed across the ceiling, engulfing the entire room. Children at the windows were hysterical, pulling and clawing each other in a mad fit to reach safety. With temperatures climbing to furnace-hot levels and flames bearing down, the children began jumping to the ground. But not all of the little fourth-graders could reach over the high windowsills that stood more than three feet off the floor. Those too short—or too weak—to pull themselves up onto the ledges fell to the floor, where they were trampled and left to die.

Diane Traynor had been sitting in the row of desks next to the windows at the back of the room. The nine-year-old would not recall hearing the fire alarm until Room 210 was entirely filled with pitch black smoke. Diane was just over four feet tall, and after running to the window she found the high ledge difficult to reach over.

Suddenly flames burst through the ceiling in the front of the room, and Diane knew she had to get out. She turned and saw one little redheaded girl sitting at her desk, frozen in fear. I'm not going to die like that, Diane thought to herself. I'm getting out. Maybe not yet. But I'm going.

She didn't wait long. Diane was struggling to reach over the windowsill when she saw one of her classmates, a boy, climb up onto the ledge next to hers and jump off. He struck the pavement hard, breaking both of his ankles. Then another little girl leaped into the air, fracturing her spine and hip when she hit the ground.

Diane's patent-leather shoes started smoking. She kicked them off. Her white socks caught fire and her hair started burning. Flames swarmed down from the ceiling and began devouring her back and shoulders. If she didn't jump immediately, she'd burn to death.

"Oh God. Please help us," she screamed.

Using her final ounce of strength, Diane pulled herself up onto the window ledge. Then, with smoke blocking her view, she somersaulted out the window.

Fortunately for Diane Traynor, her fall was broken when she glanced off the shoulders of a man standing below in the alley. She tumbled to the pavement, landing on her back. Somehow, amid the chaos in the alley, she managed to get to her feet and walk to the candy store next door. She went into the back room and telephoned her mother.

"Ma," she said, "the school's on fire, but I'm all right."

Diane left the store and sat on a wooden bench just outside the front door next to the sidewalk. She was going into shock. She got up from the bench and started to walk away.

"Grab that girl!" a woman yelled.

Someone threw a blanket over Diane and carried her to a waiting police car parked in the street. Diane felt like she was burning up inside. Her entire body ached. She was placed in the back seat of the squad car along with two other children. A policeman jumped in and took off to the hospital.

Meanwhile, for the rest of Diane's classmates still trapped inside Room 210, time had just about run out. The scorching heat was nearing its flash point and smoke had reduced visibility to less than a foot. From his spot at the window, Vito Muilli glanced one last time into the room. He couldn't see his nun or the other children at the adjacent windows. Like Diane, Vito knew he had to jump. Flames were dancing around the window frames but had not yet engulfed the center. The boy reached for the sill and pulled himself up. Suddenly he felt something hit his hand and the room exploded in flames.

Someone had placed a ladder at the window, but it was about three feet short of the ledge. Vito swung himself around and hung himself out backward. He was trying to set his feet on the top rung, but when he let go of the ledge, he missed the ladder and slid down along its beams, striking his side on the pavement.

Vito felt his body go numb. He was covered in soot and his ears felt like someone had stuck him with a thousand prickly needles. A clump of his bushy black hair was missing, burned off by flames, exposing his scorched scalp. His arms were burned and bleeding. When he looked around him he saw other children on the concrete. Some were screaming. Others lay still, motionless. At the windows above, scores of other youngsters were jumping off ledges, tumbling to the ground. Thump. Thump. Thump, they landed.

For a second, Vito shut his eyes. This can't be happening, he thought. It's too unbelievable.

A policeman was dragging kids out of the way, setting them against the wall of Barbara Glowacki's store when he spotted Vito lying on his back. "Hang on, kid," he shouted. "I'm coming."

But the frightened youngster didn't understand what the big man had said. He didn't want to. He was scared of police. He was scared of everything. He wanted his mother. Just then he regained some feeling in his legs and jumped up. He took off running, headed for his home and his bed two blocks north.

From behind his desk in the back of Room 212, John Raymond looked over to the windows, making sure the sun was still out, that clouds had not invaded the deep blue sky. He shifted his eyes to the clock on the wall next to the flag. It was 2:30. He knew it wouldn't be long before he could run home and ride his new bike, leaving all to hear the clackity-clack of the playing cards he had pinned to its spokes.

His nun, Sister Therese, was busy teaching a last-minute geography lesson to the fifty-five fifth-graders. Even though she was strict, the students adored her. Among all the sisters she displayed a delicious sense of humor. On the day before, the young nun had decorated the school's bulletin boards for Christmas. Afterward, when she returned to the convent, she crayoned a message to Sister Andrienne, her roommate, on a medicine chest mirror.

"Today is Recollection Sunday," it read. "We can't celebrate, but tomorrow we'll make whoopie."

It was a whimsical, lighthearted thought that was never fulfilled.

John was still daydreaming when another boy jumped up.

"Sister," he said, pointing to the door. "There's smoke!"

At the edges of the transoms, over the doors, black smoke curled into the classroom, fanning out along the twelve-foot-high ceiling.

That's odd, thought the nun. Maybe the chimney's backed up.

She walked to the front door and handled the doorknob. It felt unusually hot. Another boy rose from his seat and opened the back door, allowing a wave of smoke to pour inside.

"Close it," yelled the nun. "Everybody be quiet."

For a moment, Sister Therese was dumbfounded. The smoke was too dense for a backed-up chimney. It must be a fire.

They couldn't leave the room, certainly not until the fire alarm went off. That was the rule: "Never leave the building until the fire alarm rings." She remembered it from earlier fire drills and knew that it took about three minutes to evacuate the entire building—lining up the students and walking them down the stairs. What she didn't know at that moment was that the primary means of escape used during those orderly, efficient fire drills was being cut off by roaring flames and smoke in the corridor outside.

Sister Therese returned to her desk. The students looked at her, seeking direction.

"We can't go until we're told," she said. "Let's pray."

Sister Therese crossed herself. "In the name of the Father, and of the Son, and of the Holy Ghost. . . ."

Precious seconds were ticking by. The nun looked to the doors. Smoke passing through the transoms was growing denser, the smell of burning more acrid. The children were starting to cough. It was getting darker, hotter.

". . . pray for us sinners, now and at the hour of our death. Amen."

More seconds ticked by. Still no fire alarm. Suddenly the heat in the corridor shattered the large glass transom over the front door, sending a thick current of black smoke billowing into the room.

"Get to the windows!" Sister Therese screamed. "Now!"

The children obeyed, jumping up from their desks and scrambling to the four windows overlooking the alley below. They threw up the sashes, gasping for air. Smoke rolled out over their heads. There was no turning back.

"Get out on the ledges!" commanded the nun. Then, seeing no other way out, she started pushing them out. "Go! Go! Save yourselves!"

John Raymond didn't know what to do. He couldn't believe what was happening. Just a few moments before he was daydreaming about his bike. Now he found himself in the midst of a deadly panic, a bit player in a tragic production. Somehow he ended up on the floor. He started to crawl. It was like being in a tunnel. There was air near the floor and it was easier to breathe. He was crawling around desks, snaking his way toward the front of the room. He didn't know where he was going or why he was doing it, he just did it.

Where's the light? he wondered. It's getting dark in here. When he reached the front of the room, all he could see were figures. Kids were screaming for their mothers. Others were calling for the nun. She was embracing them. She was surrounded by kids, just draped with them. They were hanging from her.

"Sister," they shrieked. "Help us. Where are you?"

John looked up at the big globe lights. They probably had five-hundred-watt bulbs, but he could hardly see them. The smoke was that thick. He looked toward the windows. Outside it was bright and sunny, but he could hardly see daylight. He turned toward the front door and could feel heat at his face. It felt like being under a sunlamp.

At that point John took in a lungful of smoke. He was losing control, unable to breathe. He started to panic. "Please, God, help me," he said. He kept saying it and saying it and saying it. He was ready to pass out. "Please, God, help me. Please, God, help me."

Then he jumped up and sprang for the window. He pulled kids out of the way. Pushed them away. Dragged them away. Then he dove out. He had to. He was going to die.

Floating through the air, John felt a strange sense of relief. He knew he was falling, that he might be hurt, yet it was the greatest feeling in the world because it was air and he could breathe. He landed hard on the pavement, on his right side, and a sharp pain shot through his body. But whatever damage the fall had caused didn't matter. He was just glad to be out.

The scene in the alley where he had landed was one of utter chaos. Blood from the broken bodies of other children marked the pavement. Frantic neighbors and parents were running in all directions. They were screaming to students hanging from the windowsills, pleading with them not to jump, to wait for firefighters' ladders and nets.

John crawled the few feet to Barbara Glowacki's candy store, meeting another boy from his class. The youngster had also jumped, breaking both his ankles. He was crying; his face was turning grey.

"Jimmy," John asked. "What's wrong? Are you okay?"

When the boy didn't answer, John figured he was in shock. He just stared into space, his mouth hanging open.

Barbara Glowacki appeared with a blanket. She threw it over the two boys. "Stay here," she cried. "The ambulance will come."

John sat with his back against the bricks. His side was hurting and his throat felt like he'd swallowed a jar of tacks. He looked up at his burning school. The sights and sounds jolted his senses.

There was screaming. Women screaming. Children screaming. Kids were hanging from the sills and dropping to the ground. They landed with dull, hollow thuds, sounding like sacks of potatoes smashing on concrete. He saw a girl on fire coming down to the ground. She just stood up on the windowsill and jumped. She landed head first, cracking her skull. He saw one man break the fall of a boy, and then saw him go down after he was hit by the next falling child. He didn't get up.

When the smoke cleared for a second, John could see Sister Therese in the window. A handful of girls clutched her sleeves. Just then smoke puffed back out and they disappeared behind its oily black curtain.

John felt light-headed, like he wanted to faint. He was sick from smoke, drifting into shock, losing touch of his whereabouts. One of his aunts lived across the street on Avers. He looked over and saw people carrying injured children through the front of the building. John stood up, deciding to go there. Staggering like a drunkard, he teetered out of the alley, oblivious to the crowd of frightened faces and the terror they conveyed. Instead all he saw were mental images of his father, his two brothers, and his younger sisters. Had they made it out?

Earlier that afternoon Sister Helaine had told her class that the pastor needed about ten boys to help load donated clothes onto a truck parked outside the church. Thirteen boys in Room 211 raised their hands to volunteer their services. "All right," the nun said, "all of you can go."

About an hour later, as the class was working on its English lesson, a girl who temporarily had been out of the room rushed in the back door and went to the nun's desk. She was coughing loudly. "Sister," she said, "there's a lot of smoke in the hallway!"

Some smoke had already entered the room when the girl opened and closed the back door. Sister Helaine got up from her desk and told the students to stand and walk calmly to the front door. When the nun opened the front door, she and the eighth-graders were driven back by black smoke.

"Try the back door," Sister Helaine ordered. The rear door was opened with the same result: hot smoke poured into the room.

With both doors closed and with Sister Helaine unwilling to risk sending her pupils into the hallway in an effort to escape down the front stairs only a few feet away, the same pattern of behavior occurred in Room 211 as in other rooms in the north wing. The nun ordered her students to the windows, then started saying Hail Marys. The children joined her in prayer, but not for long.

Father Charles Hund was feeling ill.

The twenty-seven-year-old priest had celebrated Mass that morning in the parish church, and after lunch had decided to retire to his second-floor room in the rectory. It was his day to be on duty, and the effects of the flu had left him tired and sluggish. He laid himself across his bed and went to sleep.

Inside the house it was empty and quiet; his fellow religious were out. Father Alfred Corbo and Father Joseph McDonnell were away visiting patients at nearby Walther Memorial Hospital, and Father Joseph Ognibene was having lunch with friends at a neighboring parish. Monsignor Cussen, the pastor, was roaming outside on church grounds, overseeing the parish clothing drive, while the two other monsignors who shared the house, Joseph Fitzgerald and John Egan, were downtown on church business.

It didn't take long for Father Hund to nod off. He'd been napping for more than an hour when the first screams came filtering through the wall.

"Help! Please help us!"

The priest stirred and sat up, damp with sweat. He rubbed his eyes and looked at the clock. Two-thirty. Some dream, he thought. He lay back down and closed his eyes.

He heard it again.

"Help! The school's on fire!"

That, he knew, was not a dream. It was real, and it sounded close. He bolted upright in his bed. What the hell's going on?

The sole window in Father Hund's dimly lit quarters was next to his bed and faced the back of the school. He leaned over to peer through the curtains. What he saw sent him reeling. Crowding the windows directly across the narrow gangway were a dozen or so terrified faces of students, smoke pouring over their heads. The children were banging on the window frame, shouting, "Father! Save us!"

The children, he knew, were in Room 207, the "Cheese Box," so called because of its small dimensions. The classroom had once housed the school's library. It was located near the southeast corner of the north wing, next to the building's only fire escape. But Father Hund could see that the fire escape door was closed, that no one was coming down. He sprang from the bed, threw on a leather jacket over his T-shirt, and ran down the stairs. As he passed through the kitchen and headed out the back door, he could hear Mrs. Maloney on the phone, wrestling with her brogue, trying to describe the fire's location.

Father Hund ran into the gangway and looked up. Smoke was pouring out of the school. "Hang on," he shouted. "I'm coming." He slipped through the back door of the school's annex and bounded up a flight of stairs to the second floor. When he reached the landing he found the smoke so thick that he couldn't see more than a foot ahead. He remembered what he had been told as a child: If you're ever in a fire, stay near the floor. That's where the air is.

Instinctively he dropped to his knees and began crawling through the dark, narrow corridor, inching his way forward, trying to get into the north wing. But even here, near the floor, he couldn't escape the choking effect of the smoke. Heat from the fire was pressing against his face, making his eyes water. Black mucus started dripping from his nostrils. The smoke was pushing into his lungs, making him gag and cough. It felt like someone was shoving a hot rag down his throat. He thought he might vomit. He started to panic, and for a second he felt he would pass out. He knew he had to get out. To go any farther would be crazy. He'd never make it.

The young priest backed out of the corridor and retreated down the stairs, all the way to the basement. He was arguing with himself. He had to get back up to the second floor. But how?

He dashed through the chapel at the bottom of the north wing, then through a door in the boiler room that opened into the small area at the foot of the northeast stairwell where the fire had originated. Curiously, the flames here had subsided a little, though the area was super hot, with fire licking through the stairs themselves. Father Hund decided to try them anyway. He rolled up the bottom of his baggy black trousers, then started up. But he didn't go far; the inferno engulfing the upper part of the stairway stopped him short. Any farther and he'd light up like a torch. He was turning to leave when flames suddenly flared up underneath him, catching his shoes on fire. It was so hot in the stairway that he thought it would explode at any second. He had to get out, fast.

He ran back into the basement, cut off but still determined somehow to make the second floor. He returned to the annex and raced back up the same staircase he had tried the first time. His second attempt was successful, and when he reached the landing he was surprised to see the smoke had cleared a bit, though the ceiling above was now burning pretty well.

Father Hund was ducking burning embers and falling debris when a harried face appeared in the darkness. It belonged to the janitor, Jim Raymond, and he looked horrible. Raymond too had worked his way up to the smoky second floor, managing to open one window, using his flashlight to break out another. But in breaking the window he had caught his arm on a piece of jagged glass, slicing open his left wrist. He was bent over, squeezing it with his right hand, trying to stop the flow of blood.

Father Hund grabbed his arm. "What the hell's going on?"

"I don't know," Raymond replied, confused from blood loss.

The priest motioned to Room 207. "Why can't they get out?"

"They can't. The fire's too bad."

"What about the back door? By the fire escape?"

"It's locked."

"You got a key?"

"Yeah, I think so."

"Then open the damn thing."

Matt Plovanich was lying on his back, watching smoke fill up the Cheese Box.

The fifth-grader was slowly losing consciousness, contemplating the oddity of dying at ten, trying hard to remember what his nuns had always preached. "You never know when God is going to come calling on you. Always be ready for Him."

It's not that Matt wasn't ready. He was. It's just that it seemed unfair. He and his classmates hadn't done anything wrong. They were good kids, tried to do good deeds. They obeyed their nuns, listened to their parents, did their homework on time, never skipped school. They said their prayers and went to Mass, asking for God's forgiveness when they sinned. And now they were burning up in their classroom.

It was strange, but Matt felt dying wouldn't be so bad after all, just something that happens to everyone, a natural occurrence in the cycle of life. Still, he was feeling sorry for his parents. His father, Rudy, was a policeman, and his mom, Irene, a housewife. If he died, he knew they'd be sad. He hoped God would watch over them. He thought of his three brothers. Jimmy was four years old. Mike was a seventh-grader in the south wing. Danny was downstairs in the first grade.

The smoke was getting worse. It was thick and toxic, filling up the ceiling, making it harder to breathe. Matt could feel himself drifting away, like being on a life raft, floating alone in the middle of the ocean. The panic that had gripped him only moments before had dissipated, replaced by a comforting sense of serenity. Some of his classmates were still kicking and scratching each other, crying for their mothers, trying to escape the room. To Matt it seemed futile.

What good does that do? he thought. We're trapped. We can't get out.

His teacher, Sister Mary Geraldita Ennis, was somewhere inside the room, lost in the darkness amid her forty fifth- and sixth-graders. When smoke first invaded the classroom around the door cracks, she rose to investigate. The front door faced the burning stairway, and when she opened it, a wall of flame was blocking the exit.

Sister Geraldita was just five feet tall. She was strict but fair, with a good sense of humor. After closing the front door, she started quickly for the room's back door. The back exit opened into the narrow, coat-lined hallway separating Rooms 207 and 206, and led to the building's only fire escape.

But when Sister Geraldita grabbed the doorknob, it didn't turn. It was locked. She reached into her pocket, feeling for her key. It was empty. She closed her eyes, remembering now that she had been running late that morning and had left her keys behind in the convent.

Matt was sitting at his desk next to the back door. When he looked up at his nun, he saw the look of absolute terror cross her face. He knew what it meant: he and his classmates were trapped, their means of escape cut off.

"Come here," waved Sister Geraldita, gathering her students in a semi-circle near the back of the room. "We're in trouble. We must pray for help."

She began leading the class in the Rosary, but as the room turned pitch black, all control was lost. Soon the children, especially the girls, started screaming in terror. They were huddled in the back corner of the room, Matt among them, pressing their faces against the smooth wooden floor, trying to breathe. A few broke ranks and rushed to the windows overlooking the small gangway behind the school. They flung up the sashes and cried out.

"Help! Help! Save us! Save us!"

One boy picked up a planter and hurled it out the window, against the wall of the adjacent rectory. Another boy leaped out the window, landing on the fire escape below. The rest of the class stayed down on the floor, waiting uncertainly.

Smoke was banking down to the floor. Matt couldn't see. It was like nighttime. Orange flames were burning through wooden panels on the front door. It wouldn't be long now.

Just then Matt heard a tearing noise, like someone ripping apart an old T-shirt. There in the smoke stood the janitor, Mr. Raymond. Father Hund was behind him. "C'mon!" they yelled. "This way! It's clear!"

When the pair had reached the classroom, Raymond used his key to unlock the door. But he still had to push it open, for the opposite side was blocked by cardboard posters taped across the inside of the doorjamb.

For little Matt Plovanich, it was like the cavalry coming; the men might have been wearing blue hats. It was that dramatic, that close. They were on their last breaths. Time had just about run out.

Smoke rushed out the open back door as Matt and his classmates climbed to their feet. They were sluggish, unsteady, slow-moving. "Let's go!" yelled Father Hund. "Faster! Faster!" The men started grabbing the children by their collars, pulling them up off the floor, shoving them out the door.

Raymond followed them out. He was shaking, sweating, holding his bloody wrist. Squeezing his way between the children, he moved to the front of the line, then shoved open the door leading to the weighted steel fire escape ladder that dropped down into the gangway behind the school. But the youngsters, frightened and hesitant, balked. Intense heat inside their room was blowing out the windows above them, and the sound of shattering glass was scary.

"Keep going!" shouted Father Hund.

The line started moving. Soon they were down. Sister Geraldita was the last person to leave the classroom. As soon as she exited, it burst into flames. When she reached the top of the fire escape, she too hesitated. Her face was reddened and she was coughing on smoke. She turned to Father Hund, making a move to return to the room. "I can't go! They're not all out!" she screamed.

Father Hund was not entirely sure himself that all the students had made it out safely. But it no longer mattered. It was too late. The room was awash in flames. There was no turning back.

"No!" he barked. "Keep going!"

He grabbed the frightened nun by the arm and together they fled down the ladder, praying—but not yet knowing—that all the students had indeed escaped, that Room 207 would be the only second-floor classroom in the north wing not to record a fatality.

Teachers and students in the school's south wing were the farthest from the fire and the last to learn of the calamity occurring in the other side of the building. Although no deaths or serious injuries would occur in the south wing, escape from second-floor classrooms was nonetheless made difficult by waves of thick smoke drifting through the hallways.

Seventh-graders in Room 201, located in the southwest corner of the wing, were busy reading about the life of St. Joan of Arc when the tragedy struck. In her prologue, Sister Mary Andrienne Carolan described the torment of the French heroine, telling how Joan had been condemned to death and burned at the stake. The youngsters were stirred by the story. The drawings in their texts showed the Maid of Orleans perishing impressively in the flames.

Sister Andrienne had a knack for storytelling. She liked to use anecdotes to paint word pictures for her students. She was thirty-five, Irish, and proud of her heritage. "The name used to be O'Carolan," she'd smile. "Same as the last of the Irish bards."

She was in her eleventh year at Our Lady of the Angels, had charge of the altar boys, and helped supervise children who remained at school during luncheon recess. And though she was small—she weighed only 105 pounds—she still had a way of dealing with "disciplinary problems," a fact evidenced by the number of troublesome boys who were shunted to her care. But if she was strict, she was also compassionate. She had a soft spot for the children of troubled West Side families, often lending a sympathetic ear to one in need.

One girl she was particularly fond of was Mary Ellen Moretti, whose father, Michael, a former Chicago police officer, was serving a life sentence for murder at Stateville Penitentiary in nearby Joliet, Illinois.

The Moretti case had been a sordid affair, widely publicized in the press. One night in August 1951, after getting his fill in a tour of several South Side taverns, Michael Moretti had gone on a rampage, firing his gun into a parked car, killing two youths and wounding a third. Moretti, then a city patrolman assigned to the state's attorney's office, said the shootings were in the line of duty. But evidence corroborated by the survivor led to Moretti's indictment and conviction. "*Èbrutto,*"—It's ugly, he mumbled in Italian when the judge in the case sentenced him to life. After his conviction, three of Moretti's brothers were found guilty of attempting to bribe and intimidate the major witness against Michael. Six years later the family was shaken by more tragedy when another brother, Salvatore Moretti, fell victim to an unrelated gangland murder.

In the fall of 1958, at the urging of Sister Andrienne, Mary Ellen Moretti had enrolled as a transfer student at Our Lady of the Angels. The two had met during a summer religion course that the nun taught to Catholic students from local public schools. Sister Andrienne was sympathetic to Mary Ellen's plight, and their friendship blossomed. "You can't blame the children for the sins of their fathers," she'd say.

In time the two developed a pleasant rapport, and when the term began, Sister Andrienne had wanted Mary Ellen in her classroom so she could provide the emotional support she knew the girl needed. But when September arrived and Mary Ellen was assigned to Sister Canice's room in the north wing, Sister Andrienne was disappointed. Her lingering regret would turn to grief later that afternoon when the body of Mary Ellen Moretti, blond, blue-eyed, and only twelve years old, was pulled by firefighters from the charred ruins of Room 208.

But for now Sister Andrienne was finishing her talk on Joan of Arc: "On May 30, 1431, she was led into the marketplace at Rouen to be burned at the stake. She was not quite twenty years old. Her ashes were tossed into the Seine. She is the patron saint of France and of French soldiers. She is portrayed in art as a bareheaded girl in armor, holding a sword and wearing a banner with the words 'Jesus: Maria' on it."

A few boys in the room scheduled for afternoon patrol duty were getting up from their desks, putting on their bright orange patrol belts, when the fire alarm started to ring. They and Sister Andrienne looked out the windows. Nothing unusual, just a few bare tree branches reaching over the neighboring rooftops. The nun looked at the clock. It was too close to dismissal time for a fire drill. Besides, they rarely had them in such cold weather. Maybe a prankster was up to no good.

The patrol boys rushed to the door on the east end of the room. They tried pushing it open. Strangely, it wouldn't budge.

"What's the matter?" the nun asked.

"It's stuck."

Sister Andrienne looked at them, puzzled. "I'll get it for you."

The nun stepped between the boys and began pushing on the door herself. It seemed to weigh a ton. She didn't know that the door was being held shut by the tremendous draft flowing through the hallway—the fire was sucking all the fresh air from the south wing.

"C'mon, give me a hand," she said to her boys. Together they pushed against the door with all their might. It let go, sending them tumbling into the hallway, right through a cloud of thick black smoke. They realized immediately the alarm was no prank.

"Hurry, go tell the others," said Sister Andrienne, motioning the boys to neighboring classrooms. She reentered her own room. "Let's go. Everybody up."

When the students saw smoke swirling in the hallway, they became frightened. Sister Andrienne lined them up, and one by one they headed out the door for the nearby staircase. Visibility diminished rapidly. It was getting dark. They had to feel their way along. "Get on your knees," said the nun. "Start crawling!"

Heat from the fire was now at their backs, and the youngsters were coughing and gasping for breath. Some were hiding their eyes. When they reached the landing, they panicked. They were becoming disoriented and, like a bunch of frightened horses, refused to budge. In the haste of the moment, Sister Andrienne began shoving them down the smoke-filled stairway. "Don't be afraid," she urged. "Nothing will harm you."

The group started moving, and when all had reached bottom, Sister Andrienne followed. But, unbeknown to her, during the ensuing panic one of her girls had stayed behind in the classroom, slamming the door shut. The other fourteen students still inside the room reacted by scrambling to the windows.

Outside on the Iowa Street sidewalk, Sister Andrienne sensed that things didn't seem right. There were seventy children in her class, but the group seemed thin. Suddenly she realized that not all had gotten out. When she looked up to the windows, her fears were confirmed.

"Stay there!" she shouted to the students at the windows. "Don't move!"

The nun darted back into the building, running up the stairs to the second floor. The smoke in the hallway had turned decidedly worse. She dropped to her knees, feeling her way along the wall. When she reached the room she started calling for the students to follow her voice. "Hang on to each other," she said. On hands and knees they began snaking their way through the dark classroom, out into the smoky hallway. When the procession reached the stairway, Sister Andrienne stood to the side, making way for the youngsters. "Go!" she ordered. The first girl balked and the nun nudged her down. She began rolling the remaining children down the stairs like logs. One by one they bounced to the bottom. Neighbors rushing inside scooped up the youngsters and carried them outside.

When the last of the children had made it to safety, Sister Andrienne limped down the stairs herself. Smoke had penetrated her lungs, making her hack and gag. She had strained her back, and her left leg throbbed from where the children had clutched her.

Outside, above a crescendo of shouts and screams, the fire alarm was still ringing, and a siren grew near. A single fire truck, its red lights flashing, was turning the corner onto Iowa Street, trying to pass through the crowd of people in the streets. At last the firemen had arrived. But, unknown to them, they had been given the wrong location. In the confusion of the moment they were told that a blaze was burning in the rectory on Iowa Street, not in the school around the corner on Avers Avenue.

Editor's Postscript: Linda Malinski, the little girl with the premonition about being in a fire and hearing "people screaming," died in the blaze. Her brother Gerry survived.

The Circus Fire

BY STEWART O'NAN

The word "circus" cannot readily be associated with words like "tragedy" and "intense human suffering." And yet those very words exploded into the consciousness of people all across America on July 6, 1944, when a fire at the famed Ringling Bros. and Barnum & Bailey Circus in Hartford, Connecticut, seared a disaster story into the pages of history that remains unforgettable to this day. One of the reasons the events of this particular fire remain so compelling is the book *The Circus Fire*, by Stewart O'Nan. In his Foreword, O'Nan says, "I first ran across a mention of the fire ten years ago in an old *Life* magazine while I was doing research for a novel. The notion of a circus tent burning down and children inside it shocked me, as did the pictures accompanying the article." O'Nan next tried to find a book about the fire. None existed. O'Nan says he couldn't believe it. "The circus fire was the biggest disaster in the history of the state, and such a strange one. So many people had died. I couldn't believe no one had commemorated the event, set it in words for later generations."

The book O'Nan went on to write is a chronicle of the horrific events of one of America's most distrubing tragedies. In mid-afternoon of July 6, seven thousand men, women, and children were inside "The Big Top" tent when the fire broke out, small at first then burning out of control within seconds. The canvas of the big tent had been waterproofed with a mixture of paraffin and gasoline and burned like a torch. Bleacher seats were fronted by steel railings with narrow openings; the main exit near the fire was blocked by a caged chute in which leopards and lions, having just performed, raged, maddened by the fire.

This excerpt from O'Nan's book is but a small portion of the vivid and detailed portrait of what happened that fateful afternoon—the suffering, the heroism, the cowardliness, the narrow escapes, and the desperate seconds in which lives were lost and saved.

One hundred sixty-seven people died that day, hundreds of others were injured. But mere numbers do not capture the intensity of the drama, the irony of circumstances where men, women, and children out to experience intense joy and delight were slaughtered in flame and the crush of stampeding bodies. Stewart O'Nan's prose has ensured that these people will never be forgotten.

To set the scene: The time is about 2:40. The famed trapeze artists the Wallendas are performing. Here is how O'Nan describes the first few moments:

"A girl in the bleachers felt heat behind her and turned around. She turned back to her mother and asked if the tent was supposed to be on fire.

"An usher in the front row of the bleachers saw the blaze and pointed toward it—as did a man coming back up the bleachers with a Coke he's just bought from the vendor. Pointing with his bottle, the man yelled, 'Fire.'

"Some twisted around to see, but most people kept their eyes glued to the Wallendas high up in the spotlights. They didn't want to miss one second of their death-defying act."

✳   ✳   ✳   ✳   ✳

The fire was still on the untreated sidewall behind the southwest blues, directly in the center, right where the men's toilet abutted the big top, about six feet off the ground. It hadn't involved the roof yet. There was a chance if people got water on it, they could stop it here.

A trio of ushers from the north side cut behind the bleachers and grabbed the fire buckets underneath. There were four in all; each held four gallons of water, filled before every performance by a guy named Chief. The buckets were full. The first usher there hefted one and chucked it, the water splashing across the bottom of the flames.

It did nothing.

The fire was at eye level, a yard wide and five feet high. Another usher tried one bucket, then another. The third usher threw the last one, but the fire was out of reach by now. They tried to pull down the sidewall. It was too late; the flames were eating the roof, finding fuel. All they could do now was help the people at that end get out.

The blues right by the fire had already started to clear. Anna Cote remembered: "I looked up to the right over my shoulder and saw the fire. By the time I turned back around my sister and her girlfriend were gone."

The Wallendas' concentration was locked on their pyramid, the waltz playing softly so as not to startle them and upset their timing. With one wheel of the bike on the wire, Karl sensed the commotion below. From his vantage point he saw the flames creeping up behind the bleachers. Just as Henrietta on the far platform said, "Look," he signaled the others down.

Merle Evans, alert for the slightest deviation in the program, saw Karl's signal, followed where Henrietta was pointing and spotted the flames. He stopped the waltz with a flick of one hand.

From the east end, even from the north side, the fire seemed tiny, "a little ray of light across the tent." There was a moment of stunned surprise, but many in attendance had the same reaction as Detective Beckwith.

In the bleachers right across from it, William Epps said, "Look, Ma, there's a fire over there."

"Don't worry," Mabel Epps said, "they'll put it out."

Surely some circus person would come up with an extinguisher and snuff it. Yet it continued to burn.

Others thought it was part of the show, some kind of joke or surprise. Again, many failed to respond to what they could clearly see, trapped in their own anticipation of the show. They had come to see the circus, so this must be part of it. With no external cues or guidance, they fell back on their original, very narrow goals. Their failure to break out of their routine, despite evidence to the contrary, mirrors the behavior of the crowd at the Beverly Hills Supper Club in Cincinnati in 1977. Though a busboy came out on stage well before that fire had spread and used a microphone to tell everyone to leave, only a few did. They thought the warning was part of the opening comedian's act. One hundred sixty-four people died.

At the far end of the tent, Merle Evans knew the fire wasn't a joke, and he could see Joseph Walsh still had cats in his cage. Evans leaned over the band-stand and yelled to Fred Bradna, "Get those lions out—the tent's on fire."

Bradna saw the smoke by the front door and immediately whistled, calling the Wallendas down and alerting the others. His wife, Ella, headlined one of the equestrian acts coming up next; he ran for the back door to warn her.

Merle Evans cued the band and they struck up the disaster march, Sousa's "The Stars and Stripes Forever," a signal to show folks that something had gone seriously wrong. Evans chose the tune because every musician knew it by heart. The rest of the tent had no clue.

A policeman at the west end hollered at the exiting bleacher crowd, "Be calm. Walk slowly." Most were. A man halfway up with a boy shouted, "That dirty son of a bitch just threw a cigarette butt!" He dropped the boy over the side to the officer and jumped. "It was a cigarette," the man said, and ran off, the boy in tow.

One of the Wallendas' bikes fell and bounced off the sawdust.

The flames leapt up the roof, and now everybody could see the fire. No one was going to put this out.

The crowd gasped and then let loose a roar. The grandstands stood, and the chairs went over with a deafening clatter, Coke bottles rolling down the risers. Grace Smith grabbed Elliott's hand. Donald Gale stood by Hulda Grant, unsure just what was going on.

The plumed high-school horses were waiting by the back door, getting ready to perform their dressage when Fred Bradna dashed out and ordered them back to the paddock. The Ostermaiers, Los Asveras Troupe and the Bradnas tugged at their reins and whirled their mounts around. Ella Bradna's white charger spooked and backed into the dressing tent, tangling his legs in the guyropes, almost throwing her before she got him under control.

In clown alley, Felix Adler was preparing for the walkaround. "We heard a roar like applause," he remembered. "Only we knew the animal act was over and there shouldn't be applause. We knew then something was wrong. Then we smelled smoke. I got my daughter Muriel out of the danger zone. Then I thought of my pet pig and went back to get him."

Knowing the cat act had just finished, a number of performers thought a lion had gotten loose.

Emmett Kelly was in his little dressing tent, enjoying a cold beer before his star turn in the Panto's Paradise spec. "I heard someone say something about a fire. We were always very conscious of fire. I didn't see any fire. I thought at first it was the sideshow." He ran outside and saw smoke curling up from the front yard. He hoped it was only a straw fire in the menagerie, but the smoke was black—just like the smoke in Cleveland.

Inside, the Wallendas on the north platform hit the rope ladder. Helen and Henrietta first, then Joe, and finally Herman, who thought he had time to lash his bicycle fast but gave up halfway. Karl spidered down his ladder easily.

In the west cage, May Kovar still had five panthers on their stands waiting to go out. In the east cage, Joseph Walsh was breaking down his pyramid as fast as he could, keeping an eye on all six lions.

Fred Bradna ran back to the center ring, hollering for calm. Ushers and gatemen did the same. "Please keep your seats," they urged. "We know about the fire, we will take care of this."

In escape mobs, psychologists say, the behavior of a few people turns individualistic and antisocial. Lacking guides, others under extreme stress and therefore more suggestible than normal are unable to judge the situation critically and imitate these few, the effect spreading through the crowd in a process the sociologist Gustave Le Bon called a "contagion." Psychologists believe these others succumb to an "impression of universality" and, seeing the rest of the crowd all making for one exit, jettison all reason and pursue the same goals with even more fervor. The larger the crowd, the harder—necessarily—people will fight others to get out. Sociologists refer to this breakdown of societal constraints and the reversion to fight or flee behavior (and other people be damned) as "demoralization."

One reason why people panic and become a mob is a lack of leadership. In the Hartford circus fire, at least early on, Fred Bradna and the ushers and gatemen provided the crowd some exterior direction. Reassured by the voice of authority, many people in the grandstands stayed where they were. As in the Our Lady of the Angels fire in Chicago, in which the nuns told their students to pray rather than flee, people believed in the leadership of these men, and discipline held. This may have been due to the time—the war era, with its voluntary surrender of individual rights for the good of the country as a whole.

The people in the southwest bleachers needed no exterior direction. They bolted away from the flames, running east, toward the performers' entrance. The ones in the low rows had it easy, with nothing in their way—if they ran when they first had the chance. Those who hesitated were buried in the wave coming down from above.

People lost their balance on the narrow boards and fell, taking down those in front like dominos. Some went through the spaces between the seats, banging their heads on the stringers, getting wedged in between. The next wave stepped on them.

Anna Cote, who'd had the vision of her dead grandfather, said: "I couldn't stand up and walk down the bleachers so I put my hands on the bleacher and slid down to the next one. I remember doing that a couple of times and then my mind goes blank until I get outside." In fact, her sister Iva, already outside, came back in to save her. How she found her in the crowd Anna could only call a miracle.

Some people were still not moving, sitting or standing there entranced, as if none of this was actually happening—a reaction psychologists call "collective disbelief," another way of mentally minimizing or dismissing the danger because it doesn't fit with previous expectations. One survivor remembers sitting in the stands and watching a little girl trip over a rope and fall down, then get up and keep going—all of it far away, disconnected, drained of any urgency.

Above the southwest bleachers the fire suddenly flashed—like the striking of a giant match, some said. Or as one woman described it: "It was as though someone punched a button and a light went on."

The wind took the flames and pushed them up one seam. It streaked up the laces, a spear of fire headed for the top of the westernmost centerpole.

Across Barbour Street, at number 353, a neighbor was sitting on his front porch watching people mill about the grounds when he saw the fire breach the roof of the big top.

Hartford police sergeant Frances Spellman was coming up the midway, just fifty feet from the marquee, when he saw it.

Outside the front door, another policeman was talking to the man in charge of reserved seats. He heard someone yell fire and ran inside, finding circus police chief John Brice. "Yes," Brice said, "it's a fire." The policeman told Chief Hallissey he'd run for a cruiser he'd seen parked on the lot and send the alarm. As he started for Barbour Street, he could see Sergeant Spellman far down the midway, sprinting.

Circus general manager George W. Smith had gone to the yellow ticket wagon to check if the line for reserved seats had broken. He saw people coming out from under the sidewalls and thought an animal had gotten loose. He ducked inside the marquee, spied the fire, and ran out through the connection to warn the elephant men.

The cruiser parked on the lot was Sergeant Spellman's. Its radio was broken, and he knew it. As he ran toward Barbour Street, he tried to figure out who would have the closest phone. He had a choice of two houses directly ahead of him. And he had a back-up plan. If neither had one, McGurk's or McGovern's would.

The flames blazed up the laces, windblown, shooting to the roof. When the fire reached the top of the westernmost centerpole, it split, forking in three directions—straight across the top and spreading down both sides at the west end, possibly along the seams, following the richest fuel. Now the canvas itself was involved, the paraffin turning to gas and burning.

People were screaming—women, children—and the chairs banged and clashed as the grandstands began to react.

Over the PA, the announcer asked the audience to please leave their seats in an orderly fashion. The power went out, cutting him off.

The track near the front door filled with people. They'd come in that way; it was the only door they knew, and they made for it, running past other, easier exits—typical fire behavior: a reversion to the comfort of the familiar when faced with the strange. Above them, the top was solid flames, making them duck, yet still they surged, bottling up between the bleachers.

Under the marquee, a policeman yelled for the attendants to tear up the iron piping. Chiefs Hallissey and Brice pitched in. "Cut the ropes," the cop ordered, "never mind anything else." Thomas Barber had a jackknife and hacked through the one next to the ticket booth. Paul Beckwith yanked down a set connected to the bleachers, and the people poured through.

At the foot of the grandstands, it wasn't that simple. The crowd coming down piled up at the gates and pressed against the railings. "Fold 'em!" the ushers shouted, trying to jerk the rails out of the ground, but the crowd knocked them back. Gatemen came to their aid, holding the people off as long as they could. Some succeeded, some failed. They were a handful facing thousands.

Up in their assigned seats, Dr. Paul de la Vergne craned to catch sight of his wife in the crush below. He didn't see her. He should have never let Elizabeth sit by herself. He should have sat down low with her. He took his son's hand and fought his way down.

"Take it easy, take it easy, walk out quietly," the ushers were saying. Some people listened. In school, the children had learned what to do in case of an air raid, and parents pretended this was just another drill.

The Norrises were already gone. The first stampede had taken them away, leaving Mary Kay Smith beneath a pile of chairs. Mrs. Smith and Barbara were busy extricating her. The girl looked up at them, dazed, eyes wide yet not crying. Below, their neighbors were stuck at the gate. For now maybe they would be safer here.

It was a common tactic. Some people needed time to think, needed to know more information in order to assess the situation before acting—a kind of rational paralysis found in all unexpected disasters. Others still didn't consider the situation desperate yet. A man in the south grandstand explained: "I pointed it [the fire] out to my mother, and we discussed what to do with the pregnant woman who sat in front of us with one or more children. Realizing that the tent was held up by three gigantic poles [actually six], I said that we should get out of there. I feared that if the fire got to the top of the tent, the tent would collapse on all of us. The woman in front decided to stay, because she believed that the fire would soon be put out. We always wondered what happened to her."

An older gentleman sitting alone on the bleachers kept repeating, "If everybody would only keep their seats, we'll all be all right"—a denial of the reality before him, but, according to psychologists, a common reaction when presented with an unchangeable situation and no immediate options.

As the fire ate its way east, more people scrambled, bunching up, the bottom of the grandstand mobbed. One mother took her young son and wrapped his arms around her neck, his legs around her waist, and told him not to let go. Another man had his daughter stand on the riser above him and climb on his back. In S, Stanley Kurneta held his son Tony's hand and led his family down into the crush. Behind him followed Mrs. Kurneta and Betsy, Mary Kurneta and Raymond Erickson.

Outside of the railings, on the hippodrome track, it wasn't so bad early on. Folks going out the east entrance from the low rows in the middle of the south grandstands said the shoving was less than they'd experienced at baseball games. Mothers and aunts and grandmas hurried their charges along, strong-arming them when necessary.

In this first wave, the Red Cross volunteers started to move their convalescent soldiers out but then turned back to help. The canvas above the front door was fully involved, heat radiating down on top of people leaving. The men, while hampered by their injuries, could not be stopped from leading at least thirty children to safety, many of them burned. Dressed for the weather, the children were mostly exposed, their skin the bright red of sunburn. One soldier took a boy by the arm and made him cry. His hand came away wet. The child's skin had blistered; in gripping him, the soldier had ripped the blebs so they wept fluid. Outside, the Red Cross volunteers had to restrain their patients—even some in slings—from running back in.

An East Hartford mother was the beneficiary of similar heroics. She lost her six-year-old, knocked from her arms as they ran for the exit. A sailor scooped him up and carried him out, barely bruised.

There were rescues throughout the top. In the southwest bleachers, an older woman had somehow fallen through and gotten her foot caught so she was hanging upside down, her face a foot from the ground. Thomas Barber and another detective freed her and helped her outside.

On Barbour Street, Sergeant Spellman saw a woman on the far sidewalk and called to her. Where was a phone? Who had a phone around here?

There was one next door, she told him, pointing to the house on the left, 345 Barbour Street. He ran past her for the porch stairs.

In the tent, the main entrance was flooded with customers. Afraid they'd injure themselves at this rate, a ticket seller tried with some other circus employees to control the flow of people. They barreled him over, knocking him clear of the marquee.

One West Hartford father was leading his two daughters and his grandmother's nurse out the southwest exit between the bleachers and the grandstand. Several hundred people had already gone out that way. When they were about twenty-five feet from the exit, a man dressed in a circus uniform held up his hands to the crowd and shouted: "You'll have to go out another entrance." Scraps of flaming canvas were falling now, and there was a fair crowd behind them. The father realized that to go back might mean death. He shoved to the front and told the worker, "You damn fool, we're going out this way," and pushed him aside. Fewer than twenty-five people followed him, assuming perhaps that worse disaster lay that way.

In the south grandstand, George Sanford's movie camera continued to roll.

The roof over the main entrance was driving the crowd back now. One man sitting in the southwest bleachers made it to the track before the swell swept him out the northwest exit, dragging him along the animal chute that ran through there. When he got outside, he stood there watching other people come out. Two little boys asked if he was hurt badly, and he discovered blood on his sleeve. The back of his shirt was covered with it. He felt himself for a wound, but the blood wasn't his. Someone must have rubbed against him in the crush.

The fire burned eastward, the band playing over the shouts and screams, the crashing of grandstand chairs. Everyone was getting out now; there was no more heed for authority, no more waiting—even if there was nowhere to go but down into the piles at the railings. One woman pitched her high heels, dropped her pocketbook and headed down, hanging on to her son's belt. A man wrapped his daughter in his jacket.

They had to climb over piles of seats. The chairs collapsed as people tried to step on them, the wooden legs bruising and cutting shins. A foot caught in a seat, and people tripped and fell. Some stepped on the thick Coke bottles and twisted their ankles. And still there were people behind them, and more behind them, all coming down. A Hartford man explained: "There was nothing we could do. Others just walked over them in the rush."

The larger the crowd, the quicker panic spreads. Group ties in a random gathering like a circus audience are tenuous at best, and under stress people tend to react even more so as individuals, in this case with, perceptually at least, mutually exclusive goals. To the person trapped in the mob and barely moving, it seems certain that not everyone will get out. As the possibilities of escape visibly diminish—as the threat becomes larger, all-engulfing, and as more people join the crush—the more violent some people become. Those in the way become not merely obstacles but deadly enemies.

Men were flinging chairs out of the way, the discards hurtling down to strike others below. The chairs seemed deceptively light and flimsy; they each weighed eight pounds and were built to last. One husband wielded one like a machete, swinging it to clear a path to his wife. Someone surged out of the crowd and pushed him down.

Donald Gale wanted to run for it, but Hulda Grant told him to stay with her. She took his hand, and the two of them made their way down through the chairs. The boyfriend had Caroline. The crowd funneled everyone into the aisle, pushing and shoving, but they got to the bottom of the section all right.

Here the wave of people smashed against the railings, a wrack of chairs tossed off to one side. They were going nowhere when a husky sailor in a blue uniform broke through, beating his way to the front. He punched Hulda Grant in the jaw and she pitched into the chairs. Donald lost his footing, and then the people were on top of him, heavy, and he couldn't see anything.

The same thing was happening all over the tent. Someone bowled an elderly man over from behind and he landed in a tangle of seats. He got up only to be knocked down again. The younger and stronger pushed the older and weaker over chairs, knocked them down, and stepped on them. As one witness politically admitted: "It is fair to say that many people were trampled by those who had the brawn to carry it off."

Yet some did look out for others. A young mother from Hartford hit the railing of section C with her two-year-old and couldn't break loose. A thin, thirtyish man in shirtsleeves reached over from the track and lifted both of them out so they could escape. He seemed calm, and his calmness heartened her. As she ran off, he stayed there to help those remaining.

In another section, the aisle had jammed up. Some man at the bottom was holding everyone back until his wife could work her way down to him. He wouldn't let anyone out; he just kept calling to his wife. A girl ducked under the railing and gave him a good shove, and everyone started to come out.

A man from Middletown described a similar incident from a strikingly different point of view: "The people in back of us were surging down from the higher seats and I had to hold some of them back to let [a neighbor's wife] get out. This was when I hurt my leg." Once the woman and her daughter reached him, he put his elbows out like a blocker and cleared a path for them to the exit.

Don Cook took his sister Eleanor's hand and began down, but his mother caught her other hand. Now she had Edward and Eleanor. I'm going to be very calm, Mildred Cook thought, I'm going to take my time. "You go along," she told Don.

He dashed down toward the crowd but they were running over each other, and he didn't see an easy way around. He headed back up the grandstand and to his left—east, away from the fire, skirting islands of wrecked chairs.

Mildred Cook hesitated before following Don's initial move downward and lost him in the throng beneath her. "We waited a minute," she would say, "and I guess we shouldn't have." She led Edward and Eleanor down; as Don came across the top of the grandstand he looked back and saw them, part of the crowd now, surrounded. And then they were gone, lost among the others.

Across the tent, Joan Smith noticed all the seats behind her were empty. She told her mother she was going *up* the grandstand, not down. Joan was twelve and her mother trusted her. Go ahead, she said. The last Joan saw of her mother and Elliott, they were struggling down the aisle. She was halfway to the top when she realized she still had her Coke.

She tossed the bottle away and scaled the risers. The top edge of the sidewall hung right in front of her, partly slack from being let down for the breeze. She took hold of it with both hands and pushed off, swung clear and hung there a second before letting go.

She was a country kid, a tomboy who knew how to climb trees. When she hit the ground she relaxed, knees bent, and went with the impact. She was fine.

In G, Commissioner Hickey jumped up at the first sign of fire and hollered, "Be calm." Of course, no one paid any attention to him. One nephew responded by throwing his hot dog up in the air. Hickey quickly got the children under control and implemented a plan. The four boys would go down the sidepole right behind them. The two nieces and Isabel and little Billy he would accompany down the aisle and through the middle entrance on the south side. They started off, but one niece refused to move, evidently paralyzed with fear. Isabel came back and slapped her face. The girl moved.

The Alcorns chose to go over the back, the seventy-two-year-old former prosecutor leaping first, then catching the children as his son dropped them down. They met up with the Hickey party outside, Hugh Sr. realizing he'd forgotten his jacket in the rush. He'd had his wallet with $150 in it.

Going over the back of the grandstand was the best chance for those in the top rows. Parents tried to make it a game, and some children laughed as they shinnied down the poles and ropes. Adults at the bottom held the sidewall like a slide so kids could jump into it.

In the west end, the flames were overhead when one man, his wife, and their five-year-old daughter jumped down. Impressed, the little girl kept saying, "It's a shame, it's a shame. The big tent."

Some people tried to catch others jumping. One terrified woman leapt from the top; her body caught a man across the head and shoulders, toppling him, almost knocking him unconscious. "If she had been a bigger woman—she weighed only about one twenty-five—I'd have laid right there and probably have been burned to death."

The Eppses and Goffs went over the back of the northwest bleachers. Mabel Epps told her older son William to climb down a pole, then dropped Richard to him, then little Muriel Goff. Once William had the two children in hand, Mabel Epps shouted, "Go! Get out of here!" He lifted the folds of the sidewall so the other two could crawl out.

Another mother was with five children in section H. Three men below caught the children as they dropped. Thinking they were all safe, the mother leapt, but outside, counting noses, she discovered she only had four. She ran back into the tent and found one boy sitting on the edge of the grandstand, stiff with fright. She ordered him to jump, and he did, but there was no one to catch him, and he injured his back.

Outside, another man had been strolling around the grounds while his wife and two kids were inside. He saw the flames and ran for the big top.

Molly Garofolo ran a beauty salon a couple of blocks south on Barbour Street, on the corner of Westland, right beside Jaivin's Drugstore. She was giving a customer a perm, the heated rods in her hair, when they saw black smoke rolling up outside. "My two boys are at the circus!" the woman screamed, and ran out the door. The hairdresser caught up with her and made her sit on the curb while she removed the rods—another few minutes and her hair would have burned.

Inside, the band played "The Stars and Stripes Forever" over and over, as if the song might calm people knocked through the bleachers or buried under chairs. Fred Bradna pleaded with the people in the east end to leave through the side flaps, but they all clotted helplessly at the bandstand exits. Children fainted in the crush.

All the while the fire was crossing the top of the tent. It spread like a grass fire, a haystack fire, a giant orange wave. Central Connecticut residents were familiar with shade tobacco tents, how a blaze on the sheet canopies could outrun the fastest man; it was like that.

Everyone had a metaphor. The tent went up like cellophane, like tissue paper, like a fuse. A Roman candle, a sheet of newspaper. It was like tossing a piece of paper in a fireplace, like putting a match to a celluloid collar.

The wind took the fire on top and whipped it across the east grandstands. The west end was still in flames, but now people trapped in the seats and on the floor could look up and see beyond the orange and yellow line of fire—bright, strange as a vision—the clear blue sky.

Once the fire breached the roof, the tent became a chimney, sucking cooler air in through the exits and shooting it hot out the top. The paraffin acted as a constant accelerant; the vast area of the canvas provided an endless supply of fresh oxygen. The temperatures inside were rising, and likewise the panic.

One man in the middle of the grandstands plunged forward, knocking over chairs, women, children, and other men indiscriminately, stepping on them when they fell. When last seen, the man was fighting and pushing his way to get ahead of everybody else.

A Manchester woman had gone with her husband and granddaughter. The husband lifted the girl over the railing into the arena and she ran for the exit. The woman was making her way when she "was suddenly confronted with one of those heartrending problems inevitably part of such disasters. Her path was blocked by the prostrate body of a woman. [She] hesitated to step forward and walk over the body. The press of other people behind her and around her kept her from bending to be of possible aid to the fallen woman. But her sensitive indecision was ended when the burning canvas of the big top came down upon her back, badly burning her back and arms. Then she forced her way forward."

The rush was like a human waterfall, like being hurled along by a huge wave breaking. A cadet nurse at St. Francis Hospital and a friend were able to lift up an elderly woman who had fallen to her knees and to drag her along. The two held her tightly until the flow carried them far enough into the open to stumble free. They left the woman in a safe place and redoubled their rescue efforts.

The fire shot right over top of Edward Garrison and his grandmother. The crowd knocked his aunt down and people helped her up but by then they were separated. The swarm tore his grandmother's hand from his and swept her ahead of Edward. She turned around to see where he was and was dragged backwards, her eyes locked on his.

One woman remembered her mother praying out loud as they held each other, drawn along by the tide.

And still the grandstands bunched up at the gates. At one, a chair was stuck across the opening and the pressure from behind toppled those in front over it so no one could get out. Even when the gates were clear, they were purposefully narrow. Trying to squeeze through, one woman found herself caught and crushed against a steel post, half in, half out. She stretched a hand to her companion and he yanked her free, the crowd squirting through the gap, falling across the track.

Ushers continued to urge the audience to exit in an orderly fashion, though the crush was so tight that people were losing shoes. Some lost their footing and others walked on them. A woman with a child in her arms went down and the crowd closed over her. The jostling was hard. One woman dropped her pocketbook but knew if she bent down to retrieve it she'd be run over. A girl let go of her program; she wanted to stop but the current pushed her on. A boy lost his glasses and stooped over to retrieve them. A man fell over him and they both went down.

Many saw women and children being trampled, but, as a girl from West Cornwall explained: "If I stopped to pick up one of them I would have gone down in a second. We just kept going and were pushed until we got clear of the tent."

Parents had no such luxury, and took advantage of any handhold. When one mother's little boy got knocked down, she snatched him up by his overall straps. But more often when a mother bent to rescue a child, the surge buried her.

A Plainville mother had her two children and a nephew with her as she made for an exit. In the crush an unknown man suddenly reached out and took her youngest son from her arms. She managed to make her way to safety with the other two, but once outside she could find neither her son nor the man.

A Meriden man lost his wife in the scramble, then found her in a mound of bodies and hauled her off. "As I pulled [her] out I found there was a woman under her, and I believe she was dead. The fire was crawling to the center of the tent, overhead, and the heat was unbearable. By this time, the howling and yelling was beyond description."

Ushers selflessly rushed children to safety and came back for more, while at the same time other circus personnel were deliberately smashing people's cameras. They asked a *Saturday Evening Post* photographer there on assignment not to shoot, and he agreed.

Children were running around crying, trying to find their parents. Some dashed straight back into the thick of the fire.

One man hugged his son to his chest and ran past the bandstand and out into the underbrush at the east end of the lot. "Here and there could be seen men, women and children horribly burned, many wandering aimlessly about, oblivious to advice that they try to get to a doctor as soon as possible. One woman, apparently unaware that she had suffered severe burns to her arms, was trying to comfort a 9 or 10 year old youngster who was also badly burned, mostly about the legs. The child was shrieking in agony and the woman kept telling him that he would be all right as soon as his parents found him. When told by those who had just left the tent that she and the youngster should get to a doctor so that medical care could be administered, she replied, she couldn't until her family was located—she didn't know where they were. She still didn't seem to know she was badly burned. There were indications that the tents which backed up to the main tent would also go up in flames so those who escaped through the rear entrance started down through thick underbrush below, trying to find a way out. A road off to the right about 300 yards from the fire proved a haven for hundreds. From this vantage point, thick black clouds of smoke could be seen billowing skyward. Here also many men, women, and children could be seen, some burned rather seriously, others superficially."

Back in the northeast corner of the lot, way off in the woods, sat the show's water trucks. Deacon Blanchfield was supposed to make sure they were on hand during the performance with their engines turning, but somehow he'd forgotten.

The *Hartford Times* reported that the first alarm for the circus fire was turned in by a West Hartford man who detected smoke when he was buying tickets for the evening performance, but the first signal box that came in was number 82 at the corner of Clark and Westland, a good half mile from where he was standing. It rang downtown at 2:44 P.M., sending Engine Companies 2, 7, and 16, and Truck Companies 3 and 4 to the scene.

In the same minute, box 828 at Barbour and Cleveland tripped, six hundred feet from the front door of the big top, scrambling Engines 14, 4, and 3 and Truck 1.

Sergeant Spellman reached 345 Barbour Street and ran inside, only to find another officer already on the phone yet saying nothing. Fire HQ's line was busy, he explained. The woman who lived there saw the fire and rushed in from outside, thinking she'd call the police. Her seventy-seven-year-old father was at the circus. Spellman took the phone from the other officer and dialed the operator, who told him the line was busy. He explained what the trouble was and she gave him the line.

Spellman told the switchboard that the main circus tent was on fire and to send in two or three alarms. The dispatcher said apparatus was already on the way.

Spellman next called police headquarters and told them that the circus was on fire and to send all available policemen and ambulances there. Without hesitation, HQ relayed the message to the cruisers: Proceed immediately to the circus grounds—pick up every man you can and take them with you. All officers on beats to be picked up and brought to the fire.

At 2:45 box 821 at Charlotte and Barbour and box 836 at Cleveland and Hampton signaled, sending Engine 5.

John C. King, Hartford's veteran fire chief, was in his car when word came over the two-way shortwave. He was about three miles from the scene and directed his driver to go full speed through the streets.

The department's response was immediate and strong. Engine Company 16 on Blue Hills Avenue near the Bloomfield line had four men dressed and ready. In seconds they hopped on a truck and rolled.

The *Hartford Times* was wired into the fire department's signal boxes. In the city room, the alarm went off. Being an evening paper, the *Times* asked its regular reporters to work mornings so they could make deadline. They all got off at noon. The city room was empty except for a few summer interns and other cubs. Another box called in, making everyone look up from their desks. It was going to be a big one. The circus, the police confirmed. The night editor grudgingly assigned a cub to the grounds with two photographers. As they grabbed their jackets, a third alarm went off.

Don Cook ran across the top of the south grandstand. There was no one up where he was, just chairs and popcorn and Coke bottles. He reached the edge of section E and skipped across the board bridging the narrow entrance below, keeping the flames far behind him, headed for the east end of the tent where the band was still playing the same song. He glanced across the rings and saw people going over the northeast chute, vaulting the bars, crawling on top, the one pair of stairs jammed.

When Edward J. Hickey raced back in through that same narrow opening on the south side, he witnessed the same thing, but they were too far from him and the heat was too much.

The chute was chest high, the iron sections curved at the top and bolted together. Walsh's lions were still in it, even as people frantically clambered across the bars. The propmen never had a chance to move it.

A Middletown man and his family had been seated in W and hit the chute early, before the heaviest crush. As they started over, three attendants on the far side stopped them. The men had sticks to prod the last three lions through. "Get back, get back!" they yelled, waving the crowd off.

"Come on," the father yelled to his children, "go over anyhow."

He'd helped everyone across but his youngest son, who was shorter and heavier than the rest. He set him on top of the chute but the child's foot slipped through the ribs and when the boy looked down, right beneath him was a lion, snarling up, its jaws wide. The boy shied back and slid into his father's arms.

The father tried again, setting his son on the bars, but this time an attendant stopped him, shoving the child and saying, "Get back there." Why, the boy thought, would the man do something like that? The boy slipped between the chute and the edge of the grandstand, and someone knocked him to his knees.

His father reached down and with his arm around the boy's chest and one hand griping the seat of his pants, hoisted him to the top of the chute above the lions and said, "Never mind what he says. Get over there." He gave the boy a push in the back, and he landed on the far side of the bars.

At the northwest chute, the scene was even worse, the fire almost overhead. May Kovar remained in her cage to drive her five panthers out. Embers were dropping, and she was afraid the cats would turn on each other.

As people pounded down section L, the railing at the end of the grandstand gave way. A woman fell and dropped a child she was carrying on top of the chute. The child's arm dangled between the bars. An attendant prodded the nearest panther, trying to distract him, to keep him moving past, but the cat turned and clawed the child's arm, ripping off part of his sleeve. A man standing on the ribs lifted the screaming child off and passed him to someone on the far side.

The first four went easily, but the last panther in the cage turned on May Kovar. The fire was above her, flaming scraps of tent raining down. The cat was spooked by all the commotion. May Kovar circled it with her wand, giving it room to make a decision, then, when it made for the chute, closed in on it. This time the cat didn't turn. She rapped it with her wand and shoved it in, shutting the door.

The White Top, the magazine of the Circus Fans Association of America, would report that the pressure was so great at the door of her cage that May Kovar had to follow her panthers through the chute, but that's just a story, a dramatic image they couldn't resist. In reality she stepped out of the arena door and joined her cageboys shooing the cats back to the wagons.

At the rear of the grandstands, where the chute entered the tent, it changed from iron bars to wooden slats. The wooden section connected with the ramp that led to the individual wagons. Usually the animals came out one by one, separated by boards, but not today. Two panthers with a long-standing feud were surprised to find themselves together in the wooden part of the chute and decided to fight. Another cat raced back in, toward the cage, running under the fire and flaming debris, singeing its fur.

Back inside, May Kovar helped the people caught at the chute, picking up children and boosting them over, but no one would remember this. The papers focused solely on her heroics inside the cage, fighting her panthers beneath the blazing roof. A retired fire captain from New York City called her "the bravest girl I've ever seen."

But while her cats were out, and safe, the chutes were still there, and the crowd was larger now. Men tossed children across and then vaulted over, but others struggled to get a grip on the bars, catching their knees and feet. Some failed and slumped back, swallowed by the next wave. The heat from above was like being stung all over by bees.

One man on the far side caught children thrown to him, then pulled the mothers over, but that kind of cooperation was rare. Each time one young mother tried to pull herself over, people behind her searching for purchase dragged her back. She kissed her boy and told him to run, then tossed him over the top of the cage. Hands hauled her down again. When she looked up she saw her son had caught his foot between the bars. He dangled upside down, his hands not quite touching the ground on the far side. She started to pull herself up and over, but, upside down, the boy reached between the bars and untied his shoe. It fell into the chute and he was free.

The seventy-seven-year-old man whose daughter's phone Sergeant Spellman was using to call the fire department managed to crawl over the chute and stumble from the tent, but took a drubbing from the crowd. In the confusion his earphones had been yanked out and crushed. In silence, he hobbled down the midway toward home.

A couple from Meriden were sitting on the aisle down low. They hesitated, and the first rush trampled the husband. His wife helped him crawl through the narrow gap between the chute and the grandstand. Outside, they had to climb over the tongues of the animal wagons holding the big cats, who roared and paced in their cages. May Kovar stood guard over her leopards, a cageboy soaking them with a hose.

Beyond the line of wagons, people streamed back and forth along the north side, searching for neighbors and family members. Edward Garrison and his grandmother wandered among them, hoping to find his aunt and cousins. His grandmother wanted to go back inside. Just then the two sailors who'd followed them all the way from East Hartford on the bus came out of the tent, supporting the aunt and the cousins.

Inside, the fire burned east. Officers James Kenefick and Henry Griffin toiled on the far side of the northeast chute, telling people to jump, then reaching over and tugging them across. The north grandstands held nearly three thousand people, and with the west end in flames, several hundred ended up here. It was a battle, the whole crowd trying to come at once. Griffin remembered: "Boys stuck their feet through the bars, got them turned so they couldn't get away. Others were stuck or jammed so they couldn't move." They piled up on top, blocking the people behind them.

A fifteen-year-old West Hartford girl and her younger sister came tumbling out of the grandstand and into the scrum at the northeast chute. The older girl saw the officers running up and down the far side, pulling people over, and pushed her sister up on top of others who'd already fallen. As she lifted her sister, she looked down into the face of a young man slightly older than herself, unable to get up because of the layers pinning his legs.

An officer helped the younger girl across and was about to move on to someone else, but the girl held on to his hand and pulled him back toward her sister. He had to save her too, she insisted, and he did. They never knew what happened to the young man.

The Wallendas crossed the northeast chute. Herman Wallenda: "When the flames hit the roof, we saw we had to get down fast. We slid down the ropes and headed for the performer's exit, but people were so crowded there that we saw we didn't have a chance. So we climbed over the cage that lines the exit. That was easy for us—we're performers. But the public couldn't get out that way."

Herman's teenaged son Gunther was with him; they climbed over the northeast chute right by a quarterpole and headed out of the tent. When they looked back, people seemed to be getting out.

Fred Bradna, veteran of several top fires, saw the confusion at the northeast chute and ran over there. He pulled children from the pile and carried them to safety.

Dorothy Bocek, thirteen, had been sitting in the north grandstand with her married sister Stella Marcovicz and her nephew Francis, four. All three made for the northeast chute. Dorothy asked Stella what she should do. Stella, holding Francis's hand, said, "Just take care of yourself."

At the chute they got separated. Somehow Dorothy made it over, she didn't remember how. Outside, she couldn't find Stella and Francis.

The band played on, but not loud enough to drown the screaming. "They all sounded like beaten dogs," Emmett Kelly said.

Rich black smoke rolled up from the canvas. Pieces fell and caught in women's hair, ignited their light summer dresses. The unpyrolized paraffin became a flaming liquid that rained down like napalm, burning skin on contact, staying aflame until the fuel was all gone. It sizzled as it hit the skin of children in sunsuits, blisters dotting their arms like chicken pox.

The fire consumed the roof pole by pole, the heat on top of the crowd like a giant broiler, making people duck and flinch away from it. Still it found them. One girl's arm burned where she had it wrapped around her father's neck. Hair burned, and bald spots—not from flame but radiated heat. It literally cooked people.

The roof over the center ring evaporated. Ropes holding heavy tackle and trapeze equipment burned through, sending everything crashing into the rings below.

Mildred Cook lost Eleanor in the mob at the bottom of the grandstand. She hoped her daughter had followed Don. She ran with Edward for the front door, toward the fire, hoping to sneak under it.

Or, according to the missing persons report, the three of them headed for the main entrance together. The heat descended on them, making them groggy. Edward said he was tired and wanted to lie down. He did, passing out immediately. Mildred then fell unconscious, but Eleanor walked on.

After saving the lady caught in the bleachers, Thomas Barber retreated with her out the front door. There was too much heat to go back in there, so he patrolled around to the north to make sure the animals weren't loose. He'd seen May Kovar's act and unsnapped the flap of his holster just in case. That his service revolver might not stop a leopard never occurred to him. When he turned the corner, the cats were all safe in their cages.

On the midway, police cruiser number 8 nosed through the crowd streaming around it and stopped by the white ticket wagon. Chief Hallissey got on the radio and told headquarters to detail as many men as they could to the scene. One of the men headquarters then radioed was Det. William Dineen, who knew his two children were inside the tent.

Hallissey called the city authorities, and through them the War Council. They'd need to mobilize everybody on this one.

Downtown, Engine 4 turned up Ann Street and saw a pillar of heavy black smoke rising into the sky. The men on the truck wondered what the hell it could be.

The fire drove the crowd ahead of it, down toward the bandstand. People who'd thought they had time now realized they'd underestimated its speed. It was moving too fast and the east end was too crowded to get out that way. The fire was going to cut them off.

A girl was running around with her blouse on fire, batting at it. Another woman heard someone say her shirt was on fire. She felt the heat, and then a man struck her in the face and said, "This ain't no time to faint, lady."

One girl had gone to the circus for her eighth birthday. Her mother couldn't take her because she was eight months pregnant, so she went with an older neighbor. They came down the north grandstand after the first rush. People were walking on others trapped under chairs, crushed and screaming.

"We've got to help them," the girl said.

"We don't have time," the neighbor said, and she was right.

When they reached the chute, the woman took one look at the crowd and said, "We'll never get out this way," and turned around, leading the girl back up the stands, all the way to the top, right by a sidepole. There was no one else there, and the girl balked. The drop seemed far.

"You've got to jump," the woman said.

"I can't," the girl said. "I can't even climb the pole in gym."

"If you don't, I'm going to push you."

The girl jumped, grabbed on to the pole and slid down, the friction ripping the skin from her arm. The woman climbed down right behind her.

Now the crowd realized they'd never make the east end and stormed up the grandstands on both sides, searching for poles and ropes, any lifeline. At the edge, parents instructed their children to run outside and wait for them. People remember the jump as being twenty-five, thirty, even thirty-five feet, when actually it was only between ten and twelve—but they were children then, and twelve feet to a six-year-old is a long way down.

Adults at the bottom gathered to catch children, but there weren't enough of them for everybody. One man climbed down a rope with two children on his back. People leapt for the sidepoles, slid down halfway and caught their hands on the rough guyropes. The ropes burned their palms raw, and they let go from the shock and fell.

Some people jumped, not bothering with poles or ropes. One group of boys had a favorite game called paratrooper; they'd climb up on garages and—Geronimo!—fly off, bending their knees and rolling on landing, just like in the newsreels. Now they had a chance to use their new skills. But the very young and very old hadn't practiced. There were scores of bad falls. One woman went over nearly headfirst. Little girls landed on their hands and broke their wrists and arms. An older gentleman broke his leg and had to be helped away.

And there were injuries among the catchers—black eyes and strained backs, scratches and bruises from being kicked. A minor price.

But even there behind the stands people weren't out of danger. In some places the sidewall was staked down to the ground so tight there was no way to struggle under it. This was especially true behind the northwest bleachers just to the left of the marquee and the ladies' room—a natural place for kids to sneak in.

Thirteen-year-old Donald Anderson saw the column of blue sky the fire tore above his section. He hung from the top row and dropped down. He'd come with Axel Carlson, an older man, a distant cousin of his grandfather. When Donald reached the ground he couldn't find him anywhere. A mob of people were trying to squeeze out the northwest exit beside the chute, crawling all over one another—dog eat dog. Donald wanted no part of that. He had a fishing knife with him, with a good sharp blade. He unfolded it and tried to cut the rope holding down the tent; it was so thick he would have needed a hacksaw. He stuck the knife into the middle of the wall and worked it down, sawing the tough canvas until he had a fair-sized slit. Left and right at the bottom, left and right at the top, and it was a door big enough for him to get out.

He was thinking of nothing but self-preservation, but when the crowd saw it, hundreds poured through behind him. Outside now, he scanned their faces, trying to find Axel Carlson. When he didn't see him, he took his knife to the next panel, cut another door and went back in.

The old man was right there, and a little girl no more than three or four, trampled. Donald picked her up and followed Axel Carlson out.

Donald Anderson—along with May Kovar—would be remembered as a hero of the circus fire; he'd even get a medal. But all around the tent, fathers slashed at the canvas with penknives, boys wearing HiJacks paratrooper boots whipped miniature jackknives out of their scabbards, and people dashed into the cool air.

Most of the sidewalls were not staked down, however; people ducked underneath the folds into sunlight, some of them getting stepped on as they crawled out. On the north side they had to scrabble under circus wagons to get clear. On the south they had the light plant and the menagerie animals to deal with. The camels were uneasy, tethered along a rope fence tied to a wagon.

One family came out in the middle of the elephants, chained and swaying, some of them rearing. They trumpeted and shook their heads from side to side menacingly. Ralph Emerson Jr. was eighteen, an animal trainer new to the show. He'd grown up in Glastonbury and several family members had come to see him. He was working with the elephants on the south side of the main tent when the fire started "near the area that the menagerie leaned against. I saw smoke. I suppose I saw it as early as anyone. There was a V of flame in the top of the tent. I thought, How are they going to get out of this? Someone yelled, 'Get the elephants out' [possibly George W. Smith, from the connection]. There was a great sense of urgency to get the animals out of the way and to keep them from charging the crowd."

The show elephants were in the backyard, getting ready for the spec. The bull men shouted "Tails! Tails!" and the herd formed the familiar trunk-to-tail queue, one attendant for every two animals, and lumbered around the south side, squeezing between the light plant and the victory gardens. When they hesitated, their handlers whacked them with their hands and prodded them with bull hooks.

In the tent the tops of the bleachers were crammed with people. Some had fallen through the boards and gotten caught; the crowd rolled over them, pressing for the edge. Not like lemmings but *against* instinct, people jumped. Some refused to, unsure where their children were. The surge from below pushed them over. It sent one teenaged girl toppling. She fell twelve feet to the ground, breaking her back.

Waiting for a little girl in front of her to jump, one woman witnessed a man shove the child off from behind. She hadn't been going fast enough for him.

Some jumped and broke their ankles and then were unable to get up before others landed on them, knocking them out, hurting them worse. One girl remembered lighting beside a woman who couldn't move; she watched as the girl ran off. People jumped over the heads of the fallen, or climbed over them once they reached the ground. Another man recalled a lady in her thirties in a red dress whom he had to crawl over. She looked right at him, yet said nothing.

Don Cook finished his sprint across the top of the south grandstand and swung down over the railing at the end of section K. The sidewall here was loose and he slipped underneath and outside easily. People with seared faces ran choking into the underbrush. Unsure where his mother was, Don went around the east end of the tent where the biggest crowd was flowing out around the bandstand. He stood there watching everyone funnel past.

Another boy and his family ran. His father had the boy's little sister under one arm and the boy clinging to his belt. They jumped a shallow ravine where an elderly woman lay facedown in the muck. His father, never letting his sister go, reached down with one hand and pulled the old woman up and out by the back of her dress.

Another woman tore her dress going over the snow fence protecting the victory gardens. Just slats and wire, it was surprisingly strong. One young mother unable to scale the fence handed her daughter over to a man and told him to meet her on Barbour Street. "Yes," the man said, "of course I will." He ran, but once he reached the sidewalk he stopped and looked down at the girl in bewilderment. He'd been so intent on his goal that he didn't remember taking her.

And then a crowd broke out of the south side, roared across the scattered hay of the menagerie and hit the snow fence in force, bending and then flattening it, sweeping across the gardens, trampling the vegetables to mush.

Everywhere there were obstacles—wagons and stakes and crates, buckets and kegs and bales. A mother fleeing the east end tripped over a coil of rope and fell on the son she was carrying, bruising his forehead. There was chaos here with people careering out, tractors dragging wagons off, and the circus water trucks finally rolling up to fight the fire.

For people coming out the east end there was nowhere to go except down the road into the woods where there was a dump. A boy and his mother came across two older ladies sitting down, exhausted. "I wouldn't sit there," the mother said. "What if some of the animals get loose?" The ladies jumped up and took off, outstripping them.

In the confusion, rumors took on the weight of truth. The elephants were on a mad rampage. The state police had come with shotguns to hunt the lions down. Survivors pitied the animals that died in the fire; in actuality, there were none.

But, running, having just come from watching two full cages of jungle cats, naturally people assumed the worst. At this point, having escaped the tent, they were more afraid of the lions than the fire. When they finally stopped and took stock, they found they were bruised and burned and bleeding, the luckier ones just missing pocketbooks and shoes, perhaps a hat or a wristwatch. The woods were full of mothers searching for their children, the badly burned crying for help. Some didn't stop running until—blocks, neighborhoods, miles later—they made it home.

The Triangle Fire

BY LEON STEIN

Because I work in New York City, I suppose that I find tragedies that have taken place there to be particularly compelling. When you can walk or take an easy subway ride to a site such as the Empire State Building and Ground Zero of the World Trade Center and stand there, reflecting on what has transpired there in years and days past, you can't help having a particularly strong sense of sadness and bewilderment.

One such site is at the corner where Washington Street runs into Washington Square Park. Here, on a warm Saturday afternoon in March, 1911, in a span of time that amounted to less than half an hour, a sudden and literal inferno at the Triangle Shirtwaist Factory left 146 employees dead, most of them young women.

This horrific event is the subject of Leon Stein's book *The Triangle Fire*, published by Carroll & Graf in 1962.

Here's an excerpt from that work, and it captures the complete drama of those who were trapped and died, and those who somehow managed to escape.

*   *   *   *   *

The first touch of spring warmed the air. It was Saturday afternoon—March 25, 1911—and the children from the teeming tenements to the south filled Washington Square Park with the shrill sounds of youngsters at play. The paths among the old trees were dotted with strollers.

Genteel brownstones, their lace-curtained windows like drooping eyelids, lined two sides of the 8-acre park that formed a sanctuary of green in the brick and concrete expanse of New York City. On the north side of the square rose the red brick and limestone of the patrician Old Row, dating back to 1833. Only on the east side of the square was the almost solid line of homes broken by the buildings of New York University.

The little park originally had been the city's Potter's Field, the final resting place of its unclaimed dead, but in the nineteenth century Washington Square became the city's most fashionable area. By 1911 the old town houses stood as a rear guard of an aristocratic past facing the invasion of industry from Broadway to the east, low-income groups from the crowded streets to the south, and the first infiltration of artists and writers into Greenwich Village to the west.

Dr. D. C. Winterbottom, a coroner of the City of New York, lived at 63 Washington Square South. Some time after 4:30, he parted the curtains of a window in his front parlor and surveyed the pleasant scene.

He may have noticed Patrolman James P. Meehan of Traffic B proudly astride his horse on one of the bridle paths which cut through the park.

Or he may have caught a glimpse of William Gunn Shepherd, young reporter for the *United Press,* walking briskly eastward through the square.

Clearly visible to him was the New York University building filling half of the eastern side of the square from Washington Place to Waverly Place. But he could not see, as he looked from his window, that Professor Frank Sommer, former sheriff of Essex County, New Jersey, was lecturing to a class of fifty on the tenth floor of the school building, or that directly beneath him on the ninth floor Professor H. G. Parsons was illustrating interesting points of gardening to a class of forty girls.

A block east of the square and parallel to it, Greene Street cut a narrow path between tall loft buildings. Its sidewalks bustled with activity as shippers trundled the day's last crates and boxes to the horse-drawn wagons lining the curbs.

At the corner of Greene Street and Washington Place, a wide thoroughfare bisecting the east side of the square, the Asch building rose ten floors high. The Triangle Shirtwaist Company, largest of its kind, occupied the top three floors. As Dr. Winterbottom contemplated the peaceful park, 500 persons, most of them young girls, were busily turning thousands of yards of flimsy fabric into shirtwaists, a female bodice garment which the noted artist Charles Dana Gibson had made the sartorial symbol of American womanhood.

One block north, at the corner of Greene Street and Waverly Place, Mrs. Lena Goldman swept the sidewalk in front of her small restaurant. It was closing time. She knew the girls who worked in the Asch building well for many of them were her customers.

Dominick Cardiane, pushing a wheelbarrow, had stopped for a moment in front of the doors of the Asch building freight elevator in the middle of the Greene Street block. He heard a sound "like a big puff," followed at once by the noise of crashing glass. A horse reared, whinnied wildly, and took off down Greene Street, the wagon behind it bouncing crazily on the cobblestones.

Reporter Shepherd, about to cross from the park into Washington Place, also heard the sound. He saw smoke issuing from an eighth-floor window of the Asch building and began to run.

Patrolman Meehan was talking with his superior, Lieutenant William Egan. A boy ran up to them and pointed to the Asch building. The patrolman put spurs to his horse.

Dr. Winterbottom saw people in the park running toward Washington Place. A few seconds later he dashed down the stoop carrying his black medical bag and cut across the square toward Washington Place.

Patrolman Meehan caught up with Shepherd and passed him. For an instant there seemed to be no sound on the street except the urgent tattoo of his horse's hoofbeats as Meehan galloped by. He pulled up in front of 23 Washington Place, in the middle of the block, and jumped from the saddle.

Many had heard the muffled explosion and looked up to see the puff of smoke coming out of an eighth-floor window. James Cooper, passing by, was one of them. He saw something that looked "like a bale of dark dress goods" come out of a window.

"Some one's in there all right. He's trying to save the best cloth," a bystander said to him.

Another bundle came flying out of a window. Halfway down the wind caught it and the bundle opened.

It was not a bundle. It was the body of a girl.

✳   ✳   ✳   ✳   ✳

"I rang the bell," said Joseph Wexler, eighth-floor watchman for the Triangle Shirtwaist Company. He stood beside the time clock attached to the Greene Street partition, near the single exit on that side of the shop. "I was supposed to look in the girls' pocketbooks, every girl's pocketbook. I got ready. I rang the bell."

What time was it?

Quitting time on Saturday was 4:45 P.M. But Triangle, like Congress, sometimes manipulated its control clock in order to keep working.

On that Saturday, Fire Department Central received the first alarm from Box 289 at 4:45 P.M. At 4:45½ P.M., two telephone calls from 23 Washington Place reported a fire. But the first entry on the matter in the daybook of the Eighth Precinct reads: "Sgt. James Cain and eight patrolmen left for duty at Washington Place fire—4:30 P.M."

What time was it?

It was the time before sundown when bearded Jews in the East Side tenements were beginning to chant the prayer marking the end of the Sabbath. It is called the Havdallah, which means "the great divide." Its joyous words praise the Lord for creating the Sabbath and setting it apart from all the other days of the week.

Crossing back over "the great divide" and returning to the stretch of ordinary days is marked by the performance of an act forbidden during the holy day. As the sun sets, he who prays pours a small portion of ritual wine into a platter and touches fire to it. The Sabbath ends. And the flames flare up.

Those Jewish workers who had brought a strong religious faith with them to the New World—and had held on to it—paid for their piety. While others remained bent over their sewing machines on Friday afternoon, these stole glances at the sun and when it began to dip, pushed back their chairs, rose from their work and departed—losing time and earnings.

For those on whom the grip of faith had loosened, the sundown meant little. At Triangle, the Sabbath was not set apart. There was work for those who wished to work on Saturdays, and often even on Sundays.

Wexler rang the quitting bell. From where he stood, he could survey the entire shop floor, a huge square measuring about 100 feet on each side. The upper right-hand, northeast, corner of the square was separated from the rest of the shop by a wooden partition, making a vestibule 15 feet long. Behind that partition were the doors to two freight elevators and to the single staircase leading down to Greene Street and up to the roof.

"When we stepped out of the freight elevators in the morning," says Joseph Granick, who worked at Triangle as a garment cutter, "we turned to the right, walked past the staircase door and came into the shop through the single door in the narrow side of the partition. Only one person at a time could pass through that door opening. This is where the watchman stood every night to search the girls' pocketbooks."

Through the door and straight ahead was the back-yard wall. It had eight windows, the two center ones opening onto the single fire escape. Two tables on which cutters worked ran parallel to this northern wall.

The east wall of the shop had ten windows facing Greene Street, one of them behind the partition. Along its length were five more cutting tables, three of them 66 feet long, the other two about half that length, and all of them ending at the Washington Place, southern, wall of the shop. This wall had twelve windows providing plenty of light for the battery of special stitching and sewing machines lined along its length.

The fourth, or west wall, was back to back with the building housing New York University and the American Book Company. Ten feet from where it angled into the Washington Place wall, this side of the square had two passenger elevator doors and to the right of these the single door into the staircase leading to the Washington Place lobby and up to the tenth floor.

A wooden partition to the right of the stairway door enclosed the dressing room, and beyond this were the washrooms. The wall ended with three windows opening on the short wing of the L-shaped back yard across which they faced windows of the University building.

Production of Triangle's shirtwaists began on the cutting tables, where the basic economy of factory methods was achieved. It lay in the ability of the skilled craftsmen to cut many layers of fabric—several dozen at a time—with a single slicing motion.

The tables on which they worked were 40 inches wide, stood 42 inches high, and were separated by aisles that were 30 inches wide. Forty cutters, a closely knit group, were stationed in this department.

Granick remembers that his mother paid one of them, Morris Goldfarb, $25 to get her son a job at Triangle. (Goldfarb was one of Triangle's "toughies" who fought the strikers during the 1909 walkout and helped pass strikebreakers through their lines.)

He had expected to work for nothing at the start. But the $25 had worked magic, and he was hired at $3 a week plus 15 cents an hour for overtime.

Granick was working on lot number 1180 that day, cutting linings and trimmings from a thin fabric called lawn, though sometimes given a fancier name like "longerine." A cutter would pile up many layers of fabric. Then he would place his patterns on top of the pile. This was his main skill. He arranged his patterns to make the shortest possible jig-saw when he first laid them out to get the length for cutting each layer from the roll.

The less yardage he took, the more money he saved for the boss. He had to have a good eye and a strong arm because when he had all of his patterns laid out on top of the layers of fabric, minding the grain of the goods and making certain that no part of the garment was missing, he would start to cut with a short knife that looked like something fishermen use to clean fish. It had a stubby handle and a blade as sharp as a razor. With his left hand the cutter pressed palm down on the pattern while his right hand, grasping the knife, rode around the edge of the pattern, which was bound with metal to prevent nicking.

The tables were boarded up from the floor to about 6 inches below their tops, thus providing large, continuous bins. A long wire with pendant small hooks stretched directly over the full length of each table.

As he sliced out a sleeve or a bodice front, the cutter would set aside the part, hanging the pattern on the overhead wire. From time to time, he would take the cutaway fabric remaining on the table—like dough remaining after the cookies have been stamped out—sweep it together by hand, and fling it through the 6-inch slot on the underside of the table.

There was by-product value for Triangle's proprietors in the cutaways that accumulated under the tables. They were purchased regularly by a dealer named Louis Levy. Between March 25, 1910, and March 25, 1911, he removed the accumulated cutaways six times.

"I waited for an accumulation," said Levy. "The last time I removed the rags before the fire was on January 15, 1911. They came from the eighth floor. Altogether, it was 2,252 pounds."

Granick had received his week's pay and was walking toward the Greene Street exit where Wexler was stationed when he encountered Eva Harris, the sister of Isaac Harris, one of Triangle's two owners. "Eva Harris said she smelled something burning. I looked to the cutting tables. At the second table, through the slot under the top, I saw the red flames."

Eva Harris turned and ran toward Dinah Lifschitz sitting at her desk in the corner of the shop near the three western windows. Dinah handed out the work to the special machine operators on the eighth floor. Next to her desk stood short, stocky Samuel Bernstein, Triangle's production manager, who was related by marriage to both of its owners.

"I heard a cry," Bernstein said. "It was Eva Harris. She was running toward me from the middle of the shop. She was hollering, 'There is a fire, Mr. Bernstein.' I turned around. I saw a blaze and some smoke at the second table from the Greene Street windows. As I ran across the shop toward the fire, some cutters were throwing pails of water."

Another Bernstein, William, a cutter, had grabbed a pail of water that stood near the last window and had thrown it on the fire. "But it didn't do any good," he asserted. "The rags and the table were burning. I went around the partition into the freight elevator vestibule to get another pail of water. But when I tried to go back in, the narrow doorway was blocked with people rushing to the stairs."

Cutter Max Rothen had just hung his patterns on the long overhead wire, having finished the day, when he felt a punch in the back. He turned around and there was Bernstein the manager, "his face white from fright."

"At the same time there were cries of 'fire' from all sides. The line of hanging patterns began to burn. Some of the cutters jumped up and tried to tear the patterns from the line but the fire was ahead of them. The patterns were burning. They began to fall on the layers of thin goods underneath them. Every time another piece dropped, light scraps of burning fabric began to fly around the room. They came down on the other tables and they fell on the machines. Then the line broke and the whole string of burning patterns fell down."

The smoke grew thicker. Those still in the loft began to choke and cough. A half dozen men continued to fling pails of water at the fire.

"But the flames seemed to push up from under the table right to the top," Granick recalls. "I began to look for more water. I thought there might be more pails on the Washington Place side. I began to run there, then I stopped and looked back. I saw in a flash I could never make it. The flames were beginning to reach the ceiling."

Now the flames were everywhere, consuming the fabric and beginning to feed on the wooden floor trim, the sewing tables, the partitions. The heat and the pressure were rising. The windows began to pop, and down in Greene Street, Dominick Cardiane heard a sound "like a big puff."

Samuel Bernstein stood near the flames and cried out for more pails of water. One of the elevator operators came running with a pail. "He left the elevator door open. It made a terrible draft. The wind blew right through the place. We found it was impossible to put the fire out with pails."

Then Bernstein remembered there were hoselines hanging in the stairwells. "I saw Louis Senderman, the assistant shipping clerk from the tenth floor. I hollered, 'Louis, get me a hose!'"

Somehow Senderman managed to reach a hose in the Greene Street stairwell. He fought his way back into the loft, dragging the hose behind him. He reached out the nozzle to Bernstein. "As I took the hose from him, I said, 'Is it open?' But it didn't work. No pressure. No water. I tried it. I opened it. I turned the nozzle one way and then another. It didn't work. I threw it away."

Senderman tried to work the hose. So did Solly Cohen, another shipping clerk. They had as little success as Bernstein. Then a third man tried.

"He was a little fellow, I don't even remember his name, he was an assistant machinist, new in the factory. He came toward me dragging the hose. He handed it to me," Bernstein continued. "I tried it again. I hollered, 'Where is the water? where is the water?' He answered, 'No pressure, nothing coming.'

"Who was the boy? All I know is that he was lost in the fire. He was pulling me by the hand and screaming. I turned around and I looked at him and the boy was burning. He ran away from me into the smoke."

The machinist, Louis Brown, was in the men's room just north of the dressing room when he heard the cry of "Fire." He dropped the soap with which he was washing his hands and ran into the shop. The first thing he saw was Bernstein standing on one of the tables with a pail of water. He ran to join him.

"When Mr. Bernstein saw me he hollered, 'Brown, you can't do anything here. Try to get the girls out!' I saw the girls all clustered at the door to the Washington Place stairway and I ran in that direction."

Realizing that the fire was now beyond control, Bernstein jumped down from the table and hurried to the Greene Street vestibule, where he concentrated on getting the girls out.

"I wouldn't let them go for their clothes even though it was Spring and many of them had new outfits. One of the girls I slapped across the face because she was fainting. I got her out. I drove them out."

Bernstein worked now at saving the girls with the same drive and force he had used to work those same girls for the benefit of their employers.

On his way to the Washington Place door, Bernstein had opened the back-yard window leading to the fire escape. Rose Reiner had come screaming out of the dressing room, where she had been giving herself a last inspection in the full-length mirror before going home, when she heard the cries of "Fire!'"

"I saw Dinah and she shouted I should go to the fire escape. As I climbed through the window I saw Mr. Brown trying to open the Washington Place door. I went out onto the fire escape."

Filled with terror, Rose slipped and stumbled down the narrow, slatted stirs form floor to floor until she followed the girl ahead of her back into the building through the smashed window at the sixth floor. "I went down. More I don't remember."

She was one of the "clawing" women Patrolman Meehan found behind the locked door he broke down.

The flames crept nearer to her desk, but Dinah Lifschitz held her post. On her desk was a telephone and a telautograph—a duplicating script writer for sending messages—that had recently been installed by the firm. Both connected directly with the executive offices on the tenth floor.

"I right away sent a message to the tenth floor on the telautograph," Dinah said. "But they apparently didn't get the message because I didn't get an answer.

"Then I used the telephone. I called the tenth floor and I heard Mary Alter's voice on the other end. I told her there was a fire on the eighth floor, to tell Mr. Blanck. 'All right, all right,' she answered me."

Dinah stayed at the phone. She shouted to the switchboard operator to connect with the ninth floor. She was getting no answer.

But her call had given the alarm to the people on the tenth floor. They began to ring for the passenger elevators, and the operators responded to the buzzing from the executive floor. The cars began to pass the eighth floor.

The girls crushed against the eighth floor elevator doors could see the cars going up. "Some of the girls were clawing at the elevator doors and crying, 'Stop! stop! For God's sake, stop,'" Irene Seivos remembered.

"I broke the window of the elevator door with my hands and screamed, 'fire! fire! fire!' It was so hot we could scarcely breathe. When the elevator did stop and the door opened at last, my dress was catching fire."

The car could not hold all who tried to crowd in. Irene Seivos jumped on top of the girls already in the car just as she saw the door closing. Someone grabbed her long hair and tried to pull her out, but she kicked free and rode to safety.

One of those on whom she landed was Celia Saltz. When the fire had started, she was still at her machine. "All I could think was that I must run to the door. I didn't know there was a fire escape. I even forgot that I had a younger sister working with me.

"The door to the staircase wouldn't open. We pushed to the passenger elevators. Everybody was pushing and screaming. When the car stopped at our floor I was pushed into it by the crowd. I began to scream for my sister. I had lost her, I had lost my sister."

Celia fainted in the car, but in the crush remained on her feet. When she regained consciousness she was stretched out on the floor of a store across the street from the Asch building. "I opened my eyes and I saw my sister bending over me. I began to cry; I couldn't help it. My sister, Minnie, was only fourteen."

While one group of terrified girls struggled to get into the elevators, another small crowd fought to get through the Washington Place stairway door. Some ran from the elevator to the door. Then back again.

Josephine Nicolosi recalls that when she reached the door to the stairs some thirty girls were there. "They were trying to open the door with all their might, but they couldn't open it. We were all hollering. We didn't know what to do. Then Louis Brown hollered, 'Wait, girls, I will open the door for you!' We all tried to get to one side to let him pass."

Crushed against the door was Ida Willinsky, exerting all of her strength in a futile effort to push the crowd back. "All the girls were falling on me and they squeezed me to the door. Three times I said to the girls, 'Please, girls, let me open the door. Please!'

"But they did not listen to me. I tried to keep my head away from the glass in the door. Then Mr. Brown came and began to push the girls to the side."

Brown remembered that when he reached the area of the door he found all the girls screaming. "I tried to get through the crowd. I pushed my way through and tried by main strength to scatter them. But they were so frantic they wouldn't let me through. As I tried to push them to the side, they pushed back. At such a time, a thousand and one thoughts go through your mind. All I could think was 'Why don't they let me through? Why don't they understand that I am trying to get them out?'

"I finally got to the door. There was a key always sticking in that door and I naturally thought that they must have locked the door. So I turned, all I tried to do was to turn the key in the lock. But the key wouldn't turn to unlock the door. It did not turn. So I pulled the door open. It didn't open right away.

"I had to push the girls away from the door. I couldn't open it otherwise. They were packed there by the door, you couldn't get them any tighter. I pulled with all my strength. The door was open a little while I was pulling. But they were all against the door and while I was pulling to open it they were pushing against it as they tried to get out.

"They were closing the door by their pushing and I had to pull with all my might to get it open."

Brown finally got the door open, and the screaming girls squeezed themselves into the narrow, spiral staircase, pushing and falling in their fright. Brown tried to calm them as he stood at the door. Then the line downward seemed blocked. Squeezing his way halfway down to the seventh floor, he found Eva Harris slumped on the stairs in a faint. At this moment, Patrolman Meehan came panting up the stairs, lifted the girl against the wall, brought her round, and sent her down.

Sylvia Riegler was right behind Brown when he helped pick up Eva Harris. She had been in the dressing room when the fire started. She had just put on her wide velvet hat when her friend, Rose Feibush, ran into the room screaming, took her by the hand, pulled her into the shop, and began to drag her toward a window.

"I saw men pouring water on the fire at the cutting tables. The wicker baskets where the lace runners worked were beginning to burn. I was scared. Rose was pulling me and screaming.

"Suddenly, I felt I was going in the wrong direction. I broke loose. I couldn't go with her to the windows. This is what saved my life. Always, even as a child, even now, I have had a great fear of height.

"I turned back into the shop. Rose Feibush, my beautiful, dear friend, jumped from a window.

"I saw Brown get the door open. Somebody pushed me through. I don't remember how I got down. I was cold and wet and hysterical. I was screaming all the time.

"When we came to the bottom the firemen wouldn't let us out. The bodies were falling all around. They were afraid we would be killed by the falling bodies. I stood there screaming."

Two men carried Sylvia across the street into a store and "stretched me out on the floor."

She had swallowed so much smoke that they tried to pour milk into her for its emetic effect. But for one who had known hunger, milk could have only one purpose. "They gave me a lot of milk to drink to give me back my strength," is the way Sylvia Riegler remembered it almost half a century later. "But I couldn't hold it. All the time I could see through the store window the burning bodies falling."

On the eighth floor the flames had cut across the shop. Now they rose like a wall, cutting Bernstein and Dinah Lifschitz off from the Washington Place door. The corridor through the flames to the Greene Street door was perilously narrow.

"It was getting dark with smoke and there sat my cousin Dinah trying to get upstairs on the telephone or on the writing machine," Samuel Bernstein said. "She was getting no answer. She screamed 'fire' through the telephone and she screamed it so loud I stopped her. She would have scared the girl on the other end.

"We weren't getting the message through to the ninth floor. Remember, we had to make contact through the tenth floor switchboard. I said, 'For God's sake, those people don't know! How can we make them know?'"

Dinah Lifschitz cried: "I can't get anyone! I can't get anyone!"

Bernstein realized the moment of decision had come.

"I said, 'Dinah, we are the last ones,' and I ordered her to drop the phone and get out. I remembered I had relatives on the ninth floor and they were all very dear to me. I ran through the blaze and the smoke to try to get to the ninth floor.

"I don't know how I got into the Greene Street staircase. But I could not get into the ninth floor. Twenty feet from the door on that floor was a barrel container of motor oil. I suppose that was burning. I don't know. The blaze was so strong I couldn't get into the ninth floor. Then I ran up to the tenth floor. I found it was burning there, too."

On the other side of the flames, on the opposite side of the eighth floor, machinist Brown and Patrolman Meehan came back up to the eighth floor to make certain everyone was out.

"We yanked two girls out of a window and got them to the staircase," Brown said. "I went back to the window to see if anyone else was there. The people in the street saw me. They raised their hands and yelled for me not to jump. When I saw that I decided it was time for me to turn around and get out.

"But I couldn't find my way out any more. It was so black with smoke that I couldn't see. I couldn't even see the door. I knew the doorway was about fifteen feet in front of me. I got down on my hands and knees and crawled out that doorway."

Eight floors below, Fireman Oliver Mahoney of Company 72 which had arrived at 4:46½, burst into the Washington Place lobby.

"At first we couldn't even get into the lobby. As I got in, an elevator opened and another group of frightened people got out. We pushed through," said Fireman Mahoney.

Three other firemen carrying the hose on their shoulders followed him up the stairs until he reached the eighth floor landing.

"I had no water with me yet. My men were coming up with the hose. I located the proper place where I was to work. I could see the eighth floor was a mass of flames," Mahoney added.

On the Greene Street side, Captain Ruch had dashed up the stairs while his men unrolled the hoses from where they were connected to a hydrant at Waverly Place. He encountered Max Hochfield and restrained him from going back upstairs. Then he returned to the street and led his men, now carrying the hose, up to the sixth-floor level. Here they disconnected the house hose from the standpipe and connected the fire hose.

Captain Ruch carried the hose up to the eighth floor:

"I shouted, 'Start your water.' It came. The fire was so intense it was impossible to stand up. We lay down on our stomachs or on our knees to try to make an entrance. The eighth floor was a mass of fire. . . ."

✳   ✳   ✳   ✳   ✳

The nerve center of the Triangle Shirtwaist Company was the suite of executive offices on the tenth floor, which occupied the space along the Washington Place windows. About forty male and female garment pressers worked at tables lined along the Greene Street windows. The entire rear of the floor, facing the back courtyard, was occupied by a large packing and shipping room filled with hanging garments and cardboard and wooden boxes.

Also on the tenth floor was the Triangle switchboard. On that Saturday Mary Alter, a cousin of Mrs. Isaac Harris, added operation of the switchboard to her usual typing chores because the regular board operator was ill.

When Mary Alter first heard Dinah Lifschitz' buzz on the telautograph, she hurried to the machine to receive the mechanical message.

She waited, "but the pen did not move. It simply stuck in the well. As I waited for the pen to start writing, I realized that it was a new machine and that a good many of the girls did not yet know how to operate it properly. They often made mistakes and didn't connect things right. So I went back to my desk thinking that someone was fooling me."

Mary continued typing until the telephone switchboard buzzed.

"It was the eighth floor calling. At first I couldn't make out any clear sound. It was like yelling and I asked, 'What is the trouble down there? what are you yelling about?'

"Then I heard distinctly, 'There is a fire!' So I immediately got up and told Mr. Levine, our bookkeeper, to telephone the Fire Department, which he did. Then I went to tell Mr. Harris and Mr. Blanck that there was a fire on the eighth floor and to see about my father."

Mary Alter's father was the tenth-floor watchman. One of his jobs was to stand guard at the Greene Street exit at going-home time, just as Joseph Wexler was doing on the eighth floor.

Now no one monitored the switchboard. At her eighth-floor desk, Dinah Lifschitz held on to the phone, shouting into its mouthpiece for the ninth floor, getting no answer.

"I did not ring up the ninth floor," said Mary Alter.

The bookkeeper, heeding Mary's order, ran into Mr. Blanck's office, where there was a phone with a direct outside line. "I called Fire Headquarters but they had already received word of the fire so I hung up," he said.

Levine put down the receiver and turned to leave when he saw two children standing in a corner of the office, intently watching him. They were Blanck's two daughters, Henrietta, aged twelve, and Mildred, aged five. Their nursemaid, Mlle. Ehresmann, had brought them downtown for a shopping trip their father had promised. Mrs. Blanck was in Florida with the other children.

Levine told the children to stay in the office where the nursemaid had deposited them while she went to find Blanck. The bookkeeper had seen smoke rising outside the windows and had decided to get back to his own office to put the record books into the safe.

The person in charge of the shipping room was Edward N. Markowitz, and he had also seen the smoke. He was suddenly struck by the realization that on the floor below there were more than 250 persons crowded among the machines and tables. He ran to the Greene Street exit and down the stairs.

Markowitz managed to get through the ninth floor entrance to the shop just as the first wave of fright had washed over the girls. "They were standing with a sort of dazed look on their faces. They were beginning to push toward the exit and I shouted to them, 'Go nice! There is a fire! Go easy!' I don't know how long I stood in that doorway cautioning the girls. I would put my hand on their shoulders to calm them and I would say, 'One at a time and go to the stairs and get out!'"

The girls in the rear of the crowd began to press forward. Markowitz waved them toward the fire escape near where they stood and shouted to the watchman to guide them through the windows. Then he remembered he had left his order book on the tenth floor.

"That book was very valuable to the firm. I went back to the tenth floor and found it. I had the book in my hand when I turned and saw Mr. Blanck standing there in the middle of the floor. He was holding his little daughter in his arm and he held the older one by the hand. He didn't seem to know which way to turn."

Blanck had been in the shipping room—Markowitz's department—when he heard a cry: "The taxi is here, Mr. Blanck." It reminded him of his promise to the children, and he found them waiting in his office where Levine had made the call to the Fire Department.

Blanck remembered that somebody ran in and said, "Mr. Blanck, there is a little fire on the eighth floor." He left the children and started for the Greene Street side. Then it occurred to him that the children might be frightened, so he went back to get them. "At the front passenger elevator the car came up. All the pressers, all the girls were screaming, 'Save us! save us!' I told the elevator man, 'Take these girls down and come right up again.'

"But while the people were pushing in, my little girl, the five-year old, was swept into the car. I grabbed hold of her hand and pulled. I just got her out of the elevator and I held her close to me.

"The elevator operator took them down, as many as he could, and I stood there for about half a minute, seeing if he would come up again. The minute was too big for me. I started for the other side of the shop. When I saw that I was passing the door to the Washington Place stairs, I turned the handle, thinking I will go down this way.

"I heard Mr. Harris someplace in the shop hollering, 'To the roof! to the roof!' I thought I will be smarter and go down this way. I opened the door. There was so much smoke. I knew the children wouldn't be able to stand the smoke.

"I grabbed the two children and ran as far as the middle of the room, holding them. When I got to the middle of the room, I stopped. The smoke and the flames seemed to be coming from all sides."

As the bewildered Blanck stood clutching his children in the center of the turmoil, up the stairs and through the smoke came Samuel Bernstein, clear-headed and determined to save as many as possible. He had tried to enter the ninth floor only minutes after Markowitz had left it, but by that time it was impossible to get beyond the Greene Street vestibule. The flames had come to the door in the partition.

Breathlessly, Bernstein had then hurried up to the tenth floor. At first glance he saw that "they were all running around like wildcats. I shouted that the only way out was over the roof.

"I saw Louis Silk, a salesman for a textile firm, standing on a table trying to knock out a skylight. Near the table was Mr. Blanck with his two children. One of them was screaming. I went over to Mr. Blanck and told him, 'The only way you can get out is over the roof. But you better be quick about it!' Eddie Markowitz took the younger child and Mr. Blanck held the older one and we began to fight our way out of there."

When Markowitz saw Blanck paralyzed by uncertainty, he dropped his order book and picked up the smaller child. "I pulled him by the coat and I said, 'Come along, Mr. Blanck.' We went right through the loft to the Greene Street stairs. I could feel the flames in back of me. I could feel the heat of them as we went to the roof."

Blanck's partner, Isaac Harris, had posted himself at the Washington Place elevators where he remained to guide the girls until he realized that the elevators seemed to have stopped running.

At this point, "I started to holler, 'Girls, let us go to the roof!' We all rushed to the Greene Street stairs. The smoke was getting heavy and the room was getting dark."

When the girls shrank back from the smoke, Harris urged them on: "Go, one of you, two of you. If you can't all go, better at least one should get out."

Harris led the way up the stairs. Halfway up between the tenth floor and the roof was the window facing the rear yard and through it blew a blast of flame. The girls turned up their coat collars or shielded their faces with their muffs. They reached the roof, their clothing scorched, some with their hair smoldering.

On his way to the roof, Bernstein found Lucy Wesselofsky in a fainting condition. He helped her up.

Lucy was one who had tried to calm the girls "by shouting that everyone would be saved if they would stop trying to pile into the staircase all together.

"In fact, on the tenth floor, where there were about seventy people working, all were saved except one. She was Clotilda Terdanova. She tore her hair and ran from window to window until finally, before anyone could stop her, she jumped out. She was young and very pretty. She was to leave us next Saturday to be married three weeks later."

One of the first to reach the roof was Joseph Flecher, an assistant cashier. He approached the edge of the roof and cautiously peered over the side.

"I looked down the whole height of the building. My people were sticking out of the windows. I saw my girls, my pretty ones, going down through the air. They hit the sidewalk spread out and still."

The roof now became a refuge, an island surrounded by huge waves of smoke and flame. The survivors came staggering out of the structure that covered the Greene Street stairs. They were coughing, screaming, hysterical, and some stumbled perilously close to the edge of the roof.

The adjoining building on the Greene Street side was 13 feet higher than the top of the Asch building. It could be reached by climbing from the top of the staircase covering to the superstructure over the freight elevator shaft.

On the Washington Place side, the New York University-American Book Company building towered 15 feet above the Asch structure. But it too could be scaled by way of the roof over the passenger elevators.

On the tenth floor of the school building, Professor Sommer and the members of his law class had heard the screams of the fire engines. Elias Kanter, one of his students that day, remembers him as a tall, handsome redhead, "ready to adjourn at the end of class to the nearby Brevoort Hotel bar with a handful of students anxious to pursue further some fine point of the law."

Professor Sommer halted his discourse and hurried to the adjoining faculty room which had a window facing the rear courtyard.

"Some of the boys followed me," the Professor said, "and we saw that the ten-story building across the areaway was on fire. The areaway was filled with smoke. We heard ear-piercing shrieks as the girls in the factory appeared at the windows."

The screams of the engines and the girls were also heard in Professor Parsons' horticulture class on the ninth floor. He dismissed his class of forty girls at once, and while they gathered up their notes and books, he also ran to the rear window. "I was shocked by a sight more terrible than I ever could have imagined. I saw a fire escape literally gorged with girls. A great tongue of flame reached out for them."

For a moment, James McCadden, a service worker in the school building, stood beside the professor. "I saw a girl come to the edge of the roof and stand for a minute, looking down. She jumped. Her hair was in flames. I couldn't look any more."

On the floor above, Professor Sommer and George DeWitt, one of the students who had run with him to the rear window, rushed back to the lecture room and summoned the young men to follow them to the roof. There they found ladders left by painters who had been working on the roof during the week.

"We put one across the space between the coping of our building and the skylight above the elevator shaft on the Washington Place side," said De-Witt. Then they lowered a second ladder from the top of the elevator shaft to the Asch roof.

Now they formed a line up to the school roof with Charles Kramer, Frederick Newman, and Elias Kanter starting the slow procession of the frightened women from the Asch roof.

While the students continued their rescue operation on the Washington Place side, others set up a scaling relay at the Greene Street side. There somebody reached down and took Max Blanck's little girl and pulled her up. Then he handed up the older one, and after that he himself climbed up or was pulled up, he didn't remember which.

Harris had led a group from the tenth floor in a rush up the stairs past the open window—"The fire was blowing right in that window"—and once on the roof, he climbed to the adjacent Greene Street building. He and another man "ran to the door on that roof. We found it locked. So we smashed the skylight and hollered for help. A man came up and brought a ladder."

Harris then ran back to the edge of the higher building. Down on the Asch roof he saw Bernstein and Louis Senderman struggling with a salesman named Teschner weighing about 250 pounds who, according to Bernstein, was "shivering like a fish and crying like a baby," and threatening to jump. Together, the three raised him to safety.

At another time Bernstein had "pushed one man up and when he got to the next roof he began to run away instead of staying there and helping the rest of us. I yelled, 'For God's sake, stay and help us push these other people up.' He came back and helped until there were only a few left on the Asch roof.

"I saw the flames were coming right onto the roof on the Greene Street and areaway sides. And nobody was there anymore to push me up. So I ran across the roof all the way to the Washington Place side where the University is and they pushed me up onto a ladder. When I got near the end of the ladder, I looked down. I saw five or six girls falling from the windows."

In the short wing of the L-shaped back yard, the flames leaped across at the University building. They cracked the glass in the windows and set the facing rooms afire. When the Law Library began to burn, University Vice Chancellor Charles McCracken and other faculty members organized a group of students who rescued the books armful by armful.

From the roof above them, when it seemed that the last Triangle survivor had been rescued, Charles Kramer climbed down the ladder for a final inspection of the Asch roof. He groped through the thick smoke. Flames were now rising on all sides.

He came across the roof carefully. He heard someone moaning and moved in the direction from which the sound seemed to be coming. He found a girl lying across the top steps of the Greene Street stairway, her head on the floor of the roof, her hair smoldering.

"He smothered the sparks in her hair with his hands," the *Sun* reported. He lifted her in his arms and headed back across the roof toward the Washington Place ladders. "Then he tried to carry her up the ladder to the higher roof.

"But because she was unconscious, he had to wrap long strands of her hair around his hands. Dragging her, he slowly made his way up the ladder."

$$* \qquad * \qquad * \qquad * \qquad *$$

On the ninth floor, the telephone that could have alerted two hundred and sixty persons to the peril boiling up beneath them stood silently on a table in the far, inside corner of the shop. At this table, Mary Leventhal distributed the bundles of cut work brought up from the cutting department on the floor below.

The sewing machine operators who stitched the parts together worked at 240 machines that filled almost the entire area of the ninth floor. These were arranged in sixteen parallel rows running at right angles from the Washington Place wall. Each row had fifteen machines and was 75 feet long. At their far end, the lines of machines left an aisle 15 feet wide in the space between the exit to the Greene Street freight elevators and the windows facing New York University across the back yard.

The machine heads were set into a single work table running the full 75 feet. Every two tables faced each other across a common work trough 10 inches wide and 4 inches deep which connected them. The two rows thus connected formed a plant of 30 machines, and there were eight such plants on the floor.

Under each central trough, at about 8 inches from the floor, a rotating axle, spanning the full 75 feet, drew rotary power from a motor at the Washington Place end of the plant. At that side there was no through passage from aisle to aisle. Only at the far end of the machine lines was such passage possible; all aisles between the plants led only to the passage in the rear.

Fifteen workers sat on each side of the plant, rocking in the rhythm of the work. During working hours, the horizon for each was marked by the workers facing her across the trough, one a little to the right, the other slightly to the left, and by the wicker basket on the floor to her right where she kept the bundle of work to be completed. She sat on a wooden chair; her table was of wood; her machine was well-oiled, its drippings caught and held in a wooden shell just above her knees, and the material she sewed was more combustible than paper.

Each machine head was connected by leather belts to a fly-wheel on the rotating axle from which it drew motive power. The machine operators bent to their work as they fed the fabric parts to the vibrating needle in front of them. Leaning forward, each seemed to be pushing the work to the machine. In turn, the rapid stitching made a rasping whirr as the operator pressed her treadle to draw power, and as if satisfied, the machine passed the work through, sending it sliding and stitched into the center trough.

At her table, pretty, blond Mary Leventhal prepared for the end of the workday by checking the book in which she kept the record of work distributed and work returned by the operators. At her elbow stood the telephone, its yawning mouthpiece mounted on a tubelike standard with the receiver hanging on a hook at the side.

Because Saturday was payday, Mary and Anna Gullo, the forelady, had just finished distributing the pay envelops. "Mary went back to her table and I went toward the freight elevators where the button was for ringing the quitting bell. I rang the bell," Anna Gullo said.

The machinists pulled the switches and suddenly the rasp of the machines stopped. Now the huge room filled with talk as the operators pushed back from their machines. The chairs scraped, locking back to back in the aisles and with the wicker baskets filling the long passageways to the rear of the shop.

The workweek was over. Ahead was an evening of shopping or fun and a day of rest. Most of the workers good-naturedly accepted the slow progress up the aisles and around to the dressing room and the exit. Only a few impatient ones jostled ahead to be first out. Max Hochfield had learned that the way to beat the crowd was to avoid the crush in the dressing room and in the rear area of the shop. He kept his coat hanging on a nail protruding on the shop side of the Greene Street partition. When Anna Gullo reached out for the bell button, he was right beside her and out of the door as she rang the signal.

He was the first worker from the ninth floor to learn that a furnace had flamed up underneath.

When he reached the eighth floor, he could see it was all in flames. Nobody was on the stairs. He ran down another half flight and looked into the courtyard. "I saw people coming down the fire escape. I stopped. I was confused. I had never been in a fire before. I didn't know what to do."

Hochfield continued down the steps, then stopped: his sister Esther was still on the ninth floor. He turned to run back up. "But somebody grabbed me by the shoulder. It was a fireman. I shouted at him, 'I have to save my sister!' But he turned me around and ordered me, 'Go down, if you want to stay alive!'"

This had been the first week for Max and his sister on the ninth floor. On the previous Sunday the Hochfield family had celebrated the engagement of twenty-year-old Esther by giving a party. The guests had visited until early morning, and Max and his sister stayed home the next day.

When they came to work on Tuesday, they found that their machines on the eighth floor had been assigned to two other workers. "Mr. Bernstein told us if we wanted to work we would have to go to the ninth floor. That's how we came to be up there. Maybe if my sister wasn't engaged she would be alive."

The flames invaded the ninth floor with a swiftness that panicked most of the girls but paralyzed others. Pert, pretty Rose Glantz had been one of the first into the dressing room between the door to the Washington Place stairs and the windows facing the University. In high spirits she began singing a popular song, "Every Little Movement Has a Meaning All Its Own."

Some of her friends joined in and when the group finally emerged from the dressing room, giggling and happy, the flames were breaking the first windows on the ninth floor. Laugher turned to screams.

"We didn't have a chance," Rose recalls. "The people on the eighth floor must have seen the fire start and grow. The people on the tenth floor got the warning over the telephone. But with us on the ninth, all of a sudden the fire was all around. The flames were coming in through many of the windows."

Rose ran to the Washington Place stairway door, tried to open it, and when it stayed locked she stood there, screaming. But as the crowd began to thicken, she pushed forward toward the elevator door. "I saw there was no chance at the elevators. I took my scarf and wrapped it around my head and ran to the freight elevator side. I saw the door to the Greene Street stairs was open so I ran through it and down. The fire was in the hall on the eighth floor. I pulled my scarf tighter around my head and ran right through it. It caught fire. I have a scar on my neck."

She made it down the nine floors, meeting the first group of firemen as she neared the freight entrance at street level. There, firemen stopped her from going into the street as they were also doing in the Washington Place lobby with those who had come down from the eighth floor.

Finally, the firemen "escorted us out. I stood in the doorway of a store across the street and watched. I saw one woman jump and get caught on a hook on the sixth floor. I watched a fireman try to save her. I wasn't hysterical any more; I was just numb."

Where was Mary Leventhal? Her telephone did not ring to give the alarm. But Anna Gullo, as soon as she heard the screams of fire, ran across the rear of the shop toward Mary's desk. Then she was swept along with the frantic crowd heading for the Washington Place door.

At the door she tried to exert whatever authority she could command as a forelady. She shouldered the frightened girls aside and tried to open the door.

"The door was locked," she says.

Trapped, she soon shared the terror of those around her. She fought her way out of the crowd and ran to a window on the Washington Place side and tried to open it. The window stuck so she smashed the glass with her hand. Somewhere in the confusion she had picked up a pail of water, and thrown it at the flames.

"But the flames came up higher," Anna says. "I looked back into the shop and saw the flames were bubbling on the machines. I turned back to the window and made the sign of the cross. I went to jump out of the window. But I had no courage to do it."

Now Anna sought her sister. She headed back across the rear of the shop toward the Greene Street doors, shouting for her sister, Mary.

There were others who cried out for dear ones. Joseph Brenman worked with his two sisters on the ninth floor. Unable to find them, he pushed his way dazedly through the struggling crowd in the rear, calling for the younger of the two, "Surka, where are you, Surka?"

Anna fought her way to the Greene Street door. "I had on my fur coat and my hat with two feathers. I pulled my woolen skirt over my head. Somebody had hit me with water from a pail. I was soaked.

"At the vestibule door there was a big barrel of oil. I went through the staircase door. As I was going down I heard a loud noise. Maybe the barrel of oil exploded. I remember when I passed the eighth floor all I could see was a mass of flames. The wind was blowing up the staircase.

"When I got to the bottom I was cold and wet. I was crying for my sister. I remember a man came over to me. I was sitting on the curb. He lifted my head and looked into my face. It must have been all black from the smoke of the fire. He wiped my face with a handkerchief. He said, 'I thought you were my sister.' He gave me his coat.

"I don't know who he was. I never again found my sister alive. I hope he found his."

Was the stranger Max Hochfield, destined never to see his sister Esther alive again, or was it Joseph Brenman still looking for Surka?

On the ninth floor, those able to make their way up the long, obstructed aisles, pushed into the crowded rear area of the shop. Here, two tides struggled to move in opposite directions. Few knew that behind the nearby shuttered windows was the fire escape that could lead to safety.

Nellie Ventura was one of those who knew. She reached a small group at the fourth window from the left. The window had been raised, but the outside metal shutter remained firmly closed. Some banged on it with their hands. But two, working on the rusted metal pin holding the shutter closed, succeeded in lifting it. The shutters swung open. Nellie Ventura stepped over the 23-inch-high sill and down to the slatted balcony floor.

She saw thick smoke with tongues of fire at the eighth floor. "At first I was too frightened to try to run through the fire. Then I heard the screams of the girls inside. I knew I had to go down the ladder or die where I was.

"I pulled my boa tight around my face and went. I do not know how I got down to the courtyard at the bottom. Maybe I jumped, maybe somebody carried me. I remember a fireman led me through a hallway and out into the street. At first I couldn't remember where I lived. A policeman took me home."

Panic-stricken girls battled each other on that rickety, terrifying descent. Of her own flight, Mary Bucelli could recall only that "I was throwing them out of the way. No matter whether they were in front of me or coming from in back of me, I was pushing them down. I was only looking out for my own life."

The last to get to safety by way of the fire escape was quick-witted Abe Gordon who, at sixteen, had started working at Triangle as a button puncher. He loved the marvelous sewing machines, the Singers and the Willcox and Gibbs stitchers, and his dream was to become a machinist.

The steppingstone to that job was the assignment as belt boy. Then his task would be to listen for the call of an operator whose machine had lost power because its strap connecting it with the fly wheel on the axle had snapped. He would then sidle swiftly down the crowded aisle, creep under the machine table, and make the repair.

Abe saved twelve dollars out of his scant pay and bought a watch fob for the head machinist. In no time at all he was promoted from button puncher to belt boy.

Now, pushing out onto the fire escape, he sensed its inadequacy. "I could hear all the screaming and hollering in back of me. At the sixth floor, I found an open window.

"I stepped back into the building. I still had one foot on the fire escape when I heard a loud noise and looked back up. The people were falling all around me, screaming all around me. The fire escape was collapsing."

Even in the midst of the horror, some failed to grasp its finality. When Yetta Lubitz emerged from the dressing room she was surprised at the sight of the commotion. As a worker "on time" rather than "by the piece," punching out on the time clock had become a most meaningful ritual of her daily routine. She managed somehow to get through the crowd to the time clock, inserted her card in the receiving slot and pushed the punch lever. The ring of its bell seemed to awaken her to the seriousness of the situation around her. She became frightened and ran toward the dressing room.

"Then, all of a sudden, a young dark fellow—he was an operator but I didn't know his name—was running near me. I ran with him to the Washington Place door. He tried to open the door. He said, 'Oh, it is locked, the door is locked.'"

Now panic seized her. She ran back to the dressing room, then out of it to the three windows facing the school building—"the flames had knocked them out and were licking into the shop"—then back again into the dressing room.

"I just stood there crying," Yetta recounted. "The young man, the same dark one, was near me and he snapped, 'Oh, keep quiet; what's the use of crying?' So I felt ashamed and stopped it. But when he was gone, I started to scream again.

"Then I saw the girls were running to the Greene Street side and I started to run, too. The fire was burning in the aisle at the fire escape."

Unable to pass through the rear area, Yetta climbed up onto a machine table. These were 30 inches high, and the machine heads added another 12 inches. Yetta climbed over two plants of machines, past the fire in the rear area.

"I looked back and I saw one old Italian woman who couldn't jump down from the machine table. She took a few steps back and forth and she was looking down. But she couldn't get down.

"I covered my face with my skirt and ran into the Greene Street passage. I got to the roof and then it occurred to me that I had forgotten to take my time card out of the clock."

The dressing room, adjacent to the door to the Washington Place stairs, became for some the final place of decision, for others a temporary refuge before death.

Lena Yaller remembered it as being "filled with smoke; everybody was talking or screaming; some in Jewish and some in Italian were crying about their children."

When Ethel Monick looked up from her machine, she saw "fire coming in all around us. I saw women at other machines become frozen with fear. They never moved."

But Ethel, only sixteen, moved. She ran to the Washington Place stairway door, and when she saw it was locked, backtracked into the dressing room. "I was looking for something with which to smash the door. It was wired glass on top.

"In the dressing room men and women were laughing but in a strange way I could not understand at that time. I yelled at them to stop laughing and to help me find an unused machine head to smash the door."

When she left the dressing room, Ethel ran to a window, resolved to jump. "Then I saw in my mind how I would look lying there on the sidewalk and I got ashamed. I moved back from the window." Ethel headed back to the elevators.

The escape routes were closing off. Ida Nelson, clutching her week's pay in her hand, ran to the fire escape windows. She looked out and all she could see was heavy smoke laced with flames.

"I don't know what made me do it but I bent over and pushed my pay into the top of my stocking. Then I ran to the Greene Street side and tried to get into the staircase."

In the few minutes since Anna Gullo had gone down the stairs, that route had been cut off by fire. Now Ida Nelson saw that "I couldn't get through. The heat was too intense.

"I ran back into the shop and found part of a roll of piece goods. I think it was lawn; it was on the bookkeeper's desk. I wrapped it around and around me until only my face showed.

"Then I ran right into the fire on the stairway and up toward the roof. I couldn't breathe. The lawn caught fire. As I ran, I tried to keep peeling off the burning lawn, twisting and turning as I ran. By the time I passed the tenth floor and got to the roof, I had left most of the lawn in ashes behind me. But I still had one end of it under my arm. That was the arm that got burned."

Rose Cohen had already reached the roof by the time Ida came through the door. Both were sleeve setters, but in the huge ninth-floor factory they had never spoken to each other. However, Rose recalls that "there was one little girl who, like me, saved herself by running to the roof. She had wrapped white goods all around herself and one piece was still burning. I ran to her and helped her beat out the flames. Then I tried to hold back another girl who tore herself away from us and ran back into the stairway to look for her sister."

Rose had been on her way to the dressing room when she heard the cry of fire. She remembers that many of the girls still in the aisles were "caged in by the wicker work baskets." As she ran she tried to down the rising panic in her heart with the thought of what, she says, "all greenhorn immigrants like my parents used to say: 'In America, they don't let you burn.'

"I ran into the dressing room with the machinist and some of the others. The walls of the dressing room began to smoke. We ran back into the shop. Girls were lying on the floor—fainted. People were stepping on them. Other girls were trying to climb over the machines. Some were running with their hair burning.

"I followed the machinist to a window and he smashed the glass with his hand to let the smoke out—it was choking us. Instead, the flames rushed in. For a few seconds I stood at that window. My hair was smoldering. My clothes were torn. I turned and ran to the Greene Street exit.

"I put my hands on my smoldering, long hair and I started up the stairs. On the tenth floor, I went in through the door. The place was empty. All I could hear was the fire burning. Here, I thought, I would die—here was the end. I didn't realize that right above me—one more floor—was the roof.

"Then I heard some one calling, 'Come to the roof! Come to the roof!' I turned and saw him in a corner near the staircase holding an armful of record books. If not for him I would have died there on the tenth floor. My life was saved by a bookkeeper."

The red flames had raced across the big room, feeding on the flimsy fabric, the wicker baskets, the oil-soaked machines and floor. The machine tables were burning. Solid fire now pushed forward from the rear of the shop, including the Greene Street stairway. It divided the trapped ones into two groups.

One group remained cornered in the areaway in front of the Washington Place elevator doors and staircase. The stairway door remained closed, the girls clawing at it and screaming.

The second group was trapped, scattered, in the aisles between the sewing plants. Now the advancing flames forced them back down the aisles toward the windows facing Washington Place. Some climbed over the rows of machines only to get caught in the last aisle running along the Greene Street windows. The fire backed them into the windows. And in the street the crowds watched helplessly as they plunged into space.

Only the little passenger elevators continued to scoop some of the dying back to life. The Washington Place elevators measured 4 feet 9 inches by 5 feet 9 inches. They were designed to carry about fifteen passengers. Yet Gaspar Mortillalo, one of the two operators, was certain that in his last trips down from the inferno he carried twice that number.

He and Joseph Zito, both in their twenties, had been sitting in their cars at street level, waiting for Triangle—the only firm in the building still working at that hour—to check out. Suddenly, the bells in both cars began to ring insistently. They heard frantic banging up above, the sound of glass smashing, then screams.

"Gaspar didn't say anything to me and I didn't say anything to Gaspar. We both started our cars right up," said Zito.

In these elevators the cable ran through the cage. To start the car moving up, the operator reached up, took a firm grip on the cable and sharply pulled down; he reversed the procedure to descend.

It was Zito's recollection that he must have made seven or eight trips altogether. "Two of them went to the tenth floor, one to the eighth floor and the rest to the ninth. Gaspar and I must have brought down a couple of hundred girls. Twice, I went through smoke and flames that came right into the car.

"When I first opened the elevator door on the ninth floor all I could see was a crowd of girls and men with great flames and smoke right behind them. When I came to the floor the third time, the girls were standing on the window sills with the fire all around them."

Now the elevators became the last link with life. The struggle to get into them became desperate. On their last trips Zito and his partner fought to close the doors before descending.

Fannie Selmanowitz pushed herself into one of the cars as it started to move down. "There wasn't enough room for a pin in that elevator. All the way down I was being pressed through the open door of the car against the side of the shaft."

The last person to get into the last car to leave the ninth floor was Katie Weiner. "I was searching for my sister Rose but I could not find her. Then I found myself crushed against the elevator door, knocking and crying like the others for him to come up.

"He didn't come up. I was choking with the smoke. I went to a window and put my face out to get some fresh air and I calmed down. Suddenly, the elevator came up and the girls rushed to it. I was pushed back to the staircase door. I was crying, 'Girls, girls, help me!' But they kept pushing me back.

"The elevator started to go down. The flames were coming toward me and I was being left behind. I felt the elevator was leaving the ninth floor for the last time. I got hold of the cable that went through the car and swung myself in, landing on the girls' heads.

"All the way down," Katie Weiner remembers, "I was on the people's heads. I was facing downward and my feet were extending out into the shaft. As we went down, my feet were hurting horribly, my ankles were hitting the doors and I was crying, 'Girls, my feet, my feet!'"

Crushed in that elevator on that last trip was Josephine Panno. She screamed all the way down. Through all of the panicked rush to the elevators she had held firmly to the skirt of her daughter, Mrs. Jane Bucalo. But in the final surge that carried her into the car, her grip had broken.

As the elevator began its descent, she caught sight of her daughter's fear-torn face in the crowd being left behind. She screamed and struggled to raise an arm in an effort to reach out to her daughter. But her arms were pinned to her side by the crush.

"When we got to the bottom," she remembered, "girls were crying all around me as they trampled each other to get out. But I could not hear the cries of my daughter." She tried to run up the stairs and fought the policemen in the lobby until she fainted.

Where the elevator had been, there was now only a gaping hole. Sarah Cammerstein stood at the edge and watched the car slip slowly downward. "I thought the elevator was falling. It didn't seem to be driving down but only sinking slowly under too much weight. That's why I hesitated.

"But when I saw it was still at the seventh floor I knew it wasn't falling. I made the decision of my life. I threw my coat down onto the roof of the elevator and jumped for it."

Sarah Cammerstein blacked out. When she opened her eyes again she was lying face up on the roof of the elevator.

"I was alone, she says. "I was spread out on my coat and I looked straight up into the elevator shaft. I could see the flames coming out of the eighth floor. I couldn't move.

"But the elevator was moving. It was going up, straight to the flames. I began to scream. I found the strength to bang my fist on the top of the elevator."

The car stopped. For a moment it was motionless. Then it slowly descended to put its roof on a level with the exit to the lobby and Sarah Cammerstein was lifted out.

Both elevators began their final ascent. The right-hand elevator reached to just below the eighth floor where the heat of the flames pushing into the shaft had bent its tracks. It returned to the lobby. The elevator on the left, Zito's car on which Sarah Cammerstein had been lowered, never rose above the lobby. Falling bodies began to crush in its roof.

Celia Walker stood at the ninth floor opening above Zito's car, afraid of falling, seeking the courage to jump. She was proud of the fact that the other immigrant girls at Triangle considered her "a real Yankee." Celia had come to America with her parents when she was five years old. Bright and zestful, she spoke with what she liked to consider "a true American accent." Her job was to examine finished garments and to return them for cleaning or repair, if needed.

In the terror touched off by the cry of fire, Celia felt panic challenging her usual self-sufficiency. "The girls were climbing over the machine tables. So was I. The aisles were narrow and blocked by the chairs and the baskets which were beginning to burn. I jumped from one table to the next without getting down. I was twenty years old and I could jump.

"The first time I saw the elevator come up, the girls rushed in and it was filled in a second. When it came up again, the girls were all squeezing against the door and the minute it opened, they all rushed in again. This time I thought I was going to be lucky enough to make it, but just as I got to the door, the elevator began to drop down. Somebody in front of me jumped.

"Soon I found myself standing at the edge, trying to hold myself back from falling into the shaft. I gripped the sides of the open door. Behind me the girls were screaming. I could feel them pushing more and more.

"I knew that in a few seconds I would be pushed into the shaft. I had to make a quick decision. I jumped for the center cable. I began to slide down. I remember passing the floor numbers up to five. Then something falling hit me.

"The next thing I knew was when I opened my eyes and looked up into the faces of a priest and a nun. They were trying to help me. I was in a bed in St. Vincent's Hospital.

"They had found me at the bottom of the shaft on the elevator. Others had fallen on top of me. My head was injured. I had a broken arm and a broken finger. Down the middle of my body I felt the burning of the cable which had torn right through my clothes.

"One of the nurses told me she thought it was wonderful that I had enough presence of mind when I jumped to wrap something around my hands in order to save them from injury as I grasped the cable. But it wasn't presence of mind. It was a new fur muff for which I had saved many weeks. Fire or no fire, I wasn't going to lose that muff. I think the right word for my presence of mind is vanity."

Others jumped or fell through the 2½-foot opening into the left elevator shaft. Sarah Friedman had seen the elevator slide away on its last descent. She grabbed the cable at the side of the shaft. "I slid all the way down and ended up on top of the car where I lost consciousness. One of my hands was burned by the friction. When I opened my eyes I was lying in the street—among the dead."

One of the last to jump—and survive—was May Caliandro Levantini, a mother of three children. She tried to stop her fearful, relentless progress toward the elevator pit. Her hands scratched for a hold on the grating alongside the shaft opening.

But when she felt that the pressure behind her could no longer be resisted, she turned and leaped for a cable.

"I was on top of the elevator cage, face up," she said. "I saw firemen going up the stairs with a hose. One of them called to me through the grill as he went up. 'You are all right!' I kept crying, 'Look! Look!' That's all I could say. They couldn't see what I could see way up there in the shaft."

She could see others being pushed out into the shaft at the ninth floor. She rolled over toward the wall to be out of the line of their plunge.

Joseph Zito heard the bodies hit, felt his car shiver with each new impact. "A body struck the top of the elevator and bent the iron. A minute later another one hit.

"The screams from above were getting worse. I looked up and saw the whole shaft getting red with fire. I knew the poor girls up there were trapped. But my car wouldn't work. It was jammed by the bodies."

Then the car slipped down to the bottom of the shaft.

"It was horrible," Zito added. "They kept coming down from the burning floors above. Some of their clothing was burning as they fell. I could see the streaks of fire coming down like flaming rockets."

Now there was no exit. The flames roared louder, steadier. They poured up the Greene Street stairwell. They pushed out of all of the windows.

They blew into the Washington Place elevator shaft. In the center of the shop, they billowed as a single deep layer of flame. And the door to the Washington Place staircase held fast and there life screamed to an end.

"I have never been able to forget that maybe I could have saved pretty Mary Leventhal," cutter Joseph Granick says.

"Only a few minutes before the fire she came down to the eighth floor where I was cutting trimmings. She said to me, 'Joe, I have a few girls coming in tomorrow. I need a few dozen cuffs.'

"I gave her five bundles of cuffs. Why didn't I hold her back? Why didn't I talk to her a little longer? Why didn't I argue with her? If she had stayed only a few more minutes she would have escaped with us. But, no! She went back to the ninth floor to die."

PART THREE

Natural Causes: When Time and Luck Run Out

Mount St. Helens

BY ROB CARSON

Although most disasters share the characteristic of striking with little or no warning—and hence time to prepare—one of the most famous could be seen literally brewing for weeks.

The explosion of Mount St. Helens in Washington State on Sunday, May 18, 1980, was preceded by weeks when the simmering active volcano was being scrutinized by geologists and scientists who predicted an eruption was imminent. Still, the suddenness and size of the actual blast, with a force equivalent to thousands of atomic bombs, were catastrophic.

The story of what happened at Mount St. Helens, both on the fateful day of the explosion and in the weeks leading up to that awesome event, has been dramatically and engagingly told by writer Rob Carson in his book *Mount St. Helens: The Eruption and Recovery of a Volcano.* Presented with stunning photographs by photographers Geff Hinds, Cheryl Haselhorst, and Gary Braasch, the book is one of the finest ever produced on a natural disaster. This excerpt from Carson's text is but a glimpse of the excellence to be found in the complete book.

*   *   *   *   *

May 1980. The idea was to get dynamite pictures of the awakening volcano and sell them to tourists. To do that, Gary Rosenquist would have to get clear of all the crowds that had been gathering for several weeks on the south and west sides of Mount St. Helens. He would also have to find a way around the National Guardsmen who were stopping traffic on the two main routes to the mountain—the Spirit Lake Highway out of Castle Rock and State Route 503 up the south side through Cougar. The best bet seemed to be the gravel logging roads that wound from clearcut to clearcut out of the little town of Randle on the north side of the mountain. One of Gary's buddies, Joel Harvey, said he knew where there was a perfect view of the peak—a place where the mountain looked so close you could almost reach out and touch it.

Rosenquist, an unemployed taxi driver from Tacoma, had a tripod and camera he'd been using to shoot pictures of Mount St. Helens ever since the first steam and ash began exploding from the mountain in late March. So far, he'd been unable to get the close-up shots he wanted.

On Saturday, May 17, Rosenquist, Joel Harvey, Harvey's wife, Linda, their 10-year-old son Jo-Jo, and their neighbor, William Dilley, crammed themselves and their camping gear into Harvey's station wagon and set off for Randle. It was a clear, warm spring day, perfect for taking pictures. Sunday was supposed to be the same.

In Randle, they cut off on National Forest roads and drove to a ridgetop 10 miles from the mountain, a place called Bear Meadow. From there they had a straight shot at the peak. It towered over them, looking dark and sinister, its normally pure-white sides black with ash.

Rosenquist set up the camera and snapped a few shots. The mountain showed no signs of distress. They pitched the tent, and when it got dark, sat around a campfire talking. The night was clear, the sky filled with stars.

The next morning—May 18—the rising sun turned the mountain golden brown. Rosenquist set up the camera and tripod. Everything was quiet. "It felt like something was going to happen," Jo-Jo remembered later. "There was no noise, no animals—it was like a dream."

At 8:26 a.m., Rosenquist was back at the fire, eating breakfast. Dilley yelled at him from the ridge. "Something's happening!"

Rosenquist ran to his camera. The mountain looked exactly the same as it had earlier—except it seemed a little bit fuzzy, as if dust were blowing around on top. Nervous, he bumped the tripod with his leg as he fired the first shot. He looked at the mountain more closely. Something was definitely happening. He took another picture, then stared in disbelief. Half the mountain had turned to a brown, churning liquid. A jet-black plume shot out the top.

"There it goes!" Dilley yelled. Rosenquist squeezed the shutter again. The black plume spilled into the sky. Below it, a dirty, brown cloud boiled up, forming surreal cauliflowers in the air.

The five of them stood transfixed as the cloud grew. Instead of settling back down, it kept getting bigger. "Let's get out of here!" Harvey yelled.

Rosenquist snapped another picture. The clouds were boiling, galloping straight for them. He grabbed his camera and they all ran for the station wagon. Dilley scrambled in through the back door and crouched on top of the camping gear.

As they spun onto the road, Rosenquist fired his last shot. The cloud was almost upon them. It thundered over the ridge separating them from the mountain, and loomed over them, blocking out the sun.

Rosenquist started rummaging in the glove box for more film. "No, no, man," Harvey yelled. "Help me drive." The car was sliding on the gravel and the road kept disappearing, even with the headlights on. Rocks the size of marbles spattered down on the roof. The trees whipped back and forth. Lightning flashed. Hot mud and ash poured out of the sky. The light disappeared. Harvey stopped the car. "This is it," he told himself.

Jo-Jo was crying. "Daddy, are we going to die?" In the back, Dilley was talking to God, promising to be good for the rest of his life if only he could survive.

Then the storm passed. The sky was filled with ash, but there was enough light for them to see the road. They continued on, finally reaching Randle and safety. Harvey reached over, patted the camera, and smiled at Rosenquist. "I think we got it," he said.

The series of pictures Rosenquist took that day became the most famous images of the eruption of Mount St. Helens. They showed the step-by-step disintegration of the mountain, the aerial launch of more than one-half a cubic mile of rock, and the origin of the hurricane of stones and ash that turned 234 square miles of verdant forest into a grey, windswept desert.

On Thursday afternoon, March 20, two months before the devastating blast, a graduate student working in the geophysics laboratory at the University of Washington in Seattle was monitoring seismic readings routinely transmitted from Mount St. Helens. He noticed that an earthquake measuring a magnitude 4.0 on the Richter scale had originated at a point that appeared to be directly under the mountain. That was interesting—it was the strongest recorded earthquake in the southern Cascade Range since monitoring equipment had been installed there seven years earlier. But it was not remarkable.

The National Earthquake Information Center in Denver issued a routine press release, but most newspapers in the Pacific Northwest ignored it. President Jimmy Carter had announced the U.S. boycott of the Moscow Olympics the same day, and that story monopolized the news.

Aftershocks persisted the following day, as was expected, but on Saturday the number of earthquakes began to increase rather than tapering off. This was highly unusual.

The earthquakes occurred with increasing frequency on Sunday, and although monitoring techniques that indicate depth were not entirely reliable, the epicenters appeared to be rising gradually toward the surface. Excitement in the lab started to build. Thanks to a remarkably prescient report published in 1978 by U.S. Geological Survey geologists Dwight "Rocky" Crandell and Donal Mullineaux, everyone in the geophysics department knew that an eruption of Mount St. Helens was a very real possibility.

By Monday, March 24, the number of small earthquakes had jumped to more than one per minute, some as strong as 4.4 on the Richter scale. The seismograph needles twitched constantly. There was no doubt by then that something highly unusual was occurring beneath the mountain.

"The first thing I did when I came in Monday morning was call the USGS in Denver, where the volcanic hazards people were," said U.W. seismologist Steve Malone. "I talked to Rocky Crandell and told him I thought there was something significant going on at St. Helens.

"Rocky said, 'Don't worry about it. Those earthquakes are 30 kilometers away from the mountain.' He was using data from different stations than we were and couldn't tell where the earthquakes were coming from with as much accuracy. I said, 'Wrong. These suckers are right under the mountain.'"

Geologist Mullineaux was on a plane to Washington state the next day, and throughout the week more USGS geologists arrived with additional monitoring equipment and expertise. David Johnston, a young USGS geochemist and self-proclaimed volcano junkie, began working in the U.W. geophysics lab, helping interpret seismic readings. Don Swanson, an expert in predicting volcanic eruptions by measuring how mountains change shape before a blast, flew north from USGS Western Region Headquarters in Menlo Park, California.

The seismologists at the University of Washington issued a cautious press release, couched in the most guarded terms, warning that an eruption was a slight possibility. Five years earlier, warnings about a new steam vent on Mount Baker had led to extensive press coverage but no eruption, a scenario nobody wanted to repeat.

Representatives from the USGS, the Washington State Patrol, and the Washington State Department of Emergency Services held a five-hour meeting in Vancouver on Tuesday, March 25, to discuss the situation. The Forest Service sealed off the mountain above the timberline and evacuated its ranger station on Pine Creek, dangerously situated in the path of an old volcanic mudflow south of the mountain. As the Forest Service employees were leaving, geologists with metal suitcases packed with equipment were on their way in. The ground quivered beneath their feet.

Still, the mountain was barely news. Then on Thursday, March 27, Mike Beard, a traffic spotter for Portland radio station KGW, flew close to the mountain, hoping to get a fresh story idea. He found one. Near the summit, Beard saw steam and black ash spewing from a hole in the snow. "Hey, this thing's exploding!" he radioed back to his station. "There is no doubt the eruption is starting. You can see ash very, very clearly against the snow."

A black plume of steam and ash, hidden from those on the ground by overcast skies, shot 7,000 feet above the summit. When the plume subsided and the clouds cleared, aerial observers saw that a new crater, 200 feet in diameter and 150 feet deep, had opened on top of the mountain. A dark smudge of volcanic ash blackened the snow and ice around the crater. Cracks up to three miles long ran east and west near the summit, indicating the north side of the peak had begun to slump.

Mount St. Helens was on the front pages of newspapers across the country the next morning and stayed there for more than two months. The news that Mount St. Helens was stirring and could be about to burst into a major eruption brought about a curious mass reaction: People were overjoyed. Washington Governor Dixy Lee Ray, a scientist herself, remarked to the press, "I've always said for many years that I hoped to live long enough to see one of our volcanoes erupt."

Sightseers rushed to the mountain, desperate to share in the excitement. The little towns around the base of the mountain—Cougar, Toutle, and Randle—were inundated with volcano-watchers. On Sunday, March 30, the mountain put on a spectacular show for them: 93 small eruptions of steam and ash spurted from the summit during the day. Traffic on Interstate 5 stopped, jamming the main route between Portland and Seattle.

Overhead, the sky buzzed with the engines of private planes and helicopters. The Federal Aviation Administration established a five-mile restricted zone around the mountain, but so many pilots disobeyed the order that, as one of them put it, "It's like a dogfight up there." On March 30 alone, according to the FAA, 70 unauthorized planes violated the airspace restrictions over the mountain.

With the bursts of ash rose a seemingly limitless entrepreneurial spirit. Mount St. Helens T-shirt hawkers made the rounds of the best viewing points, coming up with slogans like "Mount St. Helens is Hot!" or the premature "I Survived Mount St. Helens," and a wide variety of puns on the word "ash"—"Mount St. Helens . . . Keep Your Ash Out of My Backyard." Enterprising salespeople collected samples of the volcanic ash that came gently drifting down like talcum powder, packaged it in glass vials or plastic baggies, and sold them as souvenirs.

In April, when seismometers began recording spasms of harmonic tremor, a type of continuous, rhythmic shaking that usually indicates magma moving beneath the earth's surface, the geologists' predictions grew increasingly grim. "This is like standing next to a dynamite keg and the fuse is lit, but you don't know how long the fuse is," Johnston told reporters gathered near the mountain. "If it exploded we would die."

Even so, fear seemed to be the last thing on anyone's mind. Schoolchildren in Kelso wrote songs about the volcano. One went:

Let's get the lava flowing;
It's time to light the sky.
Let's get those ashes blowing
On Mount St. Helens tonight.
Boom! Boom! Boom! Boom!

Many people regarded the idea of an eruption as a joke; evading the roadblocks was a game. "I wish it would really do a big Pompeii bit on us," one excited volcano-watcher in Cougar told a newspaper reporter.

"People went over, under, through, and around every time we tried to restrict access to what we believed were dangerous areas," Skamania County Sheriff William Closner said. "There were even maps sold showing how to get around our blockades on the mountain. People were climbing right up to the rim of the crater. It would have taken the U.S. Army to control those people."

During the weeks of April and early May, the mile-high bursts of steam and ash that had been shooting out of the top of the mountain stopped, delighting skeptics who had been pooh-poohing the whole thing, and frustrating reporters assigned to the volcano beat. The reporters' refrain, "We don't know when or if it's going to happen, but it could be any day now," grew less and less convincing. Desperate for stories, they interviewed volcano groupies. They did stories on geological history. They speculated on the volatility of other Cascade peaks. A reporter for *The Oregonian* in Portland called up 80-year-old Charles Richter, inventor of the Richter scale, at his home in Altadena, California, and asked for his prognosis on Mount St. Helens. Richter said he had no idea.

Harry Truman, a crotchety octogenarian who ran the Mount St. Helens Lodge in the shadow of the volcano, refused to leave his home at the base of the mountain and thereby became a media star. With his 16 cats, his pink Cadillac Coupe de Ville, and his Schenley bourbon, he was so perfect for the role it was as if he had been sent by a casting agency. Emboldened by the lull in activity, the National Geographic Society landed a helicopter on the mountain and took pictures. Days later, a Seattle film crew landed on the summit, filmed a beer commercial with the dark, steaming crater in the background, packed up, and flew away.

Most frustrated were the 100 or so people who owned vacation cabins in the vicinity of Spirit Lake. Governor Ray had established a "Red Zone" around the area, declaring it off-limits, and steadfastly refused to let the property owners back inside to fetch their belongings. The governor was unmoved by stories of starving cats, expensive cameras, and heirlooms left behind.

In early May, the angry property owners staged a protest at the Spirit Lake roadblock. They demanded permission to enter the restricted zone; some threatened to force their way in with guns. "We're going through that gate come hell or high water," one of the protestors, Chuck Williams, warned sheriff's deputies.

Fearing violence, Governor Ray relented—provided that the property owners sign waivers absolving the state of any responsibility for their welfare. On May 17, the day before the catastrophic eruption that buried Spirit Lake and all the cabins under 300 feet of mud and rock, a caravan of 20 property owners, many of them wearing T-shirts that said, "I own a piece of the rock," proceeded in a line up the highway to the lake. They were accompanied by a phalanx of reporters and photographers and led by a Washington State Patrol airplane. National Guard helicopters stood by for emergency evacuation. Four hours later, the property owners drove back down the valley, their backseats loaded with sheets and blankets, toasters, photographs, and radios. A second caravan was scheduled for ten o'clock the following morning—May 18.

During those weeks of outward calm, there was, in fact, significant activity going on beneath the surface. David Johnston and other geologists monitoring the shape of the mountain with laser beams noticed Mount St. Helens was growing—growing very quickly. Measurements in late April had shown an ominous bulge high on the north flank of the volcano that was increasing at a rate of five feet per day. Sections of the bulge were more than 450 feet higher than they had been weeks before, an indication that pressurized magma was being forced up through cracks and fissures in the mountain.

And then Mount St. Helens exploded.

Eleven seconds after 8:32 a.m. on May 18, as Gary Rosenquist squeezed the shutter of his camera on the ridge at Bear Meadow, a magnitude 5.1 earthquake a mile below the mountain shook the bulge loose. Weakened by the intrusion of magma and pressurized gases, Mount St. Helens literally collapsed on itself. The entire north half of the mountain slid downhill in the largest avalanche in recorded history.

At that moment, geologists Keith and Dorothy Stoffel were flying over the mountain's summit in a four-seat Cessna. "Within a matter of seconds, perhaps 15 seconds, the whole north side of the summit crater began to move instantaneously," Keith Stoffel reported later. "The nature of movement was eerie. The entire mass began to ripple and churn up, without moving laterally. Then the entire north side of the summit began sliding to the north along a deep-seated slide plane. We were amazed and excited with the realization that we were watching this landslide of unbelievable proportions. We took pictures of this slide sequence occurring, but before we could snap off more than a few pictures, a huge explosion blasted out. . . . We neither felt nor heard a thing, even though we were just east of the summit at this time."

With the plumes of the explosion blooming in the sky above them, the Stoffels' pilot put the Cessna into a steep dive and gave it full throttle, trying to outrun the cloud. Seconds before being engulfed, the tiny plane broke free and landed safely at Portland International Airport.

Instead of exploding straight up through the summit, the pent-up pressure blasted through the north side of the mountain, sending a blizzard of rock, ash, and hunks of glacial ice northward with a velocity that approached the speed of sound. A black cloud poured out of the mountain, hugging the ground as it rolled over ridges and churned down valleys. The lateral blast pulverized, incinerated, or blew away virtually everything in a fan-shaped swath of destruction that extended as far as 17 miles from the crater.

The noise of the explosion was heard as far away as Saskatchewan, and shock waves were clearly felt throughout the Puget Sound area, where many people described the impacts as "whumps." Windows rattled 100 miles away. Dishes fell from shelves; cracks opened in masonry walls. A vertical plume rose 16 miles into the atmosphere and continued unabated for nine hours.

The degrees of destruction spread northward in roughly concentric circles, beginning at the center of the volcano. In the "inner blast zone," within a few miles of the crater, the explosion vaporized every living thing. The force of the blast was so great that in places it stripped the soil from the underlying rock. Coldwater Ridge, six miles from the crater and directly in line with the blast, had been thickly forested before the eruption. Afterward, it was sandblasted to bare rock.

The force of Mount St. Helens's climactic outburst was equivalent to that of thousands of atomic bombs, yet, oddly, those closest to the volcano heard no sound of the explosion. Hikers and climbers on nearby Mount Adams, Mount Hood, and Mount Rainier watched the mountain disintegrate in eerie silence. Geologist Don Swanson, in a helicopter hovering alongside the eruptive column, compared the experience to watching a silent movie— "All that was missing was the tinkling piano." The closest observer in the blast zone who lived to tell his story was nine miles away; he reported hearing the thrashing and snapping of trees, but no sound of the explosion itself.

Meanwhile, people in the metropolitan areas of Seattle and Vancouver, British Columbia, were startled by a series of very loud bangs, which many compared to the sound of heavy artillery fired a short distance away. Residents along the Oregon coast thought they were hearing sonic booms, thunder, and dynamiting all rolled into one 15-minute barrage. The sound was heard as far away as the Canadian town of Maple Creek, Saskatchewan, 690 miles from the mountain.

Intrigued by the disparity, Clara Fairfield, curator at the Oregon Museum of Science and Industry in Portland, and John Dewey, physics professor at the University of Victoria in British Columbia, independently solicited responses from residents throughout the Pacific Northwest in the summer of 1980, asking people whether or not they had heard the eruption and, if so, what it had sounded like. On the basis of more than 5,200 responses, the scientists concluded that Mount St. Helens had been wrapped in a zone of silence that extended approximately 60 miles in every direction.

According to Dewey, the phenomenon occurs because sound waves travel faster in warmer air and tend to be refracted toward cooler temperatures. The sound waves that radiated out of the volcano were bent upward, toward cooler air at higher altitudes. At a distance of about 15 miles above the surface of the earth, in the middle levels of the stratosphere, the air temperatures begin to rise again from the radiant energy of the sun. When the sound waves reached this blanket of warmer air, they were refracted back down toward the surface of the earth, roughly in the shape of a flattened doughnut. The sound apparently bounced back and forth between the earth and the upper atmosphere a number of times, resulting in alternating zones of loudness and quiet at increasing distances from the volcano.

That much is fairly straightforward physics. The phenomenon of the zone of silence and the long-distance travel of sound has been recognized since World War I, when gunfire from the Western Front was heard as far away as London. What is more puzzling is that many people reported hearing not one explosion on the morning of May 18, but a series of them, separated by a few seconds. "We're not sure about that," Dewey says. "It could be that different pulses of sound emanated from the volcano, or possibly refraction took place at different levels in the stratosphere. There are still some uncertainties involved."

Geologist Johnston, who had been camping out on the top of the ridge, at the USGS Coldwater II observation station, barely had time to radio in one final report before he, his Jeep, his 22-foot trailer, and his monitoring equipment were swept away, never to be found. Johnston's final geological observation was perhaps the shortest of his career, but it could not have been more accurate: "Vancouver, Vancouver, this is it!" he shouted into his radio.

Harry Truman was dead, too—buried under 300 feet of avalanche debris. So was Reid Blackburn, a Vancouver *Columbian* photographer under contract to the USGS and *National Geographic,* stationed at Coldwater I observation station, two miles northwest of Johnston's station.

Beyond the inner blast zone, the trees were not disintegrated but were flash-burned and knocked down. In what came to be known as the "blow-down zone," all the trees—4.7 billion board feet of Douglas fir, cedar, and hemlock—on 86,600 acres were mowed down like tall grass. The tree trunks, some of them 500 years old and 7 feet in diameter, stayed where they landed, combed into swirls and eddies by the volcanic winds.

Outside the blowdown zone, at about 14 to 17 miles from the crater, the blast was hot enough to kill the trees but not strong enough to uproot them or break them off. There, in the "scorch zone," they remained standing, their branches shriveled and curled into delicate fleurs-de-lis.

The unexpected power of the eruption and the fact that it fired off sideways left emergency crews in utter confusion. The problems of the blast itself were compounded by waves of mud that came boiling down the mountain, and by the near-total lack of visibility caused by the airborne ash.

The intense heat of the eruption melted 70 percent of the snow and glaciers on the mountain. The water rushed down the steep slopes, combining with ash and avalanche debris to form a superheated slurry that moved at speeds of up to 80 miles an hour. The mudflows swept down several different drainages, but by far the largest and most destructive were those that tore into the upper tributaries of the Toutle River, northwest of the crater.

Picking up trees, boulders, houses, and logging trucks as it went, the mud roared into the north and south forks of the river, raising the water level of the Toutle by as much as 66 feet in places. The mud sloshed 360 feet up onto the sides of valleys and rolled over hills 250 feet high. Eight of the ten bridges across the river were jerked from their foundations or destroyed, and 37 miles of the Spirit Lake Highway were either buried or washed out. The cabins and farms in the lower Toutle River valley, some as far as 40 miles away from the mountain, were buried to their roofs. Hot mud oozed through living rooms and over vehicles like an ocean of wet concrete. At least 200 homes along the south and north forks of the river were either washed away, buried, or otherwise damaged. More than 1,000 people were evacuated. At noon, when the first wave of mud reached the Cowlitz River, 45 miles away, it was so hot that it raised the water temperature to 90 degrees. Salmon leaped out of the river to avoid the heat.

In all, more than 100 million cubic yards of sediment were deposited along the lower Cowlitz and Columbia Rivers. The water-carrying capacity of the Cowlitz was reduced by 85 percent, and the depth of the navigational channel in the Columbia decreased from 39 feet to less than 13 feet for a distance of two miles, shutting down ocean shipping. Thirty-one vessels were stranded in the ports of Portland, Vancouver, and Kalama.

Along with its load of 12 million board feet of timber, the Toutle River flood swept untold numbers of horses, sheep, cattle, and millions of fish to their deaths.

While to the west side of the mountain there was mud to contend with, the east side was confronted with a different horror: ash. When Mount St. Helens erupted, it shot a vertical column of pulverized rock 15 miles into the atmosphere in 15 minutes. It continued to pump out ash for nine hours, producing a black cloud that held somewhere between 1.7 and 2.4 billion cubic yards of material. Lightning created by colliding ash particles flashed around the edges of the cloud. Prevailing winds carried it to the north and east, dumping fine, gritty material that ranged in consistency from flour to beach sand over wheat fields in the Columbia Basin and orchards in the Yakima Valley, where some fruit trees were in blossom.

Within three hours the plume had totally blocked the sun over half the state. Light-activated streetlamps flickered on in Spokane and Yakima before noon on the day of the eruption, thereafter known as Ash Sunday. Traveling quickly on the wind, the cloud darkened Idaho, then Montana. It arrived in Boston in two days, and in 17 days had completely encircled the globe, appearing once again over the West Coast.

On Eastern Washington highways, the ash clogged the air filters of car and truck engines, leaving some 5,000 motorists stranded. Two days after the eruption, Governor Ray announced that more than half of the vehicles operated by police and emergency services were out of commission.

In some respects the dry ash was like snow—except it did not melt. When it got wet, it took on the consistency of cement. Ash closed virtually every major highway in Eastern Washington. Airplanes were grounded, trains halted, truck traffic stopped. In Spokane, work crews removed 100,000 tons of ash from the Spokane International Airport. In the town of Ritzville, 195 miles from the mountain, atmospheric idiosyncrasies caused ash to fall from the sky as if from a demonic backhoe. Fine grey ash the consistency of talcum powder lay four inches thick on roadways and lawns, and collected in drifts three feet high. More than 2,000 travelers were stranded in Ritzville on May 18, doubling the town's population for three days. People slept on church pews and gymnasium floors and in a cafe converted to a shelter. On May 21, when the roads were at last clear enough to drive, sheriff's deputies led a caravan of 1,500 drivers out of town, a giant rooster tail of ash flying up behind them.

One of the chief concerns of people in Eastern Washington was the long-term health effect of breathing the ash. At Washington State University in Pullman, 3,358 students dropped out before the end of the term, worrying about a lung ailment few could pronounce: pneumonoultramicroscopicsilicovolcanoconiosis. People appeared on the streets of east-side cities with their faces wrapped in rags or wearing industrial face masks. A chronic shortage of the masks developed, and paper coffee filters were used instead. President Carter, who flew into the state for a tour of the disaster area, promised that two million face masks would be sent immediately. The Minnesota Mining & Manufacturing Company—3M—sent its entire inventory of one million masks to the Northwest.

Meanwhile, as rescuers picked through the hot ash and downed trees in the devastated area, the number of human victims grew steadily. *The Oregonian* reported nine dead the day after the blast. As missing-person reports came in, it became clear that the actual number of those who had died would be several times higher than that. The official total took two years to determine and is now clicked off along with the rest of the eruption statistics: board feet of timber destroyed: 4.7 billion; number of feet the mountain was reduced in height: 1,313; height of the ash plume: 16 miles; persons killed: 57.

Autopsies of 25 victims of the blast—their bodies so saturated with ash that inch-deep incisions dulled scalpel blades—indicated that most died of suffocation by inhalation of volcanic ash. The gritty ash mixed with mucous and plugged their throats and noses. Doctors at the Universities of Washington and Oregon reported that the victims' hands were mummified; muscles appeared dried and frayed, and internal organs had shrunk and hardened. Those who suffocated died within minutes, the researchers said, while some of those who were burned survived long enough to walk several miles for help.

Nearly two hundred people caught in the blast made it out alive, most of them airlifted to safety aboard National Guard helicopters. The youngest survivor, three-month-old Terra Moore of Castle Rock, was trapped with her family in the ash for two days at their campsite near the Green River before they were rescued. Twenty-seven bodies were never found, and there are those who still insist the number of dead is actually higher than the official count.

Some of the victims died purely because of bad luck, others out of ignorance or because of misinformation. "I just thought some little puffs of smoke would come out and the lava would dribble down," said a survivor. One couple was killed as they watched the eruption from a viewpoint 25 miles away.

But most died seeking the sheer excitement of it all. Search crews found some victims still clutching cameras, exemplifying human characteristics that, for better or worse, set the human species apart from all others; stubbornness so entrenched that it defies all common sense, and curiosity so consuming that it continues to the very abyss.

Isaac's Storm

Today, few natural disasters provide the drama and excitement of the media coverage given to hurricanes. On sites such as The Weather Channel, we see the fledgling days of these behemoth storms when they are far away over then Atlantic, then watch them track toward the Caribbean and either track toward the U.S. or veer off.

In early September, 1900, however, there was no Weather Channel, of course, nor was there much of anything else to monitor hurricanes as they swept into our part of the world. But certain people were working on doing just that.

One such man was in Galveston, Texas. Isaac Cline was a weather scientist who believed he knew all there was to know about the motion of clouds and the behavior of storms. He was wrong—and destined to experience disaster and unbearable loss.

With Isaac Cline as its centerpiece, the book *Issac's Storm* by Erik Larson is the detailed story of the 1900 hurricane that literally wiped out the city of Galveston, in America's deadliest natural disaster. In Galveston alone at least 6,000 people—possibly as many as 10,000—would lose their lives, a number far greater than the combined death toll of the Johnstown Flood and the 1906 San Francisco Earthquake.

The jacket copy for *Isaac's Storm* provides the background for the great drama captured in the book by Larson's prose:

"The idea that a hurricane could damage the city of Galveston, Texas, where he was based, was to Isaac Cline preposterous, 'an absurd delusion.' It was 1900, a year when America felt bigger and stronger than ever before. Nothing in nature could hobble the gleaming city of Galveston, then a magical place that seemed destined to become the New York of the Gulf.

"That August a strange, prolonged heat wave gripped the nation and killed scores of people in New York and Chicago. Odd things seemed to happen everywhere: A plague of crickets engulfed Waco. The Bering Glacier began to shrink. Rain fell on Galveston with greater intensity than anyone could remember. Far away, in Africa, immense thunderstorms blossomed over the city of Dakar, and great currents of wind converged. A wave of atmospheric turbulence slipped from the coast of western Africa. Most such waves faded quickly. This one did not.

"In Cuba, America's overconfidence was made all too obvious by the Weather Bureau's obsession with controlling hurricane forecasts, even though Cuba's indigenous weathermen had pioneered hurricane science. As the bureau's forecasters assured the nation that all was calm in the Caribbean, Cuba's own weathermen fretted about ominous signs in the sky. A curious stillness gripped Antigua. One of a few unlucky sea captains discovered that the storm had achieved an intensity no man alive had ever experienced.

"In Galveston, reassured by Cline's belief that no hurricane could seriously damage the city, there was celebration. Children played in the rising water. Hundreds of people gathered at the beach to marvel at the fantastically tall waves and gorgeous sky—until the surf began ripping the city's beloved beachfront apart."

As this excerpt begins on the fateful Saturday, it is just after noon, and the exhilaration of the storm's approach of that morning is beginning to change to terror and panic as the waters rise and rise and rise.

✳   ✳   ✳   ✳   ✳

August Rollfing fought his way back into the city. With each step the water seemed to rise higher up his legs, but that was impossible—nothing could make the sea rise so quickly. The storm was much worse than it had been on his way home. Now and then powerful gusts scraped squares of slate from nearby rooftops and launched them into the air as if they were autumn leaves. He saw whole families moving slowly toward the center of the city, everyone leaning against the wind. Broadway was a river of refugees. Suddenly Louisa's desire to escape the beach did not seem so crazy.

Rollfing walked to a livery stable, Mallory's, and there hired a driver and buggy and sent them to his address with orders to pick up Louisa and the children and take them to his mother's house in the city's West End. He believed it a far safer neighborhood, perhaps because it was many blocks from the ocean beaches at the east and south edges of the city. Apparently he did not take into account the fact that the bay was only ten blocks north of his mother's home. The wind was still blowing from the north over the long fetch of Galveston Bay, and with each increase in velocity drove more water into the city. Rollfing went to his shop.

At one o'clock, the buggy pulled up in front of the family's house at 18th and Avenue O½. Louisa was overjoyed. She raced through the house collecting shoes and a change of clothing for everyone, and packed these in a large hamper, but once the driver and her children and she had all climbed aboard, she realized there simply was no room left. She had to leave the hamper behind.

She held Atlanta Anna in her arms. The driver set off for the West End, no doubt first driving north toward the slightly higher ground at the center of the city, then due west. "It was a terrible trip," Louisa said. "We could only go slowly for the electric wires were down everywhere, which made it dangerous. . . . The rain was icy cold and hurt our faces like glass splinters, and little 'Lanta' cried all along the way. I pressed her little face hard against my breast, so she would not be hurt so badly. August and Helen didn't cry, they never said a word."

The driver dodged other storm refugees and great masses of floating wreckage. Judging by the quantity, whole houses must have come apart. The sky was so dark, it looked as if dusk had arrived half a day early.

"We got as far as 40th Street and Ave. H, just one block from Grandma," Louisa said. "The water was so high, we just sat in it, the horse was up to his neck in water."

The driver turned onto 40th Street. Someone shouted for the buggy to stop. "Don't go! You can't go through." The water was too deep, the caller said—there was a large hole ahead filled with water.

The driver turned the buggy around, and asked Louisa, "Where shall I go now?"

Louisa, in a nearly submerged carriage with three young children, was at a loss. "I don't know," she said.

It came to her then: August's sister, Julia, and her husband, Jim, lived in a house at 36th and Broadway, just six blocks back toward the city. The driver gently eased his horse back along Avenue H, against the flow of water and refugees.

When Julia saw Louisa and the children, drenched and windblown, she was shocked. "My God, Louisa, what is the matter?"

Clearly Julia knew nothing of the damage along the beach. Louisa quickly described conditions in the East End and how the West End too was underwater. She paid the Mallory's driver a dollar and made him promise to tell his boss, Mr. Mallory, their new destination so that Mallory could pass the message on to August.

"I was so confident that August would go there," she said, "but he didn't."

At about two o'clock Galveston time, in the midst of Louisa's drive, the wind shifted. Until then the wind had blown consistently from the north, the weaker left flank of the hurricane. Now the wind circled to the northeast and gained intensity. Isaac noticed the change, but most people, including Louisa, did not. They were too busy seeking shelter or had battened themselves within their homes. The stories Louisa told her hosts of what she had seen on her journey frightened them. With Louisa's help, they began bracing the windows and doors. They nailed an ironing board across a window. A neighbor came over with her two children seeking shelter or company and brought the total number of people in the house to ten. They closed all the upstairs doors and gathered on the stairway. They had a pitcher of water and a lantern. Soon they heard the shattering of windows and blinds in the bedrooms behind the doors they had just closed. "It sounded," Louisa said, "as if he rooms were filled with a thousand little devils, shrieking and whistling."

She watched quietly as Julia and Jim's piano slid from one downstairs wall to another, then back.

At two o'clock in the afternoon, Dr. Sam Young started back to his house at the northeast corner of Bath and P½, one block north of Isaac Cline's house and adjacent to the Bath Avenue Public School. Thinking his family safe in San Antonio, he prepared for the storm's arrival—prepared, that is, to enjoy it, and savor every destructive impulse. Young was a member of that class of mostly landlocked men who believed God put storms on earth expressly for their entertainment.

Young's yard was a plateau of land five feet above sea level, yet by the time he got home he found the yard under two feet of water. This did not trouble him, for he had seen high water before. He took a chair on his gallery and watched the storm. The water rose gradually and soon began to climb the stairs toward him. Even this did not worry him. "My house, a large two-story frame building, stood on brick pillars about four feet high," he said, "so I had no fear of the water coming into my house."

A young black boy worked for Young as a valet. Young sent him home, then began closing shutters and windows and securing doors, intent mainly on getting these tasks done before nightfall.

Around four o'clock, he began to see that he had been wrong about the water. Two feet now covered his ground floor, and the level was still rising—not gradually, anymore, but rapidly. Visibly. Like water flowing into a bathtub.

Young had noticed the change in wind direction. "The wind had hauled further to the east and was blowing at a terrific rate." The shift accounted for the more-rapid increase in depth, Young knew. Galveston sat astride a portion of Texas coastline canted forty-five degrees toward the northeast. All morning the north wind had impeded the progress of the incoming storm tide, causing water literally to pile up in the gulf. Now, with the wind blowing from the northeast, a portion of that pent-up tide—but by no means the bulk of it—began to come ashore. The wind blowing southwest along the Texas coast pushed the sea into Galveston's East Side.

More fascinated than appalled, Young moved a chair to a second-floor window and watched the water as it flowed along Avenue P½. (He makes no mention of seeing Isaac Cline or Joseph struggling home, although the last block of their journeys would have been within his view.) The water moved fastest at the center of the street where the high curbs channeled the water and vastly increased its velocity, just like the narrow pipes used by city water systems to increase water pressure. The street had become a causeway for wreckage. Young saw boxes, barrels, carriages, cisterns, outhouses, and small shacks. He watched one barrel hold its course all the way down the street. "The flow," he saw, "was almost exactly east to west."

What he did not realize, apparently, was that the flow now included corpses.

Most likely he had stationed himself at a window that faced west or south; otherwise he would have been aware of the great damage now being done to the beach neighborhoods behind his house, where immense breakers slid over the surface of the tide and broke against second-floor windows.

It was getting dark. He found a candle, lit it, then thought better—he might need the candle later on. He blew it out. There was nothing to do, he decided, but wait out the storm. He still felt unafraid. "I found a comfortable armchair and made myself as comfortable as possible." He was very glad, however, that his family soon would be snug and dry in the train station at San Antonio. "Being entirely alone, with no responsibility on me, I felt satisfied and very complacent, for I was fool enough not to be the least afraid of wind or water."

For other fathers in homes not far from his the afternoon was playing out in rather different fashion. Suddenly the prospect of watching their children die became very real.

Whom did you save? Did you seek to save one child, or try to save all, at the risk ultimately of saving none? Did you save a daughter or a son? The youngest or your firstborn? Did you save that sun-kissed child who gave you delight every morning, or the benighted adolescent who made your day a torment—save *him,* because every piece of you screamed to save the sweet one?

And if you saved none, what then?

How did you go on?

As Louise Hopkins and her friend Martha played in the yard, they saw more strange things come floating past in the street. There were boxes and boards and bits of clothing, and now children's toys. Martha went home, fearing that soon the water would be too deep to cross, and indeed soon afterward the level rose to where water flowed into Louise's yard and into her mother's treasured garden. The sight of all that brown water destroying her mother's lovely flowers brought Louise the day's first sadness.

When Louise went inside, she saw for the first time that her mother was worried about the storm. Mrs. Hopkins was moving her great trove of cooking supplies to the second floor—her sacks of sugar, coffee, and flour (one of the most popular brands was Tidal Wave Flour). Between trips Mrs. Hopkins went to the window to watch for Louise's two brothers, who that morning had ridden their bicycles to their jobs. "She knew now with the water rising it would be impossible for them to come home the same way," Louise recalled.

Louise noticed that her kitten, a Maltese, was behaving strangely. The little thing "was restless and kept following me. I believe he was more aware of the approaching danger than I."

Her brother John arrived safely, and quickly went to work helping his mother transport the supplies to the second floor. Louise helped with the smaller things. Her brother Mason, fourteen years old, was still not home.

Once all the big sacks had been hauled upstairs, Louise's mother found the family ax and did something that just about took Louise's breath away forever. Her mother had always been so careful about the house. The house was everything. A home, an income. She kept it spotless, and polished and dusted the floors until they gleamed like the beacon of the Bolivar Light, and if you tracked mud onto these floors you knew you would not see the sunlight for the rest of your living days.

Right there, no warning, her mother lifted the ax over her shoulder and slammed it into the floor. She kept chopping until the holes were big enough to see through.

"I was amazed to see how fast the water came in under the front door and through the holes my mother had cut in the floor," Louise said. "How quickly the house was filling with water, and how difficult it was for my mother to keep her head out of the water as she reached down into the lower cabinets for the last of the groceries to be taken upstairs."

Louise looked out an upstairs window and saw that water now covered the porch rail of the house next door. Until then, she had felt mostly excitement. The morning had been full of wonders: water racing down the street, toads all over the place, her mother chopping holes in the floor, and water even inside the house. But there was something about the water so deep around her neighbor's house that took all the excitement away. "I thought of all the things that had to be left behind, and I was sad and afraid."

Her mother watched for Mason.

At precisely 2:30 p.m. Galveston time a gust of wind lifted the Weather Bureau's rain gauge from the roof of the Levy Building and carried it off toward the southwest. It had captured 1.27 inches of rain.

At 5:15, the wind destroyed the bureau's anemometer. By then the instrument had registered a maximum velocity of one hundred miles an hour.

The wind continued to intensify.

A figure approached the Hopkins home, moving against the current. The water was up to his underarms. He dodged pieces of lumber and boxes and telegraph poles. Now and then a square of slate smacked the water around him. Softer things bumped against his legs, then moved on with the current.

When Mason arrived, a lightness came over the Hopkins household. It was as if the house itself had been holding its breath awaiting his arrival. He was bruised and soaked, but smiling, and Mrs. Hopkins hugged him as she had never hugged anyone before. The storm raged and water burbled up through the holes in the floor and slid in a sheet under the front door, but everyone was home and the unspoken fear that had gripped the place was suddenly gone. "We had a warm feeling of all of us being together, safely, we believed. We went upstairs in the main part of our house . . . to wait out the storm"

All over Galveston, there was a need for light. A craving. People needed light for themselves to ease their fears, but they also needed others to know they were still in their homes and alive. Throughout Galveston, lamps bloomed in a thousand second-floor windows. We're here, they said. Come for us. Please.

The same idea came to Louise's mother. She did not want to use a lamp, however. The house was shaking too badly. She feared the lamp would fall and set fire to the house, and then all would indeed be lost.

She dragged one of the big drums of lard to the center of the room. She found a carnival flag attached to a stick, and laid the stick across the top of the drum. She saturated a strip of cloth with lard, then draped this over the stick, one end in the lard, for a wick. "When it was lighted it gave off a dim and eerie light," Louise said. "We sat and watched it flickering and listened to the banging and howling of the storm outside."

It was oddly comfortable in the room. Almost cozy.

Until her sister, Lois, screamed.

In the blocks behind Dr. Young's house, several families began moving toward the home of Judson Palmer, at 2320 P½. Anyone could see it was one of the strongest houses around. Isaac Cline himself had gauged it a perfectly safe haven against the storm. A neighbor couple, Mr. and Mrs. Boecker, arrived with their two children. Garry Burnett followed with his wife and his two children. Soon afterward another Burnett, George, arrived with his wife, child, and mother. The last couple to arrive was an unidentified black man and his wife who asked if they too might come inside until the storm passed. Palmer now counted seventeen people in his house, including his own wife and his son, Lee. The boy's dog, Youno, scampered wildly around the house, clearly delighted with the attention of so many big and small human beings.

At 6:00 P.M., Palmer and the other men rolled up the first-floor carpets and hauled them upstairs. They carried the furniture up next, an effort that caused them all to break a heavy sweat. With all the doors and windows shut and so many moist people inside, the house felt hot, humid, and stale. Once all the furniture was moved, everyone went to the second floor, which had four bedrooms and a large bathroom equipped with a tugboat-sized tub and a shower.

If a train had crossed the ceiling it could not have made more noise. With most of the slate shingles gone, the rain struck bare wood. Driven by the wind, it penetrated deep into the plaster. It grew cysts in the wallpaper, which popped like firecrackers. At 7:00 P.M., a gust of wind blew out the front door and its frame. The blast effect caused everyone's ears to pop.

Palmer estimated the water in the yard to be seven feet deep; in the parlor, two feet. He was downstairs monitoring its progress when the big plate-glass window at the front of the house exploded, along with its frame.

Palmer lit a kerosene lamp and placed it near the window of the front-most bedroom. The window shattered; the blinds disintegrated. Everyone retreated to the back of the house. Palmer brought the lamp. Here too the windows shattered. A chunk of plaster fell from the ceiling and crushed the lamp. Palmer closed a pair of big sliding doors. He suggested prayers and hymns. His son said, "I cannot pray," then reconsidered. "Dear Jesus," he said, "make the waters recede and give us a pleasant day tomorrow to play, and save my little dog Youno and save Claire Ousley."

Rain poured into the room. More plaster fell.

Garry Burnett recommended everyone squeeze into the bathroom, arguing it was the strongest, safest place in the house. George Burnett believed no room would be safe if the house collapsed into the sea. He crawled out the bathroom window onto an upended roof that had floated against the house, and persuaded his mother, wife, and child to follow. They sailed off into the storm. The Palmers joined Garry Burnett in the bathroom. The Boecker family stayed behind in the bedroom. What the black couple did is unknown.

The water rose high onto the second floor. Gusts of wind moving at speeds possibly as great as 150 miles an hour—perhaps much higher—penetrated deep into the house. Palmer held tight to his son and braced his back against the bathroom door. His wife, Mae, hugged his neck with all her strength.

Beams fractured. Glass broke. Lumber ricocheted among the walls of the hallway outside the bath. The front half of the house tore loose. The Boeckers stood in their bedroom holding each other close as the wind peeled the house away. The bedroom disintegrated.

The water rose. The Palmers climbed onto the lip of the bathtub. Judson clamped his left hand to the shower rod and held Lee circled in his right arm. Youno was gone. Mrs. Palmer grabbed the rod with her right hand, and with her left held on to her husband and son.

The house trembled, and eased off its elevated foundation. It settled in deeper water. The water was up to Palmer's neck. He fought to keep Lee's head clear.

And Lee asked, "Papa, are we safe?"

Judson could not even see his son, for the darkness. He felt the boy's small hands holding tight. His hands were cold. Maybe Judson did have time to offer his son some reassuring lie; more likely he could not speak for the great heave of sorrow that welled up within him after his son's question. He drew his son close, but could not draw him close enough.

The roof stood up and fell upon the family. They went under the water together. Palmer came up alone. He had swallowed a great volume of water. He coughed, vomited. He saw nothing of Lee or Mae. There was no light, only motion. He could not think. His mind dimmed, came back.

And he was outside, free of the house. Treading water. He felt what seemed to be ground beneath his feet but could not get purchase. A wave threw him onto a mass of floating wreckage. Window shutters—many of them, all tied together. Someone else's raft, but it was empty now.

He called for his son and wife.

They argued. Joseph wanted everyone to leave at once and head for the center of town. Isaac had faith in his house, but also argued that conditions outside had grown too dangerous, certainly for his wife, who was pregnant and ill in bed. "At this time . . . the roofs of houses and timbers were flying through the streets as though they were paper," Isaac said, "and it appeared suicidal to attempt a journey through the flying timbers." Water now covered the first floor of his house to a depth of eight inches.

At 6:30 P.M., Isaac, ever the observer, walked to the front door to take a look outside. He opened his door upon a fantastic landscape. Where once there had been streets neatly lined with houses there was open sea, punctured here and there by telegraph poles, second stories, and rooftops. He saw no waves, however. The sea was strangely flat, its surface blown smooth by the wind. The Neville house across the way now looked so odd. It had been a lovely house: three stories sided in an intricate pattern of fish-scale shingles and shiplap boards and painted four different colors. Now only the top two-thirds protruded from the water. Every slate had been stripped from its roof.

The fact he saw no waves was ominous, although he did not know it. Behind his house, closer to the beach, the sea had erected an escarpment of wreckage three stories tall and several miles long. It contained homes and parts of homes and rooftops that floated like the hulls of dismasted ships; it carried landaus, buggies, pianos, privies, red-plush portieres, prisms, photographs, wicker seat-bottoms, and of course corpses, hundreds of them. Perhaps thousands. It was so tall, so massive that it acted as a kind of seawall and absorbed the direct impact of the breakers lumbering off the Gulf. The waves shoved the ridge forward, toward the north and west. It moved slowly, but with irresistible momentum, and wherever it passed, it scraped the city clean of all structures and all life. If not for the wind, Isaac would have heard it coming as a horrendous blend of screams and exploding wood. It shoved before it immense sections of the streetcar trestle that once had snaked over the Gulf.

Something else caught Isaac's attention, as it did the attention of nearly every other soul in Galveston.

"I was standing at my front door, which was partly open, watching the water, which was flowing with great rapidity from east to west," he said. Suddenly the level of the water rose four feet in just four seconds. This was not a wave, but the sea itself. "The sudden rise of 4 feet brought it above my waist before I could change my position."

For those inside the house, it was a moment of profound terror. (Joseph claims to have been utterly calm. He says the rise occurred just after he had called his brother outside to try to persuade him, privately, that the best course was to evacuate for the center of town.) Four feet was taller than most of the children in the house. Throughout the city, parents rushed to their children. They lifted them from the water and propped them on tables, dressers, and pianos. People in single-story homes had nowhere to go. In Isaac's house, everyone hurried to the second floor. The brothers herded the refugees into a bedroom on the windward side, reasoning that if the house fell over, they would all be on top, not crushed underneath.

Isaac judged the depth of the water by its position in his house. His yard, he knew, was 5.2 feet above sea level. The water was ten feet above the ground. That meant the tide was now 15.2 feet deep in his neighborhood—and still rising. "These observations," he noted later, for the benefit of skeptics, "were carefully taken and represent to within a few tenths of a foot the true conditions." It was, he acknowledged, incredible. "No one ever dreamed that the water would reach the height observed in the present case."

One block north, Dr. Young observed the same impossible increase. Since five o'clock he had noted a change in the direction of the wind. It had begun circling to the east and gained velocity, as did the current. "The debris fairly flew past, so rapid had the tide become," he said. At 5:40 P.M., he observed a sudden acceleration of the wind. He knew the time exactly because his clock had stopped and he had just finished resetting it by his watch. (Clocks began to stop throughout Galveston, as wind burst into homes and buffeted the pendulums that drove them.) He looked out a west window at a fence he had been using to gauge the depth of the water. "And while I was looking, I saw the tide suddenly rise fully four feet at one bound."

Moments later, he saw houses on the south side of P½ between 25th and 26th—half a block north of Isaac's house—collapse into the water, among them the pretty one-story home of a man named Alexander Coddou, the father of five children whose wife happened to be off the island. The houses fell gracefully at first. One witness, watching the same thing happen in his neighborhood, said houses fell into the gulf "as gently as a mother would lay her infant in the cradle." It was when the current caught them and swept them away that the violence occurred, with bedrooms erupting in a tumult of flying glass and wood, rooftops soaring through the air like monstrous kites.

Dr. Cline's house, Young saw, was still standing, although floating debris had torn away his first and second-floor galleries.

Soon the water on Isaac's first floor was over nine feet deep. The wind tore at the house like an immense crowbar. The ridge of debris came closer and closer, destroying homes south and east of Isaac's house and casting them against his walls. Isaac's house rocked and trembled, but remained firmly footed on its pilings. Isaac at this point still believed the house strong enough to survive the assault. He did not know, however, that the ridge of debris was now pushing before it a segment of streetcar trestle a quarter-mile long, consisting of tons of cross-ties and timbers held together by rails.

Joseph knew nothing of this either. He believed the house would fail simply because the storm was too powerful.

"Strangely enough," Joseph wrote, "amid the seething turmoil, I did not feel unduly excited. In fact, I was almost calm. I was convinced that, in some way or another, I should come out of it alive. I kept thinking of an uncle of ours, who, alone of all those aboard a sinking ship, saved himself by getting on a plank when the vessel went under and [by] drifting upon this frail support five miles to shore."

Joseph may have been calm, but he was not helping anyone else achieve such peace. "Again, as strongly as I could, I warned my relatives and friends that the house was about to collapse."

Imagine it, the atmosphere in this house. Fifty terrified men, women, and children packed into one room, Isaac's wife in bed, his three daughters petrified but snuggling close to their mother for comfort. The room is insufferably hot and moist. The walls drip condensation. Now and then rain spits through the ceiling; a pocket in the wallpaper explodes. Beside the bed stands Dr. Isaac Monroe Cline, thirty-eight years old, bearded, confident the house can endure anything mere nature can muster, but even more certain that to venture outside would be like stepping in front of a locomotive. Nearby, perhaps at the other side of the bed, stands Joseph, the earnest younger brother, apprentice-for-life, who has always always always resented Isaac's insufferable pose—that *he,* not Joseph, was the man who knew weather, *he* knew when the rain would fall, *he* knew when true danger loomed. The conversation starts quietly but soon, partly because their tempers rise, partly just to be heard over the wind, rain, and barrage of debris, they start shouting. "Are you deaf, Isaac?" Joseph perhaps cries. "What do you think that is, for God's sake? An evening breeze? This house will not stand. Out there at least we have a chance."

Isaac prevailed. Joseph, frustrated, began offering advice for how best to survive the coming collapse. "I urged them, if possible, to get on top of the drift and float upon it when the dangerous moment came. As the peril became greater, so did the crowd's excitement. Most of them began to sing; some of them were weeping, even wailing; while, again, others knelt in panic-stricken prayer. Many of them were scrambling aimlessly about, seeking what, in their fright, appeared to be vantage points."

The battering continued. By now all four galleries had been torn from Isaac's house, all slate stripped from its roof.

The trestle was a yard away.

In Dallas, three hundred miles north, the telegraph operator at the *Dallas News,* sister to the *Galveston News,* realized the steady flow of cables from the Galveston paper had ceased. The two newspapers maintained a leased telegraph line that ran directly between their editorial offices. The telegrapher at the Dallas paper keyed off an inquiry, but got no response. He tried again. Again nothing. He then tried raising Galveston over public lines by relay through Beaumont, and next by sending a message to Vera Cruz, Mexico, for relay to Galveston via the Mexican Cable Company (whose Galveston agent had only a few hours to live).

Again he failed.

At that moment, City Editor William O'Leary was in the office of the Dallas paper's manager, G. B. Dealey, showing Dealey a passage in Matthew Fontaine Maury's best-selling *Physical Geography of the Sea* that seemed to show "that destruction of Galveston by tropical storm could not happen."

The wires remained dead.

Saturday evening, John Blagden, the new man temporarily assigned to Galveston, found himself alone in the office. He had been in the city all of two weeks and here he was alone in the dark, facing a storm whose intensity seemed to place it in the realm of the supernatural.

The Levy Building was four stories tall and made of brick but in some gusts, Blagden said, it "rocked frightfully." Bornkessell, the station's printer, had left for home first thing in the morning. Isaac had gone home next, followed by Joseph. Ernest Kuhnel, a clerk, was supposed to be in the office but had fled the building in terror.

The storm flag was gone, as were the anemometer, rain gauge, and sunshine recorder. The telephone had stopped ringing. There was nothing for Blagden to do but watch the barometer and try to keep himself sane. He estimated the wind at 110 miles an hour.

The hurricane had set a course toward Galveston soon after leaving Cuba, and had stayed on that course ever since, as if it had chosen Galveston as its target. It had a different target, however. The great low-pressure zone that had formed over the Pacific Coast earlier in the week had progressed to where it now covered a broad slice of the nation from Texas to Canada. The hurricane saw this low-pressure zone as a giant open door through which it could at last begin its northward journey.

The storm's track intersected Galveston's coastline at a ninety-degree angle, with the eye passing about forty miles west of the city somewhere between Galveston and the Brazos River. Meteorologists discovered this later when officers aboard an Army tug stationed at the mouth of the Brazos reported a pattern of winds that showed the eye had passed somewhere east of their position. The pattern in Galveston indicated the eye had passed to the west of the city. This was the worst possible angle of approach, for it brought the hurricane's most powerful right flank directly into the city.

Blagden knew nothing of the storm's track. What he did know was that the first shift in wind direction, from north to northeast, had brought a sudden acceleration in wind speed. And now he sensed the wind beginning to shift again, toward the east. Impossibly, the change seemed to bring another increase in velocity. Gusts struck the building like cannonballs.

Barometric pressure had fallen all day, but at five o'clock Galveston time it began to fall as if someone has punched a leak into the instrument's mercury basin. At five, the barometer read 29.05 inches.

Nineteen minutes later, 28.95.

At 6:40 p.m., 28.73 inches.

Eight minutes later, 28.70.

An hour later, the barometer read 28.53 inches, and continued falling. It bottomed at 28.48.

Blagden had never seen it that low. Few people had. At the time, it was the lowest reading ever recorded by a station of the U.S. Weather Bureau.

In fact, the storm drove the pressure even lower, although just how far will always be a mystery. The bureau's instruments in the Levy Building captured pressures well away from the center of the eye, where the pressure would have been lowest.

Barometers elsewhere in the city got widely varied readings. In Galveston harbor, the first mate of the English steamer *Comino,* moored at Pier 14, recorded in the ship's log a pressure of 28.30 inches, and noted: "Wind blowing terrific, and steamer bombarded with large pieces of timber, shells, and all manner of flying debris from the surrounding buildings." At one point the wind picked up a board measuring four feet by six inches and hurled it with such velocity it pierced the *Comino's* hull. The hull was built of iron plates one inch thick. In the train station, the scientist with the barometer—apparently unaware of his fast-eroding popularity—called out a pressure of 27.50 inches, and announced that against such impossibly low pressures "nothing could endure."

Years later, scientists with NOAA put the lowest pressure of the storm a notch lower, at 27.49.

In 1900, however, even Blagden's reading of 28.48 stretched credibility. "Assuming that the reading of the barometer reported at Galveston the evening of the 8th was approximately correct," wrote one of Moore's professors, carefully hedging for error, "the hurricane at that point was of almost unparalleled severity."

The highest speed recorded by the Galveston station's anemometer before it blew away was 100 miles per hour. The bureau later estimated that between 5:15 P.M. and 7 P.M. Galveston time, the wind reached a sustained velocity of "at least" 120 miles per hour.

Most likely the true velocity was far greater, especially within the eyewall itself. Gusts of two hundred miles an hour may have raked Galveston. Each would generate pressure of 152 pounds per square foot, or more than sixty thousand pounds against a house wall. Thirty tons.

As John Blagden sat in his office, powerful bursts of wind tore off the fourth floor of a nearby building, the Moody Bank at the Strand and 22nd, as neatly as if it had been sliced off with a delicatessen meat shaver. Captain Storms of the *Roma* had practically bolted his ship to its pier, but the wind tore the ship loose and sent it on a wild journey through Galveston's harbor, during which it destroyed all three railroad causeways over the bay. The wind hurled grown men across streets and knocked horses onto their sides as if they were targets in a shooting gallery. Slate shingles became whirling scimitars that eviscerated men and horses. Decapitations occurred. Long splinters of wood pierced limbs and eyes. One man tied his shoes to his head as a kind of helmet, then struggled home. The wind threw bricks with such force they traveled parallel to the ground. A survivor identified only as Charlie saw bricks blown from the Tremont Hotel "like they were little feathers."

All this was nothing, however, compared to what the wind had been doing in the Gulf of Mexico. Ever since leaving Cuba, the storm had piled water along its leading edge, producing a dome of water that twentieth-century meteorologists would call a storm surge.

Early scientists believed that reduced pressure alone accounted for storm tides. By the mid–nineteenth century, however, they came to understand that a one-inch decline in pressure raised the sea only a foot. Thus even a pressure as low as 27.49 inches would cause the sea to rise only two and a half feet. Yet the Galveston storm shoved before it a surge that was over fifteen feet deep.

The single most important force needed to build a storm surge is wind. A strong wind will develop a surge in any body of water. A fan blowing across a water-filled container will cause the water to swell at the downwind side. Strong winds blowing over some of Minnesota's biggest northern lakes will pile ice to the height of a McDonald's sign. One of the deadliest storm surges in American history occurred on Lake Okeechobee in Florida, in 1928, when hurricane winds blowing across the long fetch of the lake raised a storm surge that killed 1,835 people.

Another ingredient is geography. In 1876 Henry Blanford, a meteorologist in India, proposed that the configuration of the Bay of Bengal contributed greatly to the immense storm tides that came ashore during typhoons. Blanford thought of these tides as great waves. Every cyclone raised them, "but it is only when the wave thus formed reaches a low coast, with a shallow shelving foreshore, such as are the coasts of Bengal and Orissa, that, like the tidal wave, it is regarded and piled up to a height which enables it to inundate the flats of the maritime belt, over which it sweeps with an irresistible onset."

Despite such reports, Isaac and his colleagues in the bureau believed that a hurricane's most lethal weapon was the wind. They did not see the parallels. Isaac, like the famous Commodore Maury, believed the shallow slope of the seabed off Galveston would wear down incoming seas before they struck the city, and had argued in his 1891 *News* article that mainland areas north of Galveston Bay would serve as basins to capture whatever floodwaters a storm did manage to drive ashore.

The hurricane of 1900 would cause a hasty reevaluation. In October, in the Weather Bureau's *Monthly Weather Review,* one of the bureau's leading lights, Prof. E. B. Garriott, belatedly observed that Galveston's geography and topography in fact "render it, in the presence of severe storms, peculiarly subject to inundation."

A storm's trajectory can also increase the destructive power of a surge. If a hurricane strikes at an oblique angle, it spreads its storm surge over a broader swath of coast, thereby dissipating the surge's depth and energy. The Galveston hurricane struck the Texas coast head-on, at a nearly perfect ninety-degree angle, after traveling a long, unobstructed fetch of some eight hundred miles. The track focused the onshore flow directly into the city.

The track produced another lethal effect, however. It brought north winds to Galveston Bay twenty-four hours before landfall. Throughout most of Saturday, these intensified to gale force and finally to hurricane force. Due north of Galveston Island, the bay offers an unobstructed fetch of about thirty-five miles (about the same fetch as presented by Lake Okeechobee). And just as in the freak Galveston blizzard of February 1899, the wind blew the water out of Galveston Bay—this time into the city itself.

In effect, the storm's trajectory made Galveston the victim of two storm surges, the first from the bay, the second from the gulf, and ensured moreover that the gulf portion would be exceptionally severe. Throughout the morning, the north winds kept the leading edge of the gulf surge out at sea, banking the water and transforming the gulf into a compressed spring, ready to leap forward the moment the winds shifted.

The first shift, from north to east, began at about two o'clock Saturday afternoon, Galveston time. This allowed some of the gulf surge to come ashore. Water flowed over the Bolivar Peninsula and began rising within the shaft of the Bolivar Light. It flowed too over Fort San Jacinto and Galveston's East Side, where it met the floodwater already driven into the city from the bay. The reason so many men and women in Galveston began furiously chopping holes in their beloved parlor floors was to admit the water and, they hoped, anchor their homes in place.

At 7:30 P.M., the wind shifted again, this time from east to south. And again it accelerated. It moved through the city like a mailman delivering dynamite. Sustained winds must have reached 150 miles an hour, gusts perhaps 200 or more.

The sea followed.

Galveston became Atlantis.

About seven o'clock, Dr. Young heard a heavy thumping that seemed to come from a downstairs bedroom on the east side of his house. He lit the candle that he had held in reserve and walked toward the hall stairwell, the candle throwing only a shallow arc of light on the floor around him. Pistol-shot drafts penetrated deep within the house and caused the candle's flame to twist, but did nothing to cool the rooms. At the Levy Building about then John Blagden was recording a temperature of 84.2 degrees. The shock of each thump vibrated through the floor of Young's house. It was as if someone were standing in the downstairs bedroom striking the ceiling with a railroad mallet.

The stairwell appeared ahead as a large black rectangle stamped from the floor, and the closer Young got, the deeper the candlelight traveled. It should have shown him stairs and the wood slats of the banister, but he saw neither, only an orange glow undulating on the opposite wall like sunlight off a floating mirror.

Water, he realized. The sea had risen within his house nearly to the top step. The heavy thudding from the bedroom had to be furniture. A bureau, perhaps, bumping against the ceiling as the water rose and fell.

Young set the candle on the floor and walked to the door that led to his second-floor gallery. He opened it. "In a second I was blown back into the hall."

The wind snuffed the flame, then blew the candle and its holder to the far reaches of the house. From within the darkness of hall, the doorway appeared as a rectangle of wild gray air. The power of the wind shocked Young; it also inflamed his curiosity. Another man might have sought shelter in one of the second-floor bedrooms, but Young, drawn by the sheer power of the storm, fought his way back toward the door.

He kept close to the wall. He winched himself forward from doorknob to doorknob. At the door, he fastened his hands around the frame and hauled himself outside. "The scene," he said, "was the grandest I ever witnessed."

It was as if he were aboard a ship in a storm. Waves swept through his neighborhood. One witness said the waves looked like the "sides of huge elephants." Each embodied a destructive power nearly beyond measure. A single cubic yard of water weighs about fifteen hundred pounds. A wave fifty feet long and ten feet high has a static weight of over eighty thousand pounds. Moving at thirty miles an hour, it generates forward momentum of over two million pounds, so much force, in fact, that at this point during the storm the incoming swells had begun destroying the brand-new artillery emplacements at Fort Crockett, which had been designed to withstand Spanish bombardment. Debris made the waves especially dangerous. Each wave propelled huge pieces of wreckage that did to houses what the reinforced prow of Captain Nemo's *Nautilus* did to great warships. One man reported dodging a giant piano embedded in the crest of a wave, "its white keys gleaming even in the darkness."

The only other house still standing belonged to a family named Youens, with the mother, father, son, and daughter still inside. Two minutes later, Young saw the Youens house begin a slow pirouette. "It turned partly around and then seemed to hang as if suspended."

At about the same time, the wind changed direction from east to southeast, and again intensified. Young felt himself compressed against the wall of his gallery. "Mr. Youens' house rose like a huge steamboat, was swept back and suddenly disappeared," Young said. He thought of the family inside. "My feelings were indescribable as I saw them go."

Now he was alone, his house an atoll in a typhoon. The water continued to rise. "At one bound it reached my second story and poured in my door, which was exactly thirty-three feet above the street. The wind again increased. It did not come in gusts, but was more like the steady downpour of Niagara than anything I can think of."

The wind tore loose one of the posts that supported the gallery roof. The post struck Young, gashed his head, and left him dazed, but he did not fall. The wind held him in place. The door seemed about to tear loose. If the house fell, he resolved, he would grab the door, rip it free, and use it as a raft.

Slats from the gallery rail blew away "like straws." The remaining posts cartwheeled into the sea. The gallery roof lifted upward as if hinged, then blew away over the top of the house. With a shriek of wood and iron the gallery floor wrenched away and barged west.

Young remained pinned to the wall, one foot inside the doorway. He could not move. "It was an easy thing to stay there for the wind held me as firmly as if I had been screwed to the house."

The wind grew even stronger. Young estimated it reached 125 miles an hour. "The wind at 125 miles an hour is something awful," he said. "I could neither hear nor see."

He turned his head against the rain until he was looking inside the house. The rain slammed against the interior walls with such force it exploded in pixels of light. "The drops of rain became luminous," he said. It looked "like a display of miniature fireworks."

The wind grew so strong it planed the sea. "The surface of the water was almost flat. The wind beat it down so that there was not even a suspicion of a wave."

He could not open his eyes. A lion roared at his ears. That his house still stood seemed impossible. "I began to think my house would never go."

He gripped the facing of the door. He waited. He planned to kick his raft free of the house at the first sign of collapse. He did not have long to wait.

All over Galveston freakish things occurred. Slate fractured skulls and removed limbs. Venomous snakes spiraled upward into trees occupied by people. A rocket of timber killed a horse in midgallop.

At the expensive Lucas Terrace apartment building, Edward Quayle of Liverpool, England, who had arrived in Galveston with his wife three days earlier, happened to walk past a window just as the room underwent a catastrophic depressurization. The window exploded outward into the storm along with Mr. Quayle, who rocketed to his death trailing a slipstream of screams from his wife.

At another address, Mrs. William Henry Heideman, eight months pregnant, saw her house collapse and apparently kill her husband and three-year-old son. She climbed onto a floating roof. When the roof collided with something else, the shock sent her sliding down into a floating trunk, which then sailed right to the upper windows of the city's Ursuline convent. The sisters hauled her inside, dressed her in warm clothes, and put her to bed in one of the convent cells. She went into labor. Meanwhile, a man stranded in a tree in the convent courtyard heard the cry of a small child and plucked him from the current. A heartbeat later, he saw that the child was his own nephew—Mrs. Heideman's three-year-old son.

Mrs. Heideman had her baby. She was reunited with her son. She never saw her husband again.

The house shuddered, shifted, became buoyant. For a few queasy moments, Dr. Young felt himself exempt from gravity's effect. The time had come. He tore the gallery door loose and dove for the sea. Like the survivor of a sinking liner, he kicked hard to put distance between himself and the house. "The house rose out of the water several feet, was caught by the wind and whisped away like a railway train, and I was left in perfect security, free from all floating timber or debris, to follow more slowly."

The current drew him over the city. He saw few landmarks but believed he soon passed over the Garten Verein. Moments later he too careened toward the Ursuline convent, but his door got caught in a large whirlpool of water and wreckage. "I was carried round and round until I lost my bearings completely."

When the whirlpool dissipated, the inflowing sea again captured his raft. It swept him northwest for fifteen blocks until his door docked itself against a mound of wreckage. "It was very dark, but I could see the tops of some houses barely above the water; could see others totally wrecked, and others half submerged." He saw no lights, however. And no people. "I concluded that the whole of that part of town had been destroyed and that I was the only survivor."

He remained in that place aboard his door for the next eight hours. The wind rippled over his clothing. Porcupine rain jabbed his scalp and hands. Blood seeped from the gash in his head. In all that time he heard only one human voice, that of a woman somewhere in the distance crying for help. He had never been so cold in his life.

Something struck the house with terrific force. The house moved. It slid from its foundation and began to list. Joseph was standing near a window beside Isaac's oldest children, Allie May and Rosemary. "As the house capsized, I seized the hand of each of my brother's two children, turned my back toward the window, and, lunging from my heels, smashed through the glass and the wooden storm shutters, still gripping the hands of the two youngsters. The momentum hurled us all through the window as the building, with seeming deliberation, settled far over. It rocked a bit and then rose fairly level on the surface of the flood."

Joseph and the two girls found themselves on top of an outside wall. They saw no one else. "All the other occupants of that room, nearly fifty men, women and children, it appeared, were still trapped inside, for the house had not yet broken up."

The only exit from the house was the now-horizontal window through which Joseph and the children had passed. Joseph lowered the top half of his body through the window and shouted, "Come here! Come here!"

No one came. No one called out. The space below the window was utterly black. Periodically the house rose with the current, then settled, raising the water within to the level where the window glass had been. Anyone still inside would be completely submerged.

Joseph had heard that drowning men seized anything that came near. He sat on the window casing and began swinging his feet in the water. "I had hoped that some of the trapped ones within the room might catch my feet and so be pulled out," he said. "My efforts were wasted and I finally gave them up. I have no words to tell the agony of heart I experienced in that moment."

As soon as Ruby Credo's parents finished chopping holes into the floor of their parlor, they began preparations to evacuate to higher ground. If Dr. Cline planned to ride out the storm in his own house, that was his choice. Anthony Credo had no intention of doing likewise. He and his family were just about to leave when a neighbor, Mrs. Theodore Goldman, appeared at the door with her son, hoping to shelter in the Credos' house. Mrs. Goldman did not trust her own house, she said. Her husband did, however, and he was still there. He refused to leave.

The Credos put on some coffee and gave Mrs. Goldman and her son some dry clothes. In that short time, the water deepened to the point where Credo saw that leaving would be more dangerous than staying.

He had built a storm shelter behind his house, a one-room chamber atop six-foot posts. He believed, at first, that his children would be safest there. He swam them over one by one. As he watched other houses in the neighborhood disintegrate, he changed his mind. He retrieved his children. If something terrible happened, he wanted his family together. His two grown daughters were with their husbands, and he presumed them safe. His son William, visiting his fiancée, was a grown man and could take care of himself. It was the young ones he worried about most—little Ruby and her sisters, and son Raymond. The shuttling back and forth to the storm shelter unnerved him. He could carry only one child at a time.

"The water was rising rapidly to the second floor," Ruby said, "so Papa helped us climb from the outside through dormer windows to the attic bedrooms, where Mr. Goldman and his mother had moved. The water had risen so fast Mama hadn't time to grab her cherished black satin corset from downstairs." The family had little to do but watch the storm intensify. "We stood at the windows and watched the houses around us break up, wash away, and become battering rams to knock and tear others apart as they were hurled and swept about. The water kept rising; the sounds of the storm were frightening; the house creaked and groaned as if it were in some kind of agony."

Night had fallen. Ruby sat on the corner of a bed opposite Mrs. Goldman and her son. The wind accelerated. A streetcar rail pierced the roof and penetrated the floor between Ruby and the Goldmans. No one was hurt.

The house began to move. The wind lifted the roof, then dropped it. Falling wreckage pinned Ruby's mother, but Anthony Credo managed to pull her free. She bled heavily from head lacerations. Credo tore strips of cloth from her clothes to make bandages.

All this occurred in darkness.

The house eased from its foundation, slid through a shallow westward arc, then began to float. Credo gathered his family and ordered everyone out the dormer windows. The Goldmans declined to leave.

"When our house left the ground, we grabbed at anything washing by, as Papa had instructed us to do, but it was all you could do to stay on a piece of wood," Ruby said.

Waves broke upon the family and scattered them. Credo herded them together again. The cycle repeated itself.

In darkness.

The sea pushed the family north, everyone alive, everyone more or less intact, although Ruby's mother looked like a soldier wounded in the Spanish-American War.

They drifted. Credo shouted orders. Between waves, he kicked himself up from the water as high as he could, to count his family and keep anyone from straying. One wave drove a telegraph pole into the back of Raymond's head. It knocked him out and dug a severe gash in his scalp. Even in the darkness, Anthony Credo could tell the fluid pouring off his son's head was blood. Credo held Raymond with one arm and kept himself afloat with his other, struggling to hold Raymond's head out of the water and still keep track of the rest of his family.

Credo was tired. He believed his son dead, or nearly so. Several times he considered letting Raymond go. Mrs. Credo would not let him. She was not ready. She still had hope.

The storm was more intense than ever, but for a time the Credos saw a full moon behind thin clouds. An inverted roof floated past. Credo ordered everyone aboard. One daughter, Florence, helped him pull Raymond into the roof. Credo went back into the water. He did not want to risk tipping the raft. Mrs. Credo held Raymond close.

At first the roof proved an effective lifeboat, but soon it began to break apart. Credo watched for something better. An upended porch floated near. It looked sturdier than the roof. Credo shouted for everyone to abandon the roof and climb onto the porch.

Ruby's elder sisters Queeny, Vivian, and Ethel sat together, holding tight to one another's clothing. The porch was so stable, some of the children fell asleep. "We could lie back on these sections," Ruby said. "They were well-made, with no jagged nails or splinters to gash our bodies as we were tossed about."

Everyone relaxed. Raymond still did not move, but there was hope, now. The family was together. They would find Raymond a doctor. Everything would be all right. "We floated this way for an hour," Ruby said. "Then a piece of timber blown up by a wave struck my three sisters a terrific blow, knocking Vivian into the water and under heavy debris."

Vivian did not surface. The porch sailed on. The moon disappeared and lightning flared, the first lightning anyone could recall seeing. Big barrels of thunder rolled among the waves, and made the night even more terrifying. To Ruby, the rain was a particular torment. It "felt like bullets."

Ruby's sister Pearl was sitting peacefully upon the raft when a jagged spike of wood blew through her arm, just below her elbow. She screamed. Her mother held Pearl tight as Anthony Credo pulled the spike from her arm. Pearl writhed in utter agony. Credo applied pressure until the bleeding slowed, then bandaged it as best he could.

The porch beached itself against a reef of debris twelve feet high, near an intact house. Ruby and her family picked their way over the wreckage and climbed inside. Anthony Credo carried Raymond on his back.

Credo tallied the family's casualties. Vivian dead; Raymond clearly dying; Pearl hurt and now at grave risk of infection, fever, amputation, even death.

An unbearable list, but in fact it understated the true extent of the family's loss.

When the trestle struck, Isaac was at the center of the room with his wife and his six-year-old daughter, Esther Bellew. His baby. A wall came toward him. It propelled him backward into a large chimney. There was motion. He could not see it, but felt it all around. Things fell from the sky. Furniture, books, lanterns, beams, planks. People. Children. He entered the water. Something huge caught him and drove him to the bottom. Timbers held him. He opened his eyes. He felt the water but saw nothing. It was quiet. He could not move. He knew he would die. There was peace in this. It gave him time to think. He appraised things. The only course was to welcome the sea into his body. He did so. He disappeared.

He awoke to lions. Rain came like shrapnel. He was afloat, his chest caught between two large timbers. He coughed water. He sensed burden. There was something he had to do. It was like waking to a child's cry in the night. He sensed absence.

It came to him abruptly that he was now alone.

The scream had been shocking enough. What Louise Hopkins saw next caused her heart to leap halfway from her body.

Her sister, Lois, red-faced from the great energy she stuffed into that scream, pointed furiously at the place where the east wall joined the ceiling. At first Louise did not understand, but as she watched, she saw the wall begin to breathe. With each gust of wind, the wall moved out from the house until Louise could see the sky; then the wall wheezed back into position. There was a moon outside. Louise saw clouds rushing by overhead.

Louise looked at her mother. Mrs. Hopkins alone seemed not to be surprised. Apparently, she had been watching all along, but had not wanted to frighten her children any more than they already were.

It was time to leave, Mrs. Hopkins resolved. The house across the way, owned by the Dau family, looked sturdy, and there was a light inside. They would go there. Mrs. Hopkins worked out a plan. They would use a mattress as a raft. The Hopkins boys, both strong swimmers, would pull it across the street with Mrs. Hopkins, Lois, and Louise aboard. Mrs. Hopkins pulled sheets from the bed and tore them into strips, which she tied around her waist and the waists of her girls.

They assembled behind the big double front door, poised to exit. Every time the east wall and ceiling parted, Mrs. Hopkins would cry, "Let's go now."

But in the next instant the ceiling would settle, and Lois would shout, "Wait."

They could not muster the courage to cross. Water flowed wildly down the street. Bursts of spindrift erupted from the surface as missiles of slate and timber hissed back to earth.

The light across the way was irresistible. It offered safety, comfort, and company. "It doesn't seem so now," Louise said, "but there was such a consolation to know that somebody was still alive."

But this light, this beacon of comfort, began to move. They saw it dance from room to room. It moved toward the front door. They saw Mr. Dau carry the lantern out his front door and down his steps.

Leaving—the man was *leaving*. Like a ship captain ignoring a lifeboat adrift.

To Louise and her family it was as if hope itself had just departed.

Three miles down the beach, the big St. Mary's Orphanage with ninety-three children inside was under siege. It was a fortress of brick and stone that rose straight out of the grass just north of the tide line, a lonely Gibraltar shrouded most evenings in blue mist. Now waves crashed against its second story. Anyone watching from outside would have seen the lights of candles and lanterns move from room to room toward the back of the orphanage as the frontmost portions of the building collapsed into the sea like icebergs calved from a glacier.

The ten sisters who ran the place herded all ninety-three children into the chapel. Sister M. Camillus Tracy, thirty-one years old, the mother superior, ordered the other sisters to tie lengths of clothesline to the youngest children, then tie one end around their waists. They formed chains of six to eight children each, roped together like miniature climbing parties. A few older children, among them Will Murney, Albert Campbell, and Francis Bulnavic remained free. Sister Camillus led the children in hymns, including the children's favorite, "Queen of the Waves." The water rose. The children felt the concussion of each breaker as it struck the front of the building.

The sisters drew the children to the girls' dormitory at the back of the building, away from the beach. They heard the crash of wood and brick behind them as the boys' dormitory fell into the Gulf. The storm advanced through the building quickly and systematically, as if hunting the children. The chapel disappeared. Windows shattered. Hallways rose and fell like drawbridges. The children sang.

The sea and wind burst into the dormitory. In seconds, the building failed. Ninety children and all ten sisters died. Only Will, Albert, and Francis survived, all by catching hold of the same floating tree.

Later, a rescuer found one toddler's corpse on the beach. He tried lifting the child. A length of clothesline leaped from the sand, then tightened. He pulled the line. Another child emerged. The line continued into the sand. He uncovered eight children and a nun.

Sister Camillus had hoped the clothesline would save the children, but it was the clothesline, rescuers saw, that caused so many to die, tangling them in submerged wreckage.

August Rollfing sat alone in his shop on 24th Street waiting for his men to come for their pay. As the storm worsened, his anxiety increased. Water began coming into his shop. The wind accelerated. It rolled up the tin roofs across the way, then hurled them to the ground like spent shell casings. Boards and glass shrapneled the street. August had money for eighteen workers. No one came.

He locked his shop and set out to join his family, with absolute faith that the driver from Mallory's Livery had in fact done as he had asked and that now his family was safe at his mother's house. He struggled west. He got as far as the city waterworks at 30th Street between Avenue G and Avenue H, when the wind picked him up "like a piece of paper" and blew him out of the water onto a sidewalk. He hugged a telephone pole. In a lull between gusts, he crawled to the waterworks building and entered. He found the lobby full of storm refugees.

The building seemed sturdy enough. What worried the occupants was its tall smokestack, which swayed through the sky like a giant black cobra. If it fell—when it fell—everyone in the building stood an excellent chance of being crushed. Whenever the wind paused, a group of refugees would dash out onto the sidewalk.

Rollfing left, accompanied by two black men. They went first to a grocery store, which soon became too dangerous. They moved next to a private house. A beam fell and killed a man. They moved on, until they saw a light in the window of another store.

August and his companions banged on the door. At first, the occupants refused to let them in. Finally they relented.

It was nearly dark now. In the shuddery glow of lanterns and candles, August saw that the store was crowded with about eighty men, women, and children, all standing on countertops to keep out of the water. But the water was rising fast. August found a place on a counter. Soon the water was at his ankles, then his chest. August lifted someone else's son onto his shoulders as the water rose to his own neck.

He spent hours this way, until a man shouted, "The water is going down! Look at the door!"

The water had indeed reversed flow. The store owner pulled out a large jug of whiskey and passed it around the room. Men and women alike took great swallows and passed it on.

August wanted desperately to leave for his mother's house to join his wife and children and make sure they were still safe. The water receded quickly, but to him its exit seemed to take forever. Rain continued cascading from the darkness; the wind seemed little changed.

At last the water level fell low enough to enable him to leave. Outside, he saw that houses had been shattered and upended. He stumbled through deep holes gouged by the current, and over all manner of submerged debris. He dodged showers of timber and slate. It was dark, no lights anywhere. He fell, got up, fell again. The damage got progressively worse. Whole blocks had been crushed, others swept clean. He knew he was heading west—probably along Avenue H—but the darkness and devastation had eliminated all landmarks.

At intervals the moon emerged. How the moon could shine amid such wind and rain he did not know, but there it was, visible through a thin layer of cloud. A full moon, no less. It gave him light; it also gave him fear, for it showed him how vast the plane of devastation truly was. Spiky dunes of wreckage blocked his path. From the top of each, he saw that only a few homes still stood. To the south was a strange black shadow two and three stories high that stretched for miles like a mountain range freshly jabbed through the earth's crust.

At three o'clock Sunday morning he came to his mother's neighborhood. Only her house looked whole. Everything else had been destroyed, upended, or transported toward the bay. Relief poured into his heart. He burst into the house but found only his mother.

"Where are Louisa and the children? I don't see them."

The question surprised his mother. "August, I don't know," she said. "They are not here." When she realized that August *expected* them to be there, she too became afraid. "When did they go," she asked, "and how?"

He told her about the buggy he had sent at one o'clock and the instructions he had given the driver.

"Nobody could come here at one o'clock," his mother said. August started toward the door. "Wait," she pleaded. "Wait until daylight."

August made his way to his sister's house. He saw corpses. The short journey—only half a dozen blocks—took an hour. The sight made him half-crazy with dread. The house stood at a forty-five degree angle. Where Julia's kitchen had been, there was now only a jagged black hole. Every shutter had been splintered, every window broken.

But there seemed to be a light within. He pounded on the front door. The door opened. He saw Julia and her husband. He saw Louisa. He saw Helen, August, and little Lanta. "Thank God," he said.

And fainted on the stairs.

He was alone in the water. His family was gone. He flailed his arms and reached deep underwater and kicked his legs to feel for soft things, clothing, someone alive. He felt only square shapes, planks, serrated edges. He had been inside the house; now he was outside in darkness, in wind so fast it planed the water smooth. There was lightning. He saw debris everywhere, jutting from the sea. He saw a child. He shimmied free of the timbers and swam hard. The rain stung; he could hold his eyes open only a few seconds at a time. He came to her and felt his arm grow from the water and circle her and knew immediately the child was his Esther, his six-year-old. His baby. He spoke into her ear. She cried and grabbed him hard and put him under, but he was delighted. She asked for her mother. He had no answer. The house began to break up. He swam her away.

He was elated; he was distraught. He had found one daughter but lost everyone else. His memory of them would be tinted the yellow of lamplight. He tried to place them in the room, and by doing so, to place them in the sea. His wife had been with him in the center of the room with Esther. His two eldest daughters had been near the window, beside Joseph. Why had they not surfaced too?

Isaac and his baby drifted. There was more lightning. He coughed water through his nose and mouth. In the next flare, he saw three figures hanging tight to floating wreckage. Isaac swam Esther toward them against the wind.

He heard a shout.

Joseph Cline said: "My heart suddenly leaped with uncontrollable joy. In two figures that clung to the drift about one hundred feet to leeward, I discovered my brother and his youngest child."

Isaac: "We placed the children in front of us, turned our backs to the winds and held planks, taken from the floating wreckage, to our backs to distribute and lighten the blows which the wind driven debris was showering upon us continually."

Joseph: "Our little group now numbered five. We remained close together, climbing and crawling from one piece of wreckage to another, with each of the latter in turn sinking under our weight. At one time it seemed as though we were indeed lost. A weather-battered hulk that had once been a house came bearing down upon us, one side upreared at an angle of about forty-five degrees, at a height from six to eight feet higher than our drift. I was conscious of being direly frightened, but I retained sufficient presence of mind to leap as the monster reached us, and to get a grip with my hands on the highest edge of the wreck. My weight was enough to drag it perceptibly lower in the water, and I called my brother, who added his weight to my own."

Isaac: "Sometimes the blows of debris were so strong that we would be knocked several feet into the surging waters, when we would fight our way back to the children and continue the struggle to survive."

Joseph: "At one point, two other castaways, a man and a woman, joined us on the wreckage that, at that time, was serving us as a lifeboat. The strangers remained with us for some little time, until the man crawled up to where I sat, pulled the two children away, and tried to shelter himself behind my body. I pushed him indignantly away and drew the children back. He repeated the unspeakable performance. This time I drew out a knife that I carried, and threatened him with it."

They drifted for hours aboard a large raft of wreckage, first traveling well out to sea, when the wind shifted to come from the southeast and south, back into the city. For the first time they heard cries for help, these coming from a large two-story house directly in their path. Their raft bulldozed the house into the sea. The cries stopped.

A rocket of timber struck Isaac and knocked him down, but only dazed him. Joseph saw a small girl struggling in the sea and assumed that somehow Esther had fallen from Isaac's grasp. He plucked her from the water and gathered her close to the other girls. Allie May, the eldest, cried out, "Papa! Papa! Uncle Joe is neglecting Rosemary and me for this strange child!"

Stunned, Joseph took a close look at the girl. It was not Esther at all. He looked over his shoulder and saw Isaac bent over his baby, shielding her from the flying debris. This girl was a stranger.

Their raft ran aground at 28th and Avenue P, four blocks from where they once had lived. They saw a house with a light in the window, and climbed inside. Safe—although one daughter had injuries that Joseph considered life-threatening.

A miracle had occurred, Isaac knew. Nothing else could explain why he and his three daughters were still alive. Yet the enormity of what he did lose now came home to him. His children wept for their mother, but soon, out of sheer exhaustion, they fell asleep. Isaac lay awake for a time, hoping his wife somehow had survived, but knowing heart-deep that she had not.

She had been very close, as it happens. Later it would seem to Isaac as if she had been watching over her family during the entire voyage, guiding them in their passage through the night until they were safely back home.

And there was this: In the midst of the Clines' voyage, a beautiful retriever climbed aboard their raft. It was Joseph's dog. Somehow in the storm it had sensed them and swum after them. The dog was delighted to see Joseph and Isaac and the children, but sensed too that someone was missing. He went one by one to each of them, as if marking a checklist. One scent was absent. The dog raced to the edge of the raft and peered into the water. Joseph called him back. The dog stood scrabbling at the edge, obviously torn by conflicting needs. But it was clear where his passion lay. The dog ignored Joseph and prepared to jump. Joseph lunged for him, but the dog entered the sea, and soon he too was gone.

The Johnstown Flood

BY DAVID G. McCULLOUGH

One of the worst disasters to ever befall an American community occurred on Saturday, May 31,1889, when an estimated 20 million tons of water were unleashed by a broken dam on Lake Conemaugh high in the Pennsylvania Alleghenies. Down the valley, directly in the path of the roaring wall of water, was the town of Johnstown, described as "new, rough and busy" and now destined to become a legend of tragic events. Over 2,200 people were killed by the flood.

The full story of the famous Johnstown Flood and its aftermath has been told in a superb book by one of today's most distinguished historians and authors, David G. McCullough. Best-selling and highly praised biographer of such icons as Harry Truman and John Adams, and narrator of many television documentaries, McCullough turned to more dramatic material when he produced an account of the Johnstown Flood that not only is a riveting picture of the disaster unfolding, but a superb portrait of life in nineteenth century America.

The lake that doomed Johnstown, Lake Conemaugh, was dominated by the South Fork Fishing and Hunting Club, a private resort for great Pittsburgh industrialists, including Andrew Carnegie. Only an earthwork dam, long the subject of heated controversy, held back the waters of the lake from the valley below.

Jacket copy on McCullough's book describes what happened on that terrible Saturday:

"By noon of that May 31, as a result of heavy rainstorms, the dam was in serious trouble. Hour after hour work crews struggled to stave off disaster, as urgent attempts were made to warn Johnstown. Then at 3:10, the dam gave way and Lake Conemaugh, an estimated 20 million tons of water, started down the valley."

And now David McCullough describes what happened downstream.

175

*   *   *   *   *

M ost of the people in Johnstown never saw the water coming; they only heard it; and those who lived to tell about it would for years after try to describe the sound of the thing as it rushed on them.

It began as a deep, steady rumble, they would say; then it grew louder and louder until it had become an avalanche of sound, "a roar like thunder" was how they generally described it. But one man said he thought the sound was more like the rush of an oncoming train, while another said, "And the sound, I will never forget the sound of that. It sounded to me just like a lot of horses grinding oats."

Everyone heard shouting and screaming, the earsplitting crash of buildings going down, glass shattering, and the sides of houses ripping apart. Some people would later swear they heard factory whistles screeching frantically and church bells ringing. Who may have been yanking the bell cords was never discovered, but it was later reported that a freight engineer named Hugh Clifford had raced his train from above the depot across the stone bridge, his whistle going the whole way; and a man named Charles Horner blew the whistle over at Harry Swank's machine shop.

Those who actually saw the wall of water would talk and write of how it "snapped off trees like pipestems" or "crushed houses like eggshells" or picked up locomotives (and all sorts of other immense objects) "like so much chaff." But what seemed to make the most lasting impression was the cloud of dark spray that hung over the front of the wave.

Tribune editor George Swank wrote, "The first appearance was like that of a great fire, the dust it raised." Another survivor described it as "a blur, an advance guard, as it were a mist, like dust that precedes a cavalry charge." One young man said he thought at first that there must have been a terrible explosion up the river, "for the water coming looked like a cloud of the blackest smoke I ever saw."

For everyone who saw it, there seemed something especially evil about this "awful mass of spray" that hovered over "the black wreck." It was talked of as "the death mist" and would be remembered always.

The fact was there had been something close to an explosion up the river, at the Gautier works, when the water rolled over the fires there, which undoubtedly accounted for a good part of what they saw. Horace Rose, who witnessed about as much as anyone, thought so.

At the first sound of trouble he had rushed to the third floor of his house on lower Main Street and from the front window could see nearly a mile up the valley. Only a few minutes before he had been playfully teasing his neighbors' child, Bessie Fronheiser, from another window downstairs, telling her to come on over for a visit. The distance between the two houses was only about five feet, so he had put some candy on the end of a broom and passed it over to her. That was so successful that he next passed across a tin cup of coffee to Bessie's mother in the same way. She was just raising the cup to her lips when the first crash came.

From the third floor Rose could see the long line of the rolling debris, stretching from hill to hill, slicing thorough the Gautier works, chopping it down and sending up a huge cloud of soot and steam.

The sight took his breath away. Once clear of the wireworks, the wave kept on coming straight toward him, heading for the very heart of the city. Stores, houses, trees, everything was going down in front of it, and the closer it came, the bigger it seemed to grow. Rose figured that he and his family had, at the most, two or three minutes before they would be crushed to death.

There would be slight differences of opinion later as to precisely when the wave crossed the line into Johnstown, but the generally accepted time is 4:07.

The height of the wall was at least thirty-six feet at the center, though eyewitness descriptions suggest that the mass was perhaps ten feet higher there than off to the sides where the water was spreading out as the valley expanded to a width of nearly half a mile.

It was also noted by dozens of people that the wave appeared to be preceded by a wind which blew down small buildings and set trees to slapping about in the split seconds before the water actually struck them. Several men later described how the wind had whipped against them as they scrambled up the hillsides, grabbing at brush to pull themselves out of the way at the very last instant.

Because of the speed it had been building as it plunged through Woodvale, the water struck Johnstown harder than anything it had encountered in its fourteen-mile course from the dam. And the part of the city which took the initial impact was the eastern end of Washington Street, which ran almost at right angles to the path of the oncoming wave.

The drowning and devastation of the city took just about ten minutes.

For most people they were the most desperate minutes of their lives, snatching at children and struggling through the water, trying to reach the high ground, running upstairs as houses began to quake and split apart, clinging to rafters, window ledges, anything, while the whole world around them seemed to spin faster and faster. But there were hundreds, on the hillsides, on the rooftops of houses out of the direct path, or in the windows of tall buildings downtown, who just stood stone-still and watched in dumb horror.

They saw the eastern end of Washington Street, the block where the Heiser dry goods store stood, disappear in an instant. From there the wave seemed to divide into three main thrusts, one striking across the eastern end of town behind the Methodist Church, one driving straight through the center, and the other sticking more or less to the channel of the Little Conemaugh along the northern side of town. Not that there was any clear parting of the wave, but rather that there seemed to be those three major paths of destruction.

East of the park, Jackson and Clinton Streets became rivers of rubbish churning headlong for the Stony Creek. On Main and Locust, big brick buildings like the Hulbert House collapsed like cardboard while smaller wood-frame stores and apartment houses jumped from their foundations and went swirling away downstream, often to be smashed to bits against still other buildings, freight cars, or immense trees caught by the same roaring current.

Every tree in the park was torn up by the roots and snatched away as the water crossed through the center of town. John Fulton's house caved in, and other big places went down almost immediately after—the Horace Rose House, the John Dibert House, the Cyrus Elder House. The library, the telegraph office, the Opera House, the German Lutheran Church, the fire station, landmarks were vanishing so fast that no one could keep count of them. Then, perhaps no more than four minutes after the water had plunged across Washington Street, it broke past Vine on the far side of town and slammed into the hill which rises almost straight up to nearly 550 hundred feet in back of the Stony Creek.

It was as though the water had hit an immense and immovable backboard, and the result was much as it had been at South Fork when the wave struck the mountainside there. An immediate and furious backwash occurred. One huge wave veered off to the south, charging *up* the Stony Creek, destroying miles of the densely populated valley, which, it would seem, had been well out of reach of any trouble from the valley of the Little Conemaugh. Other waves pounded back on Johnstown itself, this time, very often, to batter down buildings that had somehow withstood the first onslaught.

Houses and rooftops, dozens of them with thirty or forty people clinging on top, went spinning off on a second run with the current, some to end up drifting about for hours, but most to pile in to the stone bridge, where a good part of the water headed after striking the hill, and where eventually all the water had to go.

The bridge crossed the Conemaugh River downstream from the Point where the Stony Creek and the Little Conemaugh come together. Past the bridge, another mile or so west, was the great Conemaugh Gap, the deepest river gorge between the Alleghenies and the Rockies and the flood's only way out of the mountains. But the bridge was never hit by the full force of the water. It had been built far enough down from the Point so that when the wave went grinding over Johnstown, it was shielded by Prospect Hill, and after the wave broke apart against the mountainside, the bridge had to withstand the impact of only a part of the wave.

As a result the bridge held. Had it been in the direct path and been struck full force, it would have been taken out just like everything else. But as it was, the mountainside took the brunt of the blow, the bridge survived, and the course of events for the next several hours went very differently.

Debris began building rapidly among the massive stone arches. And now it was no longer the relatively small sort of rubbish that had been clogging the bridge most of the day. Now boxcars, factory roofs, trees, telegraph poles, hideous masses of barbed wire, hundreds of houses, many squashed beyond recognition, others still astonishingly intact, dead horses and cows, and hundreds of human beings, dead and alive, were driven against the bridge until a small mountain had formed, higher than the bridge itself and nearly watertight. So once again, for the second time within an hour, Lake Conemaugh gathered in a new setting. Now it was spread all across Johnstown and well beyond.

But this time the new "dam" would hold quite a little longer than the viaduct had and would cause still another kind of murderous nightmare. For when darkness fell, the debris at the bridge caught fire.

No one knows for sure what caused the fire. The explanation most often given at the time was that oil from a derailed tank car had soaked down through the mass, and that it was set off by coal stoves dumped over inside the kitchens of mangled houses caught in the jam. But there could have been a number of other causes, and in any case, by six o'clock the whole monstrous pile had become a funeral pyre for perhaps as many as eighty people trapped inside.

Editor George Swank, who had been watching everything from his window at the *Tribune* office, wrote that it burned "with all the fury of the hell you read about—cremation alive in your own home, perhaps a mile from its foundation; dear ones slowly consumed before your eyes, and the same fate yours a moment later."

By ten o'clock the light from the flames across the lower half of town was bright enough to read a newspaper by.

The water in front of the Heiser store had been knee-deep since early in the afternoon, which was a record for that part of town. In the other floods over the years there had never been any water at all so far up on Washington Street.

People had been coming in and out of the store most of the morning joking about the weather, buying this and that to tide them through the day. The floor was slick with mud from their boots, and the close, warm air inside the place smelled of tobacco and wet wool. George Heiser, wearing his usual old sweater, was too busy taking care of customers to pay much attention to what was going on outside.

But by early afternoon, with the street out front under two feet of water, hardly anyone was about, and the Heiser family was left more or less to itself. A few visitors dropped in, family friends, and an occasional customer. Mrs. Lorentz, from Kernville, sat visiting with Mathilde Heiser upstairs. She had come by alone, without her husband, who was the town's weatherman, and, no doubt, a busy man that day.

Sometime near four o'clock George Heiser had sent his son, Victor, out to the barn to see about the horses. The animals had been tied in their stalls, and George, worried that they might strangle if the water should get any higher, wanted them unfastened.

The barn, like the storefront, was a recent addition for the Heisers. It had a bright-red tin roof and looked even bigger than it was, standing, as it did, upon higher ground at the rear of their lot. To get back to it, Victor had left his shoes and socks behind and, with a pair of shorts on, went wading across through the pelting rain. It had taken him only a few minutes to see to the horses and he was on his way out the door when he heard the noise.

Terrified, he froze in the doorway. The roar kept getting louder and louder, and every few seconds he heard tremendous crashes. He looked across at the house and in the second-story window saw his father motioning to him to get back into the barn and up the stairs. Just a few weeks earlier he and his father had cut a trap door through the barn roof, because his father had thought "it might be a good idea."

The boy was through the door and onto the roof in a matter of seconds. Once there he could see across the top of the house, and on the other side, no more than two blocks away, was the source of all the racket. He could see no water, only an immense wall of rubbish, dark and squirming with rooftops, huge roots, and planks. It was coming at him very fast, ripping through Portage and Center streets. When it hit Washington Street, he saw his home crushed like an orange crate and swallowed up.

In the same instant the barn was wrenched from its footings and began to roll like a barrel, over and over. Running, stumbling, crawling hand over hand, clawing at tin and wood, Victor somehow managed to keep on top. Then he saw the house of their neighbor, Mrs. Fenn, loom up in front. The barn was being driven straight for it. At the precise moment of impact, he jumped, landing on the roof of the house just as the walls of the house began to give in and the whole roof started plunging downward.

He clambered up the steep pitch of the roof, fighting to keep his balance. The noise was deafening and still he saw no water. Everything about him was cracking and splitting, and the air was filled with flying boards and broken glass. It was more like being in the middle of an explosion than anything else.

With the house and roof falling away beneath him, he caught hold of still another house that had jammed in on one side. Grabbing on to the eaves, he hung there, dangling, his feet swinging back and forth, reaching out, trying to get a toehold. But there was none. All he could do was hang and swing. For years after he would have recurring nightmares in which it was happening to him all over again. If he let go he was finished. But in the end, he knew, he would have to let go. His fingernails dug deep into the water-soaked shingles. Shooting pains ran through his hands and down his wrists.

Then his grip gave out and he fell, backwards, sickeningly, through the wet, filthy air, and slammed down on a big piece of red roof from the new barn. And now, for the first time, he saw water; he was bumping across it, lying on his stomach, hanging on to the roof with every bit of strength left in him, riding with the wave as it smashed across Johnstown.

The things he heard and saw in the next moments would be remembered later only as a gray, hideous blur, except for one split-second glimpse which would stick in his mind for the rest of his life.

He saw the whole Mussante family sailing by on what appeared to be a barn floor. Mussante was a fruit dealer on Washington Street, a small, dark Italian with a drooping mustache, who had been in Johnstown now perhaps three years. He had had a pushcart at first, then opened the little place not far from the Heiser store. Victor knew him well, and his wife and two children. Now there they were speeding by with a Saratoga trunk open beside them, and every one of them busy packing things into it. And then a mass of wreckage heaved up out of the water and crushed them.

But he had no time to think more about them or anything else. He was heading for a mound of wreckage lodged between the Methodist Church and a three-story brick building on the other side of where Locust Street had been. The next thing he knew he was part of the jam. His roof had catapulted in amongst it, and there, as trees and beams shot up on one side or crashed down on the other, he went leaping back and forth, ducking and dodging, trying desperately to keep his footing, while more and more debris kept booming into the jam.

Then, suddenly, a freight car reared up over his head. It looked like the biggest thing he had ever seen in his life. And this time he knew there could be no jumping out of the way.

But just as it was about to crash on top of him, the brick building beside him broke apart, and his raft, as he would describe it later, "shot out from beneath the freight car like a bullet from a gun."

Now he was out onto comparatively open water, rushing across a clear space which he judged to be approximately where the park had been. He was moving at a rapid clip, but there seemed far less danger, and he took some time to look about.

There were people struggling and dying everywhere around him. Every so often a familiar face would flash by. There was Mrs. Fenn, fat and awkward, balanced precariously on a tar barrel, well doused with its contents, and trying, pathetically, to stay afloat. Then he saw the young Negro who worked for Dr. Lee, down on his knees praying atop his employer's roof, stark naked, shivering, and beseeching the Lord in a loud voice to have mercy on his soul.

Like the Mussante family, they were suddenly here and gone like faces in nightmares, or some sort of grotesque comedy, as unreal and as unbelievable as everything else that was happening. And there was nothing he could do for them, or anybody else.

He was heading across town toward the Stony Creek. As near as he could reckon later, he passed right by where Horace Rose's house had stood, then crossed Main and sailed over the Morrell lot, and perhaps directly over where the Morrell greenhouse had been. Almost immediately after that, about the time he was crossing Lincoln Street, he got caught by the backcurrent.

Until then he had been keeping his eyes on the mountainside, which looked almost close enough to reach out and touch, and on the stone bridge. Both places looked to be possible landings, and either one would do as well as the other.

But now his course changed sharply, from due west to due south. The current grabbed his raft and sent it racing across the Stony Creek a half mile or so, over into the Kernville section, and it was here that his voyage ended.

"I passed by a two-and-a-half-story brick dwelling which was still remaining on its foundations. Since my speed as I went up this second valley was about that of a subway train slowing for a stop, I was able to hop to the roof and join a small group of people already stranded there."

When he had been standing on the roof of his father's barn, looking across the housetops at the avalanche bearing down on Johnstown, he had taken his watch out of his pocket to look at the time. It was a big silver watch with a fancy-etched cover, which had been his fourteenth birthday present from his father. He had snapped it open, because, as he would say later, "I wanted to see just how long it was going to take for me to get from this world over into the next one."

Now, on the rooftop in Kernville, realizing that he had perhaps a very good chance of staying on a little longer in this world, he pulled out the watch a second time.

Amazingly enough, it was still running, and he discovered with astonishment that everything that had happened since he had seen his home vanish had taken place in less than ten minutes.

Agnes Chapman had watched her husband walk to the front door in his bedroom slippers about four o'clock, open it, peer out, and turn around looking, as she told it later on, "pale and affrighted." The Reverend had just seen a boxcar with a man standing on top roll down the pavement in front of the parsonage. As he passed under the tree in the Chapmans' yard, the man had caught hold of a limb and swung himself up onto the roof of the front porch, from which he stepped through the second-story window directly over the Reverend's head.

The man was the ticket agent from the B & O station, across Washington Street from the Heiser store. Upon hearing the commotion up the valley, he had climbed on top of the car to see what was going on. Then the car had started running with what must have been a small but powerful current preceding the main wave. It swept the car down Franklin, across Locust, too fast for the man to do anything but hang on until he was within reach of the Chapmans' tree.

The whole scene meant only one thing to the Reverend. The reservoir had broken. He shouted for everyone to run for the attic.

Agnes Chapman, with her seven-year-old granddaughter, Nellie, Mrs. Brinker (their neighbor from across the park), Mr. Parker, and Lizzie, the cook, all made a dash up the front stairs, while Chapman ran to the study to shut off the gas fire. As he turned to go back out to the hall, he saw the front door burst open and a huge wave rush in. He ran for the kitchen and scrambled up the back stairs. A few seconds more and he would have been swept against the ceiling and drowned. The water was up the stairs and into the second floor almost instantly.

By now the whole family was in the attic, along with the B & O ticket agent and two other young men who had jumped through an open window from a whirling roof.

"We all stood there in the middle of the floor, waiting our turn to be swept away, and expecting every minute to be drowned," Mrs. Chapman said. "When our porches were torn loose, and the two bookcases fell over, the noise led us to think the house was going to pieces."

The noise everywhere was so awful they had to shout to hear one another. Outside other buildings were scraping and grinding against theirs, or crashing in heaps, and the thunder of the water kept on for what seemed an eternity.

"We knew . . . that many of our fellow citizens were perishing, and feared that there could be no escape for us," the Reverend Chapman wrote later. "I think none was afraid to meet God, but we all felt willing to put it off until a more propitious time . . ."

About then a man Chapman thought to be "an Arabian" came bounding through the window, clad only in underdrawers and a vest. He was drenching wet, shaking with cold and terror, and kept shouting at them. "Fader, Mudder, Tronk! Tronk! Two, tree hooner tollar, two, tree hooner tollar."

"I think he wanted to tell us he had lost his trunk with two or three hundred dollars he had saved to bring his mother and father over here," Chapman later explained.

The man got right down on his knees and started praying over a string of beads with such frenzy that the Reverend had to quiet him down, as he "excited and alarmed the ladies."

But despite everything happening outside, the parsonage appeared to be holding on. And when the roar began to die off, Chapman went to the window to take a look. It was, he wrote afterward, "a scene of utter desolation." With darkness closing down on the valley and the rain still falling, his visibility was quite limited. Still, he could make out the tall chimneys and gables of Dr. Lowman's house across the park, poking above what looked to him like a lake spread over the town at a depth of maybe thirty feet. There was not a sign of any of the other houses that had been on the park, but over on the left, where Main Street had been, he could see the dim silhouettes of the bank, Alma Hall, which was the Odd Fellows new building, and the Presbyterian Church sticking up out of the dark water. There were no lights anywhere and no people. "Everyone is dead," Chapman thought to himself.

Mrs. Brinker asked him to look to see if her house was still standing. When he said it was not, the others did what they could to console her. The room grew steadily darker, and from outside came more sounds of houses cracking up and going down under the terrible weight of the water.

The Hulbert House had been the finest hotel in town. It was not so large as the Merchants' Hotel on Main, but it was newer and fitted out "with all the latest wrinkles" as one paper of the day put it. Drummers made up most of the trade, and things were arranged to suit them. Breakfast was served early, dinner at noon (a custom most big-city hotels had long since abandoned), and like the other chief hotels in town, each of its rooms had a long extension table where the salesmen could display their wares. "Through some open door we can always see one piled high with samples of the latest fashions as adulterated for the provincial market," wrote a visitor from New York. It was also, for some strange reason, the only hotel in town without a bar.

Located on Clinton Street, three doors down from Main on the east side of the street, it was all brick and four stories tall. Earlier that morning it had looked to quite a number of people like one of the safest places in town.

For example, Jeremiah Smith, a stonemason who lived in a small frame house over on Stony Creek Street, brought his wife and three children (nine-year-old Florence, seven-year-old Frank, and a four-month-old baby) across town through the rain to the safety of the Hulbert House. How long Smith stayed on with them is not known, but the evidence is he soon went back home again. In any case, he and his house survived the flood. His wife and children were crushed to death when the Hulbert House collapsed almost the instant it was hit by the flood.

In all there were sixty people inside the building by four o'clock in the afternoon. Only nine of them got out alive.

"Strange as it may seem, we were discussing the possibility of the dam breaking only a few hours before it really did," one of the survivors, a G. B. Hartley of Philadelphia, was later quoted.

"We were sitting in the office shortly after dinner. Everyone laughed at the idea of the dam giving way. No one had the slightest fear of such a catastrophe."

As the afternoon passed, Hartley moved to the second-floor parlor. He was sitting there talking to a Miss Carrie Richards, Charles Butler of the Cambria Iron Company, and Walter Benford, brother of the proprietor, when they heard shouting in the streets, immediately followed by loud crashes.

"At first sound," Hartley said, "we all rushed from the room panic-stricken. Why it was I do not know, but we ran for the stairs. Mr. Butler took Miss Richards' hand. She called to me, and I took hold of her other hand. Then we started up the stairs. Mr. Benford did not go with us, but instead ran downstairs where his brother had an office. The scene in the hotel is beyond imagination or description.

"Chambermaids ran screaming through the halls, beating their hands together and uttering wild cries to heaven for safety. Frightened guests rushed about not knowing what to do nor what was coming. Up the stairs we leapt. Somewhere, I do not know when or how it was, I lost my hold of Miss Richards' hand. I really cannot tell what I did, I was so excited. I still rushed up the stairs and thought Miss Richards and Mr. Benford were just behind and I had reached the top flight of stairs and just between the third and fourth floors, when a terrific crash came. Instantly I was pinned by broken boards and debris . . ."

Hartley then looked up and saw that the building's big mansard roof had been lifted right off and he was looking at nothing more than a sullen sky. In what must have been no more than thirty seconds or so, he managed to scramble out from under the debris and climb onto the roof, which was floating to the side of the crumbling hotel.

F. A. Benford, proprietor of the house, was already on the roof, along with his brother Walter, a traveling salesman from Strawbridge & Clothier named Herbert Galager, and two chambermaids, one of whom had a dislocated shoulder. The roof floated off with the current. The rest of the building just disappeared; the walls fell in and it was gone.

Gertrude Quinn was the six-year-old daughter of James Quinn, who, with his brother-in-law, Andrew Foster, ran Geis, Foster and Quinn; Dry Goods and Notions, which stood diagonally across Clinton from the Hulbert House. The two of them, Gertrude would later say, looked like the Smith Brothers on the cough drop box.

James Quinn was one of the few prominent men in Johnstown who had been noticeably concerned about the dam since early that morning. He had been to the lake several times over the years and had a clear idea of the volume of water there. If the dam should let go, he had said, not a house in town would be left standing.

The Quinns lived in one of Johnstown's showplaces, a three-story, red-brick Queen Anne house newly built at the corner of Jackson and Main. It was surrounded by an iron fence and stood well up off the street, perfectly safe, it was to be assumed, from even the worst spring floods. There were fruit trees and a flower garden in the front yard, a kitchen garden, a barn with one cow and some ducks out back. Inside, everything was the latest—plumbing, icebox, organ, piano, Arab scarves, Brussels carpets, a marble clock from Germany on the mantel.

Besides Gertrude, there were six other children in the family. Vincent, who was sixteen, was the oldest. Helen, Lalia, and Rosemary came next; then Gertrude, Marie, and Tom, who was only a few months old. Rosina Quinn, their mother, was the daughter of old John Geis, who had started the store back in canal days, soon after he arrived from Bavaria. She had worked in the business herself before marrying and was later teased for having five of her seven children in July, which, as everyone knew, was the slow season for dry goods.

Then there was Libby Hipp, the eighteen-year-old German nursegirl, Gertrude's Aunt Abbie (Mrs. Geis), and her infant son, Richard. Aunt Abbie, who was probably no more than twenty-eight years old and a woman of exceptional beauty, had come east for her health from her home in Salina, Kansas. She had had three children in a very short time and needed rest.

James Quinn was most definitely head of the household. He was a trim, bookish man who had been an officer in the cavalry during the war and still held himself in a like manner. He was president of the Electric Light Company, a member of the school board, and, along with Cyrus Elder, Dr. Lowman, and George Swank, he was one of the trustees of the Johnstown Savings Bank. As a boy he had been taken by his father, a construction worker, to ask for a job in the Cambria mills but had been turned down because he looked too scared—for which he would be forever thankful. For a while before the war he had toyed with the idea of becoming an artist, and one of his early efforts, *Rebecca at the Well,* done in house paints, hung in the third floor of the new house on Jackson Street. (Later on, his wife would tell him, "The flood wasn't so bad, when you realize we got rid of *Rebecca* so gracefully.")

At home he was quite exacting about the use of the English language, abhorring slang and insisting on proper diction. He liked cigars. He was quiet, dignified, a strong Republican, and a good Catholic.

The advertisements he was placing in the *Tribune* that spring let it be known that Foster and Quinn were offering the finest in Hamburg embroideries, Spanish laces, Marseilles quilts, and "new French sateens." But the store also dealt in carpets, umbrellas, hatpins, flannel drawers, striped calico dresses, pearl buttons, black hose, bolsters, and pillowcases.

"I cannot separate thoughts of parents, brothers, sisters, or home from our store," Gertrude would say later. "When we went there, we became personages . . . the clerks, vying with one another for our attention, were always doing thoughtful little things for us."

The place was big and brightly lighted, with people coming and going, exchanging news and gossip. For the children it was all a grand show, from which they took home strings of stray beads or buttons or some other trinket.

For Foster and Quinn (father-in-law Geis had long since retired), the place represented an investment of about $60,000 and provided a very good living.

On the morning of the 31st, James Quinn had gone to the store early to supervise the moving of goods to higher levels. Before leaving home he had told everyone to stay inside. One of his children, Marie, was already sick with measles, and he did not want the others out in the rain catching cold. He did, however, allow young Vincent to come along with him downtown to lend a hand.

At noon, when he had returned for dinner, the water had been up to his curbstone. He had been restless and worried through the meal, talking about the water rising in the streets and his lack of confidence in the South Fork dam.

A few days before, he and his wife and the infant, Tom, and Lalia had gone to Scottdale for a christening, and Mrs. Quinn and the two children had stayed on to visit with her sister. Now Aunt Abbie and Libby Hipp were more or less running things, and he was doing his best to make sure they understood the seriousness of the situation.

"James, you are too anxious," his sister-in-law said. "This big house could never go."

In recalling the day years afterward, Gertrude felt sure that her father was so worried that he would have moved them all to the hill that morning, even though he had no special place to take them, if it had not been for Marie. He was afraid of the effect the light might have on her eyes.

After dinner he had gone back to the store, and Gertrude slipped out onto the front porch where she began dangling her feet in the water, which, by now, covered the yard just deep enough for the ducks to sport about among the flowers. Everyone who survived the flood would carry some especially vivid mental picture of how things had looked just before the great wave struck; for this child it would be the sight of those ducks, and purple pansies floating face up, like lily pads, in the yellow water.

Shortly before four Gertrude's father suddenly appeared in front of her. He took her with one hand, with the other gave her a couple of quick spanks for disobeying his order to stay inside, and hurried her through the door.

"Then he gave me a lecture on obedience, wet feet, and our perilous position; he said he had come to take us to the hill and that we were delayed because my shoes and stockings had to be changed again. He was smoking a cigar while the nurse was changing my clothes. Then he went to the door to toss off the ashes."

It was then that he saw the dark mist and heard the sound of the wave coming. He rushed back inside, shouting, "Run for your lives. Follow me straight to the hill."

Someone screamed to him about the baby with the measles. He leaped up the stairs and in no more than a minute was back down with Marie wrapped in a blanket, his face white and terrified-looking.

"Follow me," he said. "Don't go back for anything. Don't go back for anything." Everyone started out the door except Vincent. Just where he was no one knew. Helen and Rosemary ran on either side of their father, holding on to his elbows as he carried the baby. When they got to the street the water was nearly to Rosemary's chin, but she kept going, and kept trying to balance the umbrella she had somehow managed to bring along. The hill was at most only a hundred yards away. All they had to do was get two short blocks to the end of Main and they would be safe.

James Quinn started running, confident that everyone was with him. But Aunt Abbie, who was carrying her baby, and Libby Hipp, who had Gertrude in her arms, had turned back.

When she reached the top of the steps that led from the yard down to the street, Aunt Abbie had had second thoughts.

"I don't like to put my feet in that dirty water," Gertrude would remember her saying. Libby said she would do whatever Aunt Abbie thought best, so they started back into the house.

"Well, I kicked and scratched and bit her, and gave her a terrible time, because I wanted to be with my father," Gertrude said later. How the two women, each with a child, ever got to the third floor as fast as they did was something she was never quite able to figure out. Once there, they went to the front window, opened it, and looked down into the street. Gertrude described the scene as looking "like the Day of Judgment I had seen as a little girl in Bible histories," with crowds of people running, screaming, dragging children, struggling to keep their feet in the water.

Her father meanwhile had reached dry land on the hill, and turning around saw no signs of the rest of his family among the faces pushing past him. He grabbed hold of a big butcher boy named Kurtz, gave him Marie, told him to watch out for the other two girls, and started back to the house.

But he had gone only a short way when he saw the wave, almost on top of him, demolishing everything, and he knew he could never make it. There was a split second of indecision, then he turned back to the hill, running with all his might as the water surged along the street after him. In the last few seconds, fighting the current around him that kept getting deeper and faster every second, he reached the hillside just as the wave pounded by below.

Looking behind he saw his house rock back and forth, then lunge sideways, topple over, and disappear.

Gertrude never saw the wave. The sight of the crowds jamming through the street had so terrified her aunt and Libby Hipp that they had pulled back from the window, horrified, dragging her with them into an open cupboard.

"Libby, this is the end of the world, we will all die together," Aunt Abbie sobbed, and dropped to her knees and began praying hysterically, "Jesus, Mary, and Joseph, Have mercy on us, oh, God . . ."

Gertrude started screaming and jumping up and down, calling "Papa, Papa, Papa," as fast as she could get it out.

The cupboard was in what was the dining room of an elaborate playhouse built across the entire front end of the third floor. There was nothing like it anywhere else in town, the whole place having been fitted out and furnished by Quinn's store. There was a long center hall and a beautifully furnished parlor at one end and little bedrooms with doll beds, bureaus, washstands, and ingrain carpets on the floors. The dining room had a painted table, chairs, sideboard with tiny dishes, hand-hemmed tablecloths, napkins, and silverware.

From where she crouched in the back of the cupboard, Gertrude could see across the dining room into a miniature kitchen with its own table and chairs, handmade iron stove, and, on one wall, a whole set of iron cooking utensils hanging on little hooks. Libby Hipp was holding her close, crying and trembling.

Then the big house gave a violent shudder. Gertrude saw the tiny pots and pans begin to sway and dance. Suddenly plaster dust came down. The walls began to break up. Then, at her aunt's feet, she saw the floorboards burst open and up gushed a fountain of yellow water.

"And these boards were jagged . . . and I looked at my aunt, and they didn't say a word then. All the praying stopped, and they gasped, and looked down like this, and were gone, immediately gone."

She felt herself falling and reaching out for something to grab on to and trying as best she could to stay afloat.

"I kept paddling and grabbing and spitting and spitting and trying to keep the sticks and dirt and this horrible water out of my mouth."

Somehow she managed to crawl out of a hole in the roof or wall, she never knew which. All she saw was a glimmer of light, and she scrambled with all her strength to get to it, up what must have been the lath on part of the house underneath one of the gables. She got through the opening, never knowing what had become of her aunt, Libby, or her baby cousin. Within seconds the whole house was gone and everyone in it.

The next thing she knew, Gertrude was whirling about on top of a muddy mattress that was being buoyed up by debris but that kept tilting back and forth as she struggled to get her balance. She screamed for help. Then a dead horse slammed against her raft, pitching one end of it up into the air and nearly knocking her off. She hung on for dear life, until a tree swung by, snagging the horse in its branches before it plunged off with the current in another direction, the dead animal bobbing up and down, up and down, in and out of the water, like a gigantic, gruesome rocking horse.

Weak and shivering with cold, she lay down on the mattress, realizing for the first time that all her clothes had been torn off except for her underwear. Night was coming on and she was terribly frightened. She started praying in German, which was the only way she had been taught to pray.

A small white house went sailing by, almost running her down. She called out to the one man who was riding on top, straddling the peak of the roof and hugging the chimney with both arms. But he ignored her, or perhaps never heard her, and passed right by.

"You terrible man," she shouted after him. "I'll never help you."

Then a long roof, which may have been what was left of the Arcade Building, came plowing toward her, looking as big as a steamboat and loaded down with perhaps twenty people. She called out to them, begging someone to save her. One man started up, but the others seemed determined to stop him. They held on to him and there was an endless moment of talk back and forth between them as he kept pulling to get free.

Then he pushed loose and jumped into the current. His head bobbed up, then went under again. Several times more he came up and went under. Gertrude kept screaming for him to swim to her. Then he was heaving himself over the side of her raft, and the two of them headed off downstream, Gertrude nearly strangling him as she clung to his neck.

The big roof in the meantime had gone careening on until it hit what must have been a whirlpool in the current and began spinning round and round. Then, quite suddenly, it struck something and went down, carrying at least half its passengers with it.

Gertrude's new companion was a powerful, square-jawed millworker named Maxwell McAchren, who looked like John L. Sullivan. How far she had traveled by the time he climbed aboard the mattress, she was never able to figure out for certain. But later on she would describe seeing many flags at one point along the way, which suggests that she went as far up the Stony Creek as Sandy Vale Cemetery, where the Memorial Day flags could have been visible floating about in the water. Sandy Vale is roughly two miles from where the Quinn house had been, and when Maxwell McAchren joined her, she had come all the way back down again and was drifting with the tide near Bedford Street in the direction of the stone bridge.

On a hillside, close by to the right, two men were leaning out of the window of a small white building, using long poles to carry on their own rescue operation. They tried to reach out to the raft, but the distance was too great. Then one of them called out, "Throw that baby over here."

McAchren shouted back, "Do you think you can catch her?"

"We can try," they answered.

The child came flying through the air across about ten to fifteen feet of water and landed in the arms of Mr. Henry Koch, proprietor of Koch House, a small hotel and saloon (mostly saloon) on Bedford Street. The other man in the room with him was George Skinner, a Negro porter, who had been holding Koch by the legs when he made the catch. The men stripped Gertrude of her wet underclothes, wrapped her in a blanket, and put her on a cot. Later she was picked up and carried to the hill, so bundled up in the warm blanket that she could not see out, nor could anyone see in very well.

Every so often she could hear someone saying, "What have you got there?" And the answer came back, "A little girl we rescued." Then she could hear people gathering around and saying, "Let's have a look." Off would come part of the blanket in front of her face and she would look out at big, close-up faces looking in. Heads would shake. "Don't know her," they would say, and again the blanket would come over her face and on they would climb.

Gertrude never found out who it was who carried her up the hill, but he eventually deposited her with a family named Metz, who lived in a frame tenement also occupied by five other families. The place looked like paradise to her, but she was still so terrified that she was unable to say a word as the Metz children, neighbors, and people in off the street jammed into the kitchen to look at her as she lay wrapped now in a pair of red-flannel underwear with Mason jars full of hot water packed all around her.

Later, she was put to bed upstairs, but exhausted as she was she was unable to sleep. In the room with her were three other refugees from the disaster, grown women by the name of Bowser, who kept getting up and going to the window, where she could hear them gasping and whispering among themselves. After a while Gertrude slipped quietly out of bed and across the dark room. Outside the window, down below where the city had been, she could now see only firelight reflecting on water. It looked, as she said later, for all the world like ships burning at sea.

PART FOUR

Disaster at Sea: Victims, Heroes, and Doomed Voyages

The Night Lives On

BY WALTER LORD

Is it possible to become satiated with reading about the Titanic? For me, the answer is an unqualified, "No."

Because I am always anxious to grab everything about the Titanic I can get my hands on, I was overjoyed when Walter Lord followed up his classic *A Night to Remember*, first published in 1955, with a new book called *The Night Lives On*, published in 1986.

So here we go again, with new facts, new revelations. We're back to that fatal voyage of April, 1912, on the frigid Atlantic. We all *think* we know what happened. But do we?

Walter Lord has new questions, new answers, and many new reasons for us to be reading yet more about the Titanic.

*   *   *   *   *

Sunday, April 14, Gracie decided that he must get back on some sort of regimen. He bounced out of bed for a pre-breakfast warm-up with Fred Wright, the ship's squash pro. Then a plunge in the swimming pool, and up for a big breakfast. Later he attended divine service, conducted by Captain Smith, and joined the rest of those present in the "Prayer for Those at Sea."

Early afternoon, the weather suddenly turned cold. Most of the passengers stayed inside, writing letters and catching up on their reading. Gracie finished Mary Johnson's *Old Dominion* and returned it to the ship's library. Later he cornered Isidor Straus, on whom he had foisted a copy of *The Truth about Chickamauga*. The book strikes one reader as 462 pages of labored minutiae, but Mr. Straus was famous for his tact; he assured the Colonel that he had read it with "intense interest."

Despite the cold, Mrs. Candee and Hugh Woolner decided to explore the ship. A door on the starboard side of the Boat Deck was open, and hearing some clicking sounds, they looked in. "Come in, come right in and try your strength," called a cheery English voice. It was T. W. McCawley, the gym instructor, a bouncy little man in white flannels, eager to show off his domain. For the next hour they raced the stationary bicycles, rode the mechanical horses, and even took a turn on the "camel," which McCawley said was good for the liver.

But it was getting colder all the time, and they decided to go down to the lounge for tea. They settled into a green velvet settee before a glowing grate, and it reminded Helen Candee of coming back home to a fireplace after a frosty afternoon ride over the fields. Stewards arrived with steaming pots of tea and plates piled high with buttered toast, and she sensed a general feeling of total well-being and contentment—rare indeed since her son's accident.

The spell was broken by the bugle to dress for dinner. For the next hour, First Class seemed almost empty, as "our coterie" and the others struggled behind closed stateroom doors with hundreds of shirt studs and thousands of hairpins. Every steward and stewardess—every personal maid and valet—was mobilized to help.

Dinner was the social high point of the day. The elite dined in the À la Carte Restaurant, but the main dining saloon on D Deck had glitter enough. The scene might have been the Ritz in London or Sherry's in New York, with the men in white tie (except for a few daring souls in tuxedo), and the ladies shining in pale satin and clinging gauze. Tonight even the impoverished Mrs. Cassebeer looked superb, resplendent in the only snappy evening gown she had.

There's no record of what Mrs. Candee was wearing, but it's a safe guess that she looked irresistible to her six devoted swains. After a dinner of filet mignon Lili, they took a table together in the adjoining Reception Room for coffee and the nightly concert by the *Titanic's* band.

The band has become so hallowed in memory that it seems almost blasphemous to say anything critical about its music. Nevertheless, there were those in "our coterie" who did feel that it was poor on its Wagner, while others said that the violin was weak. True or not, Wallace Hartley and his men were immensely popular with the passengers, and always willing to play any request. Tonight they played some Puccini for Mrs. Candee and a little Dvorak for Hugh Woolner.

Colonel Gracie, who never recognized any number the band played now or later, used the concert as an opportunity to circulate among the crowded little tables that filled the room. He was an indefatigable celebrity collector, and liked to mention his Union Club membership and St. Paul's School background. One can imagine people wincing at his approach but putting up with him anyhow, for he was kind, courtly, and certainly meant well.

Tonight the Colonel had fewer targets than usual, for the truly big names were dining in the À la Carte Restaurant up on B Deck, where the Wideners were giving a small dinner for Captain Smith. Yet there were still plenty of attractive tables, and Gracie felt that the ladies never looked lovelier. Around 9:30 he decided to break off the evening and retire. It was still early, but it had been a long day—all that squash, swimming, and exercises in the gym—and he had reserved the squash court for another session early the following morning.

By 11:00 the rest of the crowd in the Reception Room was breaking up too, and the band finished the evening with the "Tales of Hoffmann." Soon the big Jacobean room was completely empty, except for one remaining table. Mrs. Candee and "our coterie" were going as strong as ever. But even they felt the emptiness of the room and decided to look for someplace cozier.

Somebody suggested the Café Parisien, all the way aft on B Deck. It was the showpiece of the ship, stylish but intimate. Certainly there ought to be some life there. But all they found was one other party presided over by Archie Butt, President Taft's military aide.

And it was so cold. Mrs. Candee drew her scarf close, but it made little difference. They ordered hot drinks, and a waiter appeared with a tray of grog, steaming Scotch and lemon, and (for Bjornstrom Steffanson) a hot lemonade. Even these emergency measures didn't help, and around 11:20 Mrs. Candee reluctantly went below, where there was at least an electric heater in her stateroom.

Colley also drifted off and the four remaining members of "our coterie" now went up to the smoking room, just above on A Deck. This was a male sanctuary where the ship's night owls customarily gathered and which was bound to be warm. Someone produced a pack of cards, and the foursome began to play a rather lighthearted game of bridge. There were other tables of bridge nearby, including one carefully organized by George Brayton and two of his sporting cronies. The fourth at this table was Howard Case, London Manager of the Vacuum Oil Company. Case has been selected as the sharps' next pigeon.

Several other groups sat around simply talking, and one lone traveler—Spencer Silverthorne of St. Louis—buried himself in a big leather chair, idly reading Owen Wister's *The Virginian*. It was now nearly 11:40 P.M., and the hum of conversation blended with the steady throb of the engines far below.

Suddenly an interruption. As Hugh Woolner recalled it a few days later in a letter to a friend, "There came a heavy grinding sort of a shock, beginning far ahead of us in the bows and rapidly passing along the ship and away under our feet."

It was not severe, but enough to spill gambler Harry Romaine's drink. Everyone sprang up, and several of the more curious—including Woolner and Steffanson—darted through the swinging doors aft and onto the open Promenade Deck. Steffanson's eyes couldn't adjust to the sudden darkness fast enough, but he heard one of the others call out, "We hit an iceberg—there it is!"

The bridge was as surprised as the gentlemen in the smoking room. How could the *Titanic* have collided with an iceberg so suddenly, so unexpectedly? Second Officer Lightoller wasn't on the bridge at the time, but he was senior surviving officer, and at the British Inquiry (technically the Wreck Commissioner's Court) he had an almost mystical explanation:

> Of course, we know now the extraordinary combination of circumstances that existed at that time which you would not meet again in 100 years; that they should all have existed just on that particular night shows, of course, that everything was against us.

Pressed to particularize, Lightoller pointed out that there was no moon, no wind, no swell. The Court did not seem overly impressed, but the notion has persisted that the accident was of the one-in-a-million variety, that it couldn't have been foreseen, and that the lost liner was, in fact, a helpless victim of fate.

Was she really? To find the answer, we must start back on the afternoon of April 12 as the *Titanic*—one day out of Queenstown—steamed westward across a calm, sunny sea. Around sunset a wireless message arrived from the French Liner *La Touraine* warning of ice ahead. Captain Smith gave the position to Fourth Officer Boxhall, and Boxhall noted it on the map in the chart room, but it was over a thousand miles away and far to the north of the *Titanic's* track—no need to worry.

The wireless was quiet on the 13th, but late that night the *Titanic* met the Furness Withy Liner *Rappahannock,* eastbound from Halifax to London. She had recently encountered heavy pack ice, twisting her rudder and denting her bow. Now, as the two ships passed within signaling distance, the *Rappahannock* warned the *Titanic* by blinker of the danger ahead. The great White Star

Liner, decks blazing with light, flashed back a brief acknowledgment and hurried on into the night.

Sunday, April 14, and the wireless brought a spate of fresh warnings. At 9 A.M. (*Titanic* time) the Cunard Liner *Caronia* reported "bergs, growlers, and field ice in 42°N, from 49° to 51°W." At 11:40 the Dutch liner *Noordam* also reported "much ice" in roughly the same position, and at 1:42 P.M. the White Star Liner *Baltic* reported "icebergs and large quantity of field ice in 41°51'N, 49°9'W"—about 250 miles ahead.

At 1:45 P.M. still another ice message arrived—the fourth of the day. The German liner *Amerika* reported passing two large icebergs at 41°27'N, 50°8'W. The *Amerika's* message was addressed to the U.S. Hydrographic Office in Washington, but this was beyond her own range; so, in the custom of the times, she asked the *Titanic* to relay it. This the *Titanic* did, thus adding her own voice to the chorus of warnings.

Nothing more till 7:30 P.M.; then a fifth message, this one from the Leyland Liner *Californian,* position 42°3'N, 49°9'W: "Three large bergs five miles to southward of us." The ice was now only 50 miles ahead.

Finally, at 9:40 P.M., the Atlantic Transport Liner *Mesaba*: "Lat. 42°N to 41°25'N, Longitude 40°W to 50°30'W, saw much heavy pack ice and great number large icebergs, also field ice." The *Titanic* was already in the rectangle blocked out by this warning.

Put together, the six messages indicated an enormous belt of ice stretching some 78 miles directly across the big ship's path.

But the messages were not "put together." If the recollections of the four surviving officers are any guide, most of the warnings went unnoticed on the bridge. Fourth Officer Boxhall, who was always Captain Smith's choice for marking the ship's chart, could only remember pricking off the *La Touraine's* sighting on April 12.

Of the six ice messages received on the 14th, the day of the collision, there is firm information about only the first two. The *Caronia's* sighting, received at 9 A.M., appears to have been noted by Boxhall. Third Officer Pitman distinctly remembered seeing him jot the single word "ice" on a slip of paper, with the *Caronia's* sighting underneath, and then tuck the slip into a frame above the chart room table. Other officers recalled seeing the same sighting pricked off on the chart—also Boxhall's work. And around 12:45 Captain Smith showed the complete *Caronia* message to Second Officer Lightoller, senior officer on the bridge at the time.

About an hour later Captain Smith had the *Baltic's* warning, too, but there's no evidence that he showed it to anybody on the bridge. Instead, he took it with him as he started down for lunch about 1:30. On the Promenade Deck he ran into Bruce Ismay, who was taking a pre-lunch constitutional. They exchanged greetings, and the Captain handed the Managing Director the *Baltic*'s message as a matter of interest. Ismay glanced at it, stuffed it in his pocket, and went on down to lunch.

He still had it late in the afternoon when he ran into Mrs. Thayer and Mrs. Ryerson, two of the most socially prominent ladies aboard. Ismay, who liked to remind people who he was, lost no time producing the *Baltic* message and reading them the titillating news about icebergs ahead.

Coming out of the smoking room that evening just before dinner, he again met Captain Smith. The Captain asked if Ismay still had the message, explaining that he wanted to post it for his officers to read. Ismay fished it out of his pocket and returned it without any further conversation. Then the two men continued down to the À la Carte Restaurant—Ismay to dine alone with the ship's surgeon, old Dr. O'Laughlin; Smith to join the small party the Wideners were giving in his honor. There's no evidence that the *Baltic*'s information was ever noted on the bridge before the whole affair became academic.

As for the four other ice messages received on the 14th—those from the *Noordam, Amerika, Californian,* and *Mesaba*—none of them were remembered by any of the surviving officers. The *Noordam*'s warning was acknowledged by Captain Smith, but what he did with it nobody knows. The *Californian*'s message was received by Second Wireless Operator Harold Bride, who testified that he took it to the bridge but didn't know whom he gave it to. The *Amerika* and *Mesaba* warnings were received by First Wireless Operator John Phillips, but what happened to them remains a mystery.

Almost any student of the *Titanic* knows by heart the famous scene where a weary Jack Phillips tucks the *Mesaba*'s warning under a paperweight and goes on working off his backlog of commercial traffic. Yet there's very little evidence to support the story. Lightoller said Phillips told him so while they were clinging to an upturned collapsible boat after the sinking, but nobody else on the collapsible remembered such a conversation. Even Lightoller never mentioned it at the hearings, although it was vitally important and would have helped White Star, which he was trying to do. Nor did Lightoller mention the incident to Fourth Officer Boxhall, while they were on the *Carpathia* going over together every detail of the disaster. Boxhall never heard of the *Mesaba* until he reached New York. The story first emerged in Lightoller's memoirs, 25 years later, where it should be accorded the latitude normally granted an old sea dog reminiscing.

The *Mesaba* message remains a mystery. Perhaps it did end up under the paperweight, but it seems equally possible that sometime after Lightoller went off duty Phillips passed it on to the bridge, where it received the same attention given the warnings from the *Noordam, Amerika,* and *Californian*—which was none at all.

What went wrong? To begin with, there seems to have been little coordination between the radio room and the bridge. The procedure for handling incoming messages was fuzzy at best. Any message affecting the navigation of the ship was meant to go straight to the bridge, but Phillips and Bride were no navigators; the jumble of longitudes and latitudes meant nothing to them. Their method of handling a message really depended on how it was addressed, rather than what it was about.

If the message was addressed to Captain Smith, one of the operators would take it directly to the Captain and hand it to him personally. If addressed simply to the ship, it might be delivered by a messenger, and to anyone on duty on the bridge. If sent just to be relayed on, like the *Amerika*'s alert to the Hydrographic Office in Washington, there seems to have been no standard practice at all.

Some messages were even picked up by eavesdropping, and their handling was left to the operator's discretion. The *Californian*'s warning, for instance, was addressed to the liner *Antillian*. Bride just happened to catch it, jotted it down, and took it to the bridge himself—but never knew whom he gave it to.

Nor does there seem to have been any clear-cut procedure for handling the messages once they reached the bridge. According to Third Officer Pitman, every captain had his own system, but it's hard to explain the system on the *Titanic*. Of the three messages addressed to Captain Smith personally, the *Caronia*'s was posted, the *Noordam*'s can't be traced, and the *Baltic*'s ended up in Bruce Ismay's pocket. Of the rest, there's no record that they were ever seen by any officer on the bridge.

As a result, some important information was missed altogether. The *Titanic*'s surviving officers all thought the ice lay to the north of the track, but the *Amerika* and *Mesaba* warnings clearly placed it to the south as well. Nor did the officers appear to understand the nature of the danger. Third Officer Pitman thought there was only a berg or two; Lightoller also worried about "small ice and growlers." Nobody on the bridge visualized the great berg-studded floe drifting slowly across the ship's path. The missed messages told a lot.

Above all, the cumulative effect of the messages—warning after warning, the whole day long—was lost completely. The result was a complacency, an almost arrogant casualness, that permeated the bridge.

This complacency is perhaps the most exasperating feature of the whole affair. Fourth Officer Boxhall did not even read the one message he saw. Third Officer Pitman saw the chit marked "ice" above the chart room table, but it failed to stir his interest—"I only looked at it casually." Fifth Officer Lowe also looked at the chit "casually," but once he saw the ship wouldn't reach the position during *his* watch, he put it out of his mind. Second Officer Lightoller never even saw the chit when he came on duty that last Sunday night, "because I did not look."

Strangest of all was an exchange between Lightoller and Sixth Officer Moody, who shared the watch from 8:00 to 10:00 P.M. Early on, Lightoller asked Moody when the ship would be up to the ice. Moody said about 11:00. Working it out for himself, Lightoller decided the time would really be closer to 9:30. But he never told Moody. Instead, he merely made a mental note of the Sixth Officer's lapse, as though Moody were an errant schoolboy who had made some minor mistake in math, not worth fussing over.

Later Lightoller said he thought that Moody's calculations might have been based on some other ice message that Lightoller himself hadn't seen, but this still doesn't explain his silence. Nor does it help that the collision did not occur until 11:40—well after the time even Moody expected ice. The incident remains a striking illustration of the complacency that seems to have affected the whole bridge.

Yet there was still ample opportunity to avoid disaster. Every officer on the bridge, from Captain Smith to the very junior Moody, knew that sometime before midnight the *Titanic* might encounter ice. It was with this thought in mind that the Captain left the Wideners' party shortly before 9:00 and joined Lightoller on the bridge.

The conversation was oddly laconic. As they peered into a black cloudless night, Smith remarked it was cold. Lightoller: "Yes, it is very cold, sir. In fact, it is only one degree above freezing." He described the precautions he was taking: a warning to the carpenter to watch his fresh water supply . . . another to the engine room to keep an eye on the steam winches.

Smith got back to the weather: "There is not much wind."

"No, it is a flat calm, as a matter of fact."

"A flat calm. Yes, quite flat."

Then, to the ice. Lightoller remarked that it was rather a pity the breeze didn't keep up while they were going through the danger area. Icebergs were so much easier to spot at night, if the wind stirred up some surf. But they decided that even if the berg "showed a blue side," they would have enough warning. At 9:25 the subject was exhausted and the Captain turned in: "If it becomes at all doubtful, let me know at once. I'll be just inside."

Not one word about slowing down. Why was this most obvious of all precautions not even mentioned? The usual answer is that Captain Smith thought the *Titanic* was unsinkable. But even if the ship were unsinkable, the Captain surely didn't want to hit an iceberg.

Actually, he didn't slow down because he was sure that on this brilliantly clear night any iceberg could be spotted in time to avoid it. In reaching that decision, Smith did not feel he was doing anything rash. He was following the practice of all captains on the Atlantic run, except for a few slowpokes like James Clayton Barr of the Cunarder *Caronia,* whose legendary caution at the slightest sign of haze had earned him the derisive nickname "Foggy."

Knuckling under the competitive pressure of keeping schedule, most captains ran at full steam, despite strong evidence that ice was not as easily sighted as generally claimed. Especially noteworthy was the harrowing ordeal of the Guion Liner *Arizona* in November 1879. Like the *Titanic,* she was the largest liner of her day. Eastbound off the Banks of Newfoundland, she raced through a night that was cloudy, but with good visibility. Taking advantage of the calm seas, the passengers gathered in the lounge for a concert.

Suddenly there was a fearful crash, sending everybody sprawling among the palms and violins. The *Arizona* had smashed head on into a giant iceberg, shattering 30 feet of her bow. But the forward bulkhead held; there were no casualties; and two days later she limped into St. John's. In a curious twist of logic, the accident was hailed as an example of the safety of ships, rather than the dangers of ice.

There were other close calls too. In 1907 the North German Lloyd Liner *Kronprinz Wilhelm* dented her bow and scarred her starboard side, brushing a berg in the pre-dawn darkness. In 1909 the immigrant ship *Volturno* barely escaped damage, running through a huge ice field. In 1911 the Anchor Liner *Columbia* struck a berg off Cape Race, driving her bow plates back ten feet. The jar injured several crewmen and broke one passenger's ankle. It was foggy at the time; so perhaps the accident was discounted.

Such incidents were ignored; most captains continued to run at full speed. Always dangerous, the practice became even more so with the vast leap in the size of ships at the turn of the century. It was one thing to dodge an iceberg in the 10,000-ton *Majestic,* Captain Smith's command in 1902, but quite a different matter only ten years later in the 46,000-ton *Titanic.* The momentum of such a huge ship was enormous, and she just couldn't stop suddenly or turn on a dime.

There's no record that the *Titanic* even tested her minimum turning circle during those brief trials in Belfast Lough. Nor did she ever test how long it would take to stop at various speeds, if her engines were reversed. In fact, she never went faster than 18 knots during her trials; her response to commands beyond that point remains a mystery. Once again the question arises: how much did Captain Smith really know about the great vessel under his feet?

Arguably, the practice of maintaining speed might have been a practical necessity in the days before wireless, for who knew where the ice really was? The sightings came from vessels reaching port several days later, and by that time the information was too stale to pinpoint the danger. But Signor Marconi's genius changed everything. The reports reaching the *Titanic* told exactly where the ice could be found, only hours away.

Why couldn't Captain Smith and his officers see the difference? Certainly they knew the importance of wireless in an emergency. The help summoned by the sinking liner *Republic* in 1909 proved that. But no one on the *Titanic's* bridge seemed to appreciate the value of wireless as a constant, continuous navigational aid. Basically, they still thought of it as a novelty—something that lay outside the normal running of the ship. It was a mindset tellingly illustrated by the way the wireless operators were carried on the roster of the crew. Phillips and Bride were not listed with the Deck Department; they came under the Victualling Department—like stewards and pastry chefs.

So the *Titanic* raced on through the starlit night of April 14. At 10 P.M. First Officer Murdoch arrived on the bridge to take over Second Officer Lightoller's watch. His first words: "It's pretty cold."

"Yes, it's freezing," answered Lightoller, and he added that the ship might be up around the ice any time now. The temperature was down to 32°, the water an even colder 31°. A warm bunk was clearly the place to be, and Lightoller quickly passed on what else the new watch needed to know: the carpenter and engine room had been told to watch their water, keep it from freezing . . . the crow's nest had been warned to keep a sharp lookout for ice, "especially small ice and growlers" . . . the Captain had left word to be called "if it becomes at all doubtful."

Lightoller later denied that the sudden cold had any significance. He pointed out that on the North Atlantic the temperature often took a nose dive without any icebergs in the area. Indeed this was true. The sharp drop in temperature did not necessarily mean ice, but it was also true that it *could* mean ice. It was, in short, one more signal calling for caution. After all, that was the whole point of taking the temperature of the water every two hours.

There's no evidence that either Lightoller or Murdoch saw it that way. The bitter cold and the reported ice remained two separate problems.

Lightoller had passed on all the information he could; so now he went off on his final rounds, while Murdoch pondered the empty night.

A few yards aft along the Boat Deck, First Wireless Operator Phillips dug into a stack of outgoing messages. His set had a range of only 400 miles during daylight, and the American traffic had piled up. Now at last he was in touch with Cape Race and was working off the backlog. Some were passenger messages for New York—arrival times, requests for hotel reservations, instructions to business associates. Others were being relayed for ships no longer in direct touch with the land.

At 11 P.M. the steamer *Californian* suddenly broke in: "I say, old man, we're stopped and surrounded by ice." She was so close that her signal almost blasted Phillips's ears off.

"Shut up, shut up," he shot back, "I'm busy. I'm working Cape Race." Then he went back to the outgoing pile—messages like this one relayed to a Los Angeles address from a passenger on the *Amerika:*

NO SEASICKNESS. ALL WELL.
NOTIFY ALL INTERESTED. POKER
BUSINESS GOOD.   AL.

In the crow's nest Lookouts Fleet and Lee peered into the dark. There was little conversation; they were keeping an extra-sharp lookout. At 11:40 Fleet suddenly spotted something even blacker than the night. He banged the crow'snest bell three times and lifted the phone to the bridge. Three words were enough to explain the trouble: "Iceberg right ahead."

Now it was Murdoch's problem. He put his helm hard astarboard, hoping to "port around" the ice, and at the same time pulled the engine room telegraph to STOP, and then REVERSE ENGINES. But it was too late: 37 seconds later the *Titanic* brushed by the berg with that faint, grinding jar that every student of the disaster knows so well.

The 37 seconds—based on tests later made with the *Olympic*—are significant only for what they reveal about human miscalculations. At 22½ knots the *Titanic* was moving at a rate of 38 feet a second . . . meaning that the berg had been sighted less than 500 yards away. But all the experts agreed that on a clear night like this the ice should have been seen much farther off. Lightoller thought at least a mile or so, and this undoubtedly reflected Captain Smith's opinion, for they both had gone over this very point on the bridge shortly after 9:00. The search immediately began for some extenuating circumstance that could explain the difference.

Suspicion focused first on the lookouts. How good were their eyes? Fleet's had not been tested in five years, and Lee's not since the Boer War. Yet tests after the collision showed both men had sound vision. Nor were they in-experienced. Unlike most lines, White Star used trained, full-time lookouts, who received extra pay for their work.

Next, it was the lookouts' turn to complain. They charged that there were no binoculars in the crow's nest. A pair had been supplied during the trip from Belfast to Southampton, but during a last-minute shake-up of personnel they had been removed and never replaced. After hearing numerous experts on the subject, the British Inquiry decided that it really didn't matter. Binoculars were useful in identifying objects, but not in initially sighting them. That was better done by the naked eye. Here, there was no problem of identification; Fleet knew all too well what he had seen.

Then Lookout Lee came up with a "haze" over the water. He de-scribed dramatically how Fleet had said to him, "Well, if we can see through that, we will be lucky." Fleet denied the conversation and said the haze was "nothing to talk about." Lightoller, Boxhall, and Quartermaster Hitchens, who had been at the wheel, all described the night as perfectly clear. In the end, the British Inquiry wrote off Lee's "haze" as an understandable bit of wishful thinking.

Lightoller himself contributed what became known as the "blue berg" theory. He argued that the iceberg had recently capsized and was showing only the dark side that had previously been under water, making it almost invisible. But this theory did not seem to fit the recollections of the few survivors who actually saw the berg. It was anything but invisible to Quartermaster Rowe, standing on the after bridge. He estimated that it was about 100 feet high, and he initially mistook it for a windjammer gliding along the side of the ship with all sails set.

The only explanation left was "fate." As Lightoller put it, the *Titanic* was the victim of an extraordinary set of circumstances that could only happen once in a hundred years. Normally there would have been no problem, but on this particularly freakish night "everything was against us."

But this explanation implies that Captain Smith didn't know—and couldn't be expected to know—the nature of the night he was up against. But he *did* know. He fully realized that the sea was flat calm, that there was no moon, no wind, no swell. He understood all this and took it into account in deciding not to reduce speed. Under these circumstances the collision quickly loses its supernatural quality and becomes simply a case of miscalculation.

Given the competitive pressures of the North Atlantic run, the chances taken, the lack of experience with ships of such immense size, the haphazard procedures of the wireless room, the casualness of the bridge, and the misassessment of what speed was safe, it's remarkable that the *Titanic* steamed for two hours and ten minutes through ice-infested waters without coming to grief any sooner.

"Everything was against us"? The wonder is that she lasted as long as she did.

What did the iceberg really do to the *Titanic,* and could anything have been done to save her? The report of the official British Inquiry found that "the damage extended over a length of about 300 feet," and this is generally taken to mean a continuous gash running from the bow for 300 feet along the starboard side of the ship. Countless illustrators have depicted it in books and magazines—a single, jagged slash, ugly and lethal-looking.

Actually, such a gash would have sunk the *Titanic* in less than an hour. The true nature of the damage may be partly revealed as exploration of the wreck continues over the coming years, but it will often be hard to tell what was done by the iceberg and what was caused by the avalanche of boilers that hurtled down and out of the hull during the *Titanic's* final plunge. Some of the damage may also be buried in the mud and sand where the vessel lies, hidden from the roaming eye of any video camera. Even the most sophisticated equipment will probably tell us less than a little-known witness at the British Inquiry, who was nowhere near the *Titanic* that night, but who knew her far better than any survivor or future investigator.

Edward Wilding was a naval architect at Harland & Wolff. His primary concern had been the design of the *Titanic,* and he seemed to have at his fingertips every conceivable dimension of the ship. He knew, for instance, the exact length of each watertight compartment. Using these figures, he estimated that the gash along the starboard side must have run some 249 feet—the length of the first five compartments plus the first two feet of the sixth.

Estimating the width of the gash was more complicated, but he found some clues in the testimony of various witnesses who had been on the spot. Ten minutes after the crash, Leading Fireman Fred Barrett saw eight feet of water in Boiler Room 6, which was five feet above the keel of the ship. Ten minutes later, Third Officer Pitman watched bags of registered letters floating around the mail room, 24 feet above the keel. Another five minutes and the squash court was awash, 32 feet above the keel. Fifteen minutes more, and the sea was flooding into the seamen's quarters on E Deck forward, 48 feet above the keel. Putting the evidence together, Edward Wilding estimated that 16,000 cubic feet of water had entered the shattered hull in the first 40 minutes.

What size hole would produce this result? Here Wilding's educated guess had to be built on certain basic assumptions. First, he assumed that the witnesses were accurate in their estimates of time and the depth of the water at their particular vantage point. He also assumed that the draft of the *Titanic* would be the same as that of the *Olympic* at the same stage in the voyage. All this granted, he then calculated that the area of damage had to be 12 square feet. Anything else would not fit his timetable.

But this posed a new problem. If the damage was really a continuous gash 249 feet long, then it could only have averaged 3/4 of an inch high. Nothing else would work out at 12 square feet. Since this was most unlikely, it followed that the gash was not continuous, but rather a series of separate pokes and stabs as the berg bumped along the side of the *Titanic*. Some of these stabs were great rents like the hole in No. 1 hold, where the berg penetrated 3½ feet inside the ship, ripping the protective casing of the firemen's spiral stairs. Other times the ice barely pierced the hull, like the hole in Boiler Room 5, which spouted a stream as thin as a deck hose. Occasionally, bits of the berg broke off as it brushed by, making the pattern of holes still more irregular.

Whatever the nature of the wound, there was no doubt that it was fatal. It completely flooded the first five compartments, pulling the bow down so far that the water in the fifth compartment eventually slopped over the top of the after bulkhead into the sixth, which in turn overflowed into the seventh, and so on until the ship had to sink.

Later, much was made of the fact that the watertight bulkhead between the fifth and sixth compartments went only as high as E Deck. If this bulkhead had been carried one deck higher, to D Deck, the *Titanic* would not have sunk. This is true, assuming that the only damage to the sixth compartment came from the two-foot gash in Boiler Room 5. This was easily controlled by the pumps.

But this was not the only damage to the sixth compartment. As Edward Wilding pointed out, the gash that ran from Boiler Room 6 into Boiler Room 5 couldn't help but hurt the bulkhead that stood in between. Unlike the gash, this wound was not readily visible to the firemen and engineers, but it was there all the same, and about an hour after the collision the whole bulkhead seems to have given way. From somewhere forward, a great rush of water surged into Boiler Room 5, driving out the men still on duty there.

Nor was that all. There's important, often-overlooked evidence that the next compartment aft, Boiler Room 4, suffered damage entirely independent of the gash. Initially, there was no sign of damage here, but an hour and 40 minutes after the crash, water began seeping over the floor plates from somewhere below. The flow was gradual, but more than the pumps could handle. For a while the firemen toiled on, still shutting down the boilers. The water was up to their knees when the welcome word finally came from the engineer room, releasing them from duty. They quickly scrambled up the escape ladders to the temporary safety of the Boat Deck.

It must be emphasized that this water came from below, not above. The flooding of Boiler Room 4 was not part of the process of the forward compartments filling and overflowing into the next compartment aft. Rather, it came from a separate injury to the ship, probably to the double bottom, entirely apart from the familiar gash along the starboard side. In short, the ice did even more mischief than generally thought.

The water in this compartment should also end all theorizing about what might have happened if the bulkheads had been carried one deck higher. With Boiler Room 4 gone, the ship was doomed no matter how high the bulkheads might have been carried. At best, the sinking might have been delayed—perhaps until help came—but the ultimate loss of the *Titanic* was certain.

There's no evidence of damage any farther aft than Boiler Room 4, and this poses an intriguing mystery. If, as the British Inquiry said, the *Titanic's* bow was just beginning to swing to port when the collision occurred, then the stern would have tended to slue to starboard—toward the ice, rather than away from it. This should have led to some sort of contact with the berg along the whole length of the hull.

What caused the opposite to happen and the stern apparently swing clear of the berg? One explanation might lie in the exchange between Captain Smith and First Officer Murdoch, when the Captain rushed from his quarters onto the bridge immediately after the impact.

"What have we struck?" asked Smith.

"An iceberg, sir," replied Murdoch, "I hard-astarboarded and reversed the engines, and I was going to hard-aport around it, but she was too close. I could not do any more."

Murdoch's explanation has confused many an armchair navigator. It may help to point out that in 1912 a ship's wheel was rigged so that the helmsman turned it to starboard in order to go to port—a holdover from the days when ships were steered by tillers. In 1924 the wheel was re-rigged to cater to the instincts of a generation raised on the automobile, but everyone on the *Titanic's* bridge would have been used to the old way.

At least two survivors gave testimony indicating that Murdoch did indeed try to "port around" the berg. Quartermaster Alfred Olliver, coming on the bridge right after the collision, said he definitely heard orders to put the helm hard aport. About the same time Able Seaman Joseph Scarrott, alarmed by the jar, rushed out of the forecastle onto the forward well deck in time to see the berg still passing alongside the ship. The *Titanic* at that moment seemed to be under port helm, her stern gliding away from the ice.

Scarrott undoubtedly reported what he thought he saw, but his account seems highly implausible. It would have been impossible for a ship the size of the *Titanic* to have responded to a change in helm so quickly. A motorboat yes; a 46,000-ton liner, no. Moreover, there's strong evidence that Murdoch never did actually try to carry out his plan. He intended to "port around" the berg, but abandoned the idea when he saw "she was too close." Quartermaster Hitchens, at the helm, testified that the last order he received was "hard-astarboard." Fourth Officer Boxhall, approaching the bridge just before the crash, heard only the same order, followed by the ringing of engine room telegraph bells. Reaching the bridge seconds later, he noted that the telegraph was set at FULL SPEED ASTERN—which made no sense if Murdoch still intended to dodge the ice.

Then why *did* the afterpart of the *Titanic* escape damage? Perhaps the answer lies with the other protagonist in the drama. Much has been said about what the iceberg did to the *Titanic,* but very little about what the *Titanic* did to the iceberg. It is generally pictured as a great natural force, impervious to the assault of mere man, yet we do know that the jar sent chunks of ice tumbling down onto the forward well deck of the ship. Edward Wilding, for one, thought that the same process was going on beneath the surface of the sea as the berg brushed by. If so, it seems reasonable that a large enough chunk may have broken off to end all further contact with the hull.

The first moments after the collision are among the most difficult to sort out. A series of rapidly changing orders jangled from the bridge to the engine room, but none of the surviving witnesses agreed on the exact sequence, the timing, or even the purpose. Greaser Fred Scott testified that immediately after the collision, the engine room telegraph bells rang STOP ENGINES . . . then, 10 or 15 minutes later, SLOW AHEAD . . . another 10 minutes and again, STOP ENGINES . . . then 4 or 5 minutes and SLOW ASTERN . . . 5 more minutes and once again, STOP ENGINES. This time they stopped for good.

Trimmer Patrick Dillon, the only other survivor from the engine room, thought that the signal STOP ENGINES came immediately *before* the crash, that SLOW ASTERN came *before* SLOW AHEAD, and that the time intervals were much shorter—for instance, the ship went SLOW AHEAD for only two minutes, not ten. Neither man remembered the engines being set at

FULL SPEED ASTERN, as recalled so clearly by Fourth Officer Boxhall on the bridge.

It is fruitless to turn to the bridge for clarification. Captain Smith, First Officer Murdoch, and Sixth Officer Moody were all lost; Fourth Officer Boxhall was off making a quick inspection. Quartermaster Hitchens was in the wheelhouse unable to see anything; Quartermaster Olliver was running errands most of the time. Olliver does remember the Captain telegraphing HALF SPEED AHEAD sometime during the interval when the *Titanic* lay almost dead in the water.

Many passengers, too, recall the ship starting ahead again, mostly because it seemed so comforting. Second Class passenger Lawrence Beesley, for instance, took a couple of jittery ladies into a bathroom on D Deck and had them touch the tub, where the vibration of the engines was always noticeable. Reassured, the ladies went back to their cabin.

Why the *Titanic* started ahead again, how long and how fast she went, and which direction she took are all intriguing mysteries, important in fixing her correct position when she began calling for help. It has been suggested that Captain Smith was making for the light of another ship on the horizon, but this seems unlikely for two reasons. First, there's no evidence that such a light had yet been sighted; and second, Captain Smith had no reason yet to suspect that his ship had been seriously injured. In fact, Fourth Officer Boxhall's first, quick inspection (as far down and forward in the passengers' quarters as he could go) brought the good news that he could find no damage at all.

The bad news came soon enough—from the carpenter, from Holds 1, 2, and 3, from the firemen's quarters, from the mail room, from Boiler Rooms 5 and 6. If Smith still had any hope, it was dispelled by the arrival of Thomas Andrews on the bridge. As Managing Director of Harland & Wolff, Andrews knew the ship more intimately than anyone else on board. He gave the *Titanic* "from an hour to an hour and a half."

Could anything have been done to save her? It's a favorite subject for letter-writers, and over the years suggestions have ranged from stuffing the gash with bedding to a headlong run for the light that glimmered most of the night on the horizon.

No amount of bedding could have stemmed the torrent pouring into the *Titanic*, but the possibility of using collision mats was at least considered by the British Inquiry. After a brief discussion, Edward Wilding rejected the idea on two grounds: first, it was impossible to fix the exact location of the various holes to be plugged; and second, 50 to 60 men would have been needed to rig collision mats, and they couldn't possibly be organized and deployed before it was too late to do any good.

Steaming for the light can be ruled out too, because it was not sighted soon enough. The light was first seen a few minutes after midnight, and by that time the funnels were blowing off great clouds of steam—a sure sign that the boilers had shut down for good. Even if the light had been sighted sooner, it's highly doubtful that the *Titanic's* shattered hull could have stood the strain of the dash.

Others contend that the watertight doors should have been reopened once the extent of the damage was known. This would have allowed the water to spread gradually throughout the hull, and the ship would have settled on an even keel. This way, the *Titanic* would have taken longer to sink than she actually took going down by the head. The British Inquiry agreed, but did not press the point. The damage was so overwhelming, it made little difference whether the doors were left open or shut.

Actually, there seemed to be only one moment when the *Titanic* really might have been saved, and that came at the very start of the crisis, when Lookout Fleet reported the iceberg to the bridge. If First Officer Murdoch had steamed right at the berg instead of trying to miss it, he might have saved the ship. There would have been a fearful crash—passengers and crew in the first 100 feet would have been killed by the impact—but the *Titanic* would have remained afloat.

It would have been like the *Arizona,* 33 years earlier. Tumbling out on deck, her passengers found her crumpled bow pressed against the ice. Fearing the end, they clung to each other in tears. Yet it was not the end, and when they finally realized that the *Arizona's* collision bulkhead would hold, they joined in a prayer of thanks and sang the hymn "Praise God from Whom All Blessings Flow."

The *Titanic* was not the *Arizona.* She hit the berg a glancing blow, not head on; but Murdoch could not be blamed for trying to miss it. He did what he had been trained to do—what any prudent officer would do—in the same circumstances. His great misfortune was that, in his own succinct words, "she was too close."

Now that it had happened, there was only one course left open for Captain Smith. It was almost exactly midnight—the 12:00 to 4:00 watch was just coming on deck in a last display of normal shipboard routine—when he gave the order to take to the boats.

The Last Voyage of the Lusitania

BY A. A. HOEHLING AND MARY HOEHLING

On May 1, 1915, an advertisement placed by the "Imperial German Govern-ment" in New York newspapers warned travelers to Europe that they were en-tering a war zone and were in jeopardy:

Travelers intending to embark on the Atlantic voyage are reminded that a state of war exists between Germany and her allies and Great Britain and her allies; that the zone of war includes the waters adjacent to the British Isles; that in accordance with formal notice given by the Imperial German Government, vessels flying the flag of Great Britain, or any of her allies, are liable to destruction in these waters and the trav-elers sailing in the war zone of ships of Great Britain or her allies do so at their own risk.

The Germans meant what they said. On May 7, when Britain's mag-nificent Cunard ocean liner Lusitania was eleven miles from the coast of Ire-land, the ship was torpedoed by submarine U-20. The death toll was 1,201 people, including 94 children under 12, 35 of whom were babies. One baby that perished was actually born as its mother floundered in the water. After tor-pedoing the ship, the German captain watched the helpless victims for an hour.

The story of the Lusitania is so gripping and tragic that it has attracted the interest of many excellent writers, whose books have been critically ac-claimed and widely read. Although new accounts of the sinking continue to be published, one of my favorites is the source of this excerpt—*The Last Voyage of the Lusitania* by A.A. Hoehling and Mary Hoehling, first published by Holt in 1956.

This portion of the Hoehlings' stirring book recreates the desperate plight of the passengers and crew after the torpedo had done its deadly work.

✳   ✳   ✳   ✳   ✳

lorence Padley emerged from the stair onto the boat deck to hear the staff captain calling:

"It's all right. We're making for the shore."

Land did not seem that reassuringly close to her, but neither did the chances of getting away in a lifeboat, though she saw others leaving the ship safely. Finally she saw one boat with only a few people in it, and started toward it.

When the torpedo struck, Professor Holbourn had thought of lifebelts at once. Finding none on deck, he took his twelve-year-old friend Avis Dolphin to his cabin corridor. Little Avis was feeling somewhat like Dorothy in the new *Oz* book, whose familiar and secure world had been sent topsy-turvy by a cyclone.

The professor's cabin was a mess. Such articles as his toothbrush, razor, and lotions rolled about the floor. Wide-open wardrobe doors revealed suits that hung crazily out into the room. His broad-brimmed black hat had sailed off the closet shelf and lodged itself in the corner behind the door.

Worst of all, the porthole was no longer reassuringly divided, like a well-sliced pie, into equal parts of sea and sky. It was all bright blue, motionless.

Holbourn had to pull himself up the sloping deck by grabbing first at the bed, then the wardrobe door, to which he clung with one hand as he groped on the shelf for the belts. He was afraid the wardrobe would topple over on him.

Finally he skidded back into the corridor and fastened a belt on Avis. Carrying two extras back to the deck, he and Avis met her traveling companions. One, Miss Smith, refused Holbourn's offer of a belt, reminding him that he had a wife and three children dependent on him. So he tied it on himself, under protest, as the group went in search of a boat.

Holbourn put Avis in a lifeboat as it was being swung out, then was momentarily distracted by the sight of two men, stripped naked, diving off the boat deck. They struck out toward a boat that was floating, smashed, on the water. Holbourn was amazed to see how quickly the pair were swept astern, and he deduced that the *Lusitania* was still traveling at a considerable speed.

He continued around the decks, offering lifebelts to some of Avis' friends and helping them into boats. Since he was a champion swimmer himself, he resolved he would go forward and swim for it, without trusting to the boats or the way some were being lowered.

By now Herbert Ehrhardt had reunited the girl's brother with his family. He realized from the difficulty of walking that the list was increasing more and more rapidly and that the *Lusitania* would sink before all the lifeboats were launched. It was then he "became frightened."

When the deck began to slope, he had to sit to prevent himself from losing his balance. Others were sliding down the deck all the way to the railings. Ehrhardt became still more alarmed and wondered whether he would be able to avoid bumping into people and hurting them if he slipped. As he noticed the bow awash, which caused a "tremendous turmoil in the water" it occurred to him that it might really be impossible for anyone to swim in the vortex.

This "turmoil" in the seas and the growing litter of deck chairs, empty lifeboats, and other menacing debris being tossed about, made him realize that he might be experiencing his last few seconds of life. He began to roll himself over as he slipped down the deck, hoping thus to avoid bumping anyone below him and wondering whether he would hit the rails or the water first. He remembered saying to himself:

"I'm better off than most of these as I've nobody dependent on me."

And then he started a silent, personal prayer for his fiancée and his mother.

Archie Donald was watching a fireman who poised momentarily on the rail before taking an almost professional dive into the water. Its grace, to Donald, seemed to have no fitting place in this holocaust.

Then he heard the sound of a boat running through davits and looked in time to see it smash to pieces in the water. He figured that the ropes must have been too short. He saw several people bobbing around in the water.

The fireman who had taken the beautiful dive swam until he reached the stern of the ship, then disappeared from view. Inspired by the fireman's performance, Donald decided that the "best policy" was to leave the ship, fast. When he saw an empty beer box with two handles, it occurred to him that here was a made-to-order life preserver.

First he deliberately removed his wrist watch so it would not get wet. Then, taking his pocket watch from his coat, he carefully placed both in his left-hand trouser pocket. Next he stripped off his coat.

Holding the beer case with a fierce grip, Donald started to climb the stairs to the next deck. He encountered Dr. R. J. R. Mecredy, of Dublin, whom he knew slightly, coming hand over hand down the outside of the companion-way. The young Irish physician was wearing a lifebelt and carrying another in his hand.

"Where did you get the lifebelts?" Archie Donald asked, almost in surprise.

"Down in the cabins," Dr. Mecredy answered, explaining that he had first queued up before a deck storage locker, but the supply of lifebelts had run out. He reported also that the water had been pouring through the porthole in his cabin.

Archie had not thought about belts, but luckily discovered he was on the port side of the same deck on which his cabin was situated. He noticed that a door, battened the entire voyage, had been opened. He ran through it and down the lightless passage and into his cabin. The list was so bad that he found walking extremely difficult.

He felt around in the locker and on one side of the dark cabin, and realized the belts were missing. They were gone from the other side too. He groped through the litter of the cabin that had been his home for six days until he finally found one last remaining belt. It occurred to him that if the list became worse, he might soon be walking on the walls—a thought shocking to his sense of proportion.

Archie left his cabin and continued on the port side up to the boat deck. There he saw a sight going virtually unnoticed by the other passengers. Norman Stone, of Vancouver, a veteran of General Pershing's expedition after Pancho Villa on the Mexican border, was methodically tearing all the clothing from his wife.

In the brilliant sunshine, and with the privacy of Times Square, Stone did not desist until Mrs. Stone, unprotesting, was stripped down to her stockings. Then he fastened her lifebelt securely around her, lessening to some degree her nakedness.

Donald, preoccupied as the others with his own salvation, was impressed simply with the fact that Stone "seemed to know exactly what to do." Now Stone started ripping the canvas off a nearby collapsible boat, something which the men thought should have been done long before. Archie helped him.

As he was on the port side, he noticed how terribly high the deck was above the water. He watched some people get into a lifeboat, heard its bumping-scraping descent over the plates and rivets of the sloping side. He didn't see how it could ever reach the water intact.

Archie wondered why he was not frightened. His thoughts came with a clarity that surprised him.

He decided to cross "downhill" to the First Class portion. There, he helped load a boat, fending off a group of grimy, frantic stokers who were crowding toward it.

"The women must be put in first!" he shouted. Other men joined with him in keeping the "black gang" off.

Finally, when about twenty women were in the boat, the men standing on the deck of the *Lusitania* began to lower away. This boat was lowered too fast by the forward fall, while the aft one seemed to stick in the block. Someone cut the ropes which were retarding the operation, but it was too late. Everyone had been dumped into the sea.

Donald watched the boat's passengers struggle onto a rope netting attached to a lower deck, and climb higher as the water reached them. He recognized one of them—May Bird, a stewardess. It seemed strange to see her hair streaming all over her face, her usually starched uniform clinging soddenly like wet laundry.

As he shifted his gaze back to those still on deck, he noticed Elbert Hubbard and his wife Alice. Although he had never met them, he knew at once who they were. They looked "very gray-haired" and were holding hands. He heard them refuse to be helped into a boat.

It was the same with Elbert Hubbard who, in his writings, had philosophized, "We are here now, some day we shall go. And when we go we would like to go gracefully."

Nearby was Timmins, from Texas, surrounded by a group of steerage passengers, a number of whom seemed to be Russians. While Timmins could not recognize their gabbling, he was trying to reassure them. He held up a hand, nodded his head and repeated:

"All right, all right!"

They appeared to understand. One kissed his hand. He forgot what was happening to the ship in his momentary amazement at having his hand kissed.

Timmins, like Lady Mackworth, had heard the order to empty the boats, and the assurances the ship was "safe." He did not share the optimism, although he also noticed the *Lusitania* right herself. His friend Moodie, beside him, asked:

"How about it, old man?"

Timmins shook his head. He believed the liner was even then "gone." He figured the water had surged over her longitudinal bulkheads, which would indicate that ocean was pouring in at a terrific rate. He decided against communicating his gloomy conclusions to the steerage passengers.

All the way aft on the promenade deck, Able Seaman Thomas Mahoney, who had spotted a "suspicious" object about half an hour before, was trying to help six terrified men and women down from a curious refuge. They were all perched on the awning above the veranda café, struggling to climb to the deck below.

"Get on my shoulders!" he instructed them. His height made this a very probable solution to their dilemma.

But while they were trying to obey, the awning spars broke and all six fell in a heap on top of him.

Close by, oblivious to all else, a frightened passenger, Mrs. Stewart Mason, was seeking help.

"Where's my husband?" wailed the dark-haired young bride from Boston. The tears welled in her eyes.

Oliver P. Bernard was doing his best to comfort her.

"It's all right now, we go ashore directly, so don't worry," he said.

Leslie Mason kept staring at Bernard "like one demented," as she asked, "Where's my husband?" Bernard had known her father, William Lindsey, in Boston. Now he took the girl by the shoulders and shook her.

"Stay right here," he said. "Don't move from this spot and your husband will find you here, surely, as they will be lowering the boats from this side. I'll find some lifebelts in case we need them." He told her to pull herself together.

With something to do, Bernard acquired a determination that salved his own fears. As he hurried below he kept thinking of the torpedo wake streaking toward the *Lusitania,* striking it with "a slight shock as if a tug had run into the enormous hull." He had been especially concerned about the glass roofs of the dining saloon, the lounge, and veranda café—the splinters could be as deadly as shrapnel.

As he was about to enter First Class quarters through one of the saloon doors, Bernard almost ran into Alfred Gwynne Vanderbilt. Bareheaded, dressed in a dark pinstripe suit, he was holding what looked like a lady's large jewel case. Vanderbilt appeared to the scenic artist as though he were waiting "for the next race at Ascot."

He grinned at Bernard "as if amused by the excitement." Bernard had been thinking about the multimillionaire just before the torpedo struck—"a man with nothing better to do than drive a four-in-hand to Brighton and come three thousand miles to do it."

America, Bernard believed, was "lousy with idle rich." He disliked the very wealthy with an intensity more deeply rooted than a mere distaste for their money, ostentation, yachts, and "homes like royal brothels."

The strange spectacle of existence often preyed on the thoughtful artist's mind. This morning, considering himself in the third person as was his custom, he put it this way, "If only he could believe in God, if he could only believe in life as eternal, instead of nursing a despairing conviction that life was not really worth living, that the end of all life lay in the dust, with men and women, dogs and fleas sharing the same fate as blades of grass—flourishing for a moment and then trodden into oblivion."

Bernard could not forget Vanderbilt's grin. He himself was not amused as he ran downstairs to B Deck. Preoccupied, he forgot to allow for the list. He crashed "painfully" at the bottom of the stairs, then picked himself up and limped on.

All lights were out, the passage smoky and in darkness. It was deserted. He fell several times. Once he rolled down a side passage for a few feet before he could stop. Somehow he arrived at the Masons' cabin and called:

"Stewart!"

There was no answer from the darkened, littered stateroom and so he went on. He located his own cabin readily because it was at the extreme end of the passage. He knew his lifebelt was stowed on top of the wardrobe. As he felt for it, the heavy cabinet leaned over, and he had the momentary horror that he would drown "like a rat" in the darkness.

He climbed on the berth and worked from the side of the wardrobe, finally dragging his lifebelt out. There were stairs at this end of the passage which he used to return to deck, wondering why he had not thought of them before. He found Leslie Mason had gone.

A woman spied him holding his lifebelt and screamed, "Where did you get that, where did you get it?"

He allowed her to snatch it, then continued around the decks to see what had become of the Masons. Many boats had already gone, but the deck remained crowded with people "frantic" to follow.

A stoker reeled by "as if drunk." His face was a scarlet smear and the crown of his head had been opened up like a "spongy bloody pudding." It made Bernard wonder how many others had been maimed or killed outright by the explosion. He thought of the nursery, the women in their cabins with babies they could not leave.

Now it occurred to Bernard there might not be enough boats for everyone, nor was he sure he wanted to leave on a lifeboat, considering the way some of them were handled. He'd seen at least one dump its human cargo into the water. In one of them was a girl whom a young man had persuaded to step into it.

Bernard climbed above the boat deck and onto the more narrow Marconi deck. From there he could look down upon the terrifying spectacle with almost Olympian detachment.

The strains of the "Blue Danube," which he had heard at lunch, throbbed in his brain. And he could still smell the distinctive "foody" aroma from the dining saloon. But the only question in his mind was how soon would the *Lusitania* sink?

Some distance out he spied a man swimming on his back. He was naked and paddling gently, smiling up at the ship. And that started Bernard thinking. He stood up and removed some of his clothes, first his coat, vest, collar, and necktie. He put his tiepin in his trouser pocket and then folded the clothes neatly and placed them at the base of the broad, towering funnel. It occurred to him that this following of habit was now preposterous.

With a half-weary resignation, he thought of the futility of life. He seemed to be engulfed in an "awful sadness" and thought that no matter "what fuss he'd made about life," the whole existence amounted to just nothing. His struggles and "petty attainments" were trifles which would be quickly wiped out.

He sighed and started to untie his boots.

In one tiny segment of the spectacle Bernard was watching stood Elizabeth Duckworth. Elizabeth was having trouble finding a boat, as well as maintaining her balance. Fleetingly she thought of all her meager possessions tucked in big, bulging straw suitcases, and despaired of ever seeing them again.

The mate who had picked her up after she stumbled now helped her into another lifeboat. Someone yelled as she stepped on the person's leg. The rollers wouldn't work and the sailors seemed to be having so much trouble launching it that Elizabeth gathered up her skirts and stepped out onto the sloping deck again. Mrs. Alice Scott, little Arthur's mother, was in this boat.

It was finally launched, while the weaver from Taftville stood on the deck. It went over, spewing its people into the water and against the sides of the ship, which kept plowing ahead as though it never would stop.

Elizabeth watched, horrified as Alice Scott disappeared beneath the churning green waters, heard the others cry out in terror. Alice never came up.

Now Elizabeth started to pray under her breath. "The Lord is my shepherd, therefore can I lack nothing. He shall feed me in a green pasture, and lead me beside the waters of comfort. He shall convert my soul and bring me forth in the paths of righteousness for his Name's sake. Yea, though I walk through the valley of the shadow of death, I will fear no evil . . ."

Next to her three Irish girls were singing, "There Is a Green Hill Not Far Away." They had been humming it gaily before the torpedo struck. Now they sang in cold, choking fright.

In the radio shack Marconi Operator Leith, sweating, too busy to loosen his collar, kept tapping his mariner's requiem:

Come at once. Big list. Ten miles south Old Head Kinsale.

He had to hold onto his table and the transmitter panel to steady himself against the increasing list. He prayed that his message was being received. Above him the clock read 2:20 P.M.

Charles Lauriat returned on deck wearing one lifebelt, carrying others over his arm. He went directly to the port side where he had left the Hubbards. They were gone.

He walked aft, offering his belts to those who needed them. Amazed to note that "about everyone" wore his or her lifebelt incorrectly, he busied himself readjusting them. He kept on the port side, the high one.

Lauriat paused in his work with the lifebelts long enough to walk forward again to where he had last seen the Fra and Alice. He went back more than a dozen times, in utter disbelief that the couple could have vanished so completely. He stopped Mrs. Padley, who said she had seen the Hubbards standing under a funnel.

Once a woman beside him called toward the bridge:

"Captain, what do you wish us to do?"

"Stay right where you are, Madam, she's all right," the Boston bookseller heard Captain Turner answer.

"Where do you get your information?" she persisted.

"From the engine room, Madam," Turner said. To Lauriat he sounded "severe and commanding."

The woman started aft and Lauriat fell in step with her. They tried to reassure the passengers, even though he was certain the liner's end could be measured in minutes. An Italian family, comprised of a grandmother, mother, and three children, "beseeched," him in their own tongue, for aid.

Lauriat returned to his cabin for a few personal possessions that he wanted with him even if he was to perish. This time he descended the same forward companionway Bernard had used, because the main companionway was crowded with people pushing upward.

He groped his way to his cabin through the dark, tilted passageways. Buy the flickering light of a match he searched quickly through the jumble while the *Lusitania* groaned and rumbled ominously then swayed over still farther.

With his passport and other papers stuffed in his pockets, he left his stateroom and moved back through the passage; one foot on the bulkhead, one on the deck. As he glanced down access passageways which ended with port-holes, he saw that the portholes were open. The water could not have been more than a few feet below them. He wondered why these ports had not been closed. He continued on.

When he passed the First Class lounge he noticed that the chairs had fallen over. A few were upturned, with legs straight in the air like dead, rigid horses. The painting over the marble-mantled fireplace hung askew, while the velvet window drapes hung halfway out into the lounge like starched collars strangely out of shape.

On deck, he sped a boat, filled with women and children, hanging se-curely to its davits. If it were not freed at once, the *Lusitania* would drag it down with her if she sank.

Lauriat jumped into the stern, then realized it was already afloat—the water was flush with the rail of B Deck! The sinking had gained that much momentum in the last few minutes. He freed one end, as a steward at the other hacked futilely at the thick ropes with a pocket knife.

Lauriat started forward but could make no progress over the obstruct-ing maze of oars, boat hooks, kegs of water, "and God knows what."

As the *Lusitania* continued to tilt farther, her funnels overhung the lifeboat with increasing menace. The people looked up at the four monstrous black and red specters, and blanched anew in terror. Some covered their eyes. Lauriat, caught by the swinging aft davit, was knocked into the sprawling, clawing mass of people in the bottom of the boat. He could feel a chill of panic as he struggled to an upright position and advised the others to jump for it.

"It's your only chance!"

Lauriat went into the 50-degree waters of the Atlantic, pushing several people ahead of him. In the water he urged them to put their hands on each others' shoulders to keep in a group. When he had swum about a hundred feet from the ship he blinked the cold salt water from his eyes and looked back.

The decks of the big Cunarder were still filled with people, bunched together and hanging onto stationary objects to keep their balance. As the water inched up they released their holds and clawed for upper parts of stanchions.

Many clung to the forlorn hope that they still should stay with the ship. The Charles A. Plamondons were of this desperate turn of mind. Edward Skay, a steward, spied them together on the promenade deck, refusing his en-treaties to try for a lifeboat.

One lady told Olive North that she thought she would go into her cabin and at least meet her fate in comfort. She urged Olive to keep her company.

"No, I will make a fight for my life," the English girl replied.

Olive encountered another woman cheerily packing and rearranging her suitcase in magnificent unconcern, as though the ship were now at the very mouth of the Mersey River, approaching Liverpool.

James Brooks helped all sixty of his adopted lady charges into their boat. But the *Lusitania* was listing farther as her decks became almost flush with the surface of the sea. It was hard to free the lifeboats, not from their rope falls and blocks, but from the chains that secured them to the davits. The difficulty was in loosening the clamps that disconnected the chains.

Before the boat with the sixty women could be launched, the boat's keel was afloat. The nearing waters pushed the lifeboat against the davits with a sickening crunch of wood. Most of the women were spilled into the sea.

Brooks knew it was time to go overboard. He had been watching the gathering scum of wooden debris which now was surfacing the sea for hundreds of square yards around the ship. He had no idea where it had all come from or how it had littered the water so quickly. But it made him think of the log-filled Androscoggin at home where, even before he knew much about swimming, he kept himself afloat by hanging onto timbers.

Without bothering to remove his shoes, he jumped into the sea. It did not feel any colder than the Androscoggin; in fact he thought it was "mild."

On the ship, Dr. Mecredy was patiently awaiting his chance for a line down which people were sliding directly into the water. They were making neat, regular little splashes. It seemed a climax consistent with what he considered a disorganized abandoning of the ship, where from the time of torpedoing "everything was quite chaotic."

His descent did not serve to better his opinion. It turned out that the rope was the log line (trailed out astern for recording the ship's run) and made of wire after the first six feet. It was a "very uncomfortable getaway" and he lost considerable skin from his fingers by the time he was in the water. With salt stinging the raw flesh, he struck out for a boat, overloaded though it appeared.

Not far away, the *U-20* was hushed in a silence almost sepulchral, except for the muffled whirr of electric motors. Kapitanleutnant Schwieger was noting in his log:

She has the appearance of being about to capsize.
Great confusion on board, boats being cleared and some of them lowered to the water. They must have lost their heads. Many boats crowded come down bow first or stern first in the water and immediately fill and sink. Fewer lifeboats can be made clear owing to the slant of the boat [the *Lusitania*]. The

ship blows off, in front appears the name *Lusitania* in gold letters. The stacks were painted black, no stern flag was up. She was running at a speed of twenty sea miles . . .

On the ship the remaining male passengers were making desperate, last-minute attempts to round up the children. They had seen a number being put in lifeboats, but feared many more were trapped belowdecks.

Father Basil Maturin, "pale but calm," administered absolutions to several people, then was seen handing a child into a lifeboat.

Lindon W. Bates, New York political leader crossing in connection with Belgian relief, kept dashing inside the tilting black passageways until the water rose to deck level and he could no longer go below. Then he grabbed a chair for a life preserver and ran astern. He had already seen two from his group, Marie de Page and Dr. Houghton, jump into the water. They had held on to one another.

Commander Stackhouse, explorer and organizer of the great forthcoming Antarctic expedition aboard the ship *Discovery,* was on deck with Lieutenant Frederick Lasseter, of the "King's Own Light Infantry." Stackhouse told the younger man to look for his mother.

When both Lasseters returned, wearing lifebelts, they saw Stackhouse fasten his own belt on a little girl.

"You better jump," Stackhouse advised. Lasseter, wounded in the September fighting in Flanders, decided to follow the advice. He took one last look at Stackhouse assisting women into a boat, and heard him explaining why he could not join them: "There are others who must go first."

The Lasseters jumped.

Second Steward Robert Chisholm passed Vanderbilt on B Deck "vainly attempting to rescue a hysterical woman."

"Hurry Mr. Vanderbilt, or it will be too late!" Chisholm shouted.

Vanderbilt did not heed the steward. As a matter-of-fact, one skill in particular had never been mastered by this otherwise athletic young man—he couldn't swim a stroke.

A twenty-five-year-old baby's nurse from Seattle, Alice Middleton, thought she recognized Vanderbilt as her benefactor as she accepted an offer of a lifebelt. He helped her put it on.

Others heard him telling Ronald Denyer, his valet: "Find all the kiddies you can, boy!"

Not far away on the same deck, Charles Frohman, a cigar in his mouth, was a study in calm to the trio around him. The trio included his pretty actress friend, Rita Jolivet, her brother-in-law, George Vernon and Captain A. J. Scott, an English soldier en route from India via the United States.

"Stay where you are," he had advised. "This is going to be a close call. We shall have more chance here than by rushing for the boats."

They stood arm-in-arm. Finally, forcing Frohman to put on a lifebelt, Scott unfastened his own lifebelt saying, "If you must die, it is only for once."

The producer seemed concerned primarily for the safety of the young actress. He kept looking at her and at one point warned:

"You had better hold onto the rail and save your strength." In a few moments he removed the belt the English soldier had given him and made him assist a hysterical woman into it. As the water rose closer, Frohman remarked with a smile,

"'Why fear death? It is the most beautiful adventure in life.'"

Rita recognized the quote from *Peter Pan,* by C. F.'s friend and favorite author, James Barrie. But this was no stage set. She knew they were going to have to swim for it, and started to draw her skirts higher about her. Then fear seized her as she realized that Frohman could never survive the cold waters. She stood there, clutching the rail, as the water came up.

Others, like Archie Donald, young and unimpeded by rheumatism, had no time to philosophize. When he stared up at the towering sides it seemed as though the boat deck rail and the lifeboats were "rushing" to crash down on him.

He called a steward over to help him tie the lifebelt, then put his money, about forty dollars, in the top of his sock. He bent over to take off his shoes, but decided there wasn't even time for that. The water was about twelve feet below his deck when he jumped, and he hit with a splash.

Archie felt its chilling drenching shock. Then the buoyant lifebelt brought him quickly back to the surface. Much to his surprise, swimming was "the most marvelous revelation." He had the illusion of skimming over the top of the water with incredible speed and ease, while the life preserver held his head and chest high.

He kept stroking, with one motivating desire—to get away from the ship.

Close by, a group of men who had already struggled onto a raft were huddled together like soaked terriers and singing, weakly, "Tipperary."

Herbert Ehrhardt reminded himself to keep his mouth shut as he hit the water. He must also keep eyes open and swim up toward the light whichever way the currents turned him, he thought. Then he jumped. There was at first a sensation of going farther and farther from the light in spite of swimming toward it . . . sinking, deeper and deeper.

Then the water became brighter, he broke the surface—and he was breathing again. His lungs ached. And he saw the turmoil was not yet over, for a huge wave was bearing an empty lifeboat at him.

The chemistry student raised his arms over his head to shield himself. The wave and boat passed, and he was sucked under once more. Again he struggled upward for the light, which became gradually brighter, lighter—and, finally, fresh air again filled his lungs. Now he had surfaced in an area of relative calm. He relaxed, floating quietly to catch his breath.

Matt Freeman, the British boxing champion, was in a hurry to get off, once his hand had been treated by Marie de Page. He ran to the stern, now the highest part of the ship. When he looked down, he wondered if it weren't a bit too high.

Being an athlete in peak trim, he had full self-confidence. He climbed onto the railing and dove. He struck the side of a floating lifeboat. The blow opened a deep gash in his head and he could feel the blood ooze, even under water. But it had not knocked him out, and he began to swim.

Robert Wiemann thought "a second torpedo" hit about this time. Since the liner appeared to be sinking by the bow, he knew he could do no more for the passengers. He climbed onto the stern railing in the wake of Matt Freeman, and was awestruck by the belief that it must be a hundred feet down to the water. He plunged anyhow.

When he surfaced, two men grabbed at him, so he had to duck beneath the surface again to free himself.

Thomas Mahoney, the seaman, concluded there was little more assistance he could give in lowering boats. He made for the stern and started to lower himself into the water by a rope, sailor-fashion. Halfway down he realized he was over the propellers; it looked to him as though they were still revolving slowly. He had a terrible choice—dropping between the blades or clambering back onto the deck.

He decided to "swarm" back up the rope. With considerable difficulty he shinnied up again, inch by inch, until he had finally gained the stern deck. This time he climbed onto the rail, gauged his distance down, and dove.

When he came to the surface, jarred but unhurt, he swam for a raft.

Others were jumping right after him, as though the ship's stern had turned into some macabre, monster springboard. Thomas Madden, the fireman who had finally struggled up through the ventilator, was among them. So was Frank Tower, the fireman who had swum away from the *Titanic* and the *Empress of Ireland*. It had assumed the character of a fearsome routine.

Another fireman arrived abruptly on the deck having been blown, by some lesser internal explosion, the last few feet through an escape hatch. He was sooty, bruised, and bleeding but alive. He took one look at the angle of the ship and dove over the side. Many of the engine room crew were badly scalded, presenting an appearance that stuck in many minds as far more frightful than any other aspect of the nightmare.

Passengers plunged in and swam alongside the crewmen. Fifteen-year-old Virginia Bruce Loney, whose father had returned for her from ambulance driving in France, was among them—though involuntarily—as was Florence Padley. Each had been toppled into the water by an overturned lifeboat.

Virginia Bruce was a proficient swimmer. With fast, graceful strokes she swam away from the listing ship. As she turned her head she saw her mother and father. They were standing by the rail, beside their friend, Alfred Vanderbilt, who had helped her into the lifeboat.

It hurt her deep inside with an unfathomable helplessness to look at them. She knew she would never see them again.

Lieutenant Lasseter had the same feeling as he looked back from the water to see the sturdy figure of his friend, Commander Stackhouse, standing calmly on the stern.

Avis Dolphin was also swimming. She had not remained long in the lifeboat in which Professor Holbourn had placed her. Two men had jumped into it as it touched the water, capsizing it.

She had the feeling that she was the only one to have struggled clear of the upturned boat. Soon she spied a raft nearby, with people rowing. Two other men pulled her aboard.

Some distance from her, Holbourn himself was swimming with all his might. After he first jumped, he had trouble fighting through the jumble of ropes snarling the water around the liner, like submarine nets. Once free of them, he knifed ahead like a seventy-five-yard dash professional. He thought fleetingly of the curious prophetic dreams of such a disaster he had experienced several times in New York before sailing.

Others, not necessarily old or infirm, would not jump in spite of any amount of persuasion. Patrick L. Jones, London staff photographer and reporter with the International News Service, was one of them.

Charles T. Jeffrey, a Kenosha, Wisconsin, automobile manufacturer, spied Jones on the starboard side of B Deck. His arm wrapped around a stanchion, he balanced himself further with a foot against the rail. He was taking pictures as fast as he could load and focus his camera.

"You better get off this boat!" Jeffrey shouted.

"These'll be the greatest pictures ever!" replied Jones, not pausing to look at the other man.

Jeffrey thought it "the coolest thing" he would ever see, then hastened along the deck. He was uncertain whether to jump or look for a collapsible.

Theodate Pope had abandoned hope of obtaining space in a boat for herself and Edwin Friend. As she and Emily Robinson waited for him to return with the belts, it became obvious the great Cunarder was about finished: the ship—so vast it needed telephones to connect the cabins, so ornate that the Senator from Utah thought it "more beautiful than Solomon's Temple (and big enough to hold all his wives)"—would surely sink soon.

Friend tied the belts on the women, and they stood by the ropes on the outer side of the deck in the place one of the boats had occupied. They looked up at the leaning funnels and could see the ship move. "She was going rapidly."

Now they could see the gray hull, once hidden, where the waterline began. It looked like the underbelly of a great whale.

It was time to jump.

"You go first," Theodate said.

Friend stepped over the ropes, slipped down one of the uprights, and reached the rail of B Deck, next lower. Then he jumped. The two women waited for Friend to come up.

In a few seconds they were relieved to see his head bobbing in the foamy water, then he smiled to encourage them.

"Come, Robinson," Theodate said and stepped over the ropes as Edwin Friend had before her. She slipped a short distance, found a foothold on a roll of the canvas used for deck shields, then jumped. She feared that her maid would not follow her.

She could not reach the surface. She was being washed and whirled up against something that felt like wood. Then she opened her eyes and blinked in the green water—through the murk it looked as though she were being dashed up against a lifeboat keel.

"This of course is the end of life for me," she thought as she closed her eyes again. She flailed her arms in a half-spirited attempt to come to the surface. She thought of her mother and was glad she had made a will. She started to count all the buildings she designed—the ones built and building—and hoped she had "made good."

Quietly she thought of the friends she loved, then committed herself, in "a prayer without words," to God's care. She received a sudden blow on the head, felt it crashing through the straw hat she still wore, and lapsed into unconsciousness.

As with Matt Freeman, the boxer, and Theodate Pope, striking objects proved as deadly a menace as the cold ocean. Ever since the *Lusitania* was hit, the waters were being increasingly choked with a strange, vast outpouring of debris: crushed, splintered lifeboats, deck chairs, shoring lumber—the awe-struck passengers did not know where it had all come from.

Dr. Houghton remembered hitting his head as he went underneath. The force of the water separated him from Marie de Page. He looked back for a moment, saw her struggling, then she was swept away. He lost sight of her.

On deck, Dr. Fisher returned from his quest with two lifebelts.

"I had to wade through deep water to get them," he reported to Lady Mackworth and Dorothy Conner. This news shocked them into action.

Margaret Mackworth unhooked her skirt so that it would come straight off in the water and not impede her. She watched the list of the *Lusitania*. She, as others, kept thinking it could not possibly lean over any farther. But it continued to list.

"I think we better jump into the sea," Dr. Fisher said anxiously. As he eyed the nearing waters, he wondered how the ship was keeping afloat at such a crazy angle.

Dr. Fisher and Dorothy moved to a place vacated by a lifeboat, as Theodate and Edwin Friend had done before. But there was no railing to impede them.

Margaret Mackworth followed a few paces behind, trying to summon courage for the sixty-foot jump from the boat deck to the water. She became more and more frightened. It was like leaping off a rooftop. She held tightly onto the extra lifebelt she still carried for her father.

"It is ridiculous to have a physical fear of the jump," she tried to reassure herself, "when we are in such grave danger!"

She saw others hesitating at the edge of the boat deck and reasoned they must have had the same fear. Then suddenly the water washed over the deck, and she realized she was no longer sixty feet above the ocean. In the next instant green water was swirling around her knees.

That was as far as she remembered its rising. Then she was engulfed by it.

Somewhere below, the little group that had been holding tightly onto one another—Frohman, Rita Jolivet, Captain Scott, and Vernon—had just been forcibly separated by the crush of water. The wave that smashed, frothing, into them seemed to be bearing other struggling, screaming people along with it.

Its force tore Rita Jolivet's buttoned shoes off. Like Frohman she had made up her mind to die and she was "quite calm under the water."

"The thought of God came to me—how at a time like this He was everyone's God, a living, warm all-pervading Presence. . . . The petty bickerings of creed and doctrine seemed so foolish, so futile . . ."

She was distinctly surprised when the water brightened and she floated to the surface. She reached for an upturned lifeboat and clung to it, along with at least thirty other persons, who had apparently upset it.

Others splashed over and clung desperately to the keel. The boat sank lower and lower.

Rita was seized with panic. Though she thought she had resigned herself to dying, she now wanted to live. And she was faced a second time with death.

In the wheelhouse, with its port windows pointing crazily up at the blue sky, and starboard ones awash in the sea, Captain Turner did not want to die either.

Quartermaster Hugh Johnston had sung out:

"T-w-e-n-t-y f-i-v-e degrees!" and from then on the brass indicator swung steadily to starboard. It was little use for Johnston to try to keep up with it by singing out successive lists.

Turner watched the helm and the indicator with a darkening expression. Finally he said flatly to his quartermaster:

"Save yourself."

Johnston left the helm and hurried over to the starboard bridge wing for a lifebuoy. It wouldn't be long, he thought, before he was washed right off this ship. He had never known anyone so "cool" as Captain Turner.

Marconi Operator Leith, now drenched in sweat, tirelessly flashing the SOS, knew the ship was going down. He could hardly hang onto his transmitter because of the list. Now, frantically, he altered the call:

Send help quickly. Am listing badly!

Walther Schwieger didn't think it would be long either. Aboard the *U-20*, he was recording:

3:25 P.M. It seems as if the vessel will be afloat only a short time. Submerge to 24 meters and go to sea. I could not have fired a second torpedo into this throng of humanity attempting to save themselves . . .

Just outside of the *Lusitania's* radio shack, with its outjuttings of wires and insulators, Oliver Bernard had finished untying his shoes. Although he had thought himself to be practically alone, when he looked up he saw George Hutchinson, the chief electrician, at the door of the shack talking to Leith.

"What about it, Bob?" Hutchinson asked Leith.

Before Leith could answer, an engineer ran across the deck balancing himself against the list.

"The watertight doors are all right, quite all right, don't worry," the engineer reported, breathless, to Hutchinson.

The three men grinned at each other as the engineer moved along, and the electrician reassured Bernard, "Any amount of other ships about."

The scenic artist scanned the horizon without seeing a sign of a ship, and replied, "That doesn't interest me much. I can't swim a yard and that's not enough."

Inside his cubicle, Bob Leith stood up. He pushed his swivel chair out of the door toward Bernard. He told him it would be something to hang onto later.

"No good at working water-wheels either," Bernard said. The men all laughed as the chair careened down the sloping deck and crashed against the starboard rails.

Bernard found it difficult to stand at all. The list had increased alarmingly and the bow was nearly submerged.

The wireless operator ceased sending the distress message. Now he produced a small camera and, balancing himself uncertainly on his knees, took a picture looking forward.

"What a snap this will make!" he observed to Bernard.

The men looked away from the ship and distinguished one lifeboat among the others, about a mile away, making for the clearly visible shore. There appeared to be one lady, children, and an officer in this boat, which was being rowed by sailors. The sun glinted from the gold braid on the officer's sleeve— and Bernard, the electrician and the radioman all looked at each other in bitter understanding.

It was time for them to go too. The trio, as if by unexpressed agreement, started down to the starboard rails, half sliding as they went.

To Bernard it appeared that the *Lusitania* was about to roll over and carry with her all who remained aboard. He climbed over the stairway rails and down outside them. He dropped feet first onto the boat deck, facing inward. His rubber-soled boots, which he still wore, untied, kept him from tumbling over.

The edge of the deck was awash as he slipped toward it. A lifeboat floated nearby, held by the tackle of a single davit. He recognized it as Number 2, the first of several which had dumped their passengers into the sea. Now it held new occupants, and Bernard splashed over to them, and into the boat.

Bernard helped others into the lifeboat. Among them was D. A. Thomas, who had been looking for his daughter, Margaret Mackworth, ever since the torpedo had struck. Both men then assisted a hysterical woman into the boat and halted the descent of a young boy who had made a flying leap.

The ropes from the davit were threatening to hold the lifeboat to the *Lusitania* and carry it down with her. Just in time, someone produced an ax and hacked the falls clear.

Hardly had that peril been eliminated than an incredible new danger presented itself. The liner was listing so far that the boat was caught on one of the steel funnel stays. The funnel overhung the tiny boat, threatening to tear loose and smash everyone "like flies" or at best smother them under its massive breadth—wide enough, as the advertisements lyricized, "to drive a coach and horses through."

All hands joined in a mighty effort which finally resulted in pushing the boat clear of the "tentacle"-like funnel stay . . . they watched the great liner sliding slowly away from them downward.

It looked as though she were literally going to sink under them, like a monster fish bent on a final, mighty plunge back to the depths.

At this point Quartermaster Hugh Johnston was picked up from the starboard side of the bridge, like a swimmer caught in the tide, and washed all the way across the ship. He barely missed ventilators, fans, stay wires, valve-heads, and other obstructions.

On the other side of the bridge, which was almost completely awash, Turner glanced at his watch. It was 2:28 P.M., exactly eighteen minutes after the *Lusitania* had been hit. He thought himself to be the last man on the ship—though he was not—and realized that in a few more seconds he would no longer have a command.

Here was the nightmare moment in the existence of a captain; this was ultimate heartbreak, world's end. In one instant, the planet-like substance and enduring solidity of a 32,000-ton liner; in the next, nothing, or perhaps eternity.

Turner was in full uniform, including his cap, with the gold "scrambled eggs" on the visor. On the sleeve of his coat the four wide gold stripes were tinged with the green of the sea air but still impressive.

He would go down, if he must, in courage, in pride, a man—and a Briton.

The deck assumed an impossible angle beneath him and the water surged over his legs, the green, cold, relentless water that was ruining forever the wonderful machinery of his bridge, his helm, his brass telegraph to the engine room. . . .

He pulled his cap tighter around his head so it would not come off, and started to climb a ladder leading from the bridge to the signal halyards. Les Morton, who had spotted the torpedo (or two parallel torpedo tracks, he was increasingly certain) and was now in the water swimming away from a capsized boat, looked back in time to see Turner by the halyards. Stroking for his own life as he was, it struck him as a most dramatic sight, the captain with his ship to the very last.

Now, like the apprentice of sailing-ship days, Will Turner clutched instinctively for rigging, higher, higher. The tar rolled off into the palms of his hands, and its familiar pungent smell awakened in him a nostalgia he had tried to keep dormant. Memories of long-ago, better days, flashed dizzily before him.

He wondered what in God's name he had done to deserve this.

The huge Cunarder trembled under his grasp. He heard strange, watery eruptions far below as though they emanated from the ocean's very bed. Above him the skies were blue and bright . . . from the almost horizontal funnels a bare trace of coal smoke wisped redolently upward . . . a seagull wheeled past.

He saw an oar floating toward him. He quit the rigging and struck out for it. He grabbed it, then let go and splashed over to a bobbing chair. He held onto the chair.

His cap remained on his head as he looked back at his ship. The funnels and mast tips seemed to be righting, swinging in a slow arc back toward the zenith, just where they should be pointing. An all-swallowing wave foamed past the base of the funnels, over the Marconi deck, over what remained above water of the boat deck, like heavy surf after a storm. It was one long comber.

From the stern, now that her bow was buried beneath the water, those still abord the *Lusitania* had a fleeting and bizarre perspective. It was one which they realized, even then, was unlikely to be duplicated in the infinity of time.

As the liner tilted sharply downward, the fantail soared a hundred feet into the air, exposing four nearly motionless propellers, as well as the immense sixty-five-ton rudder. And to complete the nightmare, she stopped there, frozen still, her forward motion suddenly and strangely arrested.

Those who dared not jump from the stern because of the height—including men like C. T. Jeffrey, from Kenosha, and Parry Jones, one of the Royal Welsh singers—suspected the uncanny truth. Captain Turner, pausing to gasp a lungful of air, saw it!—his great ship, poised at an unbelievable angle, "quivered her whole length." Others who did not understand one nautical term knew only that the "point end" of the liner was jutting skyward, and seemed to hang there.

Sailor and landlubber alike realized that the *Lusitania,* nearly 800 feet from stern to stern, had already hit bottom.

The pride of Cunard, first superliner to be powered by steam turbines, ventilated by "thermo-tank," with elevators, telephones, electric chandeliers, roof gardens, tapestry, 175 watertight compartments, ocean greyhound that could race at more than twenty-five knots, beat the German steamers, outrun any enemy submarine, towering 216 feet from keel to mast tips, had slid through the 300-foot depth off the Irish coast, and stuck her towering bow fast in sand and mud.

Those on the steep mountain peak of her stern heard the crashing from inside her superstructure, from her cargo spaces, engine rooms, throughout all the compartmented caverns of her stretching hull. It was as though a big hardware store had been turned upside down.

They stared below them at the swarms of men, women, and children twisting like flies and wrigglers on a lily pond, some on the surface, some just under, helpless human beings who did not know any more than Turner why God had done this to them.

The *Lusitania,* eleven miles from shore, 183 degrees, almost due south of the white lighthouse on the Old Head of Kinsale, was 270 miles from Liverpool. And she was over the same spot where a wallowing, unknown sailing schooner, the *Earl of Latham,* had been found by the submarine not many hours before.

Even Captain Turner had to admit the terrible truth—the mighty *Lusitania* shared a common mortality with all ships.

With increasingly ominous rumblings the liner began to right herself and settle lower by the stern. The wave rolled anew, flecking foam along the last exposed portions of her superstructure and decking. A few boats still hung, like broken toys, from davits.

One of the last boats that did get away carried Dr. Mecredy, who had pulled himself out of the water and over the stern. He was wet, his hands hurt and bleeding, but he was alive. Some fifty yards away, the *Lusitania*'s stern and the propellers still loomed menacingly above him. He watched her settle, not quite certain what this amazing liner might do next.

Sculling a raft close to the doctor, Seaman Mahoney watched in similar fascination, with his own interpretation of the ship's actions. She was expressing, he thought, "glorious defiance," even in her death agonies.

The occupants of her fantail, C. T. Jeffrey, Parry Jones, and others, were reluctantly leaving their last tiny island of refuge, or preparing to do so.

From another lifeboat that had barely cleared the *Lusitania,* Elizabeth Duckworth looked out on a world the like of which she had never seen before. The sea was filled with bodies as well as an indescribable mass of debris, and it was "a terrible sight." To see dead men and women was one thing. When there were children, even infants—that was something for which she was prepared neither by faith nor training. Nor did she dare to think about the many more who must still be trapped in the deep, now-flooded world of steerage.

Loud enough for those seated beside her to hear, she finished the 23rd Psalm for the second time:

". . . for Thou art with me; Thy rod and Thy staff comfort me. Thou shalt prepare a table before me against them that trouble me; Thou hast anointed my head with oil, and my cup shall be full. But Thy loving kindness and mercy shall follow me all the days of my life; and I will dwell in the house of the Lord forever."

As Archie Donald coughed out a mouthful of water he looked behind him and saw the propellers and rudder of the *Lusitania* silhouetted in mid-air. A group of survivors, in a lifeboat, placed their oars against the lower propeller and pushed themselves off.

Then, with an "explosion and rattling of all the loose material leaving her deck," the ship gathered momentum for her last lunge. She appeared to be going down sideways, with her stern toward the shore, and Donald had a great fear the mast would hit him. At the same time he wondered, curiously, whether the stay ropes were made of hemp or wire.

Whatever their composition, the ropes missed him by less than fifteen feet. Then, a three-foot-high wave picked Donald up and shot him out into the water that had been calm as a pond split seconds before. The suction of the vortex drew him down.

Archie swam against the current with a complete absence of fear that it would "get the better" of him. As he finally surfaced, an eight-by-eight-inch post and two-by-six-inch plank—measured by his appraising eye—shot up alongside like projectiles. Now he felt "guarded." He would undoubtedly have been decapitated had they been closer.

He reached the sturdy lumber which might have killed him, and hung on.

Several passengers had safely abandoned the great liner only to be met with another deadly—and not-anticipated—menace. It was the radio antenna, something which voyagers had become accustomed to watching laced high against the sky, some distance above even the funnels.

As the *Lusitania* tipped over, the wire caught Lauriat, for one, around the shoulders and dragged him under. He would not have been "as much surprised" if the submarine had surfaced with him straddling its conning tower.

Miraculously, he fought clear of the aerial and surfaced again, as did others, including Virginia Bruce Loney and James Brooks. Most, however, were badly bruised by it.

When Brooks bobbed back up again, his hand stinging from where the wire had cut in, he saw the *Lusitania*—pointed dead for the land, he thought—going down "with a thunderous roar as of the collapse of a great building during a fire." He figured that at least some of the terrible sound was caused by the turbines tearing loose from their mountings and crashing into the bow.

It seemed to him that the ship sank sideways, still listing, although Lauriat thought she had recovered "on quite an even keel" as she settled by the stern. Turner himself estimated she came back to within five degrees of even keel.

Some, like Wiemann and Mahoney, of the crew, felt a violent explosion after the *Lusitania* disappeared, as though the boilers had exploded. Mahoney was sure a vapor covered the sea momentarily before it dissipated. Wiemann was impressed with the quiet that settled over the scene of incredible destruction, which took the pattern of "a circle of people and wreckage about half a mile across."

Lauriat, however, heard "a long, lingering moan" that rose and lasted many moments; "those who were lost seemed to be calling from the very depths." And others recalled it sounded like the waters were wailing in horror.

All saw the wave surge out from the spot where the *Lusitania* had plunged, bearing a threatening flotsam of deck chairs, oars, boxes, crushed boats, a nameless "deluge."

To Professor Holbourn the spot assumed the shape of "a pork pie"—a large, whitish broken mass, caused presumably by a final explosion. While the aerial did not endanger him, the after mast barely missed shattering a lifeboat close by. Then he struck out toward the boat, taking in tow a man who was floating beside him.

Oliver Bernard, from the relative security of a lifeboat, envisioned the scene as "a boiling wilderness that rose up as if a volcanic disturbance had occurred beneath a placid sea."

Dr. Mecredy, on the other hand, found that his boat rode away very nicely. He concluded there was little undertow.

Timmins went so far under that he never saw the *Lusitania*'s final moments of anguish. His last memories were of "Niagara Falls" as the superstructure bore him down with it. Soon the water around him was "black as the inside of a cow," and the top of his head felt like a "steel plate" from increasing pressure. Something struck the crown of his head.

He figured he was at least sixty feet below the surface, which was certainly fifty feet deeper than he had ever dived before. But he remained as methodical as ever. He kept count as he swam up, fighting away from the superstructure, taking exactly thirty-one strokes before he surfaced.

Then, after "seconds which seemed like hours," the black changed to gray. Timmins blinked, looked around and figured he was about 150 yards east of the main logjam of wreckage. He was impressed by the calm—"no row, just a sort of hum over the water."

A boy of about ten floated past in the tangle of bodies and wreckage. There was no sound. He pressed his fingers to the boy's ribs, but could detect no heartbeat. Then he raised his eyes from the still form and saw the smoke of a steamer trailing across the horizon, passing on a westerly course.

Alice Middleton, the baby's nurse from Seattle, was carried far below. It seemed to her that her benefactor, Vanderbilt, had been washed off the deck, without a lifebelt, before he had finished securing hers. On the other hand, someone else thought he had seen Vanderbilt light a cigarette and saunter forward.

Beneath the surface, her head had become jammed in an opened porthole and the pressure had made her eardrums seem about to burst. It tortured her with a pain so great that she did not see how she could endure, much less survive, it.

Yet, somehow, she returned to the surface, to be appalled at once by the vast numbers of bodies—especially those of children—floating all around her. They looked like drowned dolls.

Beside her a woman was struggling. Alice stared in disbelief. The woman was giving birth to a baby, there in the water, alone. It was the most terrible thing she had ever witnessed—or would witness in her life. She became sick with a pitying horror, helpless to do anything for the woman. Soon Alice lost consciousness.

Margaret Gwyer, the bride of the Canadian minister, had been knocked out of her boat and her companions had already given her up for lost when she was scooped up by one of the funnels along with a jumble of smashed wreckage. She was sucked into it as the *Lusitania* went under.

The explosion shot her out again, as if from a cannon. The minister's lady went into the air and down into the water, landing a considerable distance from her boat and her husband.

William H. Pierpont, of Liverpool, had the same bizarre experience. He was swimming near Captain Turner when the latter saw Pierpont suddenly swallowed by a disappearing funnel. Next the "Inspector," as Turner called the gentleman, shot forth again, while the "air rushed out with a terrible hissing sound." Turner watched, incredulous, though he obtained a measure of grim humor from the sight. As Pierpont hit the water and struck out he seemed to be "swimming like ten men, he was so scared."

The incident relieved only slightly Turner's deep sense of loss. He knew now why the ship had heeled so terribly after the torpedo hit: it was, paradoxically enough, her very watertightness! With all her 175 hydraulically controlled watertight compartments, flooding between port and starboard sides had not been equalized. Not until moments before the end had the force of thousands of tons of water apparently burst through the damlike fore-and-aft bulkhead.

This very aspect of marine engineering had contributed to the debacle of lifeboat launching, compounding the terror and transforming his graceful command into a plunging, careening monster. She had been somewhat top-heavy, too, it occurred to Turner; her nine decks made her like a hotel with too many stories. Yet not until the *Lusitania* had been stricken with her mortal wounds had this fact caused any particular comment other than to give the liner the reputation of a "roller" in the minds of queasy passengers.

Will Turner hung onto his chair, dogpaddling slowly. He watched the mound of boiling water slowly dwindling to bubbles. Then the bubbles too disappeared and the sea was calm again.

Nothing remained of the *Lusitania* but a clutter of boats, debris, and people.

In eighteen minutes the liner had been utterly destroyed—obliterated, as if it had never existed, a modern Carthage.

George Kessler, sometimes called the "champagne king," stared from his boat at the same foaming spot, then after a few moments pronounced his own startled benediction:

"My God—the *Lusitania's* gone!"

Abandon Ship!
The Saga of the U.S.S. Indianapolis,
The Navy's Greatest Disaster

BY RICHARD F. NEWCOMB

One of the most poignant true war stories of all time, the sinking of the heavy cruiser U.S.S. *Indianapolis* by a Japanese submarine torpedo on the night of July 29, 1945, is a tale that will likely remain in public consciousness long after many other war "epics" have faded into obscurity. The story has everything—drama, pathos, tragedy, heroism, and even such contemporary sub-plot intrigues as cover-ups and witch hunts.

The basic facts of the disaster are these:

The battle-scarred *Indianapolis* delivered the atomic bomb that was eventually dropped on Hiroshima to the island of Tinian in the western Pacific. After pressing on to Guam, she heads for Leyte in the Philippine Islands to resume her duties as flagship of the Navy's Fifth Fleet. Her captain, an Annapolis graduate, Charles Butler McVay III, is denied a destroyer escort and ordered to get back to Leyte as fast as possible. (Despite denying McVay's request, the Navy brass knew danger lurked in the waters the *Indianapolis* was to traverse: Just two days before the *Indianapolis* departed, a destroyer was torpedoed and sunk.) On the night of July 29, clouds covered the sky, and McVay ceased the zig-zag defensive procedures in order to make better time. Unfortunately, two things happened that doomed the *Indianapolis*: the ship was headed directly for Japanese submarine I-58 and the clouds cleared. The sub fired six shots at the *Indianapolis*, and two hit. The ship went down in about twelve minutes, carrying about 300 men with her. The rest of the 1,196 men that had been on board, including Captain McVay, leaped into the oil-coated sea with their life jackets, grabbing whatever rafts they could find. Only 316 men would survive the horrific ordeal, which included shark attacks now famous in historical narratives and featured in a key scene in the famous movie *Jaws*.

The loss of the *Indianapolis* was not revealed until after Japan surrendered, and when the story began to come to light the Navy brass felt compelled to find a scapegoat. Captain McVay was charged with negligence and convicted, even though the Japanese submarine commander testified that zigzagging would have made no difference on his attack. Captain McVay later committed suicide.

Richard Newcomb's *Abandon Ship* was originally published in 1958. Republished in 2001 with Peter Maas' Introduction and Afterword, the book is stunning account of one of the war's most famous incidents and stories. This excerpt focuses on the ordeal of the crew after the ship went down and is but a small portion of the great reading to be found in the entire book.

* * * * *

The Pacific Ocean is the largest single physical feature on earth. It is greater in size than all the land above sea level on the rest of the globe. The extreme depth, about 35,400 feet, lies between Guam and the Philippines.

No one knows exactly where the *Indianapolis* went down, but the Navy accepted the spot as 134 degrees, 48 minutes East, 12 degrees, 2 minutes North. Lieutenant Commander Hashimoto fixed the position as 134 degrees, 16 minutes East, 12 degrees, 31 minutes North, or some 44 miles northwest of the Navy's position. Not that it made any serious difference; the nearest land was still some 250 miles away, directly south, the top end of the Palaus archipelago. Guam was 600 miles to the east, Leyte 550 miles west, and to the north there was nothing for nearly a thousand miles. The water at this point was probably 10,000 feet deep.

Some of the men saw their ship go down, but many did not—they were too far away. The ship, making about 15 knots at the time of the hit, slowed rapidly after the first torpedo blunted her nose, and the second one knocked out two of her four turbines. But she continued underway until almost the end, which is the reason the men were widely scattered, right from the start. The biggest group, by far, was around the hull when the stern rose straight into the air, poised there a minute, then passed straight down, never to be seen again.

Men reacted in a variety of ways. To some it was a bit of a lark; these would be the young, the high-spirited, the unstable. The badly wounded were already shielded, mercifully, by a protective blanket of shock. It was not long before the sea would close over them, ending their troubles. Fate was unkindest to those rendered unfit for the fight, but condemned to struggle unequally until the inevitable came to call them.

Every man had his immediate problems: getting away from the ship, struggling in the fuel oil, spread incredibly everywhere, finding someone else—for fear of being left alone was universal—finding a life jacket or keeping one, grabbing for a raft, floating debris, anything. Here it was all sheer luck, and each man blessed his or cursed it, in proportion to how he fared in the great last scramble.

Captain McVay was fortunate, though there were times later when he might question this. One of the few who remembered the rudiments of abandon-ship procedure, or who had time for it, he had quickly dressed. As he walked down the side of the hull—his hull, his ship, his command—a soft wave came up behind him and gently carried him into the sea. Above him towered the stern, the giant screws glinting in the fitful moonlight. For an awful second he thought the vessel might fall on him.

And in that moment the thought flashed through his mind that it might be better this way. He was an Academy man, a second-generation career man, and a third-generation Navy man, and no one had to tell him what faced him if he survived. "If the ship falls on me," he thought, "I won't have to face what I know is coming after this."

But the will to live was too strong, and he struck out swimming, away from the menacing hulk above him. After only a few strokes, a wave of oil and water washed over his head, and he turned to look. The ship was gone.

The captain struck out again, and almost immediately ran into a crate of potatoes, late tenant of the fantail. He climbed astride this, reached out and grabbed a shattered desk floating by, and almost in the same instant saw two rafts not twenty feet away. Captain McVay quickly swam to them, and as he climbed in one he heard men calling for help.

He called back and soon Quartermaster Allard swam alongside, towing two shipmates who looked more dead than alive. Allard pushed Seaman Sec-ond Class Ralph D. Klappa toward the raft and Captain McVay reached out for him, saying, "You can make it the rest of the way."

"I can't do anything," Klappa said and started to slide. Only eighteen years old, he had been to sea just fifteen days. McVay pulled him aboard and the youngster lay in the raft, vomiting oil and salt water. Meantime Allard helped Seaman Second Class Angelo Galante, twenty, over the side and then pulled himself aboard. Galante joined Klappa in retching as they lay in the raft, recovering from fright and exhaustion.

McVay and Allard lashed the rafts together and spent the night investigating their new home. They quickly discovered the rafts had fallen into the water upside down. Paddles, rations, matches, flares, and other emergency gear were all secured to the bottom. By incredible chance, they saw and heard no one else throughout the night. A man low on the water can see practically nothing, even in daylight, and particularly with a twelve-foot swell running. But at dawn they discovered another raft and floater net nearby, with five more men on it. Captain McVay directed them to come over, and soon the three rafts were lashed together with fifteen feet of line between each. This kept the party from straying but allowed enough line so the rafts wouldn't bump.

John James Muldoon, a thirty-year-old New Bedford sailor, was senior man in the second group. A machinist's mate first class, he had served in the *Indianapolis* two and a half years. In his group were Yeoman Second Class Otha A. Havins, and his buddy, Jay R. Glenn, Aviation Machinist's Mate Second Class, as well as John Spinelli, Ship's Cook Second Class, and George R. Kurlick, Fire Controlman Third Class. The twenty-year-old Kurlick was naked, but none of the men was injured. As Captain McVay surveyed his command through one eye (the other was inflamed from fuel oil and nearly closed) he thought he was seeing about him the sole survivors of the 1,196 men aboard the *Indianapolis*.

He was greatly mistaken. There were hundreds of men within a few thousand yards, all struggling for their lives, and none as well off as the captain's group. There were a number of reasons why Captain McVay could not see them, or they him.

Men left the ship in a variety of ways over a period of twelve minutes, during most of which the ship was still underway. The first off were soon left far behind, mere heads bobbing in a blanket of fuel oil, virtually undiscernible even from a ship in broad daylight. Those who stayed till the last were split into groups determined by the point at which they had left the ship, the swirling and eddying of waters around the hull, their swimming strength, and the impedimenta thrown in their way from the foundering vessel.

Once they were in the water, the sea began to separate them. The swimmers, nearly totally immersed, presented little surface to the wind and thus the prevailing current began carrying them to the southwest at about 1 knot. But those on rafts, or debris, felt the force of the 10-knot wind and were wafted off to the northeast at varying speeds. By daybreak, the groups were scattered over a line of several miles, on a generally southwest-northeast axis. A man with his eyes six inches above water can't see much in a moderately rough sea, even from the top of a twelve-foot swell. If his eyes are smarting from salt water and fuel oil, and partly blinded by a hot sun, he can see even less. Men on a raft have a better chance, but even on a crest you can't see into the troughs of other waves, and you may be scanning east when a head bobs up to the west, only to subside into a valley as you turn.

It may have seemed fortuitous that Doc Haynes, his assistant, Dr. Modisher, and Father Conway were thrown into the largest group of survivors. Actually, Haynes found soon after he entered the water that there was little medicine could do, though ministrations of the spirit might prove helpful. Hardly had the giant hulk slipped beneath the waves when the night was pierced with screams of "Doctor," "Doc," "Doctor." The thirty-three-year-old physician and surgeon, yearning to respond with the skills at his command, found he could not. For the first time he realized that his hands were painfully burned. He had been too busy to notice until now. Even had they not been, there was the fuel oil. It seemed to cover the sea everywhere, in a great viscous blanket, evil-smelling and irritating to the eyes. Men who swallowed it puked for hours, until it seemed their very stomachs would come up, inside out. Men who got it in their eyes or nasal passages cried in pain and made matters worse by rubbing in a vain effort to get rid of it. The offensive liquid was everywhere, in vast, astounding quantities, and from this endless, undulating counterpane the men struggled to get free.

In these first confused and painful hours, mercifully covered by darkness, at least twenty men, already maimed, slipped away beneath the water, unequal to the battle. These were the men without life jackets. For those who had them, but could not long survive, Doc Haynes' role quickly changed from physician to coroner. He paddled from one still form to another; it was his task to lift the eyelid, test the reflex. Finding none, he would nod to buddies nearby. They slipped off the life jacket from one who no longer needed it, and passed it to a man who had none. For the receiver, it was a gift beyond price. Fresh and new now, it held him out of the sea from the chest up, and everyone knew they were good for forty-eight hours. These good, gray vests of kapok bought two full days of life, and surely by that time help would come. There was no fighting yet, for life jackets, but no one spurned one, not even the strong, brave young men.

As dawn came, each man of the perhaps eight hundred still alive surveyed a new world. Some things were common in each man's world, and to each some things were different. Everyone saw immediately that there was nothing solid to cling to, only water on all sides and beneath—everywhere but up. Each man knew already that the sea was harshly saline, the oil sulphurously irritating, the wind and frothing comber a constant burden. Those on rafts, floater nets, or debris, a few precious inches higher than the swimmers, still could not keep entirely out of the sea.

Besides the mass reaction to this peril and discomfort, each man had his own private little problem, the problem of individually living or dying, and each reacted according to his nature. Some whimpered in terror, others were defiant, still others resigned. Many were surprised, not only at their own insouciance, but at the depths of character displayed by others. Courage blossomed in unexpected places, and cowardice in still less likely places. Now they were all in the ultimate extremity, the God-fearing and the Godless, the evil and the noble, the weak and the strong, and let us see who will survive.

Monday dawned clear and the men welcomed the sun. It seemed at first to warm them spiritually after the cold night, and promise strength and help. They took heart and, as man seems to do in any circumstance, began organizing this new watery world. There was no question of overall command, for already the groups were widely scattered. Indeed, in most cases each group knew only of its own existence and was fully occupied with its own problems. Some few small groups, finding themselves close together in the morning, did put their meager forces together. Almost from the start they fell into two large groups, and a dozen or more small isolated clusters.

In perhaps the largest group—some three hundred men that first day—Lieutenant Commander Haynes was the senior surviving officer, and by virtue of rank, training, and force of personality he took charge. Strictly speaking, he was not the senior officer, for Commander Lipski, the gunnery officer, was there. But he was clearly dying. The flesh on his hands had been burned down to the tendons, and his eyes were burned closed. Shipmates gathered round him and tried to hold his tortured body out of the stinging sea and oil, and Doc Haynes looked on in anguish, unable to lessen his pain. From somewhere, a cork life ring appeared, and they used that for the severely injured. It knew more than one tenant. A long piece of line was formed into a large circle, and perhaps 150 men clung around the perimeter. With only this flimsy line, they felt better. There were many other arrangements—one man clung to a toilet seat. Schecterle, just out of sick bay minus his appendix, latched on to a lard can, occasionally dipped into the contents to still the pangs, and alternately used the top as a heliograph. Plenty of ammunition cans were in evidence for a while, and the rubber-type, inflatable life belt was worn in several styles. Some put it around their middle, as indicated. Others wore it like a bandolier, lay across it sidesaddle, or sometimes floated—using it as a pillow. In any form, it was nearly useless, and the wise man watched for a kapok that might soon be vacated.

Off to the northwest, less than a thousand yards away at the start, was a second large group. Whatever it was at the start, by dawn Monday death had weeded it down to 120 men and perhaps eight to ten officers, senior of whom was Dick Redmayne. Now he found himself in command of three small rafts, one floater net, some 5-inch ammo cans, and other flotsam. His force included one seasoned warrant officer, three or four green ensigns, and assorted enlisted men, fortunately including a couple of chiefs. Among them was Benton, whose courage would win him the Navy and Marine Corps Medal.

To the northeast, capping the triangle, were the splendid isolationists: the men whose great good fortune it was to have nearly separate quarters on the rafts. Besides McVay's enclave of three rafts and nine men, the biggest single floating command fell to Ensign Rogers, a tall, rangy young man who had been to sea only two weeks. He had been aboard so briefly that though he was a junior officer of Turret IV, he still didn't know his duties or even how it worked. Only the night before, his roommate, the ever-efficient Ensign Woolston, had let him in on the open secret that a sub had been reported along their course. Rogers paid no more attention to this than anyone else. Anyway, he was busy writing a letter to his bride. It was their first anniversary (one month, that is), and he didn't want her to think he had forgotten it.

Rogers was one of the last to leave the ship, and when he hit the water he went down, down, down. He thought he would never come up, but he did and right in front of him was a raft. He grabbed a hand rope on the side and hung on as the ship reared above him, hesitated a moment, and then plunged. It was unbelievable that anything as big and safe and solid could disappear in a moment, but she did. After the final waves washed over him, Rogers climbed into the raft and met his new "shipmates," a mountain boy named Willie Hatfield, Seaman Second Class, from Salt Lick, Kentucky, and Chief Ferguson. During the night they picked up another man. Ferguson was suffering from his leg wounds, and Rogers put a tourniquet around his thigh. Throughout the night, he periodically released the pressure, fearing gangrene, and when dawn came he carefully unwrapped the bandage made of the mess cook's pants. There was a deep cut at the knee, and four or five inches of flesh gouged out below it, besides less serious cuts on the leg and foot. "Doc" Rogers rewrapped the wound as best he could, and cut the loss of blood to a slow ooze. Figuring rapidly, he reasoned that the ship would be missed Tuesday morning, when it failed to show off Leyte for target practice. Search would start immediately and they should be found by Wednesday morning. Ferguson could last that long, he figured. Ferguson never complained.

Daylight disclosed three other rafts nearby with men on them, and in an hour or so of paddling they were brought together. Rogers was now commander of four rafts and nineteen men, including a couple of Marines. All the men were sound, except Ferguson, but the rafts had lost all water and most of the food. One first-aid kit had been salvaged, and Rogers sprinkled sulfa on Ferguson's wounds. They tied the four rafts together for a while, but the constant bumping jarred the chief's leg painfully, and Rogers decided to cut loose from the others. The rafts drifted slowly apart, but remained in sight of each other until the end. As the sun became hotter on Monday, Rogers took off his pants and helped Ferguson wriggle into them, to protect his leg. The ensign shielded his own legs under a life jacket. So here they were, four men in a raft with one can of Spam, which appeared from somewhere. Rogers opened it and they all tried a little. The other two declined a second helping, so Rogers and the chief finished it. Hatfield began trying his luck with some of the emergency fishing gear.

During the night, the McVay rafters became scavengers, snatching from the sea any interesting-looking objects they passed. At first light, the captain began to take stock of his possessions. His wristwatch was working fine, and he decided to keep a log, using paper and a pencil stub disgorged from various pockets and wallets. The sun gave an approximate position, and fish line streaming in the water indicated drift. In spite of the wind, the rafts drifted west, and a few degrees south. The inventory revealed a relatively secure position.

There were ten twelve-ounce cans of Spam, two large tins of malted-milk tablets, seventeen cans of biscuits, but no water. At least the food would be ample for some days to come.

Paddles were retrieved from the underside of the rafts, and one carton yielded fifty small packages of Camels. Oh boy, all the comforts of home! Well, nearly. There wasn't a lighter in the crowd, and the matches from the emergency kits were soaked. Cigarettes and no way to light them; they cast the cigarettes back into the water, removing at least that form of small torture.

They also found a first-aid kit—unneeded—and, very reassuring, a can of Very flares and an emergency signaling mirror. In the can were a small pistol for firing the flares, and twelve flares in all, four each of red, green, and white. Captain McVay began to feel better. With his little convoy stretching out over seventy-five feet of water, and his signaling devices, he was confident they would be sighted by a plane on this heavily traveled track. Kurlick, who had been routed from the shower by the catastrophe, covered himself with life jackets. Allard turned to making cornucopia hats for the men from bits of canvas, and they settled down to wait. The skipper decided that for the sake of discipline they had better set a two-hour watch, and he took the 4:00 to 6:00 morning and afternoon watches. The watches were really only nominal, because everybody snapped awake when a plane went over or a shark nosed around.

They sighted another raft some 1,500 yards away on Monday morning, but the men were all too tired to try to paddle over to it. By Tuesday morning they felt stronger, and began paddling in turns. Four and a half hours later, they overtook the raft and found one man on it, happy to join them. They welcomed him because he had another can of flares. Now they were four rafts, one floater net, and ten men. There were other rafts nearby, they now knew.

They sighted them once in a while, on a wave top, and all the time they were out there they could hear whistling. But the others seemed not anxious to join them, probably because it was too exhausting trying to paddle the cumbersome rafts. Life was becoming a little grim now. The men were tired, and they ached. All soon discovered that the designer of their rafts had never had to sit on them very long. The rounded top chafed on the buttocks and soon wore them sore. Hands blistered from paddling and every cut or abrasion began to develop salt-water ulcers. There seemed no way to keep dry, even in the rafts, and the constant salt-water dousing was irritating, physically and mentally. It was uncomfortable to sit down, but if you stood up and fell, you had a new cut to contend with. Elbows were turning raw from rubbing and the skin seemed tender and sensitive all over.

At 1:00 P.M. on Monday they saw their first plane. It was a twin-engine bomber, flying high, and passed directly over them. Two hours later there was another, a B-24 or B-29, way off to the south. Nobody really expected to be seen by them, but still, it was not reassuring. The planes were pretty high, and of course they weren't looking for anything in particular. At ten o'clock that night, they saw running lights and McVay fired his first flare. The plane never wavered. Other rafts saw it too, because they fired flares plainly visible to McVay's men. One more plane passed that night, about 2:00 A.M. Tuesday, and again the flares sputtered out unseen. Tuesday they saw no planes at all during daylight hours. Toward morning the sea began to moderate, and all day Tuesday and Wednesday it was nearly calm, a blessed relief from the constant pounding and wetting of the first twenty-four hours.

In the long hours of torpor settling over them, there was little to do but think. And Captain McVay had much to think about. He was not normally an introversive type; quite the contrary, he loved life. His mind and heart were not of giant stature, and he never pretended they were, but it would be wrong to call him shallow. He loved life and he liked people, and he dreaded to think of what had happened to him, and what he faced.

He had no feeling of guilt. What had happened he had known might happen on one of those many times he traveled alone with no escort to fend for him or give alarm in case of trouble. Every precaution of the prudent man had been taken. Before he retired that night, all conceivable emergencies had been dealt with in the night orders. The ship was blacked out and buttoned as tightly as conditions permitted. The watch was in competent hands, and he himself strayed not a dozen feet from the bridge, available at any moment.

But Captain McVay did feel sorrow. He knew many of his officers were gone, but as bad as he thought it was, he still did not know the true magnitude of the tragedy. When he stepped foot on land again, he would learn that between him and his No. 32 in the chain of command not one officer survived. That of eighty-two officers aboard, only fifteen survived, barely one in six.

For a moment, he remembered the good times ashore, only a few weeks ago, his closest officers around him, and their wives. They would have to be told, and he would have to tell them. And the wives and parents of the others, too. Many of them would look at him with accusing eyes. Some would be angry, some would be numb with tragedy, and a very few perhaps wouldn't give a damn. As the hours ticked by there were even moments, in the night, when it seemed that rescue would never come, and maybe that was just as well. But that was not fair to the men with him, and when the sun rose these thoughts left him and he prepared again to face what he knew he must. He was ready, for a good commanding officer never shirks his responsibility. Captain McVay was a good commanding officer.

The *I-58* cruised slowly northward for several days, but the hunting was bad, and late on Thursday the radio operator intercepted a message from the Owada radio detachment in the Tokyo suburbs. It said: "We monitor many enemy messages in the mid-Pacific indicating the enemy is now searching for some very important ship sunk." Lieutenant Commander Hashimoto paid no attention to the dispatch, not connecting it with his kill. That would have been known on Monday. Such a large fleet unit could not have been missing for nearly four days without the U.S. Navy knowing about it. Or could it?

For the swimmers, the battle for survival began the instant they hit the water. First it was the struggle to get their heads above the water and out of the slimy, choking oil. They sputtered and coughed, some vomited for hours, spewing out the irritating substance, and many were blinded in one eye or both. Their noses, mouths, and throats smarted from the oil, and membranes became inflamed. And always there was the chop and splash of waves. By dawn, many were already seriously exhausted, but as the sun rose and they began to see others around them, the men took heart.

There was little talk among them, but a question often asked was whether a radio message got off the ship, and how soon rescue would come.

Officers who knew nothing about it assured the men around them that the distress message had gotten away. It was the least they could do, and if said with enough authority it even made them feel a little better. Even if no message got off, the ship would soon be missed and planes and vessels would come looking for them, the officers said. Everyone wanted to believe them so it didn't sound too bad, and if some men had little gnawing doubts, they kept them to themselves.

As the sun rose on Monday, the sea flattened out a little and the men felt better. The kapoks were holding them high, and the worst of the oil bath was over.

"These things'll hold you up at least forty-eight hours," they said, and everybody knew they'd be rescued before then. Some of the fellows began to get a little cocky, and cracked a joke now and then. The men around him got a kick out of Johnny Reid, swimming around in his bathrobe. It was shrinking by the hour. Schecterle pulled out his wallet and found a soggy dollar bill in it.

"Beer for the house," he said, and they all laughed.

But the mood didn't last long. The sun rose steadily, and as it glinted off the oil their eyes began to burn, and pretty soon they were nearly blind again—photophobia, worse than snow-blindness, because, even when shut, their eyes glowed like two red balls in their heads.

Little things began to be important. Doc Haynes discovered he'd tied up his life jacket wrong—higher on one side, so that the collar tilted his head to one side. It wasn't funny, and even less so when he discovered the water-soaked knots wouldn't come undone. He worked for hours picking those knots out with his fingernails until he finally got it undone and tied up right.

As the heat rose, thirst began to bother some men, particularly those who had dehydrated themselves with retching or coughing. But there was no deliberate drinking of seawater that day. The men warned one another about that, and they all knew it was bad for you. Potatoes, canned peanuts, onions, other bits of food floated on the surface in some places, but most of the men wouldn't eat anything. They were afraid of upsetting their stomachs further, or getting even thirstier. A few ate anything that came by, and even had a surplus in their pockets for later, but hunger was not a real problem yet.

It was some hours before they began to realize that sharks were among them. Suddenly a man screamed, his head bobbed for a moment, and he began flailing the water with his arms. Blood welled to the surface, and other men took up the cry. They beat the water with their arms and legs and shouted and screeched in an effort to scare the intruders away. At first they thought only of sharks, because everyone knew about sharks, and the telltale dorsal fin was often in evidence on the fringes of their circles. Gradually word spread from the older men that these warm equatorial waters were also host to carnivorous fish that could not be so easily seen.

"The barracuda has teeth like a razor and swims eighty miles an hour," one man said. "And if he slashes you going by he can cut your leg right off."

"Yeah, and what about the poisonous fish? One touch and you're dead," another man said.

Terror gradually spread, and the sea that once had seemed so friendly now became peopled with great and unknown perils.

Monday was generally a day of hope. Even the timid and the faint-hearted felt that something would happen—a ship would pass by and sight them, a plane would see them in the water, search parties must already be on the move.

"We were supposed to fire at sleeves tomorrow morning," they thought, "and even if the message didn't get off they'll miss us then and come looking." There was really nothing much to fear if one could just stay alive until Tuesday. True, it was a little disheartening when the first planes went over Monday afternoon and showed no signs of seeing them.

"I'll bet they saw us but couldn't stop," one said.

"Yeah, they radioed in and other ships will be out to look for us," said another. Nearly everybody believed that. If you could just hold on until Tuesday.

Some could not, of course. The injured who survived the first few hours were weakening now, with the sun high and hot, and the sea and the oil and their wounds all conspiring to sap their strength. It was pitiful to those around them not to be able to help, but there was nowhere to put them, nothing to give them, no way to protect them. They put some in the rafts, but there their bodies were fully exposed to the cruel sun. So they put them back in the water and tried to tie them to the rafts, if they were too weak to hold on. In these last hours of agony, those who had been spared injury gave unstintingly of their strength, their food, even their life jackets to help those who could not help themselves. But in most cases it was not enough. The burned and the maimed slipped away, one by one, and by Monday night nearly all of them were gone.

One of the last to go was Commander Lipski, whose grit had kept him alive despite his ghastly burns. Finally, now blind and nearly incoherent, he gasped out to Doc Haynes, "I'm going now, Lew. Tell my wife I love her, and I want her to marry again." They took the life jacket off his body and committed it to the sea.

It was a relief when the sun went down on Monday, but as darkness settled the wind turned cold and the men felt it as you do only in the tropics. After the blasting heat of the day the effect is devastating. It was black again now, and the men knew the full terrors of the deep. It was hard to see the man next to you, and there was the paralyzing fear of getting lost, getting separated from the group, dozing off and waking to find yourself alone in this vast sea. Sleep was becoming a peril now. During the day, many of the men had napped briefly, knowing that buddies would waken them if their heads got too near the water, or a slap from the sea would shake them up. At night, you might slip away or go under and nobody would know it. So they clung together in little knots, or held on to bits of line in the water. Some men tied their life jackets together, knotting the strings at the chest like Siamese twins.

The strongest and the bravest tried to stay alert, even riding herd on the group like swimming cowpunchers, bringing back the strays and holding the men together. More than one, in this way, used up the reserves that might have kept him alive in the final hours of agony. They were, in truth, laying down their lives for their friends.

For most men, the night was worse than the day. Man's spirit normally sinks at night, and during the long, dark hours they fell prey to fears forgotten by day. It was a grim band, indeed, that struggled through the first twenty-four hours in the water, and in the hours just before dawn a few men began to ask themselves why they fought on. A few, weak and dispirited, perhaps impelled by some previous purposelessness in their lives, may indeed have succumbed to the lassitude of despair. It was so easy just to slip down, to let go, to sink, and in a few moments it was all over. But the first streaks of morning light in the sky revived the great majority of them, and they prepared to meet the day of rescue. For surely help would come on Tuesday.

The wind dropped and the sea moderated Tuesday, and the men took it as a good omen. They were weaker than the day before, but they had hope. They realized that the kapoks were becoming waterlogged, and their chins were nearer the water, but they could last the day out, and before nightfall they could expect to be warm and dry aboard some ship. Some were beginning now to indulge in little orgies of just thinking—a dry sack, a warm place, a steak, a cold beer. A man could devote hours just to putting the trimmings around the steak, or thinking of his own bed at home and his mother saying, "Oh, let him sleep a little longer." Older men might realize that madness could lie in thoughts like these, so they tried not to think at all, or to think of something useful, or helpful, or immediate. Married men could think of their wives and children, of the good times they had known and would know again, must know again. A father couldn't afford to die, his family needed him.

Tuesday was hot again, hotter than Monday, but nobody wished for night to come. Besides the fears of the dark, ships and planes couldn't see you at night. Night was a foe. But as the daylight hours passed, nothing happened. No plane passed overhead, and no ship came plowing down on them. The strain began to show. There were quarrels at the rafts and the nets. Men were irritable and they began to bicker about turns on the raft, a fair share of the rations, where there were any. Some men said the officers were hogging the rafts, or hiding food, or eating secretly. The man who was your friend yesterday was your enemy today, because he had some potatoes and wouldn't give you any. The bosun you thought was such a good egg had been in the raft for hours and wouldn't let you in. The guy over there had two good life jackets and yours was shot, but he wouldn't give you one. Some of this was true, but much was only imagined. But my God, how much did they think a man could stand, out here in the water all this time and nobody giving a damn. Probably haven't even missed us.

Almost from the first, men began discovering that life-jacket design was an art not yet mastered. The rubber life belts were the worst.

In the first place, many refused to inflate, for a variety of causes. Even if they did, they gave little support when worn around the waist, as intended. For one reason or another, perhaps because some were old or the seawater and oil affected them, many burst in a matter of hours. They were better than nothing, to be sure, but not much. The kapok jackets, of the so-called horse-collar type, gave good support, but the collars soon began to rub the men's necks and chins, increasing their suffering as the salt water and oil inflamed the irritated parts. Salt-water ulcers set in around the skin rubbed raw by the scratchy canvas. For that matter, men soon found ulcers developing at any spot where their skin had been cut, burned, rubbed, or otherwise injured during their ordeal. Although they were painful, the ulcers did not strike them as serious at the time, but some men suffered for months afterward if, of course, they were lucky enough to survive at all.

From the first dawn, the ingenious among them—there were many— tried to devise ways to beat the sun. The fortunate, who had left the ship clothed and wearing hats, were best off, but most men had plunged into the water in the sketchiest of clothing—shorts only, shorts and skivvies, or nothing at all, if that's the way you referred to sleep or you were caught in the shower. Those who could lay their hands on bits of cloth—pants, shirt, underwear, even socks—tore them up and tried to make hats, eyeshades, noseguards, or collar pieces to protect their necks from the rubbing life jackets. But the best efforts were to little avail. Men's lips began to puff and crack, their eyelids swelled, their faces burned and burned again. The oil helped some on the upper body, but around the head it was highly irritating to delicate membranes of the eyes, nose, and mouth. By Tuesday night the swimmers were in pitiful shape. Most were nearly blind, and it was difficult to see the man nearest you, let alone recognize him, his face swollen and distorted as badly as your own. This may have accounted for some of the events of the next two days, for the man you didn't know was not merely a stranger, he was an enemy.

Thirst was more of a problem than hunger. Some men were quickly in an acute condition from dehydration, either because they had swallowed large quantities of salt water in fighting to survive the sinking or because the fuel oil and water forced them into long spells of vomiting or coughing. This dried out their systems abnormally and they began to contemplate the water all around them with more than ordinary interest. As the sun rose higher and hotter on Monday, some men began thinking of schemes for making the sea-water potable. At this stage, before dementia had set in on a large scale, and their bellies began to hurt, they talked a little of "straining" the water, or "evaporating" it.

"How about it if you hold some water in your hands? Won't the sun evaporate the salt out?"

"What do you say we strain some water through this hat a couple of times? We can catch it in this handkerchief and squeeze it through again. That ought to do it."

"Knock it off, it'll still kill you," said the clearheaded around them. But pretty soon even the clearheaded had problems of their own, and they became less careful or less watchful. Then the men who could stand it no longer took first a little drink, then a bigger one, and a still bigger one. It is a horrible death, but it comes quickly enough. During the last paroxysms, friends about them sought either to hold them or to escape from their wild thrashings, until at last the bodies subsided and became still. It was time then to salvage the life jacket and knife, mirror, or any other potentially useful object and let the body sink slowly out of sight.

If Tuesday was a day of hope, that hope died when night fell and not a single plane had flown over during daylight. It was then that men truly called upon the wellsprings of strength and courage within them. This was the night they began to see things. Some saw planes barely skimming the surface, others saw the running lights of ships bearing down on them. The latter image terror-ized some men, for they thought the Japanese sub had surfaced to machine-gun them. And as the night wind chilled them, their teeth chattered and their bodies shook with violent seizures. This was the night that most of them passed from the world of sanity into the world of fantasy. Many of them ceased to suffer in the usual sense, even as the asylum inmate may no longer suffer from a world that is too much for him. No gong rang early Wednesday to signal the end of two full days in the water, and few men even thought of time anymore. Only later did they realize that by dawn they had been fifty-five hours in this macabre world, specks on the surface of the world's largest sea, floating helpless and unhelped, as if no one knew or cared.

Wednesday was a delightful day for the swimmers. It was the day they learned the *Indianapolis* had not sunk after all. She was lying just below the surface of the water, and the gedunk stand was open, featuring six flavors of ice cream, and the scuttlebutts were pouring forth pure, sweet water as usual. The first man to discover this was so delighted with the find that he urged all those around him to go down with him and slake the terrible thirst that was driving them mad. As the word passed, a sort of frenzy ran through the swimmers and in a short time many were diving like swans, using up the last resources of strength that might have saved their lives. Some men who had not yet passed fully into the world of fantasy tried to restrain them, but it was useless.

Also, on this day, the island was discovered. It was amazing no one had seen it before, but suddenly there it was, a nice little island, with an air strip and a hotel. Some of the men were skeptical. Lieutenant McKissick called one of the men aside and asked him, honestly, if the island was really there. The fellow said sure, he knew the Chinese who ran it, but he had swum over and the man wouldn't give him any water, or even let him come ashore.

The lieutenant bided his time until nightfall, then he and his buddy started to swim over. On the way, some of the men tried to take their life jackets. The pair fought them off and swam on, but the island had moved and they became exhausted. They tied their life jackets together and slept for a couple of hours, but when McKissick awoke his buddy had gone, leaving an empty life jacket. McKissick heard him in the distance and called out, but his buddy kept going. The lieutenant never saw him again.

At dawn, McKissick started out alone for the island but soon met a couple of kids and gave them the extra life jacket. Then they passed a couple of Marines on a potato crate and invited them to come along. No thanks, said the Marines, they were swimming to Leyte.

"Well, why don't you come over to the island first and have a cold drink, then swim to Leyte?" McKissick asked. That seemed like a good idea and the Marines fell in with the party. But when they got to the island, it was under water. One boy said his mother ran the hotel, and they'd have to wait until it was open for business.

"My room's over there," he said, pointing. "My mother runs this place but I'm not very familiar with it. She's just taken it over."

He called the hotel on the telephone. A steward who used to be on the *Indianapolis* answered and said the hotel was full, but McKissick said, "Here, let me talk to that guy."

"No, he won't talk to you. He won't even talk to me, and my mother owns this place."

Then a lot of planes flew over, and the young men pointed out the air strip, but the oblivious aviators just kept going. It made the sailors mad, but they decided to lie there in their life jackets and wait for rooms at the hotel.

Another bunch of men tried to get ashore on the island, or maybe it was another island, but the Seabees wouldn't let them. So they, too, got mad and swam off. Wouldn't tell anybody where they were going, but just disappeared.

One fellow, after thinking about it steadily for a long time, announced he had figured out that he could swim to Leyte in two and a half days. With a wave of his hand, he struck out toward the west. Some fellows were quietly content where they were. Yeoman Buckett spent all day in a store filled with ice-cold watermelons. The fellow in charge told him he could eat all he wanted to. Watertender Wilcox spent Wednesday quietly, praying steadily most of the day, and crying some when he remembered his wife at home. He was determined, however, that if anyone could survive, he could. Toward nightfall, Wilcox thought that the fellows who did a lot of talking seemed to be doing better so he started to jabber to the man alongside him. The other fellow didn't mind; he was out of his head.

Lieutenant Reid dropped his car keys and dove frantically for them. He simply had to have them, so he could drive over to his farm in New Hampshire, and get some cold milk. He never did find the keys, but he noticed that his ring had slipped off his finger and gone down.

Seaman Second Class Joe Dronet, a quiet young man of seventeen from Cameron, Louisiana, remembered his boot training well, so when the sharks came around he didn't kick and scream like the others. He lay on his back quietly, and they never touched him. Others around him were slashed and bleeding, but the sharks never came near him. And then he felt that he really couldn't die. His mother had worked so hard to get him through high school and it nearly broke her heart when he went away, what with her four other boys already in service. So Joe just made up his mind he wouldn't die, and when the deck officer and twenty-five men swam off for that island, Joe just clung to his floater net. There was a time near the end when he'd take a little salt water in his mouth, but he always summoned up enough willpower to spit it out. Lack of sleep was a torture, but he had seen too many men go that way, so he resolved never to shut his eyes.

Some of the life jackets were reaching the saturation point now, and every once in a while a man would fight to get out of his before it sank, only to find that he was fatally trapped in his "life" jacket. It was horrible for the others to watch, but what could they do? There was no way to get the sodden jacket off, and they couldn't hold someone else up when their own chins were now in the water.

In truth, for the swimmers, Wednesday was a day of horror. It was a costly day in lives, for many men swam off and never came back or dived down to the ship and never came up. Still others gave their lives trying to prevent these suicidal jaunts. The big Marine, Captain Parke, swam around and around his group trying to hold it together, but toward evening he quietly sank beneath the sea, exhausted. Father Conway wore himself out in similar solicitude and on Wednesday night collapsed in delirium and expired in Doc Haynes' arms.

By contrast, Wednesday was a good day on the rafts. The sea was calm and flat, the men were well-fixed for food and shelter from the sun, and they had settled down for the long wait. Captain McVay from the start had put his faith in ships finding them, not planes, and had figured that Thursday would be the earliest they could be expected. While they had seen no planes on Tuesday, Wednesday was a big day, with eight or nine passing over. McVay's group gave them the works—Very flares, the signal mirror, two signaling flags waving wildly, yellow bunting streaming over the waves, and every available leg splashing water. But it was no good, the planes were too high.

"They aren't looking for anything down here, you know," Captain McVay told his men, trying to reconcile them. "They're busy with their radar and instruments, and even if they did look down they wouldn't see much from that altitude." The men acknowledged this, but the thought didn't make them feel any better.

As the sun sank Wednesday, the men's spirits began to decline also. They had been sleeping or quiet most of the day, except Glenn and Havins, who chatted cheerfully. One man took to moaning, but when Muldoon asked him if anything was wrong he said no, and quieted down. The captain kept telling the men that Thursday would be their day.

"They probably missed us on Tuesday, and began looking for us today," he said. "Figuring twenty-four hours to get here, they should reach us tomorrow."

At other times he told them, "There's really nothing to worry about, men. Our chances are very good. We can hold out for a long time on these rafts, and they certainly must be looking for us by now." In this way the third day ended and they passed into the fourth day on the open sea.

But among the swimmers, morale was deteriorating rapidly. There had been some fighting on the lines Tuesday night, but Wednesday night was a night of terror. When darkness fell the demented men were the victims of stark fear, and every shape became an enemy.

"There's Japs on this line," someone screamed and a little knot of men would be plunged into a melee, fighting with fists, cans, cork, anything that came to hand. Now and then a knife blade flashed in the moonlight, followed by a groan and then a struggle for a life jacket whose recent owner needed it no more.

"Here comes a Jap, he's trying to kill me," a sailor shouted. "Help! help!" The frenzied men took up the shout and began swinging wildly at anyone near. Two men climbed on Doc Haynes and dragged him under. When he struggled to the top again he tried to calm the men, but it was no use. They were too far gone for reason. Those who still possessed their senses could see the toll was terrible.

Toward morning, calm slowly returned and it was obvious the men were falling into the final stupor that precedes death. Haynes moved among the pitiful survivors, trying to rouse them for one last day's fight. He lifted head after head from the water, rolled back an eyelid, and, in some, detected signs of life. These men he slapped and cajoled into consciousness, trying to pull them back from the brink.

"This is it," he thought. "Today, or never." Looking around at what had been his three hundred men, he counted less than a hundred left, and of those still in sight not all were viable. Some floated face down and would never lift their heads again. Lieutenant Redmayne's sector was the same. In the rafts, men were piled all over each other, and those at the bottom of the heap, too weak to protest or move, were smothered by bodies above them. Bitterness among the dozens of men trying to get on or near the three small rafts directed itself, rightly or wrongly, but certainly naturally, toward the officers.

"Goddamn officers, hogging the rafts and all the food," some muttered. "I'll kill that son of a bitch when we get on shore. Drinking up all the water, and we got none."

Thursday began as a day of calm—the calm of death for the swimmers. With all strength gone, all emotion spent, they seemed nearer death than life, and indeed they were. There was little talk or movement, just a quiet waiting for the end to overtake them. Hanging in their waterlogged life jackets, their mouths and noses nearly in the water, they no longer wished or hoped for anything, not even death. The inevitable sun rose, higher and hotter, and still no complaints. They were not capable of caring anymore. A few, slightly stronger than the others, looked up occasionally or even strained to listen when they thought they heard a plane. A little before noon, with the sun still mounting, a few looked up when a plane droned by, high overhead. There was a scattering of muttered curses, even a doubled fist raised weakly out of the water. The plane passed over, to the north. They had known it would.

Then, here and there, a heart fluttered. The plane seemed to pause, to turn. Some thought it was starting down. It was, it was!

"He sees us, he sees us!" someone screamed. Others joined in, and arms and legs began to splash.

"They're coming, they're coming!" "He's turning, he's turning!" "Here he comes!"

Like sleepers roused from stupor the men began to come alive, joining in the chorus one by one. Where they got the strength no one can say, but soon the ocean was kicked into a froth, and cries echoed from many throats. Some men could only croak or grunt, their gullets swollen nearly shut, and some men didn't move or utter a sound. Too late, too late.

It was almost exactly three and a half days—eighty-four hours—since the *Indianapolis* had gone down.

They watched the plane, the blessed plane, as it came down low and circled, and some men cried and prayed, "God give us strength." They realized gradually that the plane alone could not save them. There was no telling how long it would be until ships arrived, and each man made his own plans for hanging on for the next few minutes, or hours. Now was no time for dying, help was too near. Mustn't fall asleep now, or lose your head. Just wait and be calm, be calm. Save your strength, stop kicking and shouting. He sees us, he'll get the others, the ships will come. Just hold on. Oh God, give me strength.

The big, friendly plane circled slowly and then—over the southernmost knot of men—a raft, some life jackets, and other gear spewed from the plane and fell nearby. Grateful men swam out to get the raft, careful not to overtax their strength, and when they reached it, clung to the sides, too weak to climb in. Others grabbed the fresh, dry life jackets to replace their waterlogged ones. Men for miles around watched as the plane slowly climbed away from them, and held their breath until they saw that she was not going away. It was comforting to have her there, even though she could do them no immediate good. As long as she stayed they knew she was helping them, telling someone by radio where to look, calling others to their aid.

The second plane, a PBY, arrived from the northeast a little after noon. She didn't stay long, but she dropped three more life rafts and then hurried on to the west, toward Leyte. Hope was getting stronger now; other planes would be coming, and ships. Another plane, a Ventura like the first, arrived a half hour later, and also from the south. The two Venturas orbited overhead and seemed to be talking, or planning, and watching. Then the first Ventura, their friend, their savior, took off southward, obviously going back to base to get more help. The second Ventura remained overhead, but it wasn't until nearly four o'clock, with the sun already starting down, that the next plane arrived. This was a big amphibian from the south, and after a look around she began to drop things, like an elephant littering the track at the circus. Out came rafts, one after another, and cartons of rations, dye marker, life jackets, casks of water. Some of the water casks split on hitting the water, some of the gear sank, and some was useless, but it was all welcome, if only as a symbol that help was on the way.

But day was definitely waning, and the men in the water began to wonder if still another night in the water, their fourth, would be required of them. To make matters worse, the sea was beginning to make up again. Toward sunset those few left in the southernmost group, the Haynes group, watched in wonder as the PBY slowly glided down as if to make a landing run. It looked like suicide, with the swells running nearly twelve feet high by this time. But the giant plane kept coming down and suddenly it pancaked into a trough, took three mighty bounces in a towering spray, and came safely to rest on the water.

Strangled cheers broke through sore and swollen lips and throats as the PBY began to taxi slowly around the periphery, pausing now and then to scoop a lone swimmer into its belly. Those who now had rafts, nets, or other means of support cursed at the plane as it passed them without stopping, but it was obvious what the pilot was doing—as darkness fell he was hurrying to pick up the lone swimmers, those with nothing to cling to.

It was very nearly dark now, and just as the last light began to fade a second PBY came in from the south, low and slow. This one, bearing Army markings, quickly came down to wave-top height, knifed through the tops of several swells, and cut her power, disappearing in a trough. Soon she appeared on the crest of a wave, safely landed. She seemed quite a way off from any swimmers, but maybe some could find her in the dark. Those still in the water, and there were hundreds, were alone again now, but at least they had hope, and perhaps a raft, to sustain them through the darkness.

Eight or ten miles to the north, Captain McVay and the other raft parties could see the plane activity through the afternoon. McVay was greatly cheered, not only because rescue seemed near but because the concentration of activity far south indicated there might be many more survivors than he had believed. But as the afternoon waned and the planes seemed to be working ever southward, the raft crews began to worry that they would not be seen.

Again at dusk, as he had each night, Captain McVay led the men in reciting "The Lord's Prayer." It seemed more helpful than usual this night.

McVay began to think his group must be north of the northern limit of the search area.

"We're in a fine fix now," he thought. "If they're going south all the time and we're going north, they are going to miss us."

Naturally he did not express these thoughts to his men, but they were no fools, they could figure as well as he could.

McVay's eye fell on the 40-mm. can they had retrieved at great effort, thinking it might contain provisions. It was empty, but they had kept it, and now was the time to put it to use.

"We'll make a fire in the can and see if we can't attract the planes," McVay said. They quickly tore the collars off a couple of life jackets, and cut up a rubber life preserver. These were put in the can, and McVay fired a Very rocked into the pile. The cloth and rubber began to smolder, and shortly they had a good smudge pot going. They kept it burning well past nightfall, but it seemed to have no effect. The men's spirits sank, and they began to doze.

But this was not to be a night like the others. About 9:30 some of the swimmers and rafters began to notice a light far to the south. At first it seemed it might be an illusion or a faint moon rising behind the clouds. As time passed, however, the light became stronger and within a half hour it seemed pretty definitely to be a searchlight, reflected off the clouds. By the time an hour had gone by, the light was unquestionably brighter, and coming closer, although still a long way off. By 11:00 they were sure—it was a ship coming at them, fast, and with all lights on.

One of the most powerful—and subtlest—enemies had been sleep. The human body can survive many days without food or water, under severe physical conditions, but the brain demands rest. After the first day in the water, the men passed into a sort of drunkenness of fatigue. They feared sleep and they fought it, because it separated them from the world of reality, the world in which they might be saved, and placed them at the mercy of the sea and its unknown terrors, both on the water and below it. They all dozed at times, some in the safety of a raft, others in private little havens they built of kapoks, cans, crates, anything they could put together to give a measure of safety. Others merely dropped their heads from sheer exhaustion as they bobbed up and down in the ever-lowering life jackets.

Now that help was so near, they feared sleep more than ever and were less able to fight it, being on the outer edges of oblivion.

"I mustn't sleep, I mustn't sleep," they told themselves. Men who had not once slept in eighty hours, or so they believed, vowed they would not succumb now, with help so near, so near. But the sea was rougher Thursday night, security so close, and they were so tired—not every man kept his vow.

On the rafts to the north, the men could see the searchlights off to the south, first one, then several, and finally by dawn there was great activity. But it did not move north, or so it seemed.

For the swimmers, actual rescue in the form of help from surface vessels began shortly after midnight on Thursday, exactly four days, or ninety-six hours, from the sinking of the *Indianapolis*. By chance, the first vessel approached from the south. Had she come from the north, she might have seen the men on the rafts first—the men who could wait—and delayed long enough to cost even more lives, for with the swimmers minutes counted. But the planes on the water and the accident of approach led the ships directly to the men who needed help the most, and through the black hours from midnight to dawn the rescue vessels picked up one of the most pitiful bands of men ever to escape the sea. Men suffered from burns—sun or flame—fish bites, salt-water ulcers, inflammation of the nose and throat, acute dehydration, pneumonia, fractures, and cuts and bruises from a thousand sources. But hearts still pumped and blood still flowed and from now on it would be up to medical science.

At dawn the rescue vessels began to see what they had been doing and to realize the magnitude of the appalling tragedy before them. Command and planning took over from the frantic and haphazard methods of the dark hours. They began to take stock of how many men they had aboard, how many might still be in the sea, and how best to comb the area for the last remaining survivor. On orders now, the vessels spread out in each pattern sniffing for the living among this welter of oil, debris, and bodies.

Last to be rescued were the rafters, at the north of the group. Their most anxious moments came in the last hours of Friday morning darkness, when it seemed the ships were so near and yet would miss them. But at dawn they saw planes to the north and hope rose again. The planes were obviously on box search, and coming ever closer.

At 10:00 A.M. they saw ships, and suddenly someone shouted, "My God, ships bearing down on us! The hell with the planes, we know these guys will pick us up."

Later they learned that neither planes nor ships had seen them, but one of the APD's picked up a radar pip at 4,046 yards. It was the trusty 40-mm. can, McVay's smoke pot. The vessel maneuvered skillfully alongside and gathered in the men—107 hours after the sinking.

It was the end of one of the strangest, most dramatic battles of men against the sea. It was the end, and also it was the beginning, for with these suffering and exhausted men lay the answer to the question: What happened to nearly nine hundred of your shipmates?

PART FIVE

The Hand of Man: Of Failure and Catastrophe

A Killing Wind: Inside Union Carbide and the Bhopal Catastrophe

BY DAN KURZMAN

His prose has that elusive readability of a master story-teller, but there are no yarns being spun on his pages. Dan Kurzman's engaging and illuminating books (fifteen to date) are focused on actual events that demand our attention and understanding long after they are off the front pages of our newspapers. Too numerous to mention in their entirety, Kurzman's titles have included such outstanding disaster chronicles as *Left to Die: The Tragedy of the USS Juneau* and *Fatal Voyage: The Sinking of the USS Indianapolis*. Biographies he has written include *Soldier of Peace: The Life of Yitzhak Rubin, 1922–1995* and *Ben-Gurion: Prophet of Fire*. His books of military campaigns include *Blood and Water: Sabotaging Hitler's Bomb* and *The Bravest Battle: The 28 Days of the Warsaw Ghetto Uprising*. A former *Washington Post* correspondent, Kurzman has been the winner of many outstanding literary and journalistic awards.

To tell the story of the worst industrial accident in history, there could be no more respected and distinguished writer than Dan Kurzman.

A Killing Wind: Inside Union Carbide and the Bhopal Catastrophe is a disaster classic—the ultimate account of an event so horrific its consequences have never been forgotten. The copy on the jacket of the book sets the scene perfectly, and I shall not attempt to improve upon it:

"In the early morning hours of December 3, 1984, a rolling wind carried a poisonous gray cloud past the walls of the Union Carbide plant in Bhopal, India. An estimated 8,000 or more people died (over three times the officially announced total), people whose hopes and dreams were, ironically, bound up with the technology and affluence the plant symbolized. About 300,000 more would suffer debilitating injuries from the insidious effects of the massive poisoning, while no one would say if future generations would be affected.

"*A Killing Wind*, based on hundreds of interviews and thousands of documents, reflects the passionate drama of this tragic incident. It is a tale, told in detail for the first time, of terror and torment, guilt and innocence. It is the entire Bhopal story to date—the background, the hour-by-hour events, the difficult decisions, and the bitter aftermath, in a book that matches the scope and depth of Kurzman's acclaimed *Day of the Bomb: Countdown to Hiroshima*."

Obviously, this simple excerpt from Kurzman's wonderful book can only tell you part of the story. But perhaps it will inspire you to read the full book and gain an even deeper appreciation of Kurzman's talent and dedication in laying bare the human suffering caused by this great disaster.

✳   ✳   ✳   ✳   ✳

Suman Dey felt at home in the control room, for he liked to be in control. His eyes were fixed on the gauges and indicators that showed pressure, temperature, level, and flow; on the alarm systems that warned operators of abnormal conditions and possible peril; on the interlocks that automatically shut down parts of the plant when danger threatened; and on various other safety devices.

And though Dey relished the power of the switch-puller, he—and many other workers—did not fully trust the devices, they told the author. Either the devices did not work, the workers said, or were not put to work all the time. And those that did work, they added, often were not effective; there were too few of them, and they were antiquated, ill-designed, and unsupported by modern backup systems.

The alarm on the tank, said the workers, had not been working for four years, and there was only one manual backup alarm system instead of the four-stage system they had heard was used in the United States. And since this system was not automatic, someone had to *realize* that there was a leak before the alarm would sound. The flare tower, which burned escaping gas, was being repaired, and the vent gas scrubber, which neutralized escaping gas, had just been repaired and was not yet ready for use. The refrigeration system, which would keep the MIC in the tanks cool so it wouldn't turn into gas, was lying idle to save power. Similarly, the workers said, there was often no steam to help evacuate poison from the pipes and other equipment because the management, they stated, considered it wasteful to keep the boiler operating during shutdowns.

Furthermore, according to the workers, since the chlorine storage tank valve was open to the atmosphere, chlorine escaped "nearly every day."

And chloroform did, too, through a vent line. Nor did the method used to monitor the chemical composition of MIC seem to differentiate between the phosgene and chlorine ion concentration. Only eight shutdown devices serviced the MIC unit, said the workers, though safety engineers advised triple that number. Just one level indicator, pressure gauge, and temperature gauge—which, like the tank alarm, had been out of service for four years—graced each of the three MIC tanks despite the need for at least two or three in different locations in case of an out-of-control situation. And instruments in the control room that were calibrated in pounds per square inch, the workers concluded, were interconnected with others in the plant that were calibrated in kilograms per square centimeter. Plant officials would not respond to these charges, citing the litigation.

Dey was a bit concerned about tank 610, which contained forty-one tons of liquid MIC. The pressure gauge for it registered two pounds per square inch—normal. Yet he knew that something was wrong with this tank. MIC in the tank was to have been converted into pesticide about a week earlier, but workers had been unable to pump it into the Sevin unit. When they tried to force it out of the tank by pumping in nitrogen, the nitrogen leaked. As a result, a second tank, 611, was used instead, and 610 stood nearly overflowing with MIC.

Nor did Dey know whether the temperature had risen during the previous shift, since it had not been recorded. There was no column in the log book in which to record it—perhaps because the MIC temperature was usually maintained, said the workers, at about 20 degrees Celsius (70 degrees Fahrenheit) though the operating manual called for a reading of under 4.5 degrees Celsius (40 degrees Fahrenheit). Also, the range of the temperature gauge was too limited to show critical danger. And the range of the pressure gauge was, too, they said, and therefore could not indicate when to open the relief valve so that escaping gas could go through the vent gas scrubber. UCIL would not reply, citing the litigation again, though a Danbury spokesman did say he thought the gauges were adequate.

Dey, in any case, wasn't seriously worried. Not even when he glanced at the pressure gauge at 11 P.M. and noted, he told the author, that it read ten pounds per square inch. He was puzzled, though. The log said that only a half hour before, at 10:30 P.M., it had read two pounds. An unusual rise in a half hour, he asserted. But the situation was hardly critical. The pressure was still within the normal range. And weren't the gauges often wrong anyway? No need, Dey felt, to report this curious change to the new shift supervisor, Shakil Qureshi.

Meanwhile, in a corner of the MIC area, the other operators on the new shift sat around talking and waiting for orders, when suddenly, shortly after 11:30 P.M., one of them cut in on his colleagues: He smelled MIC. The others sniffed and agreed. Their eyes were irritated, too. But nothing to get excited about—even if tearing occurred at about 2 ppm, 100 times the recommended exposure limit. They often sniffed MIC, the workers explained, though the plant managers said it leaked only occasionally. Vexed by this interruption of their leisure, they rose and, with almost apathetic calm, searched for a leak in the MIC unit area so they could plug it. After a while, they noted some liquid, cloaked in a thin haze of light-colored gas, dripping from the RVVH at a height of about fifty feet. Was that the source of the leak? Was it water or MIC? No one was sure. A minor matter, the workers say they felt, but three of them, V. N. Singh, R. K. Khamparia, and B. Mani, went to Qureshi's office across from the control room to dutifully report on the leak.

Qureshi sat behind his desk, his 220 pounds of hard flesh sprawled copiously on a chair that, it seemed, could barely support the weight. He had the massive body of a professional wrestler and the rugged face of a truck driver, fat, shrewd-eyed, pug-nosed. He was rather a gentle man—when he wasn't dealing with MIC. To Qureshi, MIC was not simply a chemical, it was a challenge. No one in the plant, he felt, indeed no one anywhere, knew MIC as intimately as he. He could control it under all circumstances, and so was never afraid of it. He couldn't imagine that it might kill him. How could it kill a man who knew its every trick, its every whim, its every weakness? MIC was his slave—and his love. For who could not love the source of his pride and strength?

Qureshi, a native of Bhopal, had handled MIC for Union Carbide since he was hired in 1974, when it was still being shipped from the United States. His experience and dedication had made him one of the most valuable men in the plant. But not one of the most popular with the workers. He was extremely qualified, they agreed—he had a master's degree in organic chemistry from Bhopal University—but, as supervisor, it seemed, he too ardently supported management policy. Yet wasn't he a simple worker like themselves who should have sympathized with their grievances? Ironically, management felt he sympathized too strongly with his men. Anyway, Qureshi gave the workers confidence by casting MIC as a challenge rather than as a threat. And now they presented him with this new, if seemingly modest, challenge.

Where was the leak coming from? Qureshi asked.

They didn't know, the three visitors said, but they had seen liquid dripping from the RVVH. V. N. Singh would later say that he told Qureshi the liquid was MIC, while Qureshi would claim that he had been told it was water. Regardless, Qureshi would have ample reason to make investigators think he had understood the liquid to be water, for he showed little sense of urgency, though he ordered the men to stop the water-washing operation just in case some water had seeped into the RVVH.

They should try to identify and plug the leak, Qureshi said, but only after teatime. No rush. MIC would not frighten him into precipitous action. He would master it as he always had—at his convenience.

The workers, while complacent themselves, were somewhat more respectful of MIC. And since there were still a few minutes before teatime, they continued their search for the leak. But at about 12:15 A.M. they ambled to the control room, where they joined Suman Dey. Dey says he was surprised to learn there was an MIC leak, for he couldn't smell it in the control room. He glanced at the pressure gauge for tank 610; the pressure remained steady. He was no more alarmed than the others.

Danbury firmly disputes this version of the atmosphere as portrayed by the workers. A spokesman quoted the tea boy as saying there was great tension in the room when he entered and that only three workers would even take tea. Why were they so tense? Because, said the spokesman, they had "learned" that a colleague had engaged in sabotage and a disaster could occur.

The workers agree that they talked about the leak, but only in a leisurely way. What was that drip of liquid? Where else could the leak be coming from? No reason to worry, though. They would find out, as they always did. Finally, at about 12:40 A.M., they departed, leaving Dey alone. They were hardly out of the room when they began coughing and choking, and their eyes, already irritated, began to burn. The MIC was out of control!

When Dey looked out the door and saw what was happening, his eyes again darted to the pressure gauge for tank 610; it had suddenly shot up past forty-five pounds per square inch and was rising rapidly. The temperature reading was just as shocking: The indicator had hit the top of the scale—77 degrees Celsius (107.6 degrees Fahrenheit), almost twice the prescribed ceiling. The liquid MIC must be turning into gas! In dismay, Dey glanced one more time at the pressure gauge and dashed to Qureshi's office, where some of the workers had gathered in panic.

"The pressure in 610 is rising to fifty-five pounds!" he cried.

Then Dey and another operator, Chandra Nath Sen, ran to the tank area about 100 feet way to investigate, with Qureshi and several other men close on their tail. Dey climbed up the ladder to the sixty-foot-long, six-foot-thick concrete slab covering the three partially sunken stainless-steel MIC tanks when suddenly it began to tremble under them and a great boiling sound in tank 610 made Dey feel he was standing on the lid of a huge, thrashing kettle. In terror Dey scrambled down and started running with the others. He looked back and was horrified. The concrete had cracked from the intense heat and gas had begun to hiss out of the crippled vent gas scrubber attached to it into the chilly night, no longer impeded by a final safety valve, which had suddenly popped off. It was 12:56 A.M.

While someone rushed to set off a glass-enclosed emergency siren, the others fled to the control room, where Dey found that both the pressure and the temperature indicators had flown off the scale. On Qureshi's order, he grabbed a microphone and screamed over the public address system: "There's a massive leak in the MIC storage area. Please take the proper safety precautions!"

At that moment, about 1 A.M., a siren wailed into the night, warning not only plant personnel but the neighboring inhabitants that a leak had occurred. However, it trailed off after a few minutes. According to the workers, that was all the time the company thought was required to signal danger; there was no need to panic the people. Anyway, management felt, the leak would be controlled before the gas could do more than irritate the eyes and skin of a few people. Critics argue that management didn't want to bring too much attention to the plant's lapses in safety. A muted "hooter" thus took over, a siren that, like the public address system, could be heard only inside the plant.

Qureshi knew that the factory had five major methods of preventing or neutralizing a runaway MIC reaction. One of them would surely work.

"Bring out the fire brigade!" Dey, on his boss's orders, cried over the loudspeaker.

Soon a truck packed with amateur fire fighters and their equipment careened into the MIC area and began spraying the hot vent line from hoses attached to nearby hydrants, since water would help to neutralize the gas. But the spray, workers told the author, could only reach to 100 feet, while the vent was 120 feet high! (The Union Carbide spokesman says other workers stated that the spray did reach the vapor.) The gas kept shooting relentlessly into the sky— just as the home office investigators feared might happen when they recommended in their 1982 report that UCIL install a more powerful spraying unit.

Maybe the next method would work.

"Start the scrubber pump!" Qureshi shouted to Dey.

Dey ran toward the vent gas scrubber, which resembled a huge sky-pointed rocket clinging to the plant. The gas now was escaping through the scrubber without being "scrubbed" by a caustic soda solution, which was to transform it into a harmless vapor as it burst into the air. One reason was that the scrubber had been under repair until recently and the pump circulating the caustic soda within it had not yet been turned on.

Dey turned on the pump, but the indicator on the caustic soda flow meter did not move. He was not sure what this meant. Was the pump defective? Was it the meter? Or was there simply not enough caustic soda in the scrubber? Whatever the case, Dey soon realized, the scrubber could not do the job. It was designed to neutralize smaller volumes of gas with temperatures up to 70 degrees Celsius (158 degrees Fahrenheit). But the gas was gushing out and its temperature had soared to 120 degrees Celsius (250 degrees Fahrenheit). Thus, even if the scrubber were in perfect shape, it would not possibly "scrub" more than about seven of the forty tons of gas in the tank.

At about this time, K. V. Shetty, the plant superintendent for the shift, who had been in another part of the plant, burst into the control room.

"What should we do?" Dey asked him.

Transfer the contents of tank 610 to tank 619 before it all turns to gas, Shetty suggested.

Qureshi, who was planning to do this anyway, agreed. Tank 619, unlike its sister tanks 610 and 611, which serviced the Sevin unit, was supposed to be kept empty for just such an emergency. A pipe connected it to tank 610, and the valves could be opened in about three minutes.

But Qureshi then shook his head in despair. This method could make matters worse, he suddenly realized. Despite the safety stipulation, he sighed, there was some liquid MIC in tank 619. Instead of slowing up the reaction in tank 610, the transfer would contaminate tank 619, turning the liquid it contained into gas, too, and compounding the disaster. There was already some reaction in that tank, he noted; the control panel showed that the pressure was rising.

Dey and Shetty, who was more administrator than technician, conceded Qureshi was right. And the desperate dialogue continued. Was it still possible to cool the remaining liquid in tank 610 so it would not vaporize? They had a thirty-ton refrigeration unit that circulated the liquid and kept it cool enough. But there was one small problem. The refrigerant, Freon 22, had been removed and the system had been closed down for five months to save on power! How long would it take to restart it again? Hours! In any case, the system was not geared for such an emergency. It was designed to keep the tanks at 0 degrees Celsius (32 degrees Fahrenheit), though the company manual specified *minus* 10 degrees Celsius (14 degrees Fahrenheit). Nor was there a backup refrigeration unit.

Now Qureshi was down to his last hope—the flare tower. This was a ninety-foot-high pipe that was used to burn toxic gases high in the air. A pilot flame in the tower was to remain lit twenty-four hours a day, according to safety rules, so it could ignite gas fed through the pipe without notice. But it was not lit now since a part of the piping that led to the tower was corroded and under repair. Could the tower, which had been out of service for more than five months, be used? No one was sure.

In the midst of the confusion, Qureshi suddenly realized that he hadn't reported to S. P. Choudhary, the plant production manager, and immediately phoned him at home to ask his advice. Choudhary was a top-rate engineer and assistant to plant manager Mukund, who seldom made a decision without consulting him. He was a jolly-natured man, whose modest chin seemed to vanish with every gleeful, cherubic smile. He perhaps smiled a lot to hide the discomfort he must have felt in the tough-fisted role he had to play occasionally to keep the plant alive. He was the link between Mukund and the technicians, and like Mukund he was sure that the staff and expenses could be cut without jeopardizing safety. It was just a matter of removing deadwood and wasteful redundancies. This was necessary for the plant's survival.

Now the plant's survival was threatened, it seemed, by those very policies that were aimed at saving it. And there was no way to hide his horror. What should the men do?

"Try the flare tower!" Choudhary cried over his bedside phone. "Control the situation as best you can, and I'll be there as soon as possible."

Go to the flare area and see if it will work, Qureshi ordered Dey.

Dey immediately dashed out, but hardly had he started when he ran into a cloud of gas. Coughing and choking, his eyes afire, he hastened back to the control room.

It's impossible, he gasped. Maybe if he had a gas mask, but with the gas swirling everywhere there could be a massive explosion if he tried to light the tower. The whole factory, if not the town, might vanish along with the gas.

Qureshi agreed; the risk was too great. And besides, he said, the flare tower probably wouldn't work with a piece of pipe missing.

It was now about 1:30 A.M., and the men grew ever more panicky as they chillingly realized there was no longer any chance of stopping tank 610 from discharging all its boiling brew into the air. There was nothing left to do but run.

Should he order the workers to evacuate the plant? Dey asked Qureshi.

Tell them to gather in the formulation area, Qureshi groaned. It was relatively safe there, since the wind was blowing from that side. But they should not leave the plant grounds since they would be needed after the emergency. Only the MIC workers were to remain at their posts, protected by gas masks. Maybe they could still do something, though he wasn't sure what.

In the chaos, no one thought of turning on the siren again to warn the inhabitants to run for their lives, a warning all the more urgent since most didn't even know that a simple wet cloth held to the face and eyes might save them. Only about half an hour later did someone finally remember to sound the alarm.

Qureshi was devastated. He had always been able to handle MIC, but now it had apparently triumphed because of an incredible series of failures. But he still refused to be intimidated. This was personal struggle, passionate and unrelenting. Even if nothing could be done, he would stay in the plant until the last molecule of gas had dissipated and then find out what happened. And his men would stay, too—if they had the guts.

As the deadly mist began to invade the control room itself, the men fled in search of their gas masks and portable oxygen tanks—all except Suman Dey, who had his safety equipment with him. Qureshi waddled to his office to get his, but when he opened the cabinet where he put these items, he found they were gone. Someone had taken them! (A Danbury spokesman claimed that witnesses saw Qureshi run to the formulation area and then back toward the MIC area, presumably to "clean up" any evidence of sabotage by a disgruntled worker. But the spokesman said that he couldn't name the witnesses, since the CBI, India's Criminal Bureau of Investigation, might intimidate and harass them.) According to Qureshi, while he was looking for his gas mask in his office, the gas began to coil around him, an unleashed force come to avenge the man who had kept it in chains. It surrounded him, blinded him, and finally frightened him.

Qureshi decided he must live—even if he had to run. He must deprive the avenger of its greatest prize. He dragged himself out the door to a plant exit and crudely calculated the direction of the wind, which, only shortly before, had dropped from less than ten miles per hour to a third that speed and, combined with the night cold, helped keep the gas close to the ground. Then he stumbled blindly into the poisoned night, unable in the dense fog to see the sky, the road, or even the factory lights. He could hardly breathe, but he plunged ahead into the thickening mist, coughing, retching, gasping in agony.

In the control room, Suman Dey, as Qureshi had ordered, shouted to the workers over the public address system: Leave your posts and gather in the formulation area!

The nontechnical people should leave first, he said, followed by the non-MIC technicians. The MIC technicians must remain as long as possible in case they were needed. Since only twenty-five or thirty MIC technicians had gas masks, they would have to share them with the others when necessary, though each portable tank of oxygen carried on the back had only a thirty-minute supply.

Dey, wearing his mask, then ran to the formulation area to repeat his instructions in person, since the public address system often didn't work. This time it did. He found most of the workers, more than 100, sitting anxiously in that area waiting for further instructions. Apparently only a few workers, including two fire fighters, fled the plant grounds, one of the firemen falling unconscious as he ran.

After repeating his instructions, Dey raced back toward the control room, but, unable to see through the thick screen of gas, he detoured to the still untainted boiler area about fifty feet way. (Union Carbide conjectures that Dey, like Qureshi, returned to "cover up" evidence of sabotage.) He removed his gas mask to save oxygen, and, in terror and bewilderment, watched the lethal cloud drift through the plant. MIC gas, he had always preferred to believe, would do little more than irritate the eyes and skin, but in the face of its full fury, he now gazed at what seemed like a microcosmic depiction of some ghastly future world, a lifeless world of iron monuments to a subdued human race.

After about fifteen minutes, Shetty came running up breathlessly. Qureshi, he moaned, had disappeared. He couldn't be found anywhere.

Dey respected Qureshi, who, despite his support of management policy, had always been fair to him, while exuding an infectious optimism that no task was impossible. And he had courage; he never feared MIC but was thoroughly convinced he could master it. He imparted to Dey himself the confidence he needed to work so intimately and unreservedly with the poison. Dey felt a sense of loyalty to Qureshi, and he would now demonstrate it.

He slipped on his gas mask, though the oxygen in his tank was already dangerously low, and vanished into the cloud to search for Qureshi, groping his way into the supervisor's office, the control room, and the storage tank area, where he could hardly see a foot ahead of him. No sign of Qureshi. He staggered back to the control room and looked at the gauges; perhaps the pressure had gone down. But the indicators were still off the scale. He then hurried back to the boiler area and removed his mask. He had virtually used up all the oxygen in his tank and the gas was still spreading. When it reached the boiler area, there would be nowhere to go. And the exits had become pockets of poison. By seeking to save Qureshi, it seemed, he had doomed himself.

Meanwhile, Qureshi had begun to think that *he* was doomed as he reeled through the fog, breathing in poison with every painful gasp. Finally, as he stumbled past the alpha-naphthol shed, he glimpsed a strip of sky cut off by the wall surrounding the plant grounds. He lurched through the opening in the steamy shroud and tottered to the wall, which stood six feet high and supported a barbed-wire fence that reached another six feet. Gathering what little strength he had left, he ponderously clawed his way onto the wall and began climbing the rusty fence, as razor-sharp steel cut deeply into his hands and knees. Bleeding profusely, struggling for breath, dizzy, and nauseous, he finally reached the top wire and tried to swing his great bulk over it to climb down the other side. But he lost his balance and plunged into a ditch on the outer side of the wall.

Qureshi, stunned, barely conscious, tried to stand up, but he could move only one leg; he had broken the other. As he lay there groaning in agony, a new wave of MIC mist filled the gap through which he had twisted. He had incorrectly guessed the direction of the unpredictable wind, and the avenger was following him. But even as he inhaled more poison and lay blinded and writhing in pain, he would not surrender.

Suddenly, Qureshi felt a drop of water on his hand and heard what sounded like a hose watering a lawn. He lifted himself on his elbows and crept toward the sound, as more drops gently kissed his flesh. Water gushing through a nearby hydrant line being used by the fire fighters was leaking from the hydrant and shooting toward him. He crawled to the hydrant, drank, washed his face, then pulled off his shirt, wet it, and held it over his nose, as he had been instructed to do in case of a major MIC leak.

Coughing and vomiting, Qureshi lay back and fell into semiconsciousness while the swirling mist continued to invade his huge hulk. Visions of his three sons, 1, 2, and 3 years old, flashed through his feverish brain, and he said goodbye to them. How had it happened? Now he would never know. For the force, he finally conceded, would have its full revenge.

Across the road about 100 yards away in the slum of J. P. Nagar, Habib Ali woke abruptly at about 1:30 A.M. while Qureshi lay by the wall battling for his life. He smelled a familiar odor. As a Union Carbide worker himself, he knew the strong scent of MIC and would have put on his gas mask if he were at work. But in his tin-roofed shanty of slats, he had no protection whatsoever.

He began coughing and his eyes burned so badly he could barely see his wife and two children as they struggled to rise from their mats. They were coughing, too, and the children retched and vomited.

In the soundness of his sleep, Ali had only half-heard the siren screaming, and felt sure that the plant was just testing the alarm system, as it often did to see if it worked. Many other people, thinking that Union Carbide was on fire, had with tragic irony rushed toward the main gate to watch the spectacle—and, as it would turn out, to die. But now, about a half hour later, he knew as he sniffed the air that the siren wasn't being tested this time. MIC gas was escaping. Thanks to Allah that it was only MIC and not phosgene, which killed people. Within seconds, however, he could hardly breathe. He was startled. No one had told him that MIC gas could be this powerful. Was his nose deceiving him? Could it be phosgene he smelled?

As his wife stumbled out the door dragging the children behind her, all of them in near-convulsion, Ali thought of the neighbors whom he had assured would never be harmed by Union Carbide chemicals. They had believed him. And now the company he served was endangering their lives. Coughing and wheezing, he ran through the settling mist from hut to hut shouting, "Run for your lives!" But even as he cried, people were staggering out on the uneven paths that divided the columns of shacks and running away. Which way should they run? Union Carbide's public address system, which might have informed them, remained silent. Most fled south, unwittingly in the direction of the wind. One neighboring family of eight that chose the east was convinced, when the fumes began to relent, that it had guessed correctly. Then suddenly, it found itself trapped as the poisoned wind shifted direction again and crossed its path. A boy of 12, Sunil Kumar Rajput, survived.

Within minutes, the trickle in each direction had matured into a stream, and the stream into a torrent of panicked humans, goats, cows, dogs. Men pushed and pulled women along and women tugged their children; they vomited and defecated as they groped through the fog, some collapsing only to be trampled or kicked aside, whether dead or alive. They beseeched Allah or their gods for help. They wept, gasped, groaned, suffocated. Flowing from the community trails onto the main road, they blended with other tortured bands of people fleeing on foot and on bicycles, and in trucks, automobiles, buses, bullock-driven carts, and motorcycle rickshaws that carved sometimes bloody paths through the thick walls of heaving flesh.

By the time Habib Ali had met his obligation to his neighbors, his family had vanished into the surging flood of humanity. Though choking and barely able to squint, Ali elbowed his way through the hysterical crowd.

"Naeem! Naeem!" he cried, praying that by some miracle his wife would hear him calling her name.

As victim after victim fell along the way, he knelt down to see if the person was his wife or one of his children, or perhaps a member of his brother-in-law's family, turning the face toward him and staring at vacant, half-closed eyes and sometimes lips bubbling with red froth. Each time he felt a sense of relief, but also of guilt for feeling such relief at the death of others' loved ones.

About 2 A.M., the Union Carbide siren belatedly sounded again, as if to mock the victims. And this time it did not stop screeching. No one in the plant worried any more about people in panic. Ali was becoming delirious as he scrambled forward searching, calling, hoping. The dreadful noise of the siren that he had hardly ever noted before pounded in his head like the laughter of the devil. He had dreamed of building a brick house for his family with his Union Carbide earnings. How could he have known that these earnings were for work that might now be contributing to his family's destruction? How could he have known that the neighbors' envy was the devil's way of deceiving him, of making him believe that he had been specially blessed?

Ali slumped to his knees once more and glanced at another waxen face. A stranger's face. How many more times could he endure the uncertainty? He felt waves of heat surge through his body, though the night was cool, about 45 degrees Fahrenheit. Then he collapsed and the horror mercifully ceased.

When the gas struck his community, Baba Lakkad Das, the sadhu, was still smoking marijuana through his *cheelum* while squatting on a mat in his tiny temple. Suddenly, he smelled something peculiar. What kind of marijuana did the dealer sell him? He heard people running past and thought it was odd for them to be running this time of night. He rose and hobbled outside.

Das began to cough furiously. No, it wasn't the marijuana. Something was in the air. He didn't know what, and nobody stopped to tell him. Nor could he ask anyone since he had vowed not to speak for five years, and he still had four years and eight months to go. But he knew that the community had been visited by some kind of poisonous plague carried by a strange mist.

"Run! Run!" people cried.

But Das didn't. He couldn't. Even with his bamboo cane, he found it hard to walk. No, he would stay, whatever the plague. It was, after all, the doing of God, who was responsible for everything. He could not know that by remaining at home, he stood a better chance of surviving than did those who ran and inhaled more poison.

Das limped to a well near his hut and sat down on the edge as the last inhabitants in the area faded from view. He was alone as he liked to be, with God. The heavier the mist became, the harder he drew on his *cheelum* and the more relieved he felt. Without his realizing it, the gas passing through the filter was apparently burned before he could breathe it in.

But soon, even the pipe couldn't help him much. He developed cramps, he choked, he could hardly see. For the first time in his life he was frightened, even though he was united with God and thus didn't have to beckon Him from afar for help. His suffering became so great that he couldn't sit still; he began stumbling around the well, groaning and choking. Finally, he threw himself to the ground, rolled in the dirt, and contorted his body in all kinds of positions, hoping to find one that would offer some relief. And all the time, he kept inhaling the marijuana and pleading with God for help.

But help did not come, and Das could stand it no more. Where was God when he needed Him most? Das didn't mind dying and taking his chance on the kind of life he would return to. But why must he suffer so before he departed? Perhaps God didn't hear him. Perhaps his misery clouded his concentration so much that he couldn't reach God, despite the mind-focusing effects of the marijuana. Yet he had to speak with Him; it was the only way to find relief. Das made a drastic decision. He would break his vow and speak aloud. He would shout to God at the top of his voice.

Das vomited, then crawled to the well and sat on the edge again, his head thrown back, his eyes popping, his mouth open. He tried to speak, but he was so choked that he couldn't. Finally, after about half an hour, he blurted into the poisoned heavens his first words in four months.

"God, why are you letting this happen? Fuck my mother!"

Das felt a sudden surge of relief. Now that he had broken his vow, he would release his innermost feelings with the relentlessness of a suddenly undammed river. Let God know how he felt. (It should be understood that the Hindus view the sexual relationship as symbolic of creation itself and consider it almost a sacrament. Sexual curses are thus not in general regarded as obscene in the western sense.)

Das took another puff of marijuana and cursed again. He kept repeating this routine for more than two hours and began to feel a little better. God was listening and had placed a benevolent hand on him to ease his misery. He understood that this simple sadhu loved Him even as he cursed Him, that cursing was natural in an extreme situation like this. That was the beauty of their relationship.

Yes, Das felt better. He couldn't open his eyes. He could barely breathe. And the pain in his stomach was unbearable.

But he felt better.

After a restless sleep, Chandabee woke with a start abut 1 A.M. in her slum neighborhood near J. P. Nagar. She felt sharp labor pains as she lay on her mat, but she suffered most now from a sore throat and burning eyes. Was this part of having a baby? She hadn't felt this way with the others. Suddenly, she heard a great rumpus outside and people crying, "Run! Save yourself!" The whole family was up now—her husband, two daughters, and mother-in-law.

"Get up! Hurry!" her husband, Isaac, cried, grabbing her by the shoulders and lifting her to her feet.

Chandabee's small body was bulging, and she found it hard to walk, but Isaac grabbed her hand and jerked her to the door and into the river of humanity flowing out of the shantytown over narrow winding paths, while members of her own family and her uncle's family, which lived in a neighboring hut, trailed behind. The extended family always stayed together in an emergency, finding strength in its numbers and unity. And never, it seemed, had an emergency seemed greater. Everyone was sick, vomiting, hardly able to breathe.

They guessed that the descending mist was smoke emanating from Union Carbide. The whole plant, it appeared, was on fire, and the flames were surely spreading to their neighborhood. Chandabee screamed as her husband dragged her along, her cries punctuated only by desperate gasps for breath. The pain in her belly was excruciating.

"I can't! Let me stay!" she pleaded.

But her husband would not release his grasp. After all, she might be carrying his son. All she had given him so far were two daughters. Though he loved his wife, he could always get another one, but who could be sure of a son? Chandabee, like himself, was a tribal, of course, and was less trained to endure pain than a Moslem woman. Somehow she would have to draw on her new faith to help her survive.

"No, you shall come!" he commanded.

Chandabee knew she had to obey her husband, especially as a Moslem wife. Why hadn't they become Hindus? Many Hindus believed that if a wife gave her husband a *roti* (a flat Indian bread) that contained flour in equal weight to her husband's left shoe, he would obey her. But now, though she was half-conscious, fighting for breath, nauseous, racked by pain, unable to see, Chandabee struggled on like some mechanical toy, stopping only to sip water from scummy ponds. Finally, she lifted her head and cried to the new deity she had adopted, though not quite sure of His powers:

"Oh God, I am dying!"

And so was the "son" she would never have. The son who was to become even more "civilized" than she so he could share in some of the rewards of life that civilized people enjoyed but were beyond the reach of simple tribes like her own, which knew only how to sing, dance, and worship nature.

Sayed Abbas was awakened shortly after 1 A.M. by a loud pounding on the door. "The factory is leaking!" neighbors cried, warning his family to join them in flight. So that was why his eyes had begun to tear before he went to sleep. And he had blamed a Sikh terrorist!

Abbas leaped from his mat. "Get the family ready to leave!" he ordered his wife, and she quickly gathered their four daughters, two sons, and his mother. But they couldn't just run out into the street like the others since his wife had had major surgery only a month earlier and could hardly walk. He would find a motorcycle rickshaw and they would all crowd in somehow. Everybody would be looking for one, of course, but he would pay whatever he had to—even his entire earnings from the television repair job he had done in Japalpur.

Abbas then dashed out the door and headed toward the main road, finding himself caught in a human stampede that trampled over everything in its way. Almost knocked down, he barely regained his balance to save himself from this fate and managed to find a relatively deserted lane where he spotted an approaching three-wheeler. He dived into it just before others could and, flashing several rupee bills, instructed the driver to take him to his house.

The driver madly twisted his way through the surging, shrieking crowds, not daring to stop even if he felt the wheels rolling over human flesh, and halted before the house. Abbas jumped out and ran inside, but when a minute later he began to lead his family out, he found that the vehicle was gone. Someone else had commandeered it!

Abbas was desperate. He had to find another vehicle before it was too late.

"Wait here for me!" he told his family.

And Abbas once more joined the throngs of running people, who were even more terrorized than the earlier ones since the mist had grown thicker. He searched every nearby path and street, but the only vehicles he saw were already swaying under the weight of their human cargo. There seemed to be no chance of stumbling on another empty one.

Meanwhile, Abbas found himself virtually blinded in the mist and he realized that he would not even be able to trace his way back. Panic now reached the brink of madness as his family apparently vanished from his consciousness and he thought only of escape. Coughing, vomiting, panting like an animal, he drove himself forward, stepping over bodies, crawling through ditches.

Abbas finally came to the railroad tracks and lurched along between the rails, a shortcut out of town. He was breathless and his leg muscles ached as he plodded ahead on bare feet that bled from the sharp stones on the tracks. Then he tripped over a crossboard and tumbled headfirst to the ground.

The young TV technician lay on the tracks unable to move. He had gravely injured his foot and, weakened by the gas, began to lose consciousness. The gas, he guessed, was entering his body through his bleeding toe. Suddenly, the plight of his family seized him again. He had to find a vehicle, he had to save his children, his mother, his wife. But then reality dawned. How could he save even himself? If the gas didn't kill him, a train probably would.

Abbas dug his fingers into the stony earth and tried to scratch his way off the tracks, but before he could succeed he blacked out.

Some minutes earlier, the Bombay-Gorakhpur Express had chugged into the Bhopal railroad station. In ten minutes it would be pulling out with new passengers and travel on the same tracks where Sayed Abbas lay—just a quarter mile away.

Actually, the train had been due at 11:30 P.M. but was almost an hour and a half late, vexing V. K. Sharma, the stocky deputy chief controller, whose cool manner shielded a passionate temperament. As the top man on duty that night, he wanted everything to run smoothly. A proud Brahman, he was a meticulous man with a sense of responsibility so profound that he even blamed himself for late arrivals, though they were beyond his control. And he didn't relish having ticket holders pester him about sudden schedule changes.

Sharma was especially irate now because of a strange physical discomfort. Shortly before 1 A.M., while he was reading the latest traffic reports to the deputy stationmaster over the phone, his eyes began to tear and he had to remove his large horn-rimmed glasses every few seconds to wipe them. Then he started coughing and could barely speak.

He soon learned that he was not the only one who felt ill. Hardly had he put the phone down when it rang again and he heard the desperate voice of the station paymaster from the platform.

"There's a lot of smoke outside," the man gasped. People waiting for the train were all coughing and vomiting.

Sharma's peon then rushed in with tea and chokingly spouted out what was causing this sudden plague. He had just come from the nearby market, where he had gone for the tea, he explained, and everyone was complaining that chili powder had been thrown into a fire and was making their eyes burn.

Chili powder? Sharma wondered. How could that cause such a strong reaction? Within minutes, Sharma's assistants were kneeling on the floor retching uncontrollably. He hurriedly phoned the railroad doctor and called him to the control room.

What was happening? Sharma asked him as he stepped in.

He didn't know, replied the doctor. But he called a colleague at Hamidia Hospital and soon found out—gas! The doctor and Sharma were horrified.

"You must wet your handkerchief and dampen your eyes and lips," the doctor advised Sharma. "That is all we can do."

The phones then jangled as railroad officers called in for instructions, and people in the station, half-dazed and sobbing, began crowding into the room. What should they do? In the chaos, women tore off their blouses and saris, and men their shirts and trousers, as if nakedness could cool their bodies and help them to breathe more easily. Some fell unconscious. Sharma's full face, somehow rendered fuller by a thin, well-groomed mustache, reflected anguish and dismay. He could barely reply to them since he himself was choking. Was everybody dying? he wondered.

Suddenly another dreadful thought seized him. What about the hundreds of passengers who were just arriving on the Bombay-Gorakhpur Express, and the hundreds more on other trains due within the next few hours? Two of them were only six miles away. Would those people die, too? He must save them.

The wheels of the express train were already grinding to a halt. Sharma had to act fast. He must get this train out of Bhopal instantly and stop the others en route, wherever they were.

Sharma phoned his two section controllers. Inform all roadside stations, he ordered, that "until further instructions from this office, no train is to be brought into Bhopal."

Then he spoke to the crew of the Bombay-Gorakhpur Express. Leave Bhopal immediately with all your passengers! he cried. Don't wait ten minutes, not even one minute!

Sharma was making drastic decisions without getting the approval of the stationmaster, though he was forbidden to do this under any circumstances.

But there was no time to call him and someone had to save lives. Besides, no one knew better than V. K. Sharma how to make things run smoothly—even in a race against death.

Despite Sharma's order, some of the passengers managed to disembark before the train pulled out of the station. Among them were Sajda Bano and her two children, the family of Ashraf Mohammed Khan, who had died in 1981 after inhaling phosgene gas in the Union Carbide plant.

Amid the frenzy in the railroad control room, a middle-aged woman burst in and struggled through the mass of hysterical people to V. K. Sharma's desk. Munnibai Balkishensingh, the water woman, cried above the din:

"I'm terrified! I think I'm going to die. I must see the doctor at once!"

Sharma gazed at her with glazed eyes after recovering from a coughing spell. The doctor, he said, had left the room and he didn't know where he was.

"What can I do?" Sharma mumbled. "Can't you see that I am also dying? We are all dying from the gas."

Munnibai was numbed. She now knew that this plague was not caused by the chili powder a vendor at the water station was pouring on his omelets. She fought her way out, unable to stop vomiting or having involuntary movements, her eyes afire. Perhaps the stationmaster knew where the doctor was. She ran to his house nearby and knocked on the door, then entered without waiting. In shock, she found the man slumped in a chair, dead, with a phone receiver dangling from his hand.

Munnibai then began a dizzying search for the doctor's house, but when she couldn't find it, started back to the control room. There by the door lay the doctor, unconscious. Unable to endure her agony any longer, she rushed back to the mist-shrouded platform and blindly jumped onto the tracks—the Bombay-Gorakhpur Express had already left—where she knew there was a water tap for the supply of the trains. As she bathed her face and eyes, the sound of water dripping reached the ears of others on the platform; they soon were swept up in a wild rush toward the tracks, and some fell or were pushed off the platform and in some cases died as they struck the ground.

Though the deadly fog still clung to the platform, Munnibai could see a little better now as she climbed back onto it. But what she saw was ghastly. Only a short time earlier, the station had been buzzing with life. Passengers were getting on and off the train. Porters were heaving baggage on carts. People were embracing, chatting, laughing. Coffee counters tinkling with cups were besieged by travelers. Motorcycle rickshaw drivers were shouting for customers. Loudspeakers were booming arrival and departure times. Beggars huddling against the chill were jiggling cans of coins to draw attention while their families slept beside them.

Now there was silence, a crushing, sickening silence, except for the sound of dripping water and the sporadic cries of despair by those who still had the strength to make their voices heard. Lying on the platform and in the adjacent waiting room in cesspools of vomit, urine, and excrement were about 600 grotesquely twisted human forms—one of them a beautiful young woman who lay with two children in her embrace. Sajda Bano and her family had returned home a little too late.

As Munnibai surveyed the endless carpet of ravaged people, about a third of them unconscious or dead, the horror was too overwhelming for her to grasp. She might have been viewing a scene from some futuristic television fantasy that she occasionally watched in a store window. In her growing delirium, she suddenly focused on the fate of her own family, but reduced to a familiar concern. What would happen to her sons—especially the elder one? Would he pass his examinations, or would he, too, be ladling out water for the rest of his life?

Like a madwoman, Munnibai stalked around the lifeless, noiseless station gazing incredulously at the human wreckage until, finally, she went totally blind and collapsed. The fantasy had come to an end.

Challenger: The Final Voyage

BY RICHARD S. LEWIS

When the Challenger space shuttle disaster occurred in January, 1986, America's space program had enjoyed an incredible string of successes, internationally televised and witnessed throughout the world. The fire during a moon launch rehearsal that took the lives of astronauts Roger Chaffee, Gus Grissom, and Ed White and the narrow escape of Apollo 13 from disaster, were the only mishaps to mar a virtually flawless record of putting men into orbit and onto the moon.

Space shuttle flights, the craft launched into orbit and eventually flown back to Mother Earth for a landing, were familiar and routine by January, '86, so much so that the Challenger launch was intended to showcase how safe and reliable space travel could be. In addition to the crew of seven, the Challenger would carry a civilian schoolteacher, selected in a highly publicized national search.

"But instead of being a showcase for the media, Challenger mission 51-L became a total and glaring failure of the world's most advanced aerospace transportation system. In a bright flash of fire, a sudden double boom and an orange fireball mushrooming across the blue sky at 50,800 feet over the Atlantic, the shuttle and its crew vanished into a rain of debris."

That quote from the jacket copy of Richard S. Lewis's remarkable book, *Challenger: The Final Voyage*, describes a disaster and traumatic event that sent shock waves throughout America and the world. The catastrophe, Lewis book points out, " ... not only jeopardized NASA's leading space project of the last decade, but called into question the future of the entire space program."

This excerpt from Richard Lewis's vivid and compelling book is an illuminating portrait of what happened on that tragic day and afterwards, including NASA's fumbling and cover-up. This excerpt cannot do justice to the complete book, but you will find it to be both dramatic and heart-wrenching.

*　　*　　*　　*　　*

Seventy-Three Seconds

The morning was clear, bright, and cold, near freezing. Busses unloaded spouses, children, and parents of the shuttle crew at VIP observation sites. Three and one-half miles away, the space shuttle Challenger stood in silhouette against the morning light on launch pad 39B like some medieval battlement, exhaling white smoke. This image acquired a glow as the sun rose out of a cold, quiet sea. It was launch day at the Kennedy Space Center: January 28, 1986.

After five days of delay filled with wind, rain, and frustration, *Challenger* was ready to go on mission 51-L, the twenty-fifth for the world's first fleet of reusable manned spaceships and the tenth of the winged orbiter *Challenger*.[1] Public interest in the flight had been focused by a strong public-relations buildup on the first private citizen to fly aboard the space shuttle. She was Christa McAuliffe, 37, a high-school teacher who had been selected from among thousands of applicants to become the first teacher in space.

Mrs. McAuliffe's assignment was to demonstrate and explain the effects of microgravity (free fall in orbit) in the context of Newtonian physics and the scientific, commercial, and industrial applications of space flight. She would address an audience of schoolchildren via television from the spaceship.

The presence of this personable and attractive young woman was calculated to add a new dimension to the public's perception of the space program: space flight in America was no longer the exclusive province of astronaut test pilots, scientists, and engineers, but an experience to be shared by the whole society.

Now in its twenty-eighth year, the National Aeronautics and Space Administration was approaching a goal of quasi–airline operations in low Earth orbit. Flight schedules were devised on a yearly basis for scientific, commercial, and military payloads. With the space shuttle transportation system, the agency was preparing to establish a permanently crewed space station. Technology developed from that enterprise was expected to provide the means of constructing a base on the Moon for scientific and industrial development and of launching a manned expedition to Mars.

The shuttle was the basic unit of the space transportation infrastructure that would be required to realize these goals. After four test flights in

---

[1]After 1983, shuttle missions were designated by the fiscal year in which they were originally scheduled, the launch site, and an alphabetical sequence. Thus 51-L referred to the 1985 fiscal year (5), the Kennedy Space Enter (launch site 1) and the mission sequence.

1981–82, the system was declared officially operational. *Columbia,* the first orbiter in the fleet, had demonstrated that despite minor problems the system was spaceworthy. *Challenger* was the second orbiter. It was followed by *Discovery* and *Atlantis.*

Challenger had been the orbiter most frequently flown. Now on the morning of its tenth launch, as it hung from its huge external propellant tank, flanked by the twin towers of its solid rocket boosters, *Challenger* represented the most advanced space transportation technology in the world. No other nation had achieved a reusable spaceship that could maneuver inside and outside the atmosphere and lift payloads with an Earth weight of up to 32 tons. *Challenger* was the exemplar of American space leadership in the 1980s, as *Apollo* had been a decade earlier.

The morning of January 28, 1986 was the coldest on which NASA had ever attempted to launch a manned spacecraft. A cold front had swept down the Florida peninsula, ending high winds and threat of rain, and now the air was clear and relatively calm. Family members, relatives, and friends of the crew and a long list of Very Important Persons invited to observe the launch were bundled up in sweaters and jackets against a damp chill in the air.

The day was warming with sunrise. Through field glasses, ranks of icicles could be seen hanging from launch pad structures. Ice had built up overnight on beams and horizontal structures from water that had been allowed to trickle out of the pad water system to keep pipes from freezing. Most of the platform ice had been cleared away by the NASA pad inspection team. The team also removed ice that had formed on the surface of the pad's overpressure water troughs. The dangling icicles created a winter scene, bizarre in subtropical Florida.

Originally scheduled for launch December 23, 1985, the 51-L mission had been postponed four times and scrubbed once. Rain and high winds had forced delays of the previous mission, 61-C, a *Columbia* flight. It carried a congressional passenger, U.S. Representative Bill Nelson (D-Fla.), chairman of the House subcommittee on space science and applications. The 61-C delays—there were six—made it necessary to reschedule *Challenger* initially to January 23. The day before, NASA's Program Requirements Board postponed the launch to January 25 and then to January 26 because of the work backlog accumulated from the delay of the 61-C launch.

NASA officials invited hundreds of guests to see the launch of 51-L, a unique mission in which *Challenger* would serve as an orbital classroom. In addition to a group of 30 VIPs flown to Florida from Washington as NASA's special guests, hundreds more were invited to witness the launch from VIP observation sites and attend briefings. The guest list included educators, corporate sponsors of the Young Astronauts Council, members of the Michigan Republican Party Organization led by E. Spencer Abraham, chairman, members of the Teacher Astronaut Selection Panel, and a delegation from the People's Republic of China.

Prelaunch briefings were scheduled for these groups during the evening of January 25. The briefers included Dr. William R. Graham, acting NASA administrator; Dr. Lawrence F. Davenport, U.S. Assistant Secretary of Education; Barbara Morgan, the teacher-in-space backup for Christa McAuliffe; Richard G. Smith, director of the Kennedy Space Center; U.S. Senator E. J. (Jake) Garn (R-Utah), who had flown as a payload specialist on *Discovery* 51-D, April 12–19, 1985; and Vance D. Brand, commander of two previous missions, *Columbia* STS-5, November 11–16, 1982, and *Challenger* 41-B, February 3–11, 1984.

The January 26 launch was postponed by a forecast of unacceptable launch weather, and many of the special guests went home. The launch was reset to the morning of the 27th, and fueling began at 12:30 A.M. The crew was awakened at 5:07 A.M. and seated in the orbiter by 7:57. The countdown proceeded until it was halted at 9:10 A.M. when the ground crew reported a problem with the exterior hatch handle. The problem was corrected at 10:30 A.M., but by this time high crosswinds had sprung up at the launch site and imperiled an emergency landing there in case the orbiter was forced to fly back by main engine failure. The high winds blowing across the three-mile runway of the Kennedy landing facility persisted, and the launch was scrubbed at 12:35 P.M.

Weather conditions allowing a safe emergency landing at Kennedy and other emergency landing sites were a requirement for launching the shuttle. During its 8½ minute ascent to orbit, the flight could be aborted only after the solid rocket boosters burned out and were dropped from the external tank. This took place at 2½ minutes. From then on, the orbiter was propelled to orbital altitude by its three main hydrogen-oxygen engines, which were fed from the big tank. If one of these engines failed, the flight could be aborted by separating the orbiter from the tank and steering it as a glider to an emergency landing strip.[2] The nearest, Kennedy Space Center, was considered safe if wind blowing across the runway did not exceed 10 knots and the skies were clear.

Depending on the velocity the orbiter reached before engine failure occurred, other emergency landing sites were available. There were two in Africa, one at Dakar, Senegal and the other at Casablanca, Morocco. Farther along the ascent track, emergency landings could be made in the Mojave Desert at Edwards Air Force Base, California or at White Sands, New Mexico.

[2]If more than one engine failed, an emergency landing was considered possible under some conditions. The alternative was ditching the orbiter in the sea.

The abort system was contingent on main engine failure. There was no abort system planned against failure of one or both solid rocket boosters during the first two minutes of the ascent. Nor was there any means of escape for the crew. Unlike *Mercury, Gemini,* and *Apollo* spacecraft, the orbiter was not equipped with a launch escape system during the solid rocket booster phase, the first stage of the ascent. Such a system had been considered during the development of the shuttle, but had been dropped, except for the temporary installation of aircraft-style ejection seats in *Columbia,* because failure of the solid rocket boosters after launch was considered highly improbable.

THE ICE PROBLEM

Following the scrub on the 27th, launch was reset to January 28. As the cold front passed through east central Florida, the winds were expected to die down, and the morning was predicted to be clear and cold. Temperatures were expected to fall to the low twenties overnight.

Mission managers assessed the possible effects of the cold weather on the launch, but the only threat they perceived to launch safety was ice on the pad structure and in the water troughs below. Ice breaking off the structure during launch could damage *Challenger's* heat shield, which consisted of 31,000 silicate-based tiles, all quite brittle. Extensive tile damage might expose the aluminum skin of the orbiter to high heat during reentry into the atmosphere.

During the night, the accumulation of ice from dribbling water pipes on the pad structures caused concern at the launch control center. An "ice team" of engineers and technicians was sent to the pad at 1:35 A.M. on the 28th. Its report was not encouraging, but launch directors anticipated that most of the ice could be cleared away before sunrise or would melt shortly thereafter.

THE CREW

The crew was awakened at 6:18 A.M., an hour later than scheduled because of a delay in the countdown caused by a fault in the ground liquid hydrogen tank fire detector. Following a somewhat leisurely breakfast, the crew received a weather briefing. There was some good and some bad news. The emergency landing site at Casablanca was declared "no-go" because of rain and a low ceiling, but weather was acceptable at Dakar, the prime transatlantic abort site. If both sites had been closed by weather, the launch would have been postponed again.

Ice conditions at the launch pad were described at the weather briefing, but if there was any concern about them, or about the effect of the unusually cold day on the performance of the shuttle at launch, it was not expressed to the crew.

The seven members arrived at the launch pad in the astronauts' van shortly after 8 A.M. and immediately rode up in the pad elevator to the white room where they entered the orbiter crew module. By 8:36 A.M., they were all strapped in their seats. Liftoff was to be at 9:38 A.M.

The ice team, meanwhile, had gone out to the pad a second time during the morning and had completed its inspection at 8:44 A.M. After hearing the team's report, the launch directorate decided to delay liftoff to allow additional time for the sun to melt ice on the pad. The ice was three inches thick on the pad's retractable service structure and covered the mobile launch platform, 160 feet long and 135 feet wide. Ice floated in the overpressure water troughs below the launch platform,[3] and icicles 6 to 12 inches long and five-eighths of an inch thick hung like stalactites from the 120- and 220-foot levels of the pad's fixed service structure. As the sun rose, the air temperature climbed from 26.1° to 36.2° Fahrenheit.

Four members of the crew were seated on the flight deck. By tradition, the forward left-hand seat was occupied by the commander, Francis R. (Dick) Scobee, 47, an Air Force-trained test pilot from Cle Elum, Washington. He had flown as pilot in *Challenger* on mission 41-C, April 6–13, 1984. The 51-L pilot in the right-hand seat was Michael J. Smith, 40, a Navy-trained test pilot from Beaufort, North Carolina. He was making his first space flight.

Although born and reared a continent apart, these two astronauts had strikingly similar physical attributes. NASA's public information dossiers confirmed that each was 6 feet tall and weighed 175 pounds. Each had brown hair and blue eyes. Both were graduates of the test pilot schools of their respective services. They appeared to express the Anglo-Saxon/North European phenotype that had been predominant in the Corps of Astronauts since its inception.

However, in the era of the space shuttle, that ethnic predominance gave way to an ethnic and gender mix that was more broadly representative of the American melting pot and that reflected the social policy of the 1980s. In these respects, the crew of 51-L exemplified the diversity of American society more nearly than any other flight team.

---

[3]Installed to prevent back pressure of rocket exhaust from moving the wing elevons, the body flap on the underside of the orbiter, and damaging struts.

The aft-center seat on the flight deck was occupied by Judith A. Resnik, Ph.D., 36, of Akron, Ohio, flight engineer. A mission specialist, she was a graduate in electrical engineering of Carnegie Mellon University, Pittsburgh, and had been awarded a doctorate in that field from the University of Maryland. She was the second American woman to fly in space, having logged 144 hours and 57 minutes in orbit on mission 41-D, the first flight of the orbiter *Discovery,* August 30-September 5, 1984. The aft right-hand seat was occupied by Air Force Lieutenant Colonel Ellison S. Onizuka, 39, mission specialist from Kealakekua, Kona, Hawaii, an aerospace engineer with a master's degree. He had served as a flight engineering instructor at the Air Force Test Pilot School, and had taken part in checking out the first two orbital test flights of the shuttle. He was the first American of Japanese descent to become a member of a flight crew.

On *Challenger's* middeck, the left-hand seat was occupied by Ronald E. McNair, Ph.D., 35, mission specialist from Lake City, South Carolina. He was a physicist with a bachelor of science degree from North Carolina A & M University and a doctorate from the Massachusetts Institute of Technology. He had become the second black astronaut to fly in space as a member of the crew of *Challenger* 41-B, February 3–11, 1984. This was his second mission.

The middeck right-hand seat was occupied by Gregory B. Jarvis, 41, a payload specialist from Detroit. He was assigned to the mission as a technical expert from the Hughes Aircraft Company to operate experiments on the behavior of fluids in microgravity (the so-called zero g). The results were expected to be useful in the design of advanced liquid propulsion systems. Hughes named its new multiple satellite launcher for him.

The middeck center seat was occupied by NASA's teacher in space, Sharon Christa Corrigan McAuliffe, a native of Boston with a master's degree in education. The Teacher-in-Space Program had been proposed by President Reagan who proclaimed it a means of communicating to the nation's schoolchildren (and to their parents) the nature and potential value of the new frontier the American space establishment was exploring.

Mrs. McAuliffe was a history and social studies teacher at the Concord High School, Concord, New Hampshire. She had been selected by NASA on July 19, 1985 and had undergone training for the flight at the Johnson Space Center, Houston. Later, a journalist was to be selected to fly a shuttle mission as an observer and narrator in the White House program of bringing space to the people.

The program of the teacher in space consisted of two classroom lessons to be televised from *Challenger* on flight day 6. The first, titled "The Ultimate Field Trip," was to describe life aboard a spacecraft in orbit. The second was to explain methods of exploring space and describe the prospects of manufacturing new products in space, where tests had demonstrated that a microgravity environment increased the purity of pharmaceuticals and the precision of microelectronic devices manufactured there.

Here was the crew of *Challenger* 51-L on the frosty morning of January 28, 1986 as the countdown approached liftoff, ready to embark on the first teaching mission of the space age.

THE CARGO

The orbiter is the largest space transport ever built. Its cargo by was designed to carry 65,000 pounds of payload into low Earth orbit, but cargoes have been considerably less than that, partly because of constraint on the weight at landing. *Challenger's* total payload on 51-L weighed 48,361 pounds.

In the cargo bay, *Challenger* carried TDRS-B, the second of three powerful tracking and data-relay communications satellites. They were designed to relay all NASA satellite communications to a central ground station at White Sands, New Mexico, for distribution over conventional telephone circuits. When completed, the TDRS system would replace most of NASA's ground stations and would provide full orbital coverage of shuttle-ground communications. The TDRS satellites, like the commercial comsats, would operate in geostationary orbit, 22,300 miles above the equator, where a satellite appears to hover in a fixed position. The first of the series, TDRS-1, was delivered to low Earth orbit by *Challenger* in 1983 and was maneuvered into its operational orbit by auxiliary thrusters after its upper-stage booster failed.

Also in the cargo bay was a 2,250-pound observatory called Spartan-Halley, which had been built to photograph Halley's Comet in ultraviolet light. It was to be lifted out of the cargo bay by the orbiter's remote manipulator arm and released over the side in temporary free flight. Tagging along with the ship, the automated observatory would make spectrographic and photographic observations for 22 orbits before being recovered by the arm and restowed in the cargo bay.

The fluid-dynamics experiments that were to be conducted by Gregory Jarvis were carried in middeck. The equipment consisted of small, transparent tanks in which the behavior of fluids could be observed during orbital flight. Fluid motions were to be recorded by video cameras as a tank was set spinning at 10 revolutions per minute and as tanks were filled at several levels.

The interaction of fluids with motions of the orbiter was to be observed. These experiments were relevant to the development of propulsion systems for orbital transfer vehicles, contemplated for moving cargoes between a space station and geostationary or lunar orbits.

The TDRS, the Halley's Comet observatory, and the fluid-dynamics experiments were of prime importance to space science and technology, but in terms of public interest, the main event of the flight would be the lessons by the teacher in space. This was an event with which millions of Americans of all ages could readily identify. The cynosure of this flight was the New England schoolteacher, a role model for young women in her profession as well as a mother of two children. Her children, her husband, and her parents were on hand with the families of her crewmates to watch the liftoff of this magnificent vehicle with pride and excitement. Mission 51-L carried a message that space was for everyone.

The ice team went out on its third inspection at 10:30 A.M., removed more ice from the deck of the mobile launch platform, and pulled more floating ice out of the water troughs with fishnets. Its measurements showed that the temperature of the left booster was 33° Farenheit while it was 19° Farenheit on the right booster. No significance was attached to the discrepancy at the time. The difference was attributed to wind blowing off the cryogenic external tank onto the right booster.

FINAL COUNTDOWN—CREW

As the five men and two women of the crew rode up the pad elevator and entered the orbiter, their banner displayed high spirits and the humor of a well-integrated team. The rain had stopped, and the sun was shining. One by one they entered the crew module and reclined in their seats, assisted by Manley L. (Sonny) Carter, Jr., the astronaut support person (ASP).

[Editor's Note: After beginning a series of preparation procedures, the crew was told the mission would be on "hold" until shortly after 11:00.]

FINAL COUNTDOWN—PUBLIC

The two-hour hold in the countdown during which the crew had been waiting restlessly for some sign that at last they might fly this day came to an end, and the crew was relieved that the long wait might not have been in vain. At the viewing sites, their families, friends, and thousands of other spectators were alerted to this juncture in the countdown by the voice of Hugh Harris, the Kennedy Space Center chief of public information, booming out of loudspeakers from the firing room. It was 11:28 A.M.

"One minute away from picking up the count for the final nine minutes in the countdown," Harris announced. "The countdown is simply a series of checks that people go through to ensure that everything is ready for flight. The countdown for a launch like 51-L is four volumes and more than 2,000 pages."

Scraps of dialogue between the *Challenger* crew and launch control filtered through the public address system, sounding impressively technical and bordering on the arcane. Hugh Harris's commentary sought to explain what was going on in the complex process of launching a spaceship.

The commentary related: "T minus 8 minutes 30 seconds and counting. All the flight recorders are turned on. Mission Control [at Houston] has turned on the auxiliary data system. The package of flight data from the aerodynamic information [system] comes back as the orbiter flies through the atmosphere.

"Coming up on the eight-minutes point. T minus 8 minutes and counting. Orbiter test conductor Roberta Wyrick has requested that Houston send the stored program commands, which is the final update on antenna management based on liftoff time and sets the system which makes the orbiter compatible with down-range tracking stations."

From *Challenger* a voice said, "Okay, that's the point."

The commentary continued: "T minus 7 minutes, 30 seconds, and the ground launch sequencer has started retracing the orbiter crew access arm. This is the walkway used by astronauts to climb into the vehicle. And that arm can be put back in 15 to 20 seconds if an emergency should arise. Coming up on the seven-minute point in the countdown. T minus 7 minutes and counting. The next major step will be when Pilot Mike Smith is given a 'go' to perform the auxiliary power unit prestart.[4] T minus 6 minutes and 50 seconds and counting."

Launch control called for voice recorders. "Roger, wilco," responded *Challenger.*

"T minus 6 minutes and the orbiter test conductor has given pilot Mike Smith the 'go' to perform the auxiliary power until prestart. He has reported back that prestart is complete. T minus 5 minutes and 30 seconds and counting, and Mission Control has transmitted the signal to start the on-board flight recorders. The two recorders will collect measurements of the shuttle system performance during flight to be played back after the mission. Coming up on the five-minute point. This is a major milestone where we go for auxiliary power unit start. T minus 5 minutes."

---

[4]The auxiliary power units (APUs) provide hydraulic pressure to move the orbiter's aero surfaces and engine nozzles for steering. They also assist deployment of the landing gear and application of the brakes.

Launch control: Let's go for orbiter APU start.
Challenger: . . . performed APU start.

Commentary: "We heard the pilot ordered to perform APU start. Lox [liquid oxygen] replenish has been terminated, and liquid oxygen drainback has been initiated. Pilot Mike Smith now flipping the three switches in the cockpit to start each of the three auxiliary power units. T minus 4 minutes 30 seconds and counting.

"The solid rocket booster and external safe and arm devices have been armed. We have had a report back from Mike Smith that we have three good auxiliary power units. Main fuel-valve heaters on the shuttle main engines have been turned on in preparation for engine start. T minus 4 minutes and counting. The flight crew has been reminded to close their airtight visors on their launch and entry helmets. And a final purge sequence of main engines is under way.

"T minus 3 minutes and 45 seconds and counting. The orbiter aerosurface test is started. The flight control surfaces are being moved in a preprogrammed pattern to verify that they are ready for launch. Orbiter ground support equipment power bus has been turned off and the vehicle is now on internal power."

THE CREW AT LAUNCH

T minus 1:47. **Smith:** Okay, there goes the lox arm [A vent arm covering the top of the external tank during liquid-oxygen loading].
T minus 1:46. **Scobee:** Goes the beanie cap [tip of the arm].
T minus 1:44. **Onizuka:** Doesn't it go the other way? [Laughter.]
T minus 1:39. **Smith:** God, I hope not, Ellison.
T minus 1:38. **Onizuka:** I couldn't see it moving. It was behind the center screen.
T minus 1:33. **Resnik:** Got your harness locked?
T minus 1:29. **Smith:** What for?
T minus 1:28. **Scobee:** I won't lock mine. I might have to reach something.
T minus 1:24. **Smith:** Oooh, kaaay.
T minus 1:04. **Onizuka:** Dick's thinking of somebody there.
T minus 1:03. **Scobee:** Uh, huh.
T minus 0:59. **Scobee:** One minute downstairs.
T minus 0:52. **Resnik:** Cabin pressure is probably going to give us an alarm.

T minus 0:50. **Scobee:** Okay.

T minus 0:47. **Scobee:** Okay, there.

T minus 0:43. **Smith:** Alarm looks good.

T minus 0:42. **Scobee:** Okay.

T minus 0:40. **Smith:** Ullage pressures are up [tank propellant pressure].

T minus 0:34. **Smith:** Right engine helium tank is just a little bit low.

T minus 0:32. **Scobee:** It was yesterday, too. [This dialogue refers to helium pressurization in orbiter main engine number 2.]

T minus 0:31. **Smith:** Okay.

T minus 0:30. **Scobee:** Thirty seconds down there.

T minus 0:25. **Smith:** Remember the red button when you make a roll call. [To assure communications when Scobee announced the shuttle was rolled to ascent attitude.]

T minus 0:23. **Scobee:** I won't do that. Thanks a lot.

T minus 0:15. **Scobee:** Fifteen.

T minus 0:06. **Scobee:** There they go, guys. [*Challenger's* main engines begin firing.]

T minus 0:06. **Resnik:** All right.

T minus 0:06. **Scobee:** Three at a hundred. [All three orbiter main engines operating at 100 percent of rated power.]

Challenger's two solid fuel boosters ignited. With a groundshaking roar and vast billows of white smoke, *Challenger* rose on pillars of orange-yellow fire. Observers watched in awe and then broke into cheers, screams, applause as the spaceship, the product of a thousand years of technical evolution, thundered majestically into the clear sky. The final flight of *Challenger* began at 11:38:00:010 Eastern Standard Time, January 28, 1986.

T minus 0:00. **Resnik:** Aaall right!

T minus 0:01. **Smith:** Here we go!

"Liftoff!" cried Hugh Harris at Kennedy launch control. "Liftoff of the twenty-fifth space shuttle mission and it has cleared the tower!"

At this point, control of the launch shifted from Florida to Texas as the Mission Control Center (MCC), Houston took over the flight. The commentary was taken up there by Stephen Nesbitt, public affairs officer (PAO) at the Johnson Space Center. Mission Control could be heard talking to *Challenger* through the public address system at Kennedy Space Center.[5]

MCC: Watch your roll, *Challenger*.

---

[5]The Mission Control communicator is usually an astronaut who speaks only to the crew. The public affairs commentator speaks to the news media. Sometimes both can be heard over the NASA communications network. Crew chatter on the orbiter intercom is not broadcast but is recorded at Mission Control.

T plus 0:07. **Scobee:** Houston, *Challenger* roll program. [The first maneuver after liftoff was to rotate the shuttle to ascent attitude, in which the orbiter was turned to face the Earth.]

Houston PAO: . . . roll program confirmed. *Challenger* now heading down range. Engines beginning to throttle down to 94 percent. Normal throttle for most of the flight is 104 percent. Will throttle down to 65 percent shortly.[6] Three engines running normally. Three good fuel cells [electric power generators]. Three good APUs. Velocity 2,257 feet per second [1,538 miles per hour]. Altitude 4.3 nautical miles. Down-range distance, 3 nautical miles. Engines throttling up. Three engines now at 104 percent.

T plus 0:11. **Smith:** Go, you mother.

T plus 0:14. **Resnik:** LVLH. [A reminder about switch configurations—local vertical, local horizontal.]

T plus 0:15. **Resnik:** [one word deleted by NASA] hot!

T plus 0:16. **Scobee:** Oooh kaay.

T plus 0:19. **Smith:** Looks like we've got a lot of wind up here today.

T plus 0:20. **Scobee:** Yeah.

T plus 0:22. **Scobee:** It's a little hard to see out my window here.

T plus 0:28. **Smith:** There's 10,000 feet and mach point five.

T plus 0:35. **Scobee:** Point nine.

T plus 0:40. **Smith:** There's mach one.

T plus 0:41. **Scobee:** Going through 19,000 feet.

T plus 0:43. **Scobee:** Okay, we're throttling down.

T plus 0:57. **Scobee:** Throttling up.

T plus 0:58. **Smith:** Throttle up.

T plus 0:59. **Scobee:** Roger.

T plus 1:02. **Smith:** Thirty-five thousand. Going through one point five.

T plus 1:05. **Scobee:** Reading 486 on mine. [Airspeed indicator check.]

T plus 1:07. **Smith:** Yep. That's what I've got, too.

MCC, Houston: Go at throttle up. [Continue at full throttle.]

T plus 1:10. **Scobee:** Roger, go at throttle up.

Racing skyward at 2,900 feet per second, *Challenger* had reached an altitude of 50,800 feet and was 7 nautical miles down range from the launch site when camera 207 on the ground saw a brilliant glow on one side of the exter-

---

[6]Power is reduced to slow ascent as the shuttle approaches the region of maximum dynamic pressure (Max Q) about one minute after liftoff.

nal tank.[7] The glow blossomed into orange-yellow flame and in seconds grew to a gigantic fireball with a nimbus of gray-white smoke that formed a multi-lobed cumulus cloud filled with streaks of fire. The cloud encompassed the shuttle, but for a moment or two the exhausts of the two solid rocket boosters could be seen through it, together with exhaust plumes from the orbiter's main engines. Vapor trails from these engines streamed behind the cloud like tattered banners.

T plus 1:13. **Smith:** Uhh . . . oh!

It was the last recorded utterance from the crew as the orbiter broke up. Houston did not hear it.

From the viewpoint of observers on the ground, a nightmare took form in the sky, visible for miles up and down the Atlantic coast. The twin solid rocket boosters began flying away from the moving cumulus of smoke and fire, diverging in fiery arcs. Screams of horror rose from thousands of watchers. Families of the crew looked at the scene in disbelief, unable at first to comprehend what they were seeing. Beyond the spreading cloud of darkening smoke, the sky was filled by debris falling into the ocean from 104,000 feet (19.7 miles), where radar showed the shuttle breaking up, to 122,400 feet (28.19 miles) peak altitude of debris.

Suddenly, the solid rocket boosters disintegrated. The Air Force range safety officer detonated their "destruct" packages of explosives by radio signal at 101,300 feet (19.13 miles). One of them, partly filled with propellant burning at 5,600° Farenheit, had been heading for the coastal community of New Smyrna Beach.[8]

The external tank collapsed like a torn balloon and was reduced to wreckage by its flaming propellant. The orbiter was nowhere to be seen. It had vanished with the crew into the fireball. Beyond the pall of smoke and descending wreckage a lone parachute appeared, drifting casually down toward the sea. It was a 54-foot drogue in the parachute descent system of one booster, a system designed to allow recovery of the boosters at sea. Highly visible against the deep blue of the sky, the parachute, still attached to the forward section, or frustrum, of the booster, led hundreds of watchers to hope that the crew was drifting down to safety and would soon be rescued. The lack of a launch escape system on the orbiter was not popularly known, and some of the radio and television commentators who were describing the scene seemed unaware that such a system did not exist.

---

[7] *Report of the Presidential Commission on the Space Shuttle Challenger Accident* (Washington, D.C., 1986) vol. 1, p. 26; vol. 2, p. L-56; vol. 3, p. O-158; Commentary, Johnson Space Center, Houston, Tex.
[8] Altitudes derived from radar data, *Commission Report,* vol. 3, p. O-158.

The white parachute went into the sea, like the flag of a sinking ship. From Mission Control came silence. Then the commentary was resumed in a tense monotone.

PAO: Flight controllers are looking very carefully at the situation. Obviously a major malfunction. We have no downlink. We have a report from the flight dynamics officer that the vehicle has exploded. The flight director confirms that. We are looking at checking with the recovery forces to see what can be done at this point. Contingency procedures are in effect. We will report more as we have information available. Again, a repeat, we have a report relayed through the flight dynamics officer that the vehicle has exploded. We are looking at all contingency operations, waiting for word of any recovery forces in the down-range field.

As Houston struggled to define the situation, a belief persisted among observers and even some NASA personnel that somehow the crew might have survived the holocaust and would be drifting in the insulated, airtight crew module. It was supposed, briefly, that it was possible for the crew to detach the orbiter from the external tank and booster and somehow survive a fall at first estimated at 9 miles into the ocean.[9] The vision of the drogue parachute had lent a few moments of hope to that supposition. But veteran observers in the press corps and NASA people for the most part were certain that all had been lost. The space agency and the nation now observed the consequences of the 1972 decision to allow a manned spacecraft to be designed and flown without a launch escape system.

In the shuttle design, the crew was committed to flight during the first two minutes of the ascent to orbit, when the boosters were firing. Only after that first stage did escape become possible through the flight abort and contingency landing system described earlier. During its first two minutes of flight, the orbiter was a death trap for the crew if a booster failed. That fact had not been publicized.

When the commentary from Houston resumed, the public affairs officer stated that the vehicle, apparently having exploded, struck the water at a point 28.64 north latitude and 80.28 west longitude.

"We are awaiting verification from—as to the location of the recovery forces in the field to see what may be possible at this point. We will keep you advised as further information becomes available. This is Mission Control."

After a pause, the commentary resumed. "This is Mission Control. We are coordinating with recovery forces in the field. Range safety equipment, re-covery vehicles intended for the recovery of the solid rocket boosters, are in

---

[9]The initial estimate was based on the first sign of the "major malfunction" at 73.2 seconds. At this time, *Challenger* had reached an altitude of 9.63 miles (50,800 feet), according to radar data.

the general area. To repeat: We had an apparently normal ascent with the data coming from all positions up through approximately the time of main engine throttle back up to 104 percent. At about approximately a minute or so into the flight, there was an apparent explosion. The flight dynamics officer reported that tracking reported that the vehicle had exploded and impacted into the water. . . . Recovery forces are proceeding to the area including ships and C-130 aircraft. Flight controllers are reviewing their data here in Mission Control. We will provide you with more information as it becomes available. This is Mission Control, Houston."

Nesbitt continued to tell as much as he was told by controllers, refraining from injecting speculation into the commentary. His was the most excruciating task in the annals of NASA public information. At NASA headquarters and the Kennedy and Johnson space centers, the public affairs people were under enormous pressure to explain the tragedy, but they knew little more than the fact that *Challenger* and its crew had vanished in an incredible disaster 73 seconds after liftoff.

REACTION

At the VIP observation sites, family members, relatives, and friends of the crew lapsed from disbelief into shock as they realized they had seen a son, a daughter, a wife, a husband vanish in the worst disaster of the space age.

Crew family members who had been waiting for the liftoff all morning joined hundreds of others at the VIP and press sites in applause and cheers as *Challenger* cleared the tower and ascended over the ocean. Launch of a manned spacecraft is certainly one of the most thrilling spectacles of the twentieth century. Then horror blossomed in the sky as the boosters tore away from the orbiter and the tank a minute too early and the fireball filled the sky.

Many family members were watching from the floor of the launch control center. There were June Scobee, the commander's wife, his son, Richard, W., 21, soon to be graduated from the Air Force Academy, and daughter, Mrs. Kathie R. Krause, and her husband, Justin; Jane Smith, wife of the pilot, and their children, Scott, 17, Alison, 14, and Erin, 9; Lorna Onizuka, wife of Ellison Onizuka, and their children Janelle, 16, and Darien, 10; Cheryl McNair, wife of Ronald McNair, their children, Reginald, 3, and Joy, 18 months, and Mrs. McNair's father, Harold Moore; Marvin and Betty Resnik, parents of Judith Resnik; Marsha Jarvis, wife of Gregory Jarvis; Steven McAuliffe, husband of Christa McAuliffe, and their children, Scott, 9, and Caroline, 6.

When it became apparent that something terrible was happening, one of the Smith children was heard to cry out: "Daddy! Daddy! I want you, Daddy! You promised nothing would happen!"

Seated in the VIP grandstand near launch control, Christa McAuliffe's parents, Edward G. and Grace Corrigan, and two sisters, Lisa and Becky, saw her disappear in an instant that would be an eternity. NASA protocol assistants gathered all the family members from the rooftop and the VIP bleachers and transported them by bus back to the crew quarters. Linda Reppert, Judith Resnik's older sister, joined their parents there and they embraced in tears.

The families were given rooms at crew quarters and served coffee and doughnuts. They rested during the afternoon. Later, Christa McAuliffe's husband, Steve, issued a statement through his Concord, New Hampshire law office: "We have all lost Christa," it said.

In the early evening, Vice President George Bush arrived from Washington with Senators John Glenn (D-Ohio) and Jake Garn (R-Utah) to speak with the families in the crew lounge. June Scobee, wife of the flight commander, spoke for the families. She thanked the visitors for their personal as well as official condolences.

Senator Garn, as was mentioned earlier, had been the first political figure to fly in space. An experienced pilot, he had accumulated more hours in aircraft than had most of the astronauts—probably, he quipped, because aircraft flew more slowly when he flew them. Senator Glenn, the first American to fly in orbit as the United States entered the space age, seemed to be able to empathize with the families more closely than anyone outside their circle of grief.

John Glenn expressed the philosophical outlook of the astronaut corps that enabled them to accept danger and the prospect of death as test pilots. During flight the astronauts were always aware that they were pioneering a new environment, one singularly unforgiving of error or oversight. Glenn told the families that he had felt a sense of loss, akin to theirs, when Virgil I. (Gus) Grissom, Edward H. White II, and Roger B. Chaffee perished in the *Apollo 1* fire just 19 years before.[10] The astronauts were an extended family in those days, but even as the corps became larger, a sense of family identification remained.

Glenn himself had been the subject of deep concern for a brief but agonizing period on February 20, 1962. Mercury Control feared that he might be doomed to perish on the first American orbital flight. An erroneous signal

---

[10]The fire in the Apollo 1 spacecraft was started by an electrical short circuit and ignited supposedly non-flammable plastics while the crew inside was running a prelaunch test on the launch pad. Unable to escape, all three crewmen were suffocated by gases from the burning plastics.

received at Cape Canaveral indicated that the heat shield had separated from the *Mercury* capsule, Freedom 7, on the second revolution of the three-orbit flight. If this had occurred, the capsule was in danger of being incinerated by the frictional heat of reentry as it plunged into the atmosphere. Although the signal seen at Mercury Control was not repeated on the spacecraft cockpit display, Glenn was instructed to keep his retrorocket package in place through reentry after the rockets had fired to accomplish the de-orbit maneuver. The package, strapped to the vehicle behind the heat shield, would thus hold the heat shield in place through reentry.

Glenn kept the retrorocket package on, although he did not appear to share the concern of the controllers on the ground. He reported that it made an impressive fireball as Freedom 7 reentered the atmosphere and landed unscathed.

Another moment of stress had occurred on the second *Mercury* orbital flight when Malcom Scott Carpenter, flying three orbits in *Mercury-Atlas* 7, overshot his Atlantic Ocean landing zone and disappeared from the space coast radar screens and Mercury Control radio. After 45 minutes Mercury Control said that he was sighted by a search aircraft that had homed in on his Sarah Beacon, an automatic beeper. He was seated in a rubber life raft that he had hitched to the floating capsule.

The crew of *Apollo 13* narrowly escaped disaster when the oxygen storage tank blew out in the *Apollo* service module during the flight to the Moon in April 1970. Aborting the planned lunar landing, the crew executed a circumlunar maneuver and, with the lunar landing module still attached, flew back to Earth, using the lunar module's oxygen supply and electric power for life support. The crew then made a successful reentry and landing in the *Apollo* command module.

The beginnings of space flight, like the beginnings of aviation, had not been free of fatal accidents. The Russians had lost four cosmonauts in the *Soyuz* spacecraft program, one in a crash landing and three as the result of accidental decompression at reentry. Since the shuttle started flying in 1981, its apparent freedom from life-threatening failures had led to the public impression that it was as safe and dependable as a streetcar. The shattering of this illusion amplified the human tragedy that send a shock wave through the nation.

From the Soviet Union, First Secretary Mikhail Gorbachev sent a message: "We share the feelings of sorrow in connection with the tragic death of the crew of the space shuttle *Challenger*. We express our condolences to their families and to the people of the United States."

Organs of the Soviet press were less diplomatic. TASS said the disaster was a symbolic warning against the militarization of space. *Komsomolskaya Pravda* shook a minatory finger, accusing the United States of setting the rate of flights unjustifiably high to accelerate the strategic defense initiative.

Historically, manned space flight had been motivated by the conviction that it demonstrated technological prowess as well as by a belief that it was the destiny of humankind to expand into the solar system and exploit its vast resources. America had been first to put men on the Moon in this context. Project Apollo had amply demonstrated American technological superiority in the late 1960s and early 1970s; the shuttle was expected to continue it as well as to provide a cost-effective means of transportation to low Earth orbit. In terms of these values, the *Challenger* accident was a national calamity. It was visible worldwide in horrifying detail, demonstrating the innate fallibility of an agency renowned for technical excellence and the fragility of its grandiose plans to extend human enterprise into the solar system.

The day of January 28, 1986, which had dawned on a scene of confident expectation for another successful mission, the twenty-fifth in a row, ended in death and despair. A Florida journalist summed it up: "The relatives now are left to cope with the sight that has linked strangers in grief: Seven people at the pinnacle of their lives, riding a symbol of national achievement in a disintegrating fireball."[11]

By the end of the day, it appeared to me, and others, that the American space program was in a state of collapse.

PART SIX

Flights that Failed: Aviation's Darkest Hours

The Sky Is Falling

BY ARTHUR WEINGARTEN

Looming 1,472 feet above Manhattan, the Empire State Building dominated the New York skyline from its construction in 1931 to the completion of the World Trade Center in 1972. Whether you are a tourist or jaded native of the city, the sight of this towering landmark creates a part of the New York signature, a statement like no other anywhere in the world.

Bordered by the Hudson and East Rivers, with both Long Island Sound and the Atlantic Ocean nearby, New York City sometimes gets fog and low-visibility conditions that reduce the grandeur of its most famous landmark. Gazing upward through the mists, one sees a stubby unfamiliar shape, its upper floors hidden behind the floating mists.

It was through such mists on Saturday morning, July 28, 1945, that a U.S. Army Air Force bomber was groping through the fog at low altitude in preparation for landing at Newark Airport a few miles away. Just before 9:55, the pilot of the B-25 was catching glimpses of the ground—the buildings of Manhattan—that he knew he should not be seeing if he was on the correct course to land at Newark. Something had gone wrong! Then, suddenly, at exactly 9:55, the image of a building filled the windscreen. In the last second left, the pilot tried to climb. But it was too late. The plane slammed into the 79th floor of the Empire State Building, on the northwest side above 34th Street.

A disaster horrible and shocking had struck the heart of New York City. Explosions, fires, and falling debris made the Empire State Building and the area around it a scene of terror and chaos. As was later written, "Brilliant orange flames shot as high as the observatory on the eighty-sixth floor of the building, 1,050 feet above Fifth Avenue, as the gasoline tanks of the plane exploded." The plane's crew of three, and eleven people at work in the building were killed in the crash. Twenty-six people in the building were injured. Miraculously, there were no fatalities to pedestrians or motorists. An estimated 25,000 people gathered in the light rain to view the aftermath of the crash.

For ten-year old Arthur Weingarten, who arrived at the scene with his father, a New York City fire marshal, the impact of the tragic vision of the accident site was unforgettable. Years later, he felt compelled to document the disaster and painstakingly reconstruct the haunting scene from interviews with the survivors throughout the country—from the pilot's widow, who had a premonition of her husband's death, to a Coast Guardsman who displayed remarkable heorism during the rescue effort.

Weingarten's book, *The Sky Is Falling*, published by Grosset & Dunlap in 1977, is a stirring account of one of the most dramatic days in New York history—a day, as it turns out, that foreshadowed the events to come on 9/11.

*   *   *   *   *

At 9:52 Bill Smith glanced down through his left window and saw the last of the airfield's perimeter slip under his wing. The bomber was now heading west, over the rippled scoop of Bowery Bay. For the second time in a little over a month he had bulldozed his way through the bramble of regulations to get where he was going.

Flying his B-17 back from England, Smith had crossed the Atlantic on instruments, letting down to refuel first at Greenland, then at Newfoundland. His navigation had been textbook-precise; the radio calls to the range stations and military airfields had been made with the exactness of a combat commander who had demanded nothing less of his own men. But on the last leg of the wearying journey home, as the Flying Fortress neared the coast of Maine, a radically different Bill Smith was behind the controls.

With Colonel Rogner in the copilot's seat, Smith had astonished his navigator by waving off the course he had plotted to their destination, Bradley Field, Connecticut. Instead, and with Rogner's wholehearted approval, Smith exuberantly announced that he could locate the field "with his eyes closed." Whooping and horsing around like a busload of teenagers on a school outing, the crew and passengers grabbed for handholds as Smith shot full-throttle, tree-level passes at six or seven airfields before locating Bradley. From Maine, through New Hampshire, down into Massachusetts and Connecticut, Smith left in his wake tower operators radioing ignored demands for the barnstorming B-17 to identify itself.

He had failed to follow his flight plan filed with the Air Transport Command in Newfoundland; disregarded his scheduled calls to range stations along the route; played roulette with the airspace around and over military and civilian fields. For one of the rare times in his life, Bill Smith raised hell. He was home, and probably for the last time flying the plane that had carried him safely through the war. At that moment it seemed perfectly natural for him to bring in his ship the way he had so many times back in England—wide-open, scooting the deck, engines screaming his joy at being alive and in command. It felt right; an allowable, if not strictly innocent, final act of bravado.

But this morning was different. Everything was estranged. The plane was not his. The weather, though foggy and rainy as it had been in England, looked and even smelled alien; the vapor formations drenched with a yellow-brown sulfurous smoke, gritty and acrid as it filtered into the cockpit. And the terrain, his surroundings, was as to a stranger. England had been palm-sized, comfortably flat; its horizon, in fog or moonless night, assured the pilots of no man-made or natural surprises. Smith had found it a human and forgiving geography.

New York was another story.

As a cadet he had traveled down from the Point on a dozen weekends, booking a room at the Barclay or staying at a classmate's apartment. No matter how often he was in Manhattan he felt a trespasser. He was a country boy used to natural contours; the rightness of a hill slope or the squirming of a river set-tling into a new bed were expectations he'd never been denied.

But New York was constructed to startle. It reached for you, he said. It was too big, on an island too small to have such dimension. And he was sensi-tive to the city's aggression—the chest-pounding power of the stone-and-glass skyscrapers; the background hum of tension that constantly played under the excitement of the bigness. No man could find his full height, stand really straight, in the city, he thought, without making comparisons—and having once made them, being diminished.

He would feel a lot easier once Manhattan was behind him.

The bomber was speeding toward the lip of Astoria Park. Smith switched on the wipers to rid the windshield of a film of soot sprayed on by the power plant's smokestacks. Just off to his right, lying under a bleak mass of fog, he caught sight of two bridges spanning a large island.

While circling La Guardia he had double-checked the map for the route he'd fly into Newark. He made a mental fix that Ward's Island, with the Triborough and Hell Gate Bridges straddling the East River channel, should be to his right. He held the B-25 on course, waiting the few seconds it would take to make positive identification of the landmark. The visibility had fallen off as he approached the East River. The ground fog was climbing to a height of several hundred feet, leaving just a narrow corridor of forward vision below the pressing clouds. With a feather touch he eased the wheel forward. The bomber's nose sank. Smith peered down to his right, across the propeller's blur, to the island less than a half-mile distant. Through the scattered cloud layer he could make out lanes of cars moving along the Triborough's roadways, the traffic emptying out onto a ramp cutting through the park directly below him.

It was Ward's Island. His left foot pressured the rudder. The B-25 dipped into a turn toward Hallets Point, a bulbous spit of land jutting a portion of Astoria into the East River. Smith watched the compass rotate as he held the plane in a banking arc to the south-southwest.

Once over the East River he would run a diagonal across Manhattan on a 240-degree heading. The flight path would take him over the Hudson River, across Jersey City, beyond Newark Bay, and into Newark Field.

The bomber leveled out of the turn and started across Hallets Point. The panel clock read just shy of 9:53.

Standing on the bow of the Erie Railroad tug *Celia C,* Dominick Mazzuco cursed the weather as he took off his glasses and began to dry them on his oil-stained sweater.

For the past few minutes, as the stubby green-and-black boat beat its way through the heavy fog along the shore of Welfare Island, Mazzuco had been on the lookout for the flashing beacon of Mill Rock Light, off Hallets Point. The tug was cautiously moving at quarter-speed up the west channel of the East River, nearing the tip of the cigar-shaped island. The deckhand glanced to his right. Between the clinging water haze and the higher layer of fog blanketing the island, he could barely see the century-old buildings of Metropolitan Hospital.

The harsh drone of an approaching plane caught his attention. It sounded low; in fact, Mazzuco could feel the deck vibrating in rhythm with its engines. He looked across the island toward Hallets Point. The sound grew louder, carrying from behind a wall of dark clouds. He slipped his glasses on just as the silver plane nosed through a break in the layer. It *was* low; maybe 400, certainly not higher than 500 feet above the east channel, and moving on a diagonal toward the tugboat. Transfixed by the thunder of its engines, Mazzuco watched as the forward section of the plane dissolved into a fog bank levitating over the east side of the island. A moment later it reappeared.

To his astonishment he saw that the plane's landing gear was being lowered.

Brushing aside a momentary fear, Mazzuco followed the bomber as it raced across the island. The pilot must know what he was doing, he thought; why else would he be flying so low into Manhattan?

Watching the panel indicator, Smith saw that the wheels were coming down smoothly. He felt the plane shudder and the airspeed fall off slightly as the tricycle gear locked into place. Reaching across the control pedestal, he adjusted the throttles to maintain his 200-mph airspeed.

Moments before, as he had cleared Hallets Point and started across the river, Smith had spotted a land mass half-hidden under a thick cover of fog and haze. Large clusters of buildings set around a landscaped park fleetingly revealed themselves on the northern edge of the island. Farther south were more buildings, and what appeared to be a large factory with several towering smokestacks. The twin peaks of a steel bridge pushed through the fog near the island's midsection.

For several reasons, Smith thought that Welfare Island was Manhattan.

As he approached the river Smith had found himself locked in a dense bank of fog. The airspace surrounding the bomber formed a solid sheet of white. He had no visual reference to the ground, yet it was of little concern; as long as he kept his heading steady on 240 degrees, he would be on course.

But fog often acts like a prism, distorting objects, disorienting even the most experienced pilots. Through thinning patches or breaks in the fog bank Smith had caught glimpses of an island. The sightings were disjointed—snatches of land crowded with large, industrial-type buildings set around a park here, factory structures and more cosmopolitan-looking buildings there; a bridge stretching ethereally into a shrouding haze.

The island lay directly between what he mistakenly took to be two distinctly separate bodies of water: the river below him, running to the left of the island, he knew was the East River; the one on the far side, to the west, therefore had to be the Hudson.

Memory and the map conspired with the distorting fog and haze to enlarge the narrow land mass; Smith saw the Metropolitan Hospital complex as taller, more densely grouped, than it was in reality. The grim overcast, the rain beading the windshield, the scattered reflections from the river's surface—all acted as a magnifying lens to swell the less-than-two-mile-long island sitting in the middle of the East River into gargantuan size.

It was Manhattan, not Welfare Island, because Smith wanted it to be.

Topography, landmarks, time, and distance were redrawn from his memory of weekends in the city to fit the immediate desire to put New York behind him. The Queensboro Bridge, ghosting black and directionless above the fog blanketing 59th Street, could logically, in Smith's mind, be either the Brooklyn or Manhattan Bridge—structures his experience told him were located much farther south, near the tip of Manhattan. But the partnership of weather and anxiety pushed Smith to accept a shifting geography. Instinct, and the vague outline of what he took to be the New Jersey shore lying behind the island, had guided his hand to the landing-gear lever. Once past Manhattan he knew that it was only six or seven miles to Newark Field.

He was flying at 500 feet as he began his letdown over the East River. Ahead, through the milky vapor whipping across the windshield, Smith saw the tall apartment buildings lining Sutton Place. The panel clock was edging toward 9:54 as the bomber cut over the center span of the Queensboro Bridge at 59th Street. Smith began to relax. Within seconds now he would be crossing into what he was convinced was Jersey City. Straining to see beyond the masking fog, he attempted to locate Newark Bay.

In her top-floor apartment on York Avenue and 61st Street, Elise Anderson was stirring milk into a steaming pot of oatmeal. Suddenly the entire kitchen seemed to explode with a deafening rumble. Pots and pans hanging on a rack over the stove began to clang like steeple bells. The frying pan danced off the burner, splattering the floor with a half-dozen basted eggs. The sheet of glass in the window facing the Queensboro Bridge rattled like a machine gun.

"My God!" she exclaimed. "It's working!" The startled reference was to the marijuana cigarette she had smoked a half-hour earlier with several fellow art students who were in the living room awaiting breakfast. Until this trembling upheaval, Elise, who had never tried the narcotic before, had thought its powers were highly overrated. She hadn't hallucinated and was feeling only the slightest bit giddy. Or so she had thought. Out of the corner of her eye she caught an object moving past the window. She turned and watched the silver plane shoot over the bridge, heading on a diagonal toward Rockefeller Center. Its wheels were down, and it looked so close that for an instant, had the window been open, she thought she probably could have reached out and grabbed its wing. Mesmerized, she stared after the retreating bomber, trying to remember if she had seen anything in the newspapers about an airport having been built on top of one of the skyscrapers. It seemed to her that she had.

Walking his beat on Lexington Avenue, Patrolman Albert Schneider had reached the corner of 56th Street when he heard a thunderous roar overhead. He, and an elderly deliveryman dragging a cash register on a dolly, looked up as the B-25 moved through a scattered layer of fog and clouds. They glimpsed only pieces of the plane as it traversed the avenue to the southwest. The old fellow winced at the echoing racket and shook his head.

"It's a wonder they don't hit one of these buildings," he said to Schneider with a nervous laugh. "I guess they must teach those guys pretty good."

"Not *that* good!" the policeman said. His eyes fixed to the overcast. Schneider was tracking the sound of the plane's engines. He lived close to La Guardia Field, and had developed an ability to determine an aircraft's distance, altitude, and direction just by its sound.

"That ship's in trouble if he doesn't get higher," he told the deliveryman. "He's heading straight for Radio City"—Schneider slapped his nightstick into his palm for emphasis—"and he aint' gonna make it!"

Something was wrong.

Even as he had crossed the bridge Smith had noticed that the buildings facing the river seemed too high, too massed together, for Jersey City. And the docks crowded with freighters and barges. And the railroad yards with their tacks running spur lines onto the piers. *Where were they?* Could he have missed them in the fog? He had a sinking feeling that he hadn't. Twice before, when he had landed at Newark Field from Sioux Falls, and again when he had taken off for Boston, he had seen the flat industrial town from the air. It lay to the northeast of Newark Field, sprawling unmistakably between the Hudson and Newark Bay. At the speed he was traveling he should have spotted the large island waterway by now.

His eyes were darting from the windshield to the cockpit's side windows. The fog was thickening. His only visibility was straight down through the left window, and even then he had just veiled sightings of rooftops and streets, an impression of a city.

"What's that?" Domitrovich was jabbing Smith's shoulder with his left hand, his right pointing directly ahead. The sergeant's voice sounded more awed than startled.

Smith drew his attention from the ground to the windshield. A point off the bomber's nose he saw the bulk of a towering object waiting behind the fog. It loomed gray and massive.

"It's a building." Smith said it as a fact, crisply, in a dead calm.

It was almost a relief to have the sighting. The skyscraper confirmed his intuition. He was somewhere over Manhattan. His left hand and foot were coordinating the bomber into a climbing left bank as he grasped the throttles with his right hand. The engines surged with increased power. He pulled his eyes from the windshield to make certain his hand had moved to the correct levers to change the prop pitch. He slammed the ganged knobs into the locked position. The changeover made the engines sound angry as the propellers took chomping bites of the air. He flicked a glance down to his right as he grasped the landing-gear lever and snapped it into the up position. He heard the hydraulics grind and begin to draw the wheels up into the fuselage. He desperately needed to be free of their drag *now*, but he knew that it would take an agonizing twenty seconds before they were sucked into place.

The building was starting to fall away to the right. He increased the bank. His eyes jumped to the altimeter. The needle was climbing past 550 feet. He tore his glance away from the dial and searched the control pedestal for the supercharger blowers. He located the levers and jerked them into the high position, then pushed the arms opening the oil-cooler shutters and the engine cowl flaps. His mind had been racing to remember the B-25's hastily learned technical orders. But now he became aware of a pounding sound coming from somewhere behind the cockpit bulkhead.

It was Perna shouting, "Look out! Look out!" as he slammed his fist against the steel partition separating him from the flight deck. He was arched forward, the safety harness cutting into his stomach as he stared through the windshield. Another building was catapulting out of the fog. It seemed less than 100 feet away, its roof level with the bomber.

Reacting to the terror in Perna's voice, Smith hauled back on the control column even before he saw the granite tower.

In her 12th-floor office at 485 Madison Avenue, Adele Halpern was conscious of the plane drawing closer. For the past half-minute the lettering pens and ink pots on her drafting table had been vibrating with its approach.

She was used to planes flying low over midtown, but this one sounded *too* low. The thought flashed through her mind that maybe it was in trouble. Lost in the fog or having mechanical problems. Diving toward her building! With a panicked urgency she swung off the high stool and started out of the partitioned cubicle. Sheets of artwork thumbtacked to a bulletin board sailed to the floor as the plane roared directly overhead. Instinctively, she ducked her head, then, realizing the danger had passed, she ran to the window and looked out across to Fifth Avenue.

For an instant she glimpsed the plane through a hazy patch in the overcast. It was pivoting on its left wing as it veered over 51st Street. Horrified, yet incapable of tearing herself away from the window, she waited for the plane to crash into the top of the International Building in Rockefeller Center.

Jan King had raced out of the lunch bar on the roof of the RCA Building. Pressing against the east parapet sixty-nine stories above Rockefeller

Center, he felt totally helpless peering into the swirling fog obscuring Fifth Avenue.

A former radio operator for Delta Airlines, King had known the ship was in trouble the instant he'd heard the props change pitch. Risking balance, he leaned farther over the low wall. The fog was impenetrable. The hammering engines grasping for altitude reminded him of a locomotive hurtling through a tunnel.

"Pull up! . . . Pull up! . . . Pull up! . . ." King continued the shouted cadence as he caught sight of the plane. It was no more than 50 feet distant and about 100 feet below him as it banked directly over the International Building's rooftop garden. The propellers cut a swath through the overcast, allowing him to see the bomber clear the building by less than 25 feet. Within a blink the fog closed in behind it.

The pulsing sound of the plane's engines had carried down to Park Avenue and 34th Street. From his bathroom window on the top floor of the Vanderbilt Hotel, David McKay was startled to see a B-25 swing out of a fog bank over the RCA Building and head down Fifth Avenue.

While shaving he had been studying the clouds and fog rolling across the midtown area. From his vantage point almost a mile to the south he saw that the overcast was scattered; portions of the city were lying under a filmy haze, while in other areas heavy fog obliterated entire groups of skyscrapers. Looking toward 42nd Street, he could clearly see the Chrysler Building's chromed spire, yet almost directly in front of his window the top third of the Empire State was invisible behind a leaden field of clouds. The area where the bomber was moving into had the lowest ceiling, less than 600 feet, McKay judged. But the airspace directly below the plane was only slightly hazy. If he could easily pick out the twin peaks of St. Patrick's Cathedral, surely the pilot could. Why, then, he asked himself with mounting apprehension, was the plane flying so low among the towering buildings?

The phone in the bedroom rang. Startled, McKay turned toward the sound, then instantly jerked his attention back to the plane. It was gone. He heard its engines coming from behind an opaque layer of clouds.

"Six twenty-five . . . six thirty-five . . . six forty-five . . ." Domitrovich was calling out the altimeter reading.

Smith eased the wheel a hair more to the right. He was cautiously, blindly leveling out of the banking left turn. "Where's the gear?" He didn't dare pull his eyes from the windshield.

The sergeant shot a look at the dial in front of him. "A third up!" Slow. Too slow. The drag was anchoring their rate of climb. He started to glance out his window.

Smith caught the movement out of the corner of his eye. "Altimeter!" he snapped. Every foot was precious.

"Six sixty . . . six seventy . . ." Domitrovich was shouting to overcome the howling engines as Smith added more throttle. "Coming through seven hundred, colonel!"

Seven hundred feet above *where*? Smith demanded of himself. Altitude was not enough. The fog wrapping itself around the plane was hiding all landmarks. He was smack in the center of Manhattan—that and only that much was certain. He gambled a fleeting look at the compass. South. Maybe a trace west of due south. The fact was useless by itself, meaningless without another reference. What was he north of? What was the fog concealing to his left or right? His eyes dropped to the airspeed indicator. The needle was quivering on 250. Another dismembered fact. Was 250 miles per hour too slow or breakneck fast for his blind flight path? The building he had just missed by a whisper was over 600 feet high. The structure directly behind it had been taller still, its top buried in the fog. Was he moving deeper into the canyons of skyscrapers, or had he already miraculously, with sheer dumb luck, passed over the city's tallest buildings? Were they clustered together, all jammed into a dense mass as he had thought on those weekend vacations from the Point? Or could they actually have been spaced farther apart, separated by channels of open air that would offer a safe passage through the aerial minefield?

He was scavenging his memory for the map he knew was imprinted in its recesses. Disjointed impressions were flashing on and off like lights on a busy switchboard. The Radio City Music Hall. Times Square. The Camel cigarette sign with the man blowing tire-sized smoke rings. Central Park. There were tall buildings, hotels, facing the park. He had stayed once at the Sherry-Netherland. Too low. The buildings around him were much higher. Forty-second Street had tall buildings, near Grand Central Station. The Chrysler Building. The Empire State.

"At the present time I can't see the top of the Empire State Building."

The message had been meaningless when the La Guardia tower operator had given him the information; isolating the landmark had had no relevance to his situation then. He had gone to the top, the 102nd floor, with his roommate, Skip Young. That was when? . . . four or five years ago. They had looked *down* on the Chrysler Building—on the entire city. The largest buildings looked like Monopoly-set pieces. Where was it? Could he have passed it?

"Wheels half up!" Domitrovich shouted. "Seven ten feet!"

"Bloody idiot!" Captain Thorolf Ingall muttered as the plane thundered overhead. The British Intelligence officer dropped the report he was reading and swiveled his chair to the window behind him. The fog and cloud layer had lowered even more than when he had last glanced through his windows on the 36th floor of the British Empire Building. Scanning the overcast across 50th Street, he located the bomber as it emerged from a rolling mass of fog. It was moving crablike to the south, angled toward Sixth Avenue.

His secretary had joined him at the window. "Look at his wheels," he said, tapping the glass. "Seem a bit off, don't they?" The wheel struts were canted inward under each wing. The secretary nodded. "I guess he must be coming in to land somewhere." Ingall watched as the plane's nose seemed to drop in a slight downward glide. Perhaps she's right, he thought. But certainly the pilot had to see that he was heading directly toward the Salmon Tower. The 700-foot building was sitting on the corner of Fifth Avenue and 42nd Street.

The B-25's pounding engines were attracting attention throughout the midtown area. Pedestrians and motorists, office workers, hotel guests, and apartment dwellers were staring into the overcast, searching for the source of their sudden apprehension. Manhattanites deaf to the cacophony of subway trains and snarled traffic, born with immunity to unending barrages of demolition and construction, insulated against the unique and unnoticing of the bizarre—all were now listening to the drama unfolding overhead.

Stopped for a light at Fifth Avenue and 45th Street, Stan Lomax, the sports announcer for radio station WOR, glanced up through his rain-spotted windshield and searched the sky. He felt the pavement under his tires shake with the plane's closeness. Even before he spotted the bomber racing toward the Salon Tower, he was climbing out of the car and jumping onto the running board. He heard himself pleading: "Climb, you damn fool, climb!"

Annette Dutton was having difficulty breathing. Standing in the doorway of the shoe store where she worked on Fifth Avenue and 43rd Street, she watched the silver plane slice above a row of towering office buildings. The turbulent overcast and the menacing engines brought back her memories of the London blitz. For three years she had lived through the firebombings and German rockets. It had been only in the last few weeks that her nightmares had begun to taper off. "He's going to hit it sure as hell!" shouted a man standing next to her. He sounded superior in his safety, a spectator more than half-hoping to see a fall from the high wire. Annette turned to him with the thought of overcoming her shyness and telling him to shut up. Instead, she felt her hand pummeling his face, saw his glasses shatter and a ribbon of blood start down his cheek. She found herself screaming exactly as she had in her nightmares.

In his 16th-floor room in the Hotel Commodore, Mort Cooper was sitting on the bed fitting a new flint in his lighter. The Boston Braves pitcher was listening to music, relaxing before taking a cab to Ebbets Field for his afternoon game against the Dodgers. He had subconsciously picked up the drone of the plane when it was still far off, then became annoyed as the rumbling engines began to echo down 42nd Street. Now his room was literally quaking, as if an avalanche were descending. Bolting to the window, Cooper looked up to his right. He recognized the bomber as a Billy Mitchell. Through a shifting break in the fog he watched the plane's left wing dip almost imperceptibly, then the angle deepened slightly. Thank God! Cooper thought, he's seen the building. He waited for the plane to heel more to the left. To his horror he saw the wing abruptly come back up to a level position. The bomber was moving over 43rd Street.

Coming out of Grand Central Station, Walter Daniels, the *New York Times* day cable editor, stopped under the canopy to light his pipe. Suddenly he became aware of a great movement on both sides of 42nd Street. People were surging toward Fifth Avenue, their faces turned upward, some pointing off to the west. Then he heard the plane. The engines had been so loud, the noise seemingly so close at hand, that he had dismissed it as normal. Con Edison and the phone company were always jackhammering the streets. His reporter's instinct triggered, he fell in with the crowd. "What is it? What's happening?" Daniels asked a heavy-set woman running alongside. She was cradling two net shopping bags overflowing with old newspapers. "I don't know," she puffed. "Somebody said a plane's gonna crash." Daniels stopped. He watched the woman shove her way through the mass of people racing toward the ominous thunder. He hesitated, then looked up. The plane, appearing to him more like a shadow skimming the fog, was about to collide with the Salmon Building.

Old John Feather Merchant was approaching 42nd Street at four miles a minute. An instant past, over 44th Street, Smith had committed himself to turning east, heading back to La Guardia Field.

With his visibility still totally obscured, he had leveled out of the climb, risking that he had enough altitude to clear any surrounding buildings lurking behind the fog. The left wing had just started to dip when he glimpsed metal suspended in a shallow patch of haze. It had been angled to his left, at eye level. At first he thought it was a reflection off his prop blades. Then, as he deepened the bank, he made another veiled sighting. Stone! And rows of windows! He kicked right rudder, aborting the turn. That path was closed. He would have to find another.

The bomber continued on past the Chrysler Building.

In his 39th Street office, James Jagger slipped a fresh plastic recording disk into the Sound Scriber and continued his dictation. "And so, in conclusion, any encouragement you can give would be greatly appreciated. Sincerely." The civil engineer placed the letter on top of a pile sitting on his desk and picked up another. Settling deeper into his leather chair, he scanned it for a moment, then began: "Letter to Dean Crawford, University of Michigan. Dear Dean Crawford. I have just discovered . . ." The drone that had set his windows vibrating moments ago had suddenly become shockingly loud. With singular concentration Jagger ignored the intrusion and proceeded. ". . . that my schedule precludes the visit I had hoped . . ." It was impossible to continue. As it was, he had caught himself almost shouting into the microphone. Normally unafflicted with curiosity, Jagger rose and crossed to the window, wondering if he should issue a complaint. The city was noisy enough, he thought, without some fool adding to it. He looked across toward the Salmon Building. Just as he had suspected—a plane. A bomber from the look of it. He watched, his head shaking in disapproval, as the aircraft seemed to teeter crazily, its wings dipping first to the right, then to the left as it barely scraped over the top of the buff-colored building. It continued a boomerang climb over the 42nd Street Library, then leveled out and headed down Fifth Avenue. It struck Jagger that the pilot would most likely play the same juvenile game when he reached the Empire State. He turned back to his dictation.

It was as if the air above the city had become partitioned, a Byzantine maze. For the three men traveling in the fog, time and direction ceased to exist. The compass pointed south. The altimeter registered 725 feet. The artificial horizon indicated that the aircraft was in a slight climbing attitude. The panel clock reported seconds less than 9:55. The bomber was closing the seven-block distance to the Empire State Building at 127 yards per second.

Nanette Morrison had been struggling with the press release for the last ten minutes. The weather boiling past her tower windows overlooking

Fifth Avenue and 40th Street had an urgency and beauty far exceeding the description of the stock venture in her typewriter. The rampaging sound of the plane's engines gave her new reason to search the sky. Over 41st Street she saw a cloud tear open and the bomber appeared. It was startlingly close, its left wing bridging the distance to her window with a stepping-stone gap. Like suction plumps the propellers dredged the fog clear of the fuselage, allowing her to see the men in the cockpit. Through his open window, the pilot was peering toward the ground. She raised her hand in the start of a wave, then froze. The bomber shot past, creating a shock wave that toppled a crystal bud vase sitting on her desk to the floor. Overcoming her numbed horror, she threw the window open and leaned out, oblivious to her lifelong dread of heights. The plane seemed to be climbing, its twin tail slightly lower than the nose as it crossed 38th Street. The climb was so agonizingly slow that Nanette Morrison felt she might go mad watching the bomber, as if on a cable, being pulled toward the Empire State. At 37th Street she heard the engines suddenly grow louder. The plane seemed to hover momentarily in its climb, then the left wing dropped violently. At 35th Street, too slow, too late, she watched it begin a turn to the east. Her hands intertwined, fingers working like rosary beads, she began to chant a whispered "Oh no . . . Oh no . . . Oh no . . . Oh no . . ."

The claxon blast of the stall-warning horn filled the cockpit as Smith pulled the last inch of the control column into his chest. The bomber's nose was almost vertical now, the right wing vaulted perpendicular to the face of the building. At 975 feet above 34th Street the windshield was being filled with pockmarked blocks of limestone and chrome mullions dividing windows. And behind the windows, on the 79th floor of the Empire State Building, the men in the bomber could see people seated at their desks.

Gripping the troopship *Winnipeg's* bow rail, Major Jean Mayer swept the shoreline for the target of the explosive thud. A split-second before the hollow, crumping sound had carried across the Hudson, Mayer had been watching the fog shrouding the tall buildings around 34th Street. Allowing for the distance and sound-distorting characteristics of water, the major was nevertheless certain that somewhere in the city a bomb had gone off. So were the men around him. Hundreds were pressing the starboard rail, their voices rising in anxiety as they searched the skyline.

In a sudden rush, the clouds that had been secreting the top of the Empire State vanished. With perfect clarity, Mayer saw an arrow of orange flame streak out from the north face of the building—high up, near the observation deck, narrow, rolling outward as if being spit from a chemical flamethrower. There was a second explosion, massive this time, a full four or five seconds after the first. The concussive blast seemed of unmistakable origin to the men on the *Winnipeg*.

"Rockets!" a young GI standing next to Mayer shouted. "The Japs are bombing the city!" His panicked cry raced through the troops massed on the deck. "They're using German V-2s!" yelled another man. Mayer was being crushed against the rail as a wave of bodies pushed onto the bow. The flames had mushroomed over the tower mast, predominantly black now, flecked with splotches of deep, hot orange. As the ship moved past the building, Mayer saw rivers of fire sluicing down the center section, pieces falling off in jellied clumps and dropping down onto 34th Street. Throughout the harbor, ships were sounding their horns and whistles in emergency blasts. Tearing his attention away from the holocaust, the major looked off toward the dock where his wife was waiting. He thanked God that so far none of the rockets had fallen in that area.

For seconds after the bomber crashed an eerie silence surrounded the building. In contrast to the ear-shattering roar of the plane's approach, the sound of the impact had been curiously muffled.

To Patrolman Harold Voelbel, directing traffic at the intersection of 34th Street and Fifth Avenue, it had been a distant door slam; in fact, at fist Voelbel thought the plane had missed the building, that the hollow boom had been an echo of its engines. For Theodore Eusebi, parking his car on the south side of 34th Street directly beneath the building, the crash was not unlike the sound of a tire running over a tin can, a sudden metallic flattening. Emerging from McCreery's, where he had just finished washing the inside of the large display windows, Horace Walters had the impression of a thunderclap rumbling across from New Jersey. On an inspection tour along Fifth Avenue, Fire Lieutenant William Murphy had just reached Alarm Box 681 when he heard what he took to be an auto accident, the crunching grind of fenders suddenly meeting.

Reaching the door of the barber shop on 33rd Street, Ed Cummings and Jack McCloskey had heard a dull, scraping sound echo under the engines' thunder. Cummings turned and looked across Park Avenue to the Empire State. At that instant he saw the clouds surrounding the tower blown away. A gusher of flame was shooting out of the north face, just beneath the 86th-floor observation deck. McCloskey had opened the door and was starting inside.

Cummings gripped his arm. "Oh, my God, Jack—look!" McCloskey turned and peered off in the direction of Cummings' outstretched arm. Within the moment it took for him to grasp that the building was on fire, McCloskey's normally florid face had drained white. "Holy Mother of . . ." he started. An explosion, unbridled, from deep within the flaming section, cut him short. The men saw large, odd-shaped chunks of debris hurled with volcanic fury into the space over 34th Street. Rivulets of molten fire were running down the northeast corner of the structure.

Coatless, bearing traces of shaving cream on his face, Father Swanstrom pushed past the men and stared up at the building. As if attempting to mask the damage, the clouds and fog had again settled over the tower area. With grim urgency, the priest was silently reckoning the stories below the charred billows of smoke that poured through the cloud layer. "Do you think it's our offices, Father?" Cummings asked quietly. He was shaking. Swanstrom continued to stare at the building, certain that if answered immediately he'd burst into tears. "Whoever's they are," he finally managed, "they'll need help." He turned to Cummings. "Go to St. Francis. Ask them to send over as many priests as they can. Tell them to bring their holy oils." Without waiting for McCloskey, Swanstrom took off on a dead run for the building.

In the time between the bomber's impact and the second explosion, a yellow-and-red Desoto Skyview cab had entered the intersection commanded by Patrolman Voelbel. Behind the wheel, Raphael Gomez was watching the traffic officer perform a series of startling maneuvers. With his hands raised over his head, Voelbel was bent at the waist, his feet making small, shuffling hops around a manhole cover like a Navajo rain dancer. Then, spinning around, he straightened and turned his face to the sky. One of his white-gloved hands was thrust out in a shielding gesture. Gomez started to laugh, his eyes darting to the rear-view mirror. "Hey, you see that?" he asked his passenger. "What's that crazy guy doing?" The taxi's forward motion was suddenly diverted into a sickening skid as a flaming bar of metal cleaved the hood. The rear end of the cab jumped inches with the impact. Gomez was fighting the wheel, flooring the brake pedal, as the vehicle, its wheels locked, slid like an ice boat across Fifth Avenue. It leaped the curb at precisely the moment of the second explosion and came to a jarring halt against a fire hydrant. The blast deafened Gomez; he thought his cab had been squarely hit by an artillery shell. Recalling the days in Havana when Batista had taken over the government, Gomez scrambled from the taxi and, wild-eyed, raced off shouting, "Madre mia! La Revolucíon!"

For at least five hundred people, the intersection had taken on the terror of a battlefield. Chunks of stone and flaming metal rained down on the four corners bordering Fifth Avenue. Skeletal sections of the plane—wing ribs, fuel tanks, a 58-pound piece of the tail structure, a 109-pound portion of the landing gear—crashed down in an area hundreds of yards in all directions. Jagged shards of glass shattered against the sidewalks, trickled along the gutters; miniature lakes erupted exploding like grenade shrapnel on the roofs of passing cars. Like a biblical rain of fire, hundreds of gallons of blazing gasoline showered down from the blackened sky. Puddles of reddish high-octane fuel formed in the streets, on the sidewalks, trickled along the gutters; miniature lakes erupted into flaming islands as burning drops of fuel set them off in a chain reaction.

About to begin washing the outside of McCreery's display windows, Horace Walters set his long-handled brush into the bucket of soapy water. The second blast knocked him off balance. Startled, still thinking the tremendous roar was thunder, he looked over his shoulder to the clouds above the Empire State. He never saw the hurtling slab of wing flap that exploded the 10-foot-square sheet of glass less than two yards to his left. He felt a stabbing pain in his right hand.

Dodging the falling debris, Voelbel began evacuating the screaming, panicked pedestrians from the area. He herded a woman whose cheek had been flayed open by glass into a doorway. An elderly man, wailing incoherently, refused to get off the sidewalk, where he had been dropped by a shaft of metal lancing his leg. Voelbel picked him up with a scooping motion and deposited him in the doorway of Altman's department store. A woman standing on the northwest corner was screaming that she couldn't see. A man was rolling on the pavement in front of the Oppenheim Collins store, his suit jacket still smoking from burning fuel. Like a performer in a ballet written by Dante, Voelbel was leaping across patches of flaming concrete, running through clouds of oily black smoke, warding off hailstorms of glass in his rescue efforts. In passing, he saw Patrolman Harold Kennedy throw open the police call box in front of McCreery's.

Staring numbly at the streams of liquid fire running down the face of the building, Kennedy heard the desk sergeant's voice come over the phone with a stale "Midtown South—Sergeant Phalen." Kennedy's mind suddenly went blank. He opened his mouth and made a coughing sound. He tried again, with the same result. A third time produced the best and most succinct statement he could muster: "This is Kennedy—Badge 3772. I just want to report a very unusual occurrence. I think a plane just hit the Empire State Building." There was a long pause, then the sergeant blandly asked: "Kennedy, where are you?"

Seconds before the crash, Mrs. Oswald Hering had been standing in her penthouse living room in the Waldorf Building, drawing on a pair of white gloves. The approaching plane had set up a series of vibrations through the old structure. The wood floorboards and plaster walls were oscillating in tempo to the quickening thunder. The panes in the skylight overhead joined in with an ominous timbre. At the very peak of the engines' crescendo the elderly widow heard a metallic thump, as if an empty oil drum had tumbled from a distant height. Then silence.

It was the sudden, unexpected silence that caused her to glance through the skylight to the Empire State. *That's ridiculous,* Mrs. Hering thought, *the plane couldn't have possibly hit the building.* She searched the sky on either side of the towering structure, certain that the aircraft would momentarily appear through the fog.

She saw it first as a tiny flicker of orange darting through the clouds obscuring the observatory level. Then, as the gray shroud abruptly lifted, Mrs. Hering saw a section of the building explode open. Massive chunks of masonry were hurtling out of a tunnellike hole just below the 86th floor. Behind the cascading boulders she caught sight of something being catapulted out of the building. The large object was flaming, trailing a plume of oily black smoke as it plunged over 33rd Street, heading directly toward her penthouse.

In his 12th floor office in the Waldorf Building, Joseph Bing gave a startled cry as he was lifted out of his chair and pitched to the floor. The entire building was shuddering under the impact of the bomber's 1,100-pound forward landing gear and a 340-pound section of an engine.

The room seemed to be coming down around him. Slabs of plaster and wooden joists tore loose from the ceiling, threatening to bury him in a choking rubble. The windows had shattered, sending shreds of glass pinging off the walls like snipers' bullets. The room was beginning to fill with smoke, black and heavy with the smell of gasoline. And above the confused shouts of his workers Bing heard Mrs. Hering screaming in the penthouse directly above him. Staggering to his feet, he grabbed the fire extinguisher off the wall and groped his way out of the office. With several workers falling in behind, Bing bolted up the flight of stairs leading to the roof.

He was greeted with utter devastation. Through a suffocating wall of smoke he saw flames raging out of Henry Hering's studio. The skylight and three of the walls had been blasted open, littering the roof with a maze of bricks and timbers. In the very center of the holocaust, rising like a phoenix, was the sculptor's plaster model of his famous statue *Pro Patria*. By some quirk the 22-foot statue had remained standing, virtually untouched. The acrid fumes were searing Bing's lungs as he strained to see through the smoke to Mrs. Hering's penthouse. The flames roaring out of the studio had ignited a pile of timbers and furniture strewn in front of her apartment.

"Mrs. Hering!" Bing shouted. "Are you all right?" There was silence. Handing the extinguisher to one of the men, Bing tied his handkerchief around his nose and mouth and plunged across the roof. Three times he stumbled to his knees over obstacles hidden by the blinding smoke before reaching her door. He pounded on it. "Mrs. Hering! Are you in there?" No answer. Thinking it locked, Bing threw his shoulder against the door. It flew open. Through the smoke pouring in from the shattered skylight he saw the old woman standing rigidly against the far wall. A glance told him that she was in shock, numbed and incapable of moving. As he started toward her, Bing noticed that she was staring blankly at an object lying on the rug in front of her.

"You're safe now, Mrs. Hering," Bing said gently. He took her arm and attempted to lead her toward the door. She stood rooted, resisting his pressure. Her eyes remained fixed on the object. Bing glanced down, then quickly turned away and gagged. It was a woman's hand, torn off at the wrist. A gold wedding band remained firmly on the ring finger. The red nail polish still retained its gloss. Keeping his eyes averted, Bing took a stronger grip on Mrs. Hering's arm and pulled her out of the penthouse.

In the minute remaining before the bomber crashed into the building, the workers on the 79th-floor office of the Catholic War Relief Services had settled into a well-trod rhythm.

In the north section Paul Dearing was nearing the end of his story on the returning war veterans. Moments before he had called the dock master to check on the arrival times of the troopships. He was surprised to learn that they were expected ahead of schedule. If anything, it seemed to him that clouds and fog cutting off his uptown view of Fifth Avenue had grown thicker. But experience had cautioned him against the folly of attempting to judge the weather from his perch 975 feet above the city. There were days when the sun could be streaming through his windows, while just a few floors below a layer of clouds released a deluge on the streets.

"Paul, got time for coffee?" Kay O'Connor asked. She was leaning into the office, her arms straddling the doorway. Dearing swung around, glancing at his watch. "Are you having it sent up?"

She extended her finger toward the floor. "Walgreen's with Mary. Soon as I finish the mail." Dearing hesitated, then shook his head. "I don't think so. I've got to wrap this up. Thanks anyway." She nodded and started off. "Hey, I almost forgot," Dearing called out. Kay popped her head back in.

"Do you know if Monsignor O'Boyle got around to checking that press release I left on his desk yesterday afternoon?"

"Last night, just before quitting time, naturally. I put in a half hour overtime typing the ditto."

"What did he think of it?" Dearing asked.

"For a reporter, he said you write like Shakespeare."

Dearing threw his hands up in mock helplessness. "That bad, huh? Well, at least I'm moving up in class. Last week it was Walter Winchell."

Moving back into the central office, Kay selected two letters from the dwindling stack of mail and crossed to John Judge's desk. He was leaning back in his chair with his eyes closed, dictating to Jeanne Sozzi in a low monotone. Kay dropped the envelope into his "in" basket, then turned and looked across the room toward Mary Kedzierska's office. The cubicle was empty. Through the glass partition she saw a cigarette burning on the lip of an ashtray.

"Where'd Mary disappear to?" she asked Anne Gerlach.

Planting her finger on a line of the report she was reading, Anne looked up with a befuddled expression. "She's right here," she said, pointing to Mary Lou Taylor seated at the next desk.

"She means Mary K., Miss Gerlach," Mary Lou said. "I saw her heading back to the files just a second ago. Do you want me to get her for you, Miss O'Connor?"

Kay shook her head with an appreciative smile. "I'll be going back there in a minute." Since coming to the charity as a summer replacement secretary, Mary Lou had become a favorite of Kay's. Aside from her spontaneity and cheerful outlook on life, Kay found that of all the young girls in the office, Mary Lou was the only one who consistently had the good manners not to address her elders by their first names. For a moment it crossed her mind to invite Mary Lou down to the drugstore for coffee; then she decided against it. Mary Kedzierska was peculiar about fraternizing with anyone on the staff who wasn't an executive. Instead, Kay made a mental note to ask Mary Lou to lunch one day. She was curious to learn why someone so vivacious and attractive had decided to enter a convent at the end of summer.

Joe Fountain was on the phone, peering at the fog eddying past his windows as Kay entered the office. She waved several envelopes to gain his attention, dropped them on the desk, and started out. Fountain snapped his fingers and held his hand up, signaling for her to wait. A few words told her that he was talking to his wife, pregnant with their fifth child and due to give birth any day now.

Fountain was surveying the litter of reports and budget sheets lying on his desk. "I'll be home around four, honey," he said into the phone. "If you feel up to it, maybe we'll get a sitter and go out for a bite and a movie. See you later." He hung up and motioned Kay over to the window.

She had already broken into a smile. Fountain was an inveterate practical joker, a man truly blessed, Kay thought, with a sense of humor that allowed him to locate the improbable or incongruous in most situations and translate it into fun.

He had picked up a coffee mug from the desk and was offering it to her. "Feel like a drink?" he asked with a sly wink.

A little early, isn't it? What's the occasion?"

He pointed in a direction across Sixth Avenue. "Can't turn it down when it's on the house."

Through the window Kay saw a huge Four Roses liquor bottle hovering above the cloud layer just beyond Macy's department store. It was tilted at a pouring angle, a stream of golden liquid flowing out of the mouth. The rest of the billboard and its scaffolding was completely hidden by the clouds and fog.

"You nut!" Kay laughed, playfully punching Fountain's arm.

In the reception foyer, Lucille Bath was struggling to finish the last chapter of *Bugles in Her Heart,* a romantic novel of frontier days.

It was a toss-up which was more boring—the book or sitting behind the switchboard. She released a long-suffering sigh and closed the volume as Kay swept through the wooden gate.

She read the youngster's morose look and offered a cheering grin. "Buck up, Lucille, only two more hours till the cell doors open."

Lucille returned a halfhearted smile. "It sure is dragging this morning. It must be the weather. Whenever it rains I feel like staying in bed all day." She loosened another plaintive sigh, reaching for a cable to quiet the buzzing switchboard. *Ah, youth,* Kay laughed to herself. Only a teenager like Lucille could contort boredom into excruciating pain. She suddenly felt jealous for the memory.

Entering the south portion of the office, Kay spotted Mary Kedzierska at the far end talking to Ellen Lowe and crossed to her.

"I'm done. You ready to go now?" Kay asked.

Mary reached up and adjusted the pearl stickpin in her turban. "Can you wait a couple of minutes? I've just got to check some figures." She turned back to Ellen. "I need the complete Mexican budget, not just the quarterly. Okay?" She flashed the young, blond secretary a smile meant to prepay the act.

Only Ellen's voice, a touch brittle, hinted at her annoyance. "Can I finish this letter? It'll take just a minute or two."

"I really need it now, dear," Mary said, her smile just slightly less generous. She turned to Kay. "If you want to go down, I'll meet you there in about five minutes."

"No problem," Kay said. "I've got some filing that's just screaming to be done."

Ellen waited until Mary was out of earshot. "I swear, that woman must think she runs this place. She's got her own secretary." She pushed her chair back in a miff and started toward the row of wooden file cabinets resting against the opposite wall.

"Mary probably has her drowning in work," Kay said, feeling a need to soften her friend's somewhat officious manner.

Ellen pulled open a drawer and began rummaging through the crowded files. "The least she could've done was waited for it. I'm not her maid, you know."

Kay was listening to the rumbling sound grow louder. She had picked it up seconds before, while it was still a distant, muffled drone. It seemed to come from the north end of the office.

"I wonder what *that* is!" she said. The vibrations shooting through the floor made her voice sound quavery.

Therese Fortier looked up from her typewriter. "Sounds like a subway train, doesn't it?" she said with a startled laugh.

Paul Dearing was the first to see the bomber. It was banking out of a cloud layer in an almost vertical climb less than twenty yards away. He leaped to his feet and started to turn from the desk when the plane hit. The sudden concussion jerked him backward and hurled him through the closed window. His body fell seven floors before coming to rest on the roof of the 72nd-story setback.

At 250 miles per hour, the 12-ton plane was invading the building with astonishing effortlessness. The blunted Plexiglas nose had made the initial entry through a row of windows directly behind John Judge's desk. Both Judge and Jeanne Sozzi were crushed instantly as the fuselage continued to gouge deeper into the office.

Because its left wing was dropped slightly below the 78th floor, the B–25 was tearing through the War Relief Services office at an upward angle. The raised cockpit flattened like an egg carton as it made contact with a 16-inch beam imbedded in the ceiling just behind the windows. The 2,000-pound column of steel, yielding with a memory of its once molten state, arched up into the 80th floor, slicing open the top of the fuselage as it traveled through the widening passage. The right wing, almost perpendicular to the 20-foot hole in the limestone facing, sheared off in sections. The fuel tanks burst open, spewing hundreds of gallons of the pinkish gasoline ahead of the furnace-hot engine.

Until then, there had been no fire.

During the first second of its rampage, the bomber's impact alone had claimed six lives: the three men in the plane, Bill Smith, Christopher Domitrovich, and Albert Perna; and in the office, Paul Dearing, John Judge, and Jeanne Sozzi. But now, as the remaining portion of the right wing slammed into a vertical steel column, the engine exploded from its mounting. Like a bolt of Greek fire, it catapulted through the office in a southerly direction.

Drenched by the shower of fuel while seated at their desks, Mary Lou Taylor, Anne Gerlach, and Patricia O'Connor were just reaching the entrance to the reception foyer when the blazing engine caught up with them. The incinerating geyser of flame was so intense that it melted the glass and metal partition. Hissing smoke rose from the fused elements of flesh and metal. The fire now raced back into the office to consume the unburnt fuel lying ankle-deep on the linoleum.

The six bright yellow oxygen tanks had been hurled from the disintegrating bomber. Two of the canisters had flown on a diagonal trajectory into the cubicle shared by Maureen Maguire and Margret Mullins. An instant before the flames swept through the office, the women had stumbled out of the glass enclosure. Dazed and bleeding from deep cuts inflicted by exploding metal and glass, they saw Mary Kedzierska standing in the doorway of her office.

"Mary!" cried Margret Mullins. She started toward the slim, dark-haired woman just as a wave of flames rolled across the room. Reaching to the ceiling, the fire cascaded over Mary. She remained standing in the doorway for what seemed the longest moment, then slowly, almost casually, as if she had decided to sit on the floor, her body folded onto the ground. Maureen Maguire had time to scream "Oh my God!" before three of the oxygen tanks lying in the middle of the inferno erupted.

The sudden blast, a thousand times brighter than the sun, created a momentary vacuum in the reception foyer. Halted in midflight only a foot or two from the hallway door, Lucille Bath was sucked backward into the rapidly expanding ball of orange fire.

Some ninety feet south of the bomber's point of entry, Kay O'Connor had just started out of Monsignor O'Boyle's office with a handful of letters. The resulting shock wave knocked her off balance. "Hey!" she yelled with startled surprise. Her feet were carrying her in small, shuffling steps back into the desk. She had become aware of a deafening roar, a terrible wrenching sound of metal tearing apart. And of wood and glass splintering. The small office seemed to be swaying; then Kay realized the sickening motion wasn't confined just to the room. *The entire building was moving!* Yawing off center, trembling with a side-to-side, up-and-down motion. Earthquakes aren't supposed to happen in New York, she thought. The horrible sound had grown louder. She felt that if it didn't stop instantly, her head would explode.

The jolt had spun Therese Fortier around in her chair. Facing the north portion of the office, she saw the boiling mass of orange flame rolling out of the reception foyer. It was moving directly toward her. She began to scream. For some reason she was unable to get out of the chair. A dead weight seemed to be pressing on her shoulders, anchoring her to the seat.

Occupying the desk to the left of Therese, Theresa Scarpelli was crying hysterically, her eyes clamped shut as she attempted to thrust her ample weight past her coworker. "Fire!" she began to scream over and over. "Fire!" She was leaning across Therese, pushing down on her in a desperate attempt to squeeze past. Charlotte Deegan, standing next to Ellen Lowe at the file cabinets, was watching Theresa's struggles with what appeared to be an amused look. Her hands were clutching her hair on either side of her head, and her mouth was frozen into a horrified grin. She was moaning an "Ohhhhh" sound as she rocked back and forth, her voice rising and falling with the motion like a wailing siren.

Stumbling out of her office, Anna Regan, the personnel manager, seemed unaware of the blood flowing down the right side of her face. She had been gashed by a shard of glass that had flown into her office through the open door. Standing less than twenty feet from the oncoming wall of fire, she glanced first to the five secretaries huddled at the rear of the office, then turned and, in a daze, started moving toward the flames. After a few steps she halted, looked back toward the women, and placed her right hand over her forehead. She hesitated, then continued toward the fire.

"Anna!" screamed Kay O'Connor. "Come here! This way!" There was a sudden rumbling sound, Kay saw a burst of thick, black smoke shoot through the center of the orange flames. For an instant the fire seemed to be halted in its forward movement. Anna turned from the fire and, still holding her forehead, walked toward Kay. Except for the heavy flow of blood streaming down her face, her skin was colorless. Kay was certain that she had been mortally wounded, that only the reflex of shock was forcing her legs to function.

Ellen Lowe shrieked and covered her face with her hands. In that instant, as Joe Fountain walked out of the raging flames, she was left with no doubt that they would all die.

He moved slowly, with deliberate steps, as if cautiously picking his way over uncertain ground. Both of his arms were raised at shoulder level, the hands dangling limply at the wrists. The skin on the back of each hand had risen from the bone structure and was hanging in flaps by bare threads of tissue. His face was a mass of blood and charred skin, the once prominent features now all but unrecognizable. He had been wearing a white shirt and tie when the fire erupted. As he came through the flames, Ellen had seen only singed patches of cloth clinging to his bare arms and chest. In that instant sighting she saw that his entire upper torso had turned an ebony brown. Small, bright yellow blotches of skin remained on his chest, just flecks, like the splattering of paint from a brush. But most of all, it was Fountain's face that she was seeing behind her closed eyes. His hair had been completely burned off. In its place a mass of yellow blisters had swelled the skull to unhuman proportion. Below the narrowed eyes his mouth was open, the lips pulled back in a gesture of agonized surprise.

"Oh, Joe!" Kay O'Connor cried. "Oh, Christ in Heaven! Look at what's happened to Joe!"

He continued toward the women, a ghostly somnambulist exiting the fires of Hell. Kay ran to him and without thinking placed her hand on his shoulder.

His body went rigid, as if charged with a jolt of electricity. "Please . . . please don't touch me!" He was begging, the words forced out in breathless sobs. The horrible pain had seemed to bring him into focus. "Go into Father Swanstrom's office," he ordered Kay. The women remained where they were, unmoving, gaping at him. Suddenly, Theresa Scarpelli burst past him and ran shrieking into Swanstrom's corner office. The spell broken, the rest of the secretaries bolted in after her. With his arms still elevated, Fountain followed them with small, jerky steps. The flames behind him were now hidden by a curtain of midnight black smoke.

Waiting for Fountain in the office doorway, Kay started to cough as billows of the dense smoke began to fill the rear section of the office. "Shut the door!" Fountain said as he moved into the room. "Get some window open!"

How he could walk, how he could take command of the situation—how he was *alive!*—stunned Kay.

Charlotte Deegan was struggling to open one of the windows facing Sixth Avenue. "It's stuck!" she yelled in panic. "I can't get it open—it won't budge!" She began to cry hysterically as she yanked on the window handles. Fountain crossed to the window. "Let me do it," he said in a voice that had taken on a hoarse, bubbling quality. As he pulled up on the window, pieces of charred flesh dropped away from his hands. Anna Regan gasped and fainted.

The small room was rapidly filling with the black, acrid smoke seeping in under the door. The heat, already intense, was rising. Therese Fortier pushed her way to the east window and opened it halfway. A cooling draft of air rushed over her. She stuck her head out and breathed deeply. Ellen Lowe moved in beside her. "Thank God for some air," she said. "I thought I was going to pass out."

"Ladies," Fountain called out, "get hold of yourselves and listen to me." The women turned toward him. He was standing next to the west window, his head propped against the wall. The skin had continued to swell and now it seemed too heavy for his body alone to support. "I don't know what's going to happen to us, whether we'll live or die. But we're all Catholic, and this is the moment the church has prepared us for."

Theresa Scarpelli let out a screech and drummed her fists on Father Swanstrom's desk. "Oh, my God! Oh, Jesus Christ, save me, save me!" she wailed hysterically. Ellen Lowe turned to Theresa and, in pique of anger that surprised even her, shouted: "Shut up! Stop all that damned screaming!" Shocked by the outburst, Theresa quieted down to a sobbing whimper.

Fountain continued, "Let's pray and ask for God's forgiveness. I want all of you to say the Act of Contrition with me."

In a whisper, barely audible above the rumble of flames outside the door, Fountain closed his eyes and made the sign of the cross. "Oh my God, I am heartily sorry for having offended Thee . . ." One by one, the five women crossed themselves and joined in. ". . . and I detest all my sins, because of Thy just punishments, but most of all because they have offended Thee, my God . . ." Charlotte Deegan began to cry quietly. She raised her face toward the ceiling and dropped to her knees, clasping her hands together. ". . . who art all good and deserving of all my love. I firmly resolve with the help of Thy grace, to sin no more and to avoid the near occasions of sin. Amen."

The lowered forward landing gear and the left wing had torn into the unoccupied 78th floor. The outer section of the wing cleaved off, dropping in a solid piece onto a setback over 34th Street. Relieved of the encumbrance, the 1,100-pound nose wheel and the 2,700-pound engine separated from the fuselage, which was entering the War Relief Services office a floor above.

Spraying hot fuel from the ruptured gas tanks onto the paint cans and canvas tarp William Sharp had left under the window, the engine, sparking as it passed, touched off a blaze. Within seconds the large drum of turpentine exploded, sending a gusher of blackened flames shooting straight up the north face of the building. Hundreds of gallons of aviation fuel raced along the floor in a flaming torrent. At the stairwells it turned left and found entry under the closed doors. The steel stairs, floor by floor below the crash site, became drenched with the high octane fuel and erupted into brilliant orange flames.

Traveling at a speed of more than 200 miles an hour, the landing gear strut, with its 47-inch wheel still attached, rocketed down the center corridor. Impaled on the front of the gear, fused by the enormous force of the impact, were the engine's oil cooler and a large section of the oil tank. Moving on an unswervingly straight line for almost a hundred feet, the flaming mass of metal and rubber blasted through the south wall and began its plunge to the roof of the Waldorf Building on 33rd Street.

The engine took a diagonal route to the right, heading directly toward the G bank of elevators. It struck an eight-inch brick wall enclosing the vent shaft of the fire tower stairwell, skipped across the four-foot shaftway, and cut through another eight-inch brick wall. Its speed was barely diminished as it entered the steel and brick shaft enclosing elevators 6 and 7.

On the 80th floor, elevator operator Mary Scannell was standing just inside the open doorway of car Number 7. In her rich brogue, larded with a generous amount of dramatic embellishment, she was putting Sam Watkinson into stitches.

Only a few minutes before, she related to the observatory ticket taker, Carla Haines had asked Mary if she could switch cars with her. The starter had assigned the young, inexperienced girl to car Number 7, which had a left-hand control. Carla, pleading helplessness when it came to doing anything with her left hand, had asked Mary if she could take over car Number 2. "Just until my coffee break," Mary mimicked. "Then she said she'd practice up real hard with her left hand and switch back with me!" She slapped Watkinson on the shoulder and broke into a lusty laugh.

"Maybe she should try tying her right hand behind her back for a week," Watkinson said between wheezing chuckles. "Or better still, we could ..."

Simultaneously with the sound of an explosion somewhere in the shaft beneath her, Mary felt a violent shudder race through the floor of the car. Suddenly, the roof and the rear wall of the cage blew open. An orange mass of flame, driven by hurricane-force air currents in the narrow shaft, catapulted her off her feet. She sailed across the corridor and slammed into the wall. Stunned almost into unconsciousness, she rebounded and stumbled back into the burning car. Molten drops of steel were dripping on her head, setting her hair on fire. Through the flames she saw Watkinson writhing in agony on the corridor floor. His brown uniform pants had been torn away at the knees and blood was gushing from cuts on both of his legs.

Forcing herself to a sitting position in the center of the blazing car, Mary screamed, "Get away from here, Sam! It's going to explode!" *How strange,* the thought raced through her mind, *that I'm not feeling any pain.* Here she was, being burned alive, and yet she felt nothing. Time seemed to have halted. She was aware of everything—minute details, like one of her shoes lying in the corridor burning; a black smear on the opposite wall that reminded her of a globe her teacher had kept on her desk; a light bulb loosened from the ceiling fixture, dangling just by its filament. She saw Sam Watkinson dragging himself along the corridor, away from the burning car, his blackened face contorted with pain.

Flattening her hands on the floor of the car, she felt the molten metal dissolve the skin on her palms. She pushed herself into a half crouch and staggered out of the flames. A few feet across the corridor she saw the Caterpillar Tractor Company office. Screaming hysterically, Mary burst through the glass-paneled door.

The sudden rush of super-heated air instantly wilted a small cactus plant sitting on John Norden's desk. The executive had been knocked to the floor by the bomber's impact. He was just gaining his feet as Mary staggered into the office. Wild with pain, screaming at the top of her lungs, she ran blindly past him into his assistant's office.

Arthur Palmer had also been toppled from his chair to the floor. Still dazed, thinking that the building had been hit by a bolt of lightning, he stared blankly at Mary for a long moment. Then it registered that the woman standing in his doorway had been horribly burned. Her face and bare arms were pouring blood. Large patches of her bright red hair had been burned down to the scalp. The sight triggered Palmer into action. Overcoming her flailing arms, he forced her into a chair, then ran into Norden's office.

"What the hell happened?" he asked Norden. Seeing the older man's ashen face, he suddenly began to shake.

Norden shook his head. "I don't know, but we better get out of here fast." He crossed the hall door and opened it a crack. Even before he saw the flames raging in the corridor, the blast of furnace-hot air and black smoke that rushed into the office told him that they were trapped. He quickly closed the door and turned to Palmer. "Art, guess this is the end. There's no place to go." The two men stared at each other, then Palmer smiled ruefully. "We could always try the windows."

Feeling strangely calm, Norden laughed and glanced to his left. For the first time he noticed that all the windows had been shattered. Waves of thick black smoke were pouring into the offices. "I wonder which'll get us first, the fire or the smoke?" As if in answer, Palmer began to cough. He reached into his pocket and took out his handkerchief. "Maybe if we wet these and cover our faces, we'll last until the firemen can reach us." Even as he was crossing to the water cooler, Palmer had rejected his idea as futile. He went through the motions anyway, soaking his handkerchief and Norden's. The bottled water was almost hot as it poured out the spigot.

Mary's screams had risen in pitch and intensity, forcing the men to remember her presence. "What can we do for her?" Palmer asked. Norden started to answer, "We're all going to the morgue, so what's the . . ." He halted in mid-sentence, a startled look sweeping his face. Without a word, he turned and ran to the small supply closet at the far end of the office. He tore the door open and pulled out a claw hammer. "I forgot I put it in there last week!" he said triumphantly. Palmer studied the tool doubtfully. "What're we going to do with it?" he asked with a shrug. Norden was moving toward the south wall of the office. "Maybe if we bang on the wall loud enough, somebody, a tenant or . . . somebody, will hear it. It's worth a try," he said. He raised the hammer and pounded it against the wall. A small chunk of plaster broke loose with the impact. Palmer watched his boss deliver a few more blows, then he turned and, with a resigned look, went into his office. If nothing else, he thought, he could at least make the elevator operator's last minutes a bit more comfortable.

Mary was doubled over in pain. The small office had become filled with the choking smoke. Between cries she was coughing. Suddenly, she screamed, "I can't breathe!" Before Palmer could stop her, Mary leaped to her feet and thrust her body far out the window. Thinking that she was about to jump, Palmer grabbed hold of her waist and hauled her back into the chair. He pulled off the handkerchief covering his nose and mouth and attempted to tie it about her face. Mary whipped her head from side to side, thrusting him away with her burned hands. "Don't touch me!" she pleaded. The pain had become unbearable. Each time the damp, hot cloth came into contact with her raw skin she prayed that she would lose consciousness.

"Art—come here!" Norden shouted. "Get in here and help me!" Palmer hesitated. He was afraid to leave Mary alone. "Don't go near the window," he told her firmly, "understand?" Getting a nod from her, Palmer ran into Norden's office. The smoke had cut the visibility in the room down to near zero. Following the sound of the hammer blows, Palmer located Norden kneeling on the floor.

"Look!" Norden said excitedly.

Palmer bent close to the hole Norden had chopped in the plaster. Behind the jagged two-foot opening he saw shattered pieces of white tile. He was unimpressed. "What about it?" he asked.

"Look closer," Norden ordered. "It isn't brick, it's tile—just a thin layer of fireproofing. Look through here!" Norden jabbed his finger at a small opening in the squares of tile. Palmer pressed his face close to the tile and squinted into the tiny aperture. He found himself looking into another office. It was free of smoke and appeared undamaged. Without a word, he began tearing at the plaster with his hands as Norden hammered away at the tile.

Seconds before the hurtling engine was to tear into the shaft of car Number 6, Betty Lou Oliver glanced at her watch. It read 9:55, five minutes short of her ten o'clock coffee break.

She slowed the car to a halt on the 79th floor and opened the doors for Morris Needleman.

"I'm going to miss you, Betty," the large, gray-haired man said with a serious shake of his head. "Nobody gives me as smooth a ride as you." He hesitated, then awkwardly leaned over and gave her a gentle peck on the cheek.

"I'll miss you too, Mr. Needleman," she said, certain that his broad smile was the result of her sudden blush. She felt ridiculous; here she was, a twenty-year-old married woman, and still she couldn't control her emotions!

"You make sure you come back and say hello now and then," Needleman said as he exited the car. "And bring your sailor boy. Tell him he can pick out any belt in the place." Betty returned his wave and watched him move down the corridor to the Hickock showroom. She pulled the brass handle back, standing to the side as the doors rushed shut.

Moving the handle all the way back, she slid to the floor of the car as it started down. She stretched her legs out, cleared her throat, and in a high-pitched monotone began to sing the "St. Louis Blues." Since her first day on the job, six weeks before, Betty had discovered that an empty elevator was the perfect place to indulge her passion for singing. From childhood on she had self-consciously forced herself into the role of a "listener"—silently mouthing the words to everything from "Happy Birthday" to "Jingle Bells" to avoid the embarrassment of having family and friends laugh at her squeaky, one-note renditions. But in an empty elevator, secure in the metal, high-ceilinged cage, she was free to sing as loud as she liked. Songs that she once had only dared to hum ever so faintly under her breath—"Dancing in the Dark," "Small Hotel," "Don't Sit under the Apple Tree"—now were given daily airings as she shot up and down the thousand-foot shaft. Adding a dash of growling vibrato to the lyrics, she felt a sadness come over her. In two hours she would not only be saying goodbye to her friends on the staff, but from then on she'd never again have the opportunity to belt out a song with such abandon—and privacy—as now.

The car had begun to pick up speed. As it approached the 76th floor, Betty heard a concussive sound echo high in the shaft. The car lurched, then began rocking from side to side. Startled, she clutched the handle tighter and stared up at the roof of the car.

Thirty feet above car Number 6, the exploding engine had just severed the first of the six braided steel lifting cables attached to the top of the shaft.

Deflected after having slammed into the base of Mary Scannell's car and jamming the massive counterweight into the brake rails, the motor was now traveling horizontally. It sliced through the wrist-thick cables like a rotary buzz saw and rebounded off the steel fire wall. Blazing white-hot like the head of a meteor, the engine began its last journey toward the roof of car Number 6.

She had been pitched to the opposite side of the cage, the handle torn from her grasp as the car skipped from one wall of the shaft to the other. Betty opened her mouth to scream. She discovered it was physically impossible. Her head and stomach were shooting apart at literally breathtaking speed.

Out of the corner of her eye she caught sight of the red lights flashing on the panel indicator. 76 . . . 75 . . . 74 . . . The numbers were running into a vertical blur.

She was pressing her back against the wall in an attempt to stand when the roof caved in with a blinding explosion. The car filled with flaming chunks of metal and acrid, oil-black smoke. With all her strength, Betty pushed herself to a standing position. She was wondering how she could reach the emergency switch, when a burning piece of cable whacked her over the shoulders. She flung herself across the car, raising her hands above her head to ward off the flaming debris that poured through the hole in the roof.

The overhead light flickered and went out. Guided by the flames, she found the emergency switch and jerked it to "Stop." The car continued its plunge. She snapped it back and forth a half-dozen times. If anything, she felt the car moving faster. She couldn't breathe, and now she became aware of a weightless sensation. It was becoming difficult to keep her feet on the floor. Her hand fumbled for a hold and located the telephone receiver. For a reason unattached to the realty of her situation, Betty found herself pulling the phone to her ear and jiggling the hook. The line was dead—and even if it hadn't been, she suddenly realized, what in God's name could the starter down in the lobby do to end her nightmare?

She was going to die. The possibility hadn't occurred to her until now. She dropped the phone and moved to the rear corner of the car, pressing her hands tightly against the walls. The blistering metal seared her palms. She held on a second longer, then let go. As she felt her feet lift off the floor, she started to cry. Slowly, as if caught in a gentle but persistent updraft, her body was being pulled toward the roof of the car. Glancing up, she saw an inferno. Which was quicker, she found herself wondering—death by fire or being crushed?

Two thoughts, one tumbling upon the other, suddenly pushed death out of her mind: her husband Oscar, and the new suit she had bought for his homecoming. A picture flashed before her eyes. Oscar was standing at the rail of his ship, searching the crowded dock for her. He was deeply tanned from the South Pacific sun, and happy, so happy to be home. The image broke apart as she felt herself being sucked up the side of the wall faster. The car was filled with a strange howling sound.

Running across the Empire State lobby, Donald Molony paid scant attention to the howling echo. Between the sirens of the converging fire engines and the panicked shouts of the people pouring out of the building, the unnerving sound had no special meaning to the young Coast Guardsman.

Seconds after the crash Molony had braved the falling debris and darted across Fifth Avenue into the building. He didn't stop to ask directions. A hunch—a sudden sixth sense—led him directly to the ground floor Walgreen's drugstore.

The startled clerk behind the pharmaceutical counter, Charles Wilson, found himself instantly obeying the seventeen-year-old's snapped orders. "A first aid kit—the largest and most complete you've got!" Molony had demanded. And sterile bandages, burn ointment, alcohol—"lots of it!"—gauze rolls, cotton, and some adhesive tape!

While the clerk hurried to gather the items, Molony had darted around the counter and rummaged through the small safe in which the nar-

cotics were stored. He snapped open a paper bag and tossed in four vials of
morphine, a syringe, and several dozen needles. Then, slinging the pack Wilson
had assembled over his shoulder, Molony had headed for the elevators. He was
determined to reach the crash site. This was the moment he had spent eight
months training for.

As he approached the G bank of elevators he became more aware of
the howling echo. It was growing louder. From a vague, indistinct sound that
had merged into the background clamor, it now took on a chilling familiarity.
The young man felt the hairs on the back of his neck rise in a sudden shiver. It
was a human voice! A woman's!

Molony halted and scanned the crowded lobby for the source. He
spun around and faced the elevators. All of the doors, with the exception of
one, were closed. The Coast Guardsman saw an elderly elevator operator standing in the doorway of his car, wondering, as Molony himself was, where the
banshee wail was coming from.

At the moment of impact, John Monte and his handful of passengers
were unaware that disaster had struck. The car had been somewhere around
the 30th floor, the whistling noise of its rapid descent masking the horrific explosion that was taking place far above.

Now Monte was awaiting orders from the starter, Chauncey
Humphrey. The elevator staff had been given emergency training. Each man
and woman was to remain at his or her car, standing ready for orders from
the starters to aid in the orderly evacuation of the building. On the run,
Humphrey had shouted at Monte a few seconds earlier to hold tight, not to
move from car Number 8 until he checked with the other starters to learn
where the most elevators would be needed.

The eerie sound was now coming from just over his head, and to the
right. With a sudden start, Monte realized that it was reverberating from the
shaft of Number 6. He was about to start out of the car when the world went
black.

Molony had been staring at Monte when the anguished howl abruptly
ended in a shattering explosion somewhere below him. In the time it took for
the shock wave to race through the marble floor beneath his feet, Molony saw
John Monte's car suddenly plunge from sight. Black smoke was curling out of
the open shaft, and, although unseen, Molony caught the unmistakable odor of
an oil fire. He urgently searched the lobby for a way down to the sub-
basement. His training had taught him that the first thirty seconds in a chemi-

cal fire were the most critical. Deadlier than the flames, smoke and chemical fumes claimed most victims trapped in a disaster such as this. He was moving toward the far end of the lobby, pushing his way through the mass of people who were making frenzied exits from the stairwells.

"Sailor!" The shouted cry brought Molony up short.

He turned and saw a squad of firemen running toward him. Dragging coiled lengths of hose, several of the helmeted men broke off and made for a brass standpipe connection near the elevators. The chief, Arthur Massett of the Seventh Battalion, continued on to Molony. He had caught sight of the first aid kit slung over the seaman's shoulder and correctly guessed that the youngster was a trained medical corpsman.

"Two elevators crashed to the basement!" Molony blurted out. "I think they're both on fire."

Massett turned and waved to a half-dozen of his men. "This way!" he ordered. Grabbing Molony's arm, he guided him through the crowd to a door leading down to the sub-basement.

The elevator shaft compartments under the G bank were pitch black. The electrical conduit cables had been severed by the invading engine. The confined area was thick with bitter smoke. Deep orange flames darted up through the mass of twisted wreckage.

"Bring some lights this way!" Massett shouted to his men. Molony let out a sharp gasping sound as the portable spotlights flared on. No part of his intensive training had prepared him for the sight greeting his eyes. Steel beams, wide as a doorway, had been snapped in two, twisting into grotesque shapes, and tossed like matchsticks over piles of burning rubble. He spotted an arm and part of a leg stabbing out from the shaft that moments before had housed John Monte's car.

Two of the firemen had also spotted the victim. Climbing over the flames, they began pulling at the debris with their asbestos-gloved hands, tossing heavy pieces of steel and smoldering cable to the side as another man played a steady stream of water over their work area. Geysers of dazzling white steam hissed up, shrouding the rescuers in a dreamlike mist.

"Sailor!" Massett shouted, "Over here. Quick!"

Molony stumbled over the wreckage to the spot where the fire chief and two of his men were huddled around the shaft of car Number 6. Under the glare of the spotlights Molony saw that the elevator had smashed through the concrete floor, driving itself anther three or four feet into the ground. Looking down through the gaping hole in the roof, he saw that the bumper mechanism—a large, round rubber device employed to cushion a car's sudden drop—had been thrust up through the floor. Not even God's Child could have survived a fall like that, Molony thought to himself as he looked questioningly at Massett.

"Do you think you can make it through that hole?" the fire chief asked. He adjusted the spotlight beam, focusing it directly on the jagged passage.

"Sure, I guess so," Molony answered.

"It's too small for any of us, but I think you could squeeze through." Massett was slipping the first aid kit off Molony's shoulder. Almost as an afterthought he added: "We heard her moan. You'll probably have to pull a lot of stuff off to find her."

The Coast Guardsman stared at Massett incredulously for a moment, then quickly scrambled down onto the roof of the car. The hoseman sprayed a stream of cooling water over the opening as Molony eased himself through feet first. He dropped on top of one of the pancaked walls.

"Move the lights," he shouted up. "I can't see where I'm going." He was lost in darkness for an instant, then the interior of the car was brilliantly illuminated. Molony looked up and saw the chief hanging over the edge of the hole, a spotlight in each hand. The stream of water continued to shower over him as he climbed through the wreckage. A glance told him that the operator was not lying on the surface of the rubble. That she had escaped instantaneous death—if the chief weren't mistaken—was miracle enough. But for anyone to survive under the crushing weight of the twisted beams and mountains of brick was a sheer impossibility, Molony thought.

"What's that over there to your right?" Massett called out. Molony turned and saw nothing but a pair of smoking cables and shattered remnants of the car.

"No, no—*there!*" the chief said brusquely. He rotated one of the lights to target the area he meant. Molony turned and followed the beam. There *was* something. A patch of brown cloth and, although difficult to make out until he got closer, perhaps a hand. He ducked under a lean-to of crisscrossed beams and knelt. The chief was right, it was the operator. She was lying face down, all but completely covered by a blanket of bricks and cable. Two steel beams had fallen across her back and legs.

But she was alive! Molony felt a rush of excitement as he saw her try to move her head. She moaned faintly with the effort. He bent close to her ear. "Lie still. Don't try to move," he said softly. "We're going to get you out of here." He straightened and turned toward the chief. "She's alive. Throw down the first aid kit."

Massett tossed the kit down int the car. "What shape is she in?" he called out. Molony had picked up the first aid pack and was moving back toward Betty Lou. "I won't be able to tell until I clear some of the small stuff off her. We'll need a stretcher and a body board, something to lay her down flat on. And you'll have to get that hole widened."

He knelt next to the semiconscious operator and opened the first aid kit. Before he could begin extracting her from the wreckage she'd need a shot of morphine. It was clear, even from his hurried glance, that her legs were broken. What concerned him even more was the way her body lay angled under the beams. He prayed that he was wrong, but there was a strong possibility that her spine had been either fractured or crushed. Moving quickly but methodically, Molony had the syringe prepared with a dose of morphine. Clearing some rubble away from her arm, he tore loose what little was left of her uniform sleeve and swabbed her skin with a wad of cotton saturated with alcohol.

She began to moan loudly as Molony injected the painkiller. She moved her head toward him, her mouth struggling to form words. Molony leaned close.

"What did you say?" he asked.

"Drowning . . . drowning," she muttered, the words barely decipherable.

Puzzled, he was about to dismiss the effort as meaningless. Then he realized what she meant. He turned and shouted to the firemen: "Hey, turn off that hose!" As the drenching shower moved to another part of the wreckage, Molony saw that her face had been submerged in a hollow filled with water. He carefully shifted her head. "Is that better?" he asked. She had passed out. The Coast Guardsman began to lift the wreckage off her body.

The Last Nine Minutes:
The Story of Flight 981

BY MOIRA JOHNSTON

This is the story of an airline disaster that was an immediate "first" in two categories of horror: It was the first crash of a so-called "widebody" jet, and the loss of life was the largest in a single crash in aviation history up to that time, 334 passengers and a crew of 12. The plane was an American-built McDonnell-Douglas DC-10, owned and flown by Turkish Airlines as Flight 981, operating from Paris' Orly Airport with a destination of London's Heathrow Airport. Nine minutes after takeoff on Sunday, March 3, 1974, it crashed into the Ermenonville Forest with no survivors.

Moira Johnston's book *The Last Nine Minutes: The Story of Flight 981* is a superb chronicle of that accident and the investigation into its causes. Told in prose that captures both pathos and drama, *The Last Nine Minutes* is a stunning book that carries the reader through the painstaking details of how inattention to an improperly designed and operated cargo hold door doomed the passengers and crew of Flight 981. Fifteen months before the Orly crash, another DC-10 had barely missed being lost after a cargo hold door blew out over Windsor, Ontario. Only luck and the skill of the pilots saved the craft. In the case of the Orly disaster, critical hydraulic lines were destroyed in the cargo door explosion and the airplane dove into the forest at over 500 miles an hour, the crew unable to regain control.

Long after Orly, the DC-10 continued to write headlines of disaster. In July, 1989, the center engine of a United flight exploded over the mid-west, and critical hydraulic lines were lost. In making an emergency landing at Sioux City, Iowa, superb flying by the crew could not prevent the plane from cartwheeling on the runway, killing 111 people.

Now, however, our focus is on Paris. We are going on board Flight 981 to relive "The Last Nine Minutes."

＊　　＊　　＊　　＊　　＊

With its rear engine speared on the tail like a silver cigar and poised over 30 feet above the ground, the big plane was the most commanding sight at Orly airport.

But Prudence Pratt had no time for tail watching. She was rushing to get home to Stephen after a week-long modeling job in Spain. These trips were always tiring—on location at dawn, trying to dress in a cramped trailer with all the models grabbing for mirrors and accessories, trying to stay fresh and glamorous in wilting heat. But to be delayed a whole day by French incompetence! Air France had overbooked her Malaga-Paris-London flight and bumped her. She had made her way to Paris and called Stephen the night before to tell him what had happened. He'd be at Heathrow to meet her. If she could make her way to the plane through this madhouse.

Swinging the big, soft bags that were a model's trademark, she and the others pressed into the crush of people who were all trying to get back to London. It was like the last train from Berlin—this anxious army of people dashing from ticket counter to ticket counter, trying to get confirmation, change flights, get aboard with friends. What a shambles strikes created. The ground engineers' strike at Heathrow that had caused this chaos was apparently already over. But it had put them so far behind in servicing planes that all BEA and Air France flights to London that day had been canceled. And now thousands of people were being shuffled, with the urgency of Dunkirk, aboard every available craft.

But even in the confusion, Prudence and her friends were a commanding sight. Simply coming home from work, they were playing their looks very low key. Prudence was wearing the flared jeans overalls she'd picked up in New Mexico under her blue military greatcoat and her black boots. But when seven models and their coterie move through an airport on their way to or from a modeling assignment, an aura of glamour and excitement spins up around them. Prudence had matured well beyond thinking that life was all about turning heads in a restaurant. But it was impossible not to feel heads turn and be pleased by it. And when you had Prudence's theatrical flair, and a shiny mane of red hair flying behind you, every airport scene was like the disembarking of a movie star from the old *Queen Elizabeth*.

She and her friends had got tickets on Turkish Airlines' Flight 981 that would be leaving at noon—the four girls and three male models, the stylist, fashion buyer, and editor of the mail-order catalog they had been shooting in Spain.

A pretty, brisk American-looking mother held tightly to her little girl's hand, steering her through the crowd. Her two other children stayed close, as the husband led them through the maze of check-in, security, and boarding passes.

Fay Wright was eager to get home, too. There was school tomorrow, and it was her turn for car pool. The family had had a week's vacation in Spain. Tom had just been made managing director of Merrill Lynch-Brown Shipley Bank's corporate finance activities in London, and Fay had finally been able to break him free of his obligations at work. American corporate families living abroad, as they were, were always under strains of ambition, absence, alien customs. They had needed this week to be together and get in touch. Stranded in Marbella by the strike, they'd had the option of flying to Manchester and taking the train down to London, or flying home via Paris. They'd discussed the alternatives with friends they'd run into at the airport in Spain. The friends had gone to Manchester. They had decided on Paris.

Several other families from the American School in London were coming home from Turkey and the Alps. It was a difficult place for children that day. The crowds of men flying home from the England v. France international rugby match the day before gave Orly-Sud terminal the atmosphere of a pub at closing time. Men had come from rugby clubs all over England. Among the dozens of young men trading jokes and tickets were the team and officers of the Bury St. Edmunds rugby club—eighteen men. At that moment, they should have been pulling on their rugby shirts, getting ready to run on the field for an exhibition game against a French team—the windup to their big weekend in Paris. But the strike had made an evening flight home so uncertain that they had canceled the game and grabbed seats on the Turkish plane.

The quiet orderliness of a large group of young Japanese men was like a collective frown at the boisterous rugby boys. All in their early twenties, their purposes were far loftier than a rugby game. For the thirty-eight men, this was a brief educational hiatus between graduation from university and the beginning of work for the companies that would employ them for the rest of their lives—a chance to travel and see at first hand the sights and the corporate and industrial techniques of Europe. An academic elite chosen from thousands of applicants for the jobs they were about to begin, all had prospects of senior management opportunities before them. And each was the focus of family pride and obligations that surpass anything known in the Western world.

There were other Japanese faces in the crowd. Atsuko and Takehiro Higuchi had been married less than a month, and were honeymooning in Europe before Takehiro returned to his architectural practice and, as eldest son, to heavy family obligations.

Prudence rushed aboard with the rest, 216 of them—196 at first, and then a last-minute flurry of twenty people who were hurriedly found seats, delaying the flight half an hour. Changes kept being made until the moment the doors were locked—changes that would mean life and death. Several people got on, and then got off and gave their tickets to others. One man got word after he had boarded that his wife had surprised him by flying to Paris, and he dashed from the plane to meet her. Ticket switching was easy to do, as immigration does not check the name on the passport against the name on the ticket. Friends flipped coins to see who'd get aboard. Two men with hangovers missed the plane. In the rush, few knew or cared what kind of plane they were boarding. But on the phone the night before, when Prudence had told Stephen that she was coming on Turkish Airlines, he had made some comment about flying on "that" airline, implying that Turks might be better at flying carpets. But she knew it was just that he hated flying. He loathed and feared it as much as she loved it. And yet he traveled all the time.

He was a partner in a successful law practice that negotiated claims for Lloyd's of London underwriters, and he often flew to Hong Kong, the Bahamas, New York, or Beirut on business. He frequently packed off on the trail of lost emeralds, silver coins . . . deteriorating frog's legs, of damaged, delayed, or stolen shipments of all kinds, protecting Lloyd's interests. It was delicate work, carrying Lloyd's rigorous ethics and reputation for fair and fast payment of claims through a maze of conflicting stories, international smuggling, networks of thieves, and sophisticated attempts at fraud. Lloyd's was a legend. But it was also a business. Its cases called for discretion, shrewd judgment, and able help.

Whether in a suit or with his dark hair curling over the collar of an open-necked print shirt, he displayed an enigmatic air he carefully nurtured. His good looks and lazy charm made him compellingly attractive. And with his head lowered over a glass of wine and a cigarette, he could make even the description of a boxing match sound sensuous and conspiratorial. But as he talked of his days in Muscat, of drinking with mercenary soldiers on their way to Biafra, dressing for dinner in borrowed "Gulf rig," probing the pink desert city for ways to liberate a trapped shipment of Kuwaiti dinars insured at Lloyd's, he could laugh at his own role in a bad movie.

He did not want his relationship with Prudence to end up as a bad movie. They had been together for two years now, two cautious and independent personalities, and it had worked. They both resisted a relationship based on need. Need made you vulnerable, something neither of them wanted to be. If they did marry, it would never be to hold each other up. He felt the trips were good. He had had a previous relationship where there had been no chance to escape, and he sometimes wondered if trips didn't operate as a pressure valve, preventing tensions or, worse, boredom.

As he hurried into Heathrow airport, he checked with BEA, which acted as handling agents for Turkish Airlines. The flight was late, and Stephen waited. He had spent much of his life waiting for planes. He settled in with the Sunday papers, a London ritual. He lit a cigarette and flicked ashes from his suit. He wondered why he'd worn a suit. He'd even shaved. He supposed it was a spontaneous gesture of pleasure at her coming home. He flipped through the color supplement and spotted a picture of Prudence as a housewife. Or was it Prudence? He was embarrassed to admit that he wasn't always sure. Several times he'd congratulated her on some pictures in such and such a magazine only to be told that they were of somebody else. Prudence played her roles so well—the seductress, the chic matron, the bride. He only knew her natural style, which was one of "cultivated casualness," of blue jeans and battered mini cars. His favorite picture of her was one he had taken the day they'd gone to Brighton—a color snap of her in blue jeans and macintosh, standing on Brighton Pier with her red hair blowing free, the strong jaw giving her face character, the blue-green eyes laughing. Brighton had been one of their very best days together—a silly, spontaneous day when they'd done all the things they *never* did—take a day off, ride the train to Brighton like daytrippers, hike the honkey-tonk Pier in pouring rain, eat slimy fish and chips doused in ketchup, and buy mildly pornographic mementos. The picture would shatter the illusions of the hundreds of thousands of housewives who would revel vicariously in sun-drenched glamour when they read the catalog she'd shot in Spain. He wanted her home. He wanted to see the ivory heart and silver letter *P* he'd given her around her neck. Their symbol of commitment. He checked with BEA again, and they told him the plane was still over forty-five minutes away. It was only a fifty-minute flight, and it sounded to him as if she hadn't even taken off yet. He decided to drop in on friends who lived nearby and have a drink.

The DC-10 was still a novelty in Europe in the spring of 1974. Many eyes at Orly followed it, fascinated, as the tail with the red streaks and symbol of Turkish Airlines wove its way through the Caravelles, 707s, and Tridents in the stately gavotte of the modern jet.

They read the strip of words that ran the length of the fuselage—*THY TURK HAVA YOLLARI—TURKISH AIRLINES TC-JAV.* En route to London from Istanbul that first Sunday in March, the Turkish DC-10 did have a commanding presence. With its huge rear engine apparently pierced by the fin—a phallic symbol—it was the most virile aircraft around. Clean and workmanlike, it had its vital power source right up where you could see it. Functional, direct, the DC-10 moved the air in a straight line from intake to exhaust. No sacrifice of efficiency for visual elegance.

It was the youngest in the distinguished family of Douglas aircraft, successor to the legendary DC-3, the -4, the -6, and the -7, and the pure jets, the DC-8 and -9. It had been tested more than any of Douglas's previous planes, all to achieve the mission of "building an airplane that's not going to cause the guy any trouble," as a Douglas executive had described it. Douglas, like the rest of the aviation industry, was driven by the concept of *mission*—the striving for goals as if for the Holy Grail. Douglas was proud of the DC-10. It was their baby.

It had had some problems, but all new planes had a debugging period. Debugging was built into cost estimates. Certain cautious passengers stayed away from any new plane for the first two years on general principle, for everybody in aviation knew that an airplane got better as it got older. The DC-10's cargo door had been causing some operational delays—something airlines didn't like. And a door had blown out over Windsor, fifteen months ago. . . .

But pilots loved the plane. The two Turkish pilots had landed Turk Hava Yollari's Flight 981 at 11:02 that morning, completing the first and longest leg of the journey to London. As TC-JAV nosed into the arrival gate, a telescoping ramp moved out to meet it. Fifty of the passengers disembarked. Men from the service company, Samor, attacked the cargo holds. They left the front compartment untouched, unloaded the center one of empty pallets and mail bags, and began to load on the baggage of passengers who were boarding at Paris. With passengers still buying tickets, last-minute luggage would have to go later, on another plane. Four Samor men unloaded baggage and mail from the rear cargo compartment, and when it was empty, one of them, a big young Algerian named Mohamed Mahmoudi, called out from the hold to his supervisor to ask if there was any more baggage to load. The supervisor hollered back "No." Mahmoudi climbed out of the hold onto a conveyor belt that had been driven over for him and proceeded to close the door as he had forty or fifty times before. He pressed the toggle switch that electrically closes the door and, he later claimed, kept his finger on it until he heard the characteristic "click" and saw the usual light go out. He reached up and pulled down the handle that locks the door. The handle stowed easily, confirming closure. The small truck carrying the conveyor belt moved Mahmoudi swiftly away from the plane. It must not obstruct the plane at departure.

He had closed the rear cargo door at 11:35, just 33 minutes after landing and 5 minutes after completion of the refueling. The door had delayed them before when they couldn't get it closed, and sometimes the baggage handlers had had to close it manually. There had been nearly a dozen recorded cargo door delays in the past year. But this morning, it would not be the door causing delays. From the chaos at the ticket counters, it was clear that it would be the passengers.

Captain Nejat Berkoz would undoubtedly have welcomed the delay and a chance to stretch. It had been a long flight from Istanbul. The rest of his cockpit crew got up and moved around the airplane. They were virtually pioneers on the airline's DC-10s. All three—Berkoz, his cocaptain, Oral Ulusman (in Turkey, all pilots are captains), and his flight engineer, Erhan Ozer, had been sent to the manufacturer's plant at Long Beach, California, for simulator training on the same day, January 24, 1973, just over a year before, and just six weeks after Turk Hava Yollari had taken delivery of the first of its three DC-10s.

Now flights were routine. Berkoz had 438 hours on the DC-10, Ulusman had 628, and Ozer had 775 hours, a respectable body of experience. The plane itself had 2,955 hours and 52 minutes, still just the beginning of the 60,000 flight hours she'd been built for.

Berkoz would have checked his watch. The stop in Paris was running over schedule. Loading of passengers would delay them half an hour. Departure was now set for 12:30. The crew settled back into the cockpit to prepare for the 50-minute flight that would complete their long mission. At 12:11 and 30 seconds, they made their first contact with Orly Control and began the preflight procedures and checklists, getting routing, altitudes, checking fuel, weather, systems. Everything was going smoothly. There was no hint of trouble. Pilots are acutely aware of air safety, always—as they like to joke—the first ones at the scene of an accident. They have a fierce will to live and a positive attitude toward flight. Though Ozer had talked of death to his wife through his poetry, he worked to deny it by these methodical preparations for flight.

On the ground, the service men had loaded all the baggage they were going to load and closed the doors of the center hold at 12:10, but the loading of passengers was continuing. By 12:18, they had their clearance from Orly Control, the first of four control agencies that would monitor TC-JAV, handing it from one to the other as it moved out to the runway and through the first stages of flight. At 6,000 feet, Orly Control would hand the big plane off to Paris Control.

Departure from the gate had been delayed at the last minute, as the twenty extra passengers rushed aboard and hunted for the few remaining seats.

With no seat assignments, it had been everyone for himself, and the 8 cabin attendants were smilingly plying the aisles trying to get everyone seated in the three big compartments, settling and soothing the people who had boarded at Paris, stowing parkas and coats, checking that children were strapped in. Semra Hidir, who had been with the airline for a year, was anticipating London as much as the passengers. She had already made out her shopping list for the gifts she wanted to buy for her family.

Most of the passengers pressing aboard that morning had never flown in a DC-10, but there was casual assumption of a safe flight. In the sixty-five years since Louis Blériot had made the first precarious crossing of the English Channel by air, the awe had gone out of it. Psychologically, Paris to London was now a shuttle run. The passengers, nearly two hundred of them British, began to lean back and settle in. The final weight and balance forms were handed into the cockpit. Even with all the extra passengers, they were still well within their maximum weight allowance of 430,000 pounds.

At 12:19 the cabin door was locked, closing out the confusion of the airport and severing almost the last of the physical support links with the ground. The most symbolic act of any flight, the closing of the door shifts almost baronial powers and obligations to the captain's shoulders, and gives each flight its own unique dynamic. To an engineer, the closing of the doors gives the aircraft a sealed pressure vessel ready to test itself in the thin, alien air of cruising altitudes. And to him, the humbler act of closing the rear cargo door is as important as the more symbolic closing up front.

Mahmoudi, the baggage handler, had completed that 45 minutes ago at the rear of the DC-10. The amber light in the cockpit that warns of an improperly locked door was out. The wheel chocks were removed, and at 12:20, a tractor pushed TC-JAV back from the gate. The aircraft taxied out to Runway 08, escorted to the threshold by two mobile gendarmes. Berkoz would take off to the east. He was cleared to climb initially to 4,000 feet, and then to 6,000 feet. Weather conditions were good. Temperature was 43 degrees Fahrenheit, chilly but well above freezing. Light cumulus clouds between 1,500 and 3,000 feet. Visibility more than 9 miles.

He taxied onto the runway and held, waiting for takeoff clearance. Momentarily still, he kept his right hand firmly on the throttles, adjusting his grip and flexing his fingers, waiting. The cocaptain's hands performed a deft cockpit ballet, moving with graceful precision over the final buttons and switches, double checking. 334 passengers and the crew of 12 were strapped in for takeoff.

The takeoff roll started at 12:31. As the captain pushed the throttles decisively forward, three mighty turbo-fan engines, each with 40,000 pounds of thrust, accelerated the DC-10 down the runway. The plane reached V1—the go/no go speed—the speed at which they could still have chopped the throttles and aborted. Everything checked out. Past V1, the captain moved his right hand swiftly from the throttles to the wheel, irreversibly committed to flight. They raced on, gaining a speed of 143 knots and rotated, lifting the nose into the air at a speed 4 knots below the precalculated takeoff—or V2-speed—when the airplane could safely take off even with the loss of an engine. The great bird lifted easily. Flight 981 was committed to the last leg of its long mission. It was almost 12:32.

Still under Orly Control, the plane climbed through lofty cumulus and light winds to 6,000 feet. Berkoz would follow Departure Number 18, which would vector him to three checkpoints—Tournan, Coulommiers, and Montdidier. At 12:34, Flight 981 contacted Orly Departure Control to report reaching 6,000 feet and was handed off to Paris Control. Flight 981 contacted Paris Control at 12:36—4 minutes into the flight—and was cleared to Flight Level 230—an altitude of 23,000 feet. They were then instructed to turn left, toward the Montdidier checkpoint. Flight 981 turned to the northwest on a heading of 345 degrees. At 12:37, the flight called in to report reaching 7,000 feet, its last coherent transmission.

They climbed swiftly through 7,000 feet . . . 9,000 feet, at an airspeed of 300 knots—345 miles per hour.

In the cabin, everyone was relaxing after takeoff, lighting cigarettes, and chatting. The young rugby fans would have carried their high spirits with them into the air, with laughing and joking up and down the aisle. Steve Backhouse, traveling with friends from the Davenport Rugby Club, had headed to the airport in a very happy mood, according to a friend who had seen him off in a taxi. Two of the rugby boys from Bury St. Edmunds hadn't got out of bed and had missed the flight.

With so many men aboard, it was impossible for the four models not to be actively looked at. Prudence had never liked being "chatted up." She was intent on London and knew Stephen would be on his way to Heathrow.

There were six people at the rear of the plane whose random choice of seats beside each other would cast them in a special destiny, one that was to become symbolic of the special fears that haunt a plane crash. Omer Faruk Afir had been on the plane since Turkey. One of a number of young Turkish students aboard, he was on his way to London to attend medical school and looked forward to becoming a doctor like his father. In Paris, others had taken the seats around him. Three women and two young Japanese men. Daniele Cam-ha Nguyen Thi was a twenty-three-year-old Vietnamese girl studying in France; and Georgiana Byatt, a forty-six-year-old primary schoolteacher from Middlesex returning from a holiday in Spain, traveling with a friend, Bessie Brown, a crossing guard at the same school. The two Japanese men were new friends on the trip—Tsukuro Yoshitake, who would be joining the Tomen trading company, and Tadaharu Sakata, who would join a bank. Sakata would have to make his own way in the business world, unaided by money or position. His only brother had died five years earlier in a gas leak accident, and now it would be his duty to support his father, already sick with diabetes. But he had finished fifth out of eight hundred in his graduating class. And like the rest of the thirty-eight young men, he had been tapped to become part of the managerial elite of Japan.

The six sitting at the left rear of the fuselage in two banks of triple seats were a random sampling of any international flight in Europe. Their choice of seats bound them to a macabre destiny.

The plane climbed through 9,000 . . . 10,000 feet into the thinner air that makes climbers and skiers gasp, their hearts palpitate. But passengers sat back breathing normally, taking for granted the sophisticated environmental control system that maintained the air in the plane at comfortable pressures. Now it meant simply comfort. But at 40,000 feet, this cocoon of thick, compressed air meant survival for the human organism.

But who notices air? Innocent. Invisible. Apparently the same on both sides of the window.

There was no way to see or to feel that, with every foot of altitude, the air trapped in the fuselage was growing more frustrated by containment. It was roiling with eagerness to expand, to escape. And as it responded to the suck of the partial vacuum outside, it pressed out, putting stress on every rivet, latch, and window, every square inch of the thin, silvery skin. Pushing against the shell with several times the force of a hurricane, it searched for a way out.

The plane climbed through 11,500 feet, sprinting up at 2,200 feet a minute toward its assigned flight level, with the pressure differential between the cabin and the air outside building rapidly.

At 12:39 and 56 seconds*—a moment frozen in time by the plane's cockpit voice recorder—the air found its escape route. In one explosive microsecond, the caged hurricane burst through the rear cargo door, shearing off the

---

*There is a 30-second discrepancy between this time taken from the cockpit voice recorder and times taken from the flight data recorder. Both, however, are in agreement on duration of flight and crisis.

bolts that held it to the fuselage, and flinging it—with six passengers still in their seats—down to the quiet French countryside.

On radar, stunned controllers watched, helpless. A battery of radar screens had been monitoring the moving blip that was Flight 981. At the instant the door came off, the image on the screens changed. On secondary radar, the blip simply vanished, leaving for several seconds the imprint of its altitude—13,000 feet. On the primary radar screen, the controller watched in horror as the image of Flight 981 split in two and became a double image. He had "seen" the door come off. As he watched, the two blips separated from each other on the screen. One stayed fixed at 24 miles northeast of Orly, frozen on the screen for two or three minutes. It was the door and the bodies free falling to the freshly plowed fields of St. Pathus. The second image followed a trajectory to the left, reached a heading of 280 degrees, to the northwest, and vanished. It disappeared from his screen 77 seconds after the image had split.

Shortly after the image spilt, there were alerts by radio, too, that something had gone wrong with Flight 981. At 12:40 and thirteen seconds, Paris Control heard a garbled transmission of Turkish voices above the blaring of the depressurization alarm and, then, the overspeed Klaxon. All transmissions ceased as the blip disappeared from the screen.

The controller tried to reach Flight 981. "981, come in . . . 981 do you read me? . . . Come in, 981 . . . 981 . . ." Eight times he tried to reach them. There was no response. After 9 minutes of flight, she had vanished.

In the cockpit, the crisis had hit the crew like a lightning strike. There was the sudden, thunderous noise of decompression as the air evacuated and violent jolts kicked the plane sideways. An explosive burst of dust and debris flew up into the cockpit, temporarily blinding them. From a climb of 3 or 4 degrees, the nose pitched down violently into a dive. The plane yawed hard left because of a 10 degree rudder deflection, forcing the left wing down. The autopilot disengaged instantly and the crew grabbed for control. Scanning instruments with ferocious speed and intensity, they had no idea what had happened, though Ulusman snapped out, "The fuselage his burst!" They did not know that the cabin floor had collapsed, severing and jamming the control cables that ran through the floor from cockpit to tail—their lifeline. They knew they were yawing hard left. And that elevators were forcing the nose down, jammed, inoperative—their prime means of pitch control. Within 22 seconds, the nose was down 20 degrees. They had to get the nose up. Berkoz yelled, *"Bring it up . . . pull her nose up!"* Ulusman pulled back with all his strength on the controls. But he could not overpower the dive. *"I can't bring it up. She doesn't respond!"*

Speed, increasing with pitch, had risen viciously from 300 to 362 knots. Number 2—the mighty engine on the tail—was already out. Dead. Windmilling uselessly. Now they cut the power on the underwing engines 1 and 3 in a desperate effort to stop the buildup of speed. But speed kept rising. They were diving at over 10,000 feet a minute. They would crash in seconds unless they could get the nose up. They were fighting for their lives, and for the lives of 334 passengers. But the rudder was jammed left. Elevators had locked the nose down. Number 2 engine was out. The exchanges were terse, as they worked frantically for an answer. *"Nothing is left."* Thirty-four seconds into the crisis. Speed was still rising . . . 400 . . . 410 knots. The aerodynamic scream was jerking up heads of Sunday strollers in the woods below. *"7,000 feet!"* Forty seconds to impact at the speed of their dive. *"Hydraulics?"* Hydraulics powered all their controls. Were they all gone?

But maybe something was left. For gradually the nose was coming up. It was coming up! Was it the one-in-a-thousand chance that they were flying the plane through the autopilot, using its limited authority to save them from crashing? Or was it simply the effect of the increasing speeds, for speed itself will pull the nose up. It came up from 20 degrees to 10, 9 . . . to 6, 5. They were leveling out. And speed had stabilized at 430 knots. But it was too late. They were too low. Flight 981 was a doomed and helpless bird. There were the desperate words, *"We've lost it."* The straight pines of Ermenonville Forest were rushing toward them like spears as they came in, left wing 17 degrees low, pitch nearly level, 4 degrees down, and speed at 423 knots. The final voiceless emission from Flight 981 ended at 12:41 and 13 seconds. At impact.

Impact is an experience that is beyond integration. An event so violent that the mind refuses it.

Disintegration of the fuselage began instantly. Number 1 engine, hung from the low left wing, impacted first, and began to break up immediately. As it impacted with a large tree, the stage 1 fan disk acted as a punch die, cutting a core right through the tree and driving it, like a wooden plug, into the bore of the engine where it was later found. The rear engine told a story of even more appalling violence. As the momentum that had built up at a speed of almost 500 miles an hour was suddenly slowed by the convulsive impact of the hull, the massive rear engine, poised on the tail like a stone in a slingshot, was catapulted in an arcing trajectory at two thirds the speed of sound for half a mile beyond the main impact area. The same forces ripped off the rear of the hull and sent it, with ninety-five passengers, hurtling along the same path.

Within ten seconds, the hull—stripped of wings and engines—thundered through half a mile of forest, disintegrating progressively as it decelerated, literally raked to bits by the stiff pines. Before the bodies had even completed initial reaction to impact—feet shooting up and hips jamming down into the seat—the violent destruction of their protective envelope, the turmoil of flailing, crushing, and wrenching, of impaling by flying beams, metal, and sharp trees, would have killed all but the ninety-five catapulted to the far end of the crash site when the rear of the fuselage snapped off. For them annihilation of sensation would be doubly guaranteed by lethal whiplash.

Within ten or fifteen seconds, the last piece of metal would have tumbled to rest, and there would have been no more sound. A small hand lay on the snow, still clutched by a larger female hand. For that child, for her mother—for all the humans who perished with them—there had been no "agony of death." Only agony for those left behind.

In those last few seconds of silence and certainty of death, the poem Flight Engineer Ozer had written just weeks before to his wife took on an unbearable poignancy:

I want to call you,
I want you to hear me.
I wonder if you can feel
One day my last breath.

Before the initiation of the 77 second nightmare, all had been perfectly normal in the cabin. Babies frightened by the noise and unfamiliarity of takeoff were probably fussing. Mothers would be trying to comfort them. Flight attendants would be moving up the aisles within six or seven minutes of takeoff, pitched forward as if walking against a wind. But passengers would still be in their seats. The NO SMOKING sign would have gone off shortly after the gear was raised, and many would already have lit up a cigarette. Between eight and nine minutes into the flight, a contagious click of seatbelts would riffle through the cabin, as a sense of confidence began to spread. The FASTEN SEAT BELT sign would probably still be on, though, and most passengers would be loosening, rather than unbuckling, their belts. People who had been apprehensive at takeoff would be relaxing tensed muscles, still going through a period of adjustment. They would be settling back, interested primarily in comfort, unprepared for emergency as they might be at landing, the most dangerous phase of flight.

When the decompression hit, it would not be the sound of a bomb or gun blast, but a more thunderous rush, as if a car window had been suddenly opened at 350 miles an hour. The explosive blast of escaping air would sweep loose objects with it, pull down ceiling panels and pop panels up from the floor. As the pressure and temperature dropped, fog would fill the cabin, making many think, "SMOKE . . . FIRE!" The initial response would be the startle reflex, with arms and legs snapping out, spread-eagled, muscles tensing. Fingers would go straight, though anyone already gripping the armrest would probably dig his fingers in harder, instinctively trying to hold the plane up. In the shock, air would escape from the lungs, making people say a dead "Oh." If some panicked at decompression, they would probably not try to undo their seat belts and run from the threat; they would sit silent, paralyzed from action. Simultaneous with the first reflex bodies would be jerked up hard against their seat belts, as the nose suddenly dropped. For an instant, they would experience negative G, the sensation of cresting a hill on a roller coaster, or of going over a big rise in the road—the sensation that hits you in the pit of the stomach and makes children scream "Wheeee!" It may have lifted them out of their seats. Then, torsos would lean, perhaps flail, to the right as the airplane yawed and the left wing dropped. But the yaw would not be precipitous; it would not be a convulsive, heart-stopping movement. But the two events combined—the wing down, and a dive angle that was many times steeper than anything most would ever have experienced, and getting steeper—would be alarmingly abnormal.

Though most would not panic, a general feeling of anxiety would sweep the pressure vessel. Bodies would become hyperactive, muscles tense, senses supersharp. Awareness and memory would become acute. Stress would shrink the range of vision to a narrow focus in which each detail would be seen and remembered. Time would snap into a new dimension, with seconds lengthening to vivid detail-filled lifetimes in the remarkable phenomenon that lets a fighter pilot take an hour to describe a three-minute aerial battle. Life's vignettes would be relived as if time had stopped. Physical movements would be discoordinated as people tried to handle their newly hypertense bodies. Stress would strip them of the ability to judge their own forces, and movements would be overdone, like bad acting.

All would be alert, intent on "What's happening? What hit us?" trying to figure it out, waiting for the next event. In an instant, the initial violence would pass, and they would fall back into their seats as almost normal G forces returned. There might be a certain sense of relief. And *hope* would be heard in a flurry of comments that put danger in the past tense, behind them—"What do you think it was?" "I wonder what hit us?" But there would be no end to the anxiety, for wasn't the plane going faster? The dive getting steeper?—a sensation exaggerated by the banking of the plane. Everyone would be vibrantly alert now to any abnormality, retrieving more rapidly than a computer any information that could help them figure out what was happening. What had they seen, read, heard, been taught? They would search for clues. But there were few physical references to help them. The seat in front. The people immediately adjacent. No answers outside the small windows.

Most would think "MIDAIR!" Seeing the fog, some would think "SMOKE!" and search for signs of fire. All would release tension in their own way, grasping desperately for normalcy, exaggerating it. There would be nervous laughter. Mothers would hug and soothe their children, diverting their own fears. The dependent would be more dependent; strong husbands more reassuring. Strong relationships would be reconfirmed by holding hands tightly, quietly. No protestations of love. Mostly silence, as minds raced. Cigarettes would be grabbed. And magazines. The strongly religious might pray, or handle beads or crosses. Cultural differences would become distinct. People from the Middle East, Italy, or any of the Latin countries might cry out and fling their arms; a man from the northern Anglo-Saxon countries might bolster his own self-control by saying with disgust, "What a bloody fuss she's making!" Others would be drawing on every four letter word they knew. People are profane in crisis. Some would run a frantic checklist of all the eventualities, finding comfort in the process of elimination. Others would find security in tightening their seat belts, or in pulling their clothes around them. A bloodied parka proved to Japanese parents that their son had pulled his hood up over his head.

There would be a compulsion to act to overcome the danger, but few actions were possible. As they quickly discovered that there was nothing constructive to be done, they might hurl hostility at the pilot and crew. "Why doesn't he come on and tell us what's happening?" He was their window on the world. What was he doing up there? And yet, things were not getting worse. Some might be conscious of an increase in speed and the rapid loss in altitude, but at least the dive wasn't getting any steeper. In fact, was it only wishful thinking . . . or was it actually decreasing? Gravity forces would be pressing them forward so gently that many would not notice it. Some would think, "He's diving to a lower altitude." For safety.

And then, before impact, the nose was clearly coming up. And up! "We're leveling off, we're pulling out!" "Whew! Thank God!" Mothers would squeeze small hands with hope. "It's going to be all right, darling . . . going to be all right." Relief would wash through the pressure shell.

Most of the 328 passengers still aboard Flight 981 were probably look-ing around, apprehensive but hopeful, as they came into the trees, unaware that these were the last moments of their lives.

The experience of the six who fell from the plane was quite different; images of their ordeal will always haunt the crash. The collapse of the floor was violent enough to tear loose one of the flight attendants' seats and two banks of triple sets, to hurl them and their six passengers into the cargo hold below to be sucked out into the slipstream. The three men and three women at the left rear had no time to think about their fate. As seats and bodies ripped past shat-tered metal beams, torn cables, sharp floor panels, and out the hole, the six were almost certainly knocked unconscious, or killed. The young Turk was still strapped in and fell attached to his seat. Reportedly, all except him suffered se-vere and similar head damage that suggests death may have been caused during the terrible exit. Probably all were spared awareness as they were whipped into the slipstream.

If any were swept out cleanly, without damage, there could have been consciousness, but not awareness in the normal sense. For the mind would throw up protective walls around the delicate human mechanism. The initial experience would be so violent that there would be complete disorientation, with a rush of events the mind would not begin to catalog and comprehend in any rational way. Within seconds, this could be replaced by panic, the negative panic that throws people into a catatonic state. Eyes could close. The mind would either blank out or race uncomprehendingly. Thoughts or words, if there were any, would be repeated over and over. In this state, they could have fallen the 2 miles insulated from awareness. For others, the initial disorientation could have passed in four or five seconds, and awareness could have returned. But in crisis, it could have been a detached awareness, allowing a passenger to view the incomprehensible events happening to her as if she were a dispassion-ate observer: "Mary's falling. She's bleeding. I hope she survives. She wants it to be over." If there was blood—if Mary had been damaged by the tumult of exit—she would not feel it; for there would be too many other more acute sensations fighting for dominance, crowding out the sensation of pain. The fall could even have been euphoric, silent, with no sensation of plummeting to earth. The earth would not rush up until the final seconds, and Mary might have imagined herself suspended, perhaps from the plane.

Yet the six had fallen fast, reaching a maximum speed of 135 mph and impacting at a terminal velocity of about 120 mph in the denser air of lower altitudes. Attached to their seats, or falling free, they would have tumbled un-controllably, probably never regaining clear orientation to events or their environment, never seeing the ground. In spinning, blood pressures could have dramatically altered consciousness. But if any had been aware and clearly oriented to their situation, they would have fought for life, turning every fiber of mind to finding a way out. For "the habit of living has become an addiction." But attempts to fight back would be thwarted by the complete physical helplessness of their situation. There was nothing to grasp. No way to control the fall. No hope that they could survive it. Not prepared as skydivers would have been, they would not know to flip onto their backs and spread-eagle as they fell to distribute the energies at impact, or to use the half-mile circle-of-choice they had to maneuver away from trees and pavement to green or plowed fields. It was chance that brought them down in plowed fields, a factor that could conceivably have worked toward their survival. Though the odds of preparedness making any difference are very slim indeed, people have fallen remarkable distances and lived. A Russian stewardess survived a fall of 3,000 feet; a Russian pilot has survived a fall of 29,000 feet. A navy parachute rigger jumping in a test program free fell 16,000 feet with only his streaming unopened chute slowing his fall, and recovered to become a flight instructor and charter pilot.

Pilots fight all the way down for their own lives, and for the ship's. Unlike passengers, they are actively in command of their fates and keep very busy. When they do realize that, for reasons known or unknown, they have lost control—blown it!—they respond with frustrated resignation. Though the words are always edited out for the sake of the surviving families, it is well known that the pilot's last words on the cockpit voice recorder are often "Oh, shit!" It is said as if he had just hit his thumb with a hammer. Or missed the last train.

With no survival tasks to preoccupy them, there would be loss of hope for those falling. And then, knowledge of death. This is the part that would cause nightmares to the families. But from the little we know, it seems that in that flash of transition from the fight for life to the recognition of imminent death, another threshold is leaped. Fighter pilots coming in for a crash have described it as a state of anticipation, of exhilarated fascination with "What will it be like?" A woman, brought back by doctors from "death," resented the interference with her dying. It has been described as "a remarkable sensation of detachment, of an extraordinary sense of peace, calm, and total painlessness. . . ." The dying appear to go through a withdrawal, a preparation for death, as though intuitively familiar with the process." The renowned physician William Osler believed that there was "no agony of death."

Impact in the field at St. Pathus would have occurred at almost the same moment as impact in the forest. Death would have been instantaneous. There would be no conscious screams of terror. If there were human sounds, they would be the involuntary expulsions of air. If anything had been heard as they neared the ground, it would more likely have been the vibration of their clothes at high speed, making the tumbling bodies sound like an approaching artillery barrage. Then, a thud, as they impacted deeply into the earth.

Aboard the plane, there would have been a ring of panic around the hole where the seats had vanished. A zone of partially collapsed floor, seats askew, people hanging from their seat belts, trying to resist the suction that would continue through the flight, terrified to breathe or move. There would be a tangle of shiny bent or snapped cables that any mechanically aware passenger would quickly guess were vital to control. Here, there would probably be no noise or movement. Only the blanked minds and physical paralysis of negative panic. People resort to the mobile panic glorified in disaster movies only when there is a clearly marked exit to safety, and it is blocked, as when crowds jam the door from a burning theater. There would be no stampede toward this exit.

In the cockpit, the crew would be obsessed with "What the hell is happening?" and with saving the plane.

After the crash, there were rumors that, in crisis, Turkish pilots would throw up their hands and await the will of Allah. There were fears that they might have reverted to old culture patterns. Pilots who had trained with them in NATO remembered that "flying wing" on a Turk was a "near-*kamikazi*" experience; that they would shrug off incredible errors with a resigned, "I didn't understand." And maybe they didn't. Turks are not yet fully at home with twentieth century technology, as demonstrated by the training of DC-10 flight engineers who would prepare for takeoff with 40,000 pound errors in takeoff weight, and without fuel logs. But with experience, they can be among the world's best—highly motivated and intelligent. Clearly, they would fight to save a plane. With origins as barbarous steppes horsemen, Turks have historically been the most aggressive of the Islamic groups, long in contact with the West's adversary spirit. The captains of Flight 981 were seasoned military and commercial pilots with well over 12,000 flight hours between them—enough for imprinting sound crisis responses. Turkish pilots are potentially perhaps even better than U.S. pilots because they obey rules and more easily suppress their egos for the good of the mission. If the Turkish crew *did* engage the autopilot to try to use its limited control to recover from the dive—a remote but tantalizing possibility—it was a cool and positive response. Without final proof that they had lost all hydraulics that powered the autopilot, there will always remain the intriguing possibility that they were flying her out on autopilot at the moment of impact.

On March 3, 1974, a cargo door failure had initiated a series of secondary failures that, in 77 seconds, had brought a giant plane screaming down at nearly 500 mph into the pine trees of Ermenonville Forest, 23 miles northeast of Paris. With the sturdy pines acting "like a giant shredding machine," the aircraft and its occupants had been utterly destroyed.

It was the worst, the largest, the most unspeakable crash in aviation history. It was the crash that had been haunting the aviation insurers since the 747 had started commercial flights in 1970. The crash of a fully loaded wide-body airplane.

Statistically, it was overdue. The loss of one wide-body plane had been predicted for the first year of operation.

But when it came, only a small, highly specialized group of professionals was ready to respond. Of all those who may have speculated, few had really accepted the possibility. Compulsive Peter Pans, Westerners have tried to deny death in any form. But death by air crash has a special terror.

There is still a mystique about moving through the skies. And our ability to get us up there has raced ahead of our ability to handle it emotionally. As Canadian author Hugh McLellan suggested, perhaps our technological society has "outtraveled its own soul." Getting into a plane is an act of faith in high technology. And when a transport falls from the sky, we suffer not only the shock of loss, but also a shaken faith in the mechanistic way. A faith that must be reaffirmed. So a frantic search for cause follows. "Fixes" are made. And we try to believe it will never happen again. We keep trusting that if the wax is going to melt, it won't be on *our* wings.

Committed to the perfectibility of men and machines, we force air safety up to higher and higher levels, until flying becomes safer than taking a bath. Yet we fly suspecting that flight itself is a violation of one of the most tyrannical of all physical forces—gravity—and knowing that implicit in getting off the ground are some basic compromises, one of which is the compromise with perfect safety. One of the most popular pieces of received wisdom in aviation is: "Sure, we could build a perfectly safe plane. But it wouldn't fly."

An air crash is a public, highly visible event. And this was the most visible of all air crashes. The glare of public attention would be on it from minutes after the crash. The grim horror of it would be brought to many families by television hours before they had any idea that they would be involved.

From the stark lights that lit the barren hangar where the wreckage was examined, to the white-hot scrutiny by journalists, investigators, lawyers, and governments, the DC-10 crash would become a prisoner held under harsh lights until he has told everything he knows.

From the moment of impact, the *Paris Air Crash,* as it quickly became known on legal briefs, would become the most publicized, most controversial, and potentially most influential aviation disaster in history. The world's shock at the enormous loss of life would put unprecedented pressure on getting at the truth. And before the last ripples died away, the search for cause and culpability would carry us far beyond the testing of the structural integrity of a cargo door and the pressure vessel it should have sealed, to the testing of the most basic institutions, systems, strengths, and values of all the nations and individuals involved.

Aviation's Greatest Disaster

BY DAVID GRAYSON

When Boeing's behemoth 747s began plying the skies in the late 1960s, it did not take much imagination to picture the colossal disaster a crash would be. Depending on the individual airline configurations, the planes were carrying upwards of 350 people. The prospect of losing that many souls in a single accident was something very bitter to contemplate.

The thought of two fully loaded 747s colliding on the ground was one of nightmarish proportions—almost incomprehensible. Yet, that is exactly what happened on March 27, 1977, at Las Palmas Airport at Tenerife Island in Spain's Canary Islands. One plane was a KLM 747 carrying 234 passengers and 14 crew members, all of whom perished. The other 747 was a Pan Am flight with 16 crew members and 378 passengers. Nine Pan Am crew members and 317 passengers died in the collision.

How can such a monstrous disaster occur? How could two giants of the skies collide on the runway with professional, highly experienced crews at the controls and talking to the airport's tower about clearances and takeoff instructions?

You're about to find out, in a revelation of pilot error (human error, whatever you want to call it) of unparalleled proportion.

This detailed description of what happened that fateful day at Las Palmas is a chapter from David Grayson's excellent book, *Terror in the Skies: The Inside Story of the World's Worst Air Crashes*, published in 1988 by Citadel Press, a division of Lyle Stuart, Inc.

*　　*　　*　　*　　*

I n the previous chapter, the flight crew thought they were doing the right thing by ordering the emergency evacuation when the flaming aircraft screeched to a stop. Unfortunately, as a result of what initially appeared to be a sound decision, four people perished and 29 other Hawaiian-bound passengers were seriously injured.

We now turn to another vacationing group, also traveling on a jumbo airliner, where an unsound decision by the captain (according to the investigating authorities) was primarily responsible for the resulting catastrophe. The events leading up to this major accident were as follows:

On March 27, 1977, a bomb exploded in the passenger terminal at Las Palmas Airport in the Canary Islands, Spain, temporarily closing the airport to all traffic. All aircraft with a Las Palmas destination were diverted to the nearby airport on the island of Tenerife, less than 70 miles away.

One of the airliners re-routed to Tenerife awaiting the reopening of Las Palmas was a Pan Am 747 originating from Los Angeles, California, with 16 crew members and 378 passengers, mostly vacationers. Also at Tenerife, awaiting permission to take off and land at its primary Las Palmas destination, was another giant four-engine 747, a KLM jet from Amsterdam with 14 in crew and 234 passengers.

The delay, so far, had lasted more than two hours. Although everyone was impatient to get going, the KLM captain was especially anxious to depart. His crew had already flown sufficient hours so that any further delay could put them in the position of possibly exceeding their limit of continuous crew time for that tour of duty. Since these limits are strictly enforced, this would compel them, with their passengers, to remain (most unhappily) overnight in Tenerife.

A short time later, to the applause of the passengers, the stranded aircraft received the welcome news that Las Palmas was now open for landings. At about 5:00 P.M. (local time), the KLM 747 received radio permission to taxi out on the runway (Tenerife only had one runway) to the very end where it would make a backtrack (a 180 degree turn) and prepare for a takeoff in the direction from which it had just taxied. This one runway, normally used only for takeoffs and landings, had to be utilized for taxiing since all the taxiways running parallel to the runway were clogged with aircraft diverted from Las Palmas.

Immediately after the KLM started taxiing down the runway, the 747 Pan Am received permission to taxi behind the KLM—but with the instructions to turn off at one of the exits midway down the runway (actually, the third one). This was necessary to move the Pan Am 747 out of the way of the KLM 747, which it was following, since the latter would be turning around at the end and taking off in the opposite direction on the same runway.

It is important to note here that, when the planes originally landed, the weather was sunny and clear. Now, however, low-lying clouds had rolled in and visibility was limited to a few hundred yards. Therefore, the controller in the tower could not see the planes nor could either of the 747 pilots see the other aircraft.

We therefore have a situation in which the KLM 747, in this patchy fog, is taxiing down to the end of the runway with instructions to turn around at the end and await permission to take off in the direction it just came from. Taxiing behind the KLM is the Pan Am 747 (also with very limited visibility) with orders to turn off at the third runway exit (a little past the halfway point on the runway) so it can be safely off the runway when the KLM 747 receives permission to take off.

It is now time to hear the actual conversations taking place in the cockpit between crew members among themselves and with the controller in the tower. This information comes from tapes taken from both aircrafts' cockpit recorders and transmission tapes furnished by the Tenerife Control Tower. Some of the conversations have been deleted to maintain continuity. Also some words were inserted [in brackets] for purposes of clarification.

TIME 5:02:03 (seconds) P.M.

Pan Am Co-Pilot: We were instructed to contact you and also to taxi down the runway. Is that correct?

Tower: Affirmative. Taxi onto the runway and leave the runway third [exit], third to the left.

Pan Am Co-Pilot: Third to the left, okay.

Pan Am Captain: Third, he said.

Tower: [Th . . .]ird one to your left.

Pan Am Captain: I think he said first.

Pan Am Captain: I'll ask him again.

Pan Am Captain: [To another crew member] What really happened over there [in Las Palmas] today?

Pan Am Unknown Voice: They put a bomb in the terminal, sir, right where the check-in counters are.

Pan Am Captain: Well, we asked them if we could hold [wait out the delay by flying a holding pattern] and I guess you got the word, we landed here.

TIME 5:02:49 P.M.

Tower: KLM 4805, how many taxiways did you pass?

KLM: I think we just passed Charlie 4 [the fourth and last taxiway] now.

Tower: Okay, at the end of the runway make 180 [degree turn] and re-port [when] ready for ATC [Air Traffic Control] clearance.

TIME 5:03:09 P.M.

Pan Am Co-Pilot: The first one [taxiway] is a 90-degree turn [to get off the runway].

Pan Am Captain: Yeah, okay.

Pan Am Co-Pilot: Must be the third. I'll ask him again.

Pan Am Captain: Okay, we could probably go in, it's . . .

Pan Am Co-Pilot: You gotta make a 90 degree turn . . .

Pan Am Captain: Yeah.

Pan Am Co-Pilot: . . . 90 degree turn to get around this. This one down here [is] a 45 [degree turn to exit off the runway].

Obviously, there was confusion in the Pan Am cockpit.

TIME 5:03:29 P.M.

Pan Am Co-Pilot: [To tower], would you confirm that you want the [Pan Am] Clipper 1736 to turn left at the thirrrrrrd intersection?

Tower: The third one, sir; one, two, three; third, third one.

Pan Am Captain: Good.

Pan Am Co-Pilot: Very good, thank you.

Pan Am Captain: That's what we need, the third one.

Pan Am Engineer: Uno, dos, tres.

Pan Am Captain: Uno, dos, tres.

Pan Am Engineer: Tres, sí. We'll make it yet.

Tower: Pan Am, report [when] leaving the runway [via the third taxi-way exit].

The Pan Am 747 crew acknowledged the most recent instructions and while looking for the third turn-off from the runway, busied themselves with the checklist and reviewed departure procedures. So far, they had passed the first two exit turn-offs.

By now, the KLM crew had reached the end of the runway, turned around and was making takeoff preparations.

TIME 5:04:58 P.M.

Tower: KLM and [Pan Am] Clipper 1736. For [both] your informa-tion, the centerline lighting is out of service.

KLM: I copied that [message acknowledged].

Pan Am: Clipper 1736 [message acknowledged].

TIME 5:05:22 P.M.

Pan Am 747 continues taxiing along the runway looking for the third taxiway exit.

Pan Am Captain: That's two.

Pan Am Engineer: Yeah, that's a 45 [degree turn-off] there.

Pan Am Captain: Yeah.

Pan Am Co-Pilot: That's this one right here.

Pan Am Engineer: Okay, next one is almost a 45 [degree turnoff].

Pan Am Captain: But it goes . . . ahead. I think (it's) gonna put us on [the] taxiway.

Pan Am Engineer: Yeah, just a little bit, yeah.

Pan Am Co-Pilot: Maybe he counts these [for] three.

The Pan Am crew remained confused. They missed the third turnoff and continued taxiing down the runway searching for their designated exit.

At about the same time, the KLM 747 crew had completed their cockpit procedures, and were apparently awaiting permission to take off. However, the digital flight data recorder on the KLM indicated a slight forward movement of the aircraft due to opening of the throttle at:

TIME 5:05:41 P.M.

KLM Co-Pilot: [To KLM Captain] Wait a minute. We don't have ATC [Air Traffic Control] clearance.

KLM Captain: No, I know that. Go ahead, ask [for it].

KLM Co-Pilot: [To Tower] Ah, the KLM 4805 is now ready for take-off and we're waiting for our ATC clearance. (This communication was also heard in the Pan Am cockpit since both aircraft are tuned to the same tower frequency.)

Tower: KLM, you are cleared to . . . (Instructions are given as to the turns to be made after takeoff, the altitude to climb to and the heading to take towards Las Palmas radio station.)

As a matter of procedure, the receipt of an Air Traffic Control clearance does *not* give an aircraft permission to take off. It has only received the routing and altitude the plane will fly when it does depart. The pilot must first receive another radio command that he is cleared to take off *before* he is allowed to start his takeoff.

TIME 5:06:09 P.M. to 5:06:17 P.M.

During this time period, the co-pilot of the KLM confirms the ATC clearance by reading back the clearance instructions to the tower. However, while the co-pilot is talking to the tower, the flight data and Cockpit Voice Recorders indicated (in that same eight-second time interval of above) that the KLM Captain released the brakes, told his crew "Let's go," advanced the throttles for forward thrust and started his takeoff before the co-pilot finished his readback. (A note of interest here is that the 50-year-old KLM captain was his airline's Chief-of-Pilot Training, a position of great respect and authority. The other KLM crew members were aware that they were flying with one of the pilots of greatest prestige in the company and were not likely to challenge his authority.)

TIME 5:06:18 P.M.

The KLM co-pilot had just finished his readback and as his aircraft starts to move, now hurriedly says:

KLM Co-Pilot: [To Tower] We are now at takeoff. (The normal interpretation is that he is at the takeoff position and still needs radio permission to actually start his ground run.)

Tower: Okay [KLM]. Stand by for takeoff. I will call you.

TIME 5:06:18 P.M.

Pan Am: [To Tower] We are still taxiing down the runway, the Clipper 1736. (This Pan Am transmission partially blocked out the tower's message to KLM.)

(Due to the blocked transmission, the only word from the tower that the KLM heard clearly was "Okay." KLM did not hear, "Stand by for takeoff. I will call you.")

TIME 5:06:25 P.M.

Tower: Pan Am 1736, report runway clear [when you are clear of the runway].

Pan Am: Okay, we'll report when we're clear.

Tower: Thank you.

(These transmissions from Pan Am to the tower were audible in the cockpit of the KLM which had already started its takeoff run.)

TIME 5:06:32 P.M.

KLM Engineer: [In the KLM cockpit] Is he [the Pan Am] not clear, then?

KLM Captain: What do you say?

KLM Engineer: Is he not clear, that Pan American?

KLM Captain: Oh yes!

TIME 5:06:32 P.M.

Pan Am Captain: [In Pan Am cockpit] Let's get the hell right out of here.

Pan Am Co-Pilot: Yeah, he's anxious, isn't he?

Pan Am Engineer: Now he's in a rush.

TIME 5:06:40 P.M.

Pan Am Pilot: There he is . . . Look at him! Goddamn! That-son-of-a-bitch is coming!!

Pan Am Co-Pilot: Get off! Get OFF!! GET OFF!!!

The Pan Am 747 applied full throttle as it frantically tried to turn off the runway at a 45-degree angle relative to the center of the runway. The KLM 747 crew, finally aware of the other 747, desperately attempted to pull their aircraft into the air up and over the Pan Am airplane. The KLM actually managed to get entirely airborne; however, it was not enough. Although the nose and front landing gear of the KLM just managed to clear the Pan Am, the main landing gear smashed against the Pan Am fuselage.

Each aircraft weighed approximately 700,000 pounds!

TIME OF IMPACT 5:06:50 P.M.

The KLM, after destroying the top of the Pan Am fuselage, desperately attempted to gain altitude. Like a staggering bird, the 747 struggled and strained in an effort to remain airborne—but to no avail. After 500 feet of flight, it gave up, fell back to the runway and slid an additional 1,000 feet before coming to a complete stop. The aircraft then caught fire suddenly and with such force that emergency evacuation operations could not be employed.

Although the body of the KLM 747 remained substantially intact, there was no sign of movement from the aircraft. The doors stayed shut. All that could be heard was the roaring and raging fire. There were no survivors.

In the Pan Am 747 aircraft, the first-class lounge disintegrated as a result of the impact. The lounge floor also gave way which meant that the crew had to jump to the first-class section and get out through a hole in the left wall. This hole was also the main escape route for the passengers located in the forward part of the aircraft.

At the center and rear of the Pan Am plane, the twisting of metal sheets of the fuselage, along with the fire that suddenly broke out, formed a kind of trap preventing forward exit of the passengers. Those who survived managed to jump to the ground through an opening on the left side or through an open door from a height of 20 feet. Despite a fire under the left wing, some of the passengers managed to escape by jumping off this wing onto the grass.

Of the 16 crew members and 378 passengers aboard the Pan Am 747, only 59 survived. All of the survivors suffered injuries.

There were unusual circumstances surrounding this disaster. The weather conditions with its fog patches prevented this accident, despite its magnitude, from being directly visible from the control tower. Actually, when the control tower heard one explosion followed by another, it was unable to pinpoint them on the airfield and also unable to determine the cause of the explosions. It was some moments later when an aircraft located on the parking apron advised the tower that it had seen a fire, without specifying the exact place or its cause. Still not being able to locate the fire, the tower alerted the fire service.

The firemen headed for a bright light through the fog. When they came closer, although they were as yet unable to see the flames, they were hit with the effects of strong heat radiation.

When there was a slight clearing, they saw for the first time that there was a plane (the KLM 747) totally enveloped in flames, the only visible part being the rudder. After they had already begun to fight the fire, a greater clearing in the fog took place and they saw a bright light further away, which they thought at first was a part of the same plane which had broken off and was also burning.

They divided up the fire trucks and, on approaching what they thought was only an additional segment of the same fire, discovered a second plane on fire (the Pan Am 747). The firemen immediately concentrated their efforts on this second plane because the first was already totally beyond salvaging.

Meanwhile, in all this time, because of the dense clouds surrounding it, the tower was still unaware of the exact location of the fire and whether one or two planes had been involved in the accident. It was some time before the confusion dissipated and the account of what actually occurred started to emerge.

The most horrifying fact was the size of the death and injury toll. The total number was the largest ever recorded in an aircraft accident. The figures for each aircraft broke down as follows:

KLM 747

	CREW	PASSENGERS	TOTAL
FATAL	14	234	248
INJURIES	0	0	0

PAN AM 747

Fatal	9	317	326
Injuries	7	61★	68★

Adding the casualty list of both 747 aircrafts comes to a mind-boggling total of 583 killed and 59 injured as a result of one aircraft impacting another. These numbers are especially hard to assimilate when we realize that this catastrophe occurred when the wheels on the main landing gear of one airplane *just did not quite clear* the fuselage of the other on takeoff.

Five hundred eighty-three people died. Not even taking into consideration the considerable number of injured, how can we possibly grasp the

---

★Of the 61 passengers injured, nine subsequently died as a result of the injuries received.

enormity of that number of deaths from one accident? Five hundred eighty-three people.

In an attempt to come to grips with what could be viewed by some as merely a statistic, consider the following comparisons: 583 deaths comes to more individuals than all of the players on 64 baseball teams; or, as many athletes on 53 complete football teams; or, more than all the teammates on 116 basketball teams. In fact, the number is about the size of an entire school body of a small-town high school, or the entire seating capacity of an average-sized movie theatre house. Obviously, a number too large to easily comprehend.

What about the ramifications of these numbers? How about the relatives of these unfortunate victims? The spouses, children, parents, sisters, and brothers? And even boyfriends, girlfriends, fiancées (and fiancés)? How about employers or key employees of the deceased? Or business partners? And, besides shattered family and business relationships, consider the loss by good friends, neighbors, organizations, charities, etc. The almost endless circle of people significantly affected runs into the many, many thousands.

Three hundred fifty tons of aircraft hurtling down the runway at 175 miles per hour toward anther 350-ton monster. The Pan Am cockpit recorder indicated that the crew saw the KLM 747 approximately nine seconds before the impact. What was going through the minds of both crew members in those few seconds? Could the KLM captain be saying, "Dear God, I was too hasty—I never expected the Pan Am to still be on the runway!" How about the KLM co-pilot or engineer, "I don't care if you are the captain. I told you that we must not take off until absolutely certain that the Pan Am is clear of the runway!" What were the thoughts of any of those passengers on both aircraft who were able to see the other 747 only seconds before the impending crash?

Naturally, there was an extensive inquiry. Investigators from Spain, the Netherlands, and the United States participated in trying to determine the cause of this tragic accident.

In addition to all other phases of the investigation, they listened to the tapes recovered from the cockpit recorders of the two aircraft as well as the tower tapes. The most significant evidence came from the cockpit recorder of the KLM.

Of course, listening to the tapes was only part of the investigation. It was only after every aspect of the accident was thoroughly examined that a number of conclusions were reached. Following is the Official Report of Conclusions by the authorities:

The fundamental cause of the accident was the fact that the KLM captain:

1. Took off without clearance.
2. Did not obey the "stand by for takeoff" from the tower.
3. Did not interrupt takeoff on learning that the Pan Am was still on the runway.
4. In reply to the flight engineer's query as to whether the Pan Am had already left the runway, replied emphatically in the affirmative.

Now how is it possible that a pilot with the technical capacity and experience of the KLM captain, whose state of mind during the stopover at Tenerife seemed perfectly normal and correct, was able, a few minutes later, to commit a basic error in spite of all the warnings repeatedly addressed to him?

An explanation may be found in a series of factors which possibly contributed to the occurrence of the accident:

1. A growing feeling of tension as the problems for the captain continue to accumulate. He knew that, on account of the strictness in the Netherlands regarding the rules on the limitations of duty time (he may be prosecuted under the law if he exceeds the limits), if he did not take off within a relatively short space of time, he might have to interrupt the flight—with the consequent disruption for his company and inconvenience for the passengers.
2. The fact that two transmissions took place at the same time. The "Stand by for takeoff . . . I will call you" from the tower coincided with Pan Am's "We are still taxiing down the runway," which meant that the transmission was not received with all the clarity that might have been desired.
3. Inadequate language. When the KLM co-pilot reported the ATC clearance, he ended with the words, "We are now at takeoff." The controller, who had not been asked for takeoff clearance and who consequently had not granted it, did not understand that they were taking off. The O.K. from the tower, which preceded the "Stand by for takeoff" was likewise incorrect—although irrelevant in this case because takeoff had already started about six and a half seconds before.
4. The fact that the Pan Am had not left the runway at the third intersection. This plane should, in fact, have consulted with the tower if it had any doubts, and this it did not do. However, this was not very

relevant either since Pan Am never reported the runway clear, but to the contrary, twice advised that it was taxiing on it.

5. Unusual traffic congestion which obliged the tower to instruct aircraft to taxi on the active runway—a procedure which can be potentially dangerous.

That was the official report released by the investigating authorities. However, there are four additional items of interest worth mentioning which involved making a crucial decision:

1. The KLM flight was part of a charter series operated on behalf of a Holland Travel group. Accompanying this group was a company travel guide. This lady decided to remain on Tenerife and did not return on board the KLM for the fatal flight to Las Palmas. Can we believe that at one time in every person's life, he (or she) will be faced with a decision on a course of action that will have a major impact on his future?

2. The Pan Am flight allowed two additional company employees to board the plane at Tenerife and sit on the cockpit jumpseats for the flight to Las Palmas. These two Pan Am employees escaped death but were injured in the accident. Another decision by two people with a severe impact on their lives.

3. The Tenerife airport itself is set in a sort of hollow between mountains. Therefore, on account of its altitude and location, the airport has distinctive weather conditions with frequent presence of low-flying clouds affecting visibility. Visibility before and during the accident was both minimal and quite variable. There was a threat of even a further reduction of the already precarious visibility. Faced with this threat, the way to meet it was either by taking off as soon as possible or refraining from taking off—a possibility which certainly must have been considered by the KLM captain. His decision—takeoff.

4. Before taxiing out, the KLM took an extra 30 minutes to refuel. Its tanks were filled with almost 15,000 additional gallons even though the 747 had more than enough fuel for its flight to Las Palmas. If we bear in mind that the Tenerife-Las Palmas flight is only one of about 25 minutes in duration, the taking on of this additional weight of fuel leads us to suppose that the KLM captain wished to avoid the difficulties of refueling in Las Palmas, with the resulting delay, because a great number of planes diverted from Tenerife

would be going there later. Question: How much less runway would the KLM 747 have used to become airborne if it had not taken on this extra load (almost 100,000 pounds) of fuel? Perhaps enough to completely clear the fuselage of the Pan Am 747? This decision, in the light of what happened, could have been the most crucial and devastating of them all.

Deadly Departure

BY CHRISTINE NEGRONI

When a disaster such as the loss of a jumbo jet and its passengers and crew occurs in the New York City area, media coverage is so immediate and intense that the event is thrust into national attention within seconds.

When TWA Flight 800 exploded in mid-air over the ocean minutes after taking off from JFK on the evening of July 17, 1996, search-and-rescue personnel had barely arrived on the scene of burning fuel slicks, floating debris, and a few bodies and other human remains when the airwaves were already full of spectacular and lurid wild guesses about what had happened. There was talk of a terrorist bomb—with understandable reason: It was a terrorist bomb that had brought down Pan Am Flight 103 over Scotland in 1988. Now the mystery and speculation surrounding the crash included vivid images of not only the explosion in the sky, but of missile-like streaks supposedly seen renting the sky amid the torrent of fire and debris raining through the evening twilight. And the tragedy of human suffering—men, women and children strapped in their seats while the aircraft broke apart and plunged earthward— was heightened by the heart-wrenching revelation that a group of high school students on a class trip to Paris had been aboard the plane.

The actual facts of what happened that afternoon were slow in coming, but after weeks and months of investigation, the National Transportation Safety Board's dedicated and thorough investigation team found the answer to what caused the tragedy. To do so, they cut through layers of hysteria, media pundit guesses, and political infighting involving the FBI. The NTSB stuck to the facts: It had both the flight data recorder and the cockpit voice recorder (the infamous "black boxes") and they had enough debris to reconstruct a great deal of the plane in a hanger.

Christine Negroni's book *Deadly Departure* is an account of stunning revelations and a terrifying recreation of one of aviation's most tragic disasters.

＊　　＊　　＊　　＊　　＊

In a matter of seconds, the men in the cockpit realized they were going to die. In the minute that passed before the plane hit the water, fifty-seven-year-old pilot Steven Snyder was probably astonished that the Boeing 747, a plane he knew intimately and trusted completely, was failing him. Oliver Krick, the twenty-five-year-old flight engineer on the verge of becoming a commercial airline pilot, was likely feeling a different and unfamiliar emotion. For the first time in a life filled only with accomplishments, Oliver Krick felt helpless.

Thirteen minutes into the flight, the plane was still climbing out of New York airspace. There had been an explosion closely followed by a disorienting tempest of unrecognizable sounds. The force behind the noise shook the flight deck. When a quick fog of condensation filled the cockpit, the men grabbed for their oxygen masks and set the control knobs to the emergency position to begin a flow of pressurized oxygen.

Pilot training always includes time in a flight simulator practicing for in-flight emergencies, but there's no practice for the situation that was facing the pilots of TWA Flight 800. They did not know it, but the plane had split apart.

Desperate, Captain Snyder ordered Flight Engineer Krick to check essential power, looking for some reason why the battery in the electronics bay beneath the cockpit wasn't supplying an emergency source of energy for the flight control instruments. Krick was confused, unable to comprehend the sudden shift from normal to unimaginable. It might have crossed his mind that he'd done something wrong, and he was frantically reconstructing his actions.

Struggling against the cockpit's wild pitching, Training Flight Engineer Richard Campbell eyed the panel by Krick, noting that the emergency battery switch was already in the "on" position. It should be providing electricity to the cockpit instruments. Yet dozens of amber flags had popped up in the flight control dials, indicating they were powerless. So was the crew.

On July 17, 1996, the Boeing 747-100 that was TWA's Flight 800 to Paris was one day younger than Oliver Krick. It had come off the assembly line in Everett, Washington, on July 15, 1971, the 153rd 747 made, and given the tail number N93119. Twenty-five is young for a man, but it's old for an airplane. Though this 747 still looked modern from the outside, its technology was essentially the same as that of the first 747 flown in 1969. The Boeing 747 and twin-engine 737 are the oldest commercial Boeing designs still in production.

N93119 had been scrupulously inspected by TWA under an FAA program to prevent age-related structural weaknesses, but the plane's systems were as old as the plane, including hundreds of miles of wiring that hadn't been examined since the day it was installed. The cockpit was a quaint array of yesterday's technology, dials and knobs, toggle switches, and analog gauges. There were no color graphical displays, no whiz-bang computers capable of improving on the calculations of the human flight engineers in a fraction of the time. This model 747, referred to as a "747 Classic," is one of the few remaining commercial jetliners still requiring a third crew member, like Flight Engineer Krick, to monitor the amount of fuel in the tanks and the operation of the engines.

In its twenty-five years, the jumbo jet had made 16,000 flights. It had flown 100,000 miles in just the last two weeks, making twenty-four transatlantic flights. It checked out fine as pilots Snyder and Ralph Kevorkian, and Campbell and Krick prepared it for the scheduled 7 P.M. departure to Paris. Reports filed by the pilots who'd brought the plane to New York from Athens showed nothing unusual during their nine-hour-and-forty-five-minute flight.

The ground crew at Kennedy noted that the Athens to New York leg had drained the fuel tank located between the wings down to the last fifty gallons, but since that tank would not be needed for the shorter trip to France, it was not refilled. Thirty thousand gallons of Jet A kerosene would be pumped into the plane's six wing tanks only. The wing tanks held enough fuel to get the plane to Paris: Filling the center tank would have increased the plane's weight, making the flight more expensive to operate.

TWA would have been pleased with more passengers. In the height of the summer vacation travel season, the 433-seat wide-body was carrying only 176 fare-paying passengers. The fifty-four others on flight were TWA employees and their families working the flight or enjoying free travel, the benefit of working for an airline.

Snyder, Kevorkian, Campbell, and Krick were not planning to fly Flight 800 to Paris. Their scheduled trip to Rome on TWA Flight 848 was canceled, so both passengers and crew were switched onto the Paris flight, which would continue to Rome after stopping in France.

Rather than go as passengers, a practice known as deadheading, as TWA schedulers had arranged, Krick and Captain Kevorkian were flying because Captain Snyder convinced New York's chief pilot, Captain Hugh Schoelzel, to let them get the experience. Kevorkian would be completing his last supervised flight.

"These fellas are on check rides, Hugh," Captain Snyder pleaded. "Why not give us this trip and let 800's original crew deadhead into Paris?"

And so it was that Oliver Krick, lucky from the day he was born, found himself in one of the best seats in the sky, two miles above the rustic shorelines of southern Long Island and climbing.

Philip Yothers made the three-hour trip from central Pennsylvania to JFK Airport hundreds of times in his fifteen years driving for Susquehanna Trailways bus line. It wasn't his favorite assignment: New York traffic was always heavy, and sitting on a slow-moving highway, his right foot riding the clutch, could make his muscles sore for a day or two.

The passengers on his bus on July 17, 1996, were high school French students headed for a week in Paris. He was drawn into their good humor and was soon participating in the banter of the kids sitting up front near his seat at the wheel of the big motorcoach.

Yothers, sixty-six, had never been to Paris, never traveled farther than he could drive. Even if he had the opportunity, he wasn't sure he would make such a trip. Yothers was the kind of man who liked to be home at night.

Earlier in the day, with the bus idling in the parking lot of Montoursville High School, he heaved luggage into the bins beneath the bus. Over the low rumble of the engine, and the high-energy chatter of teens starting an adventure, he'd overheard the French teacher tell a friend she really didn't want to go. Deborah Dickey and her husband, Douglas, were leaving two young daughters behind with their grandparents. Yothers, a father and a grandfather, understood her hesitation.

By the time the bus finally pulled up to the curb at the airport, Yothers noticed Deborah Dickey had caught the excitement. Students and their five chaperones burst out of the bus, snatching worn duffel bags and bulging backpacks from the luggage bins so fast that Yothers hardly had the chance to help. When he lowered the doors and turned to wave good-bye, every single one of them had already disappeared into the airport terminal.

If she hadn't been so eager to get back to Rome, Monica Omiccioli would have been excited by an unexpected trip to Paris. After all, Paris was fashion and fashion was Monica's other love. When she and her new husband, Mirco Buttaroni, arrived at Kennedy International Airport from Santo Domingo to learn their flight to Rome was canceled, it was just a frustrating delay for the honeymooning couple on their way home.

Monica was as colorful and dramatic as the clothing she designed in art school; she'd sketched a classic pinstripe suit rendered in scarlet, and fringed cowboy palazzo pants slit to the thigh. The twenty-five-year-old from Lucrezia, Italy, was always mixing things up in her work, in her life.

On June 23, 1996, she married Mirco Buttaroni, a banker she'd known since both were sixteen years old. Four days later they left for their three-week honeymoon. It was their first trip abroad, their first trip on an airplane. Devoted to the Catholic Church and to their large extended families, they planned to raise their own kids in the small village where they grew up.

Monica worked with her uncle at his design house, J Cab, in Fano, in northeastern Italy, producing men's fashions for an international market. Having graduated with honors in accounting from Luiss University in Rome, Mirco worked at a bank in the same town.

On their wedding day, guests took photographs of the beaming couple. Less than a month later, the snapshots were heartbreaking evidence of how quickly joy can turn to grief.

Boarding Flight 800, even novice flyers like Monica and Mirco had to give some thought to their vulnerability to terrorists. Security at Kennedy International Airport was heightened in the summer of 1996 because of the federal trial of Ramzi Ahmed Yousef in a courtroom in Manhattan. Yousef was on trial for conspiring with notorious Saudi millionaire terrorist Osama bin Laden to put bombs on U.S. carriers flying into Asia. Passenger security checks and questioning by ticket agents is intended, in part, to help passengers recognize their role in keeping air travel safe.

But on July 17, no one was questioning the plane itself. The 747, an icon of the jet age, inspired confidence and awe.

As they prepared for the trip in the pilots' meeting room at Hangar 12, the airline's run-down operations building, TWA's economic troubles were very much on the minds of the pilots. Snyder was keen on figuring out how various operating procedures could reduce fuel consumption and help the airline get the most out of every gallon. His plan for saving fuel by making hourly adjustments to the plane's trim, its position in the sky, was referred to by some pilots as "Snyderizing" the plane. Since TWA's annual fuel budget comes close to $1 billion, a small savings adds up when multiplied by 300,000 flights a year.

At TWA, Snyder was considered the "godfather of the 747," an expert in the plane's fuel consumption. Some pilots wondered about his obsession with the subject, noting that he kept voluminous records detailing the fuel burn on each airplane he flew.

Seated on the flight deck, Snyder waited to depart, delayed because a computer could not match a checked suitcase to a passenger boarding card. Security precautions resulting from the 1988 Christmas bombing of Pan Am 103 over Scotland forbade unaccompanied baggage on international flights. When the bag's owner was found on the plane and the suitcase reloaded in the cargo hold, the luggage loader broke down, blocking the 747 at the gate. More time passed before a tow truck could move the machine.

Restless passengers shifted around the cabin, finding better seats, looking for empty rows where they could bed down for the overnight flight. Some had been served drinks and were already using the bathrooms. Others were taking down their carry-on luggage, rummaging for an aspirin or a new CD. Getting things restowed and passengers belted back into their seats would not be quick or easy.

The flight was an hour behind schedule when the door to the cockpit opened.

"Hello darlin'," Krick drawled to the flight attendant who was giving him a thumbs-up.

"Everybody seated?" he asked, confirming her gesture. "Thanks."

"Amazing," Captain Kevorkian mumbled, relieved to be ready for takeoff.

Kevorkian, fifty-eight, was worried about how to explain the delay to passengers. There wasn't any good reason. The owner of the unidentified luggage had been on the plane all along.

"We won't bother telling them that," he said to the others on the flight deck. "You don't mind, huh?" he asked them, smiling.

Krick was working only his sixth flight with TWA, but he piped up, "We'd have a mutiny back there."

Had it been necessary to calm frustrated passengers, though, Krick would have been up to the job. Handling people was one of the things he did best. Flying planes and playing sports were the other two. He'd been competing in athletics since grade school. Water and snow skiing, soccer, hockey, golf, football, volleyball, basketball, even darts. In a boyish display, he'd wedged the plaques and trophies he won over the years into every inch of available space on the bookshelves in his bedroom. The only other decoration was an equally impressive collection of books, tapes, posters, and computer programs about flying.

Before joining TWA, Krick had been a flight instructor and corporate pilot and had recently been accepted in the Air National Guard for flight training on the F-15. He continued to live at home with his parents and younger brother in suburban St. Louis, but owned property on a lake in rural Missouri where he planned to build a house in the future. That future included Tiffany Gates, a woman he'd met in college and had dated steadily for five years. Ollie Krick was attractive, talented, and much loved. It occurred to him often how much he'd been blessed.

Charles Henry Gray III, the chief operating officer of the Midland Financial Group, missed his flight from Hartford to Washington's Dulles Airport, where he was scheduled to fly out to Paris, because his driver got lost on the way to the airport. He was rescheduled onto TWA Flight 800 along with his travel companions.

Later, as he waited in the airline's first-class lounge, his anger still in low idle, Gray called Elena Barham, the company's chief financial officer. "Damn, Ebie," he said, complaining about the screw-up in Hartford. Barham, who was also Gray's best friend, cheered him up, as she often did.

Gray had a thick shock of sandy brown hair, clear blue eyes, and a lop-sided smile. He was tall and kept himself fit with daily five-mile runs. Raised in Arkansas, he developed a taste for good wine and well-made clothes once he left home. At forty-seven, he'd made and lost three fortunes and four marriages. There was something about his recklessness that, rather than alienating others, made him more endearing. He was a less-than-attentive parent. He didn't often see his two sons by his first and second wives when they were young. When Hank IV and Chad entered their teens and joined their dad in his perpetual adolescence, the relationship got going.

Gray had a custom twin-turbo Corvette that he would take to an un-interrupted five-mile stretch of Tennessee back road. With the boys in the car, he would run it up to 190 miles an hour and scream over the roar of the engine and the buffeting wind, "This is how I'm gonna go, boys, I'll die before I'm fifty and I'm gonna be goin' fast when I go." And though young Hank and Chad heard him say this many times, they never detected a hint of regret in their father's voice.

At six foot three, Gray had to duck his head slightly to board the plane. He settled in seat 2A in the first-class section. His mood had improved, courtesy of the champagne he'd been served in the TWA Constellation Club and the knowledge that this trip to Paris could make him very wealthy.

Gray was sitting in front of Kurt Rhein, with whom he was traveling to Europe to find financing for a merger of their two companies. A year earlier, Gray and Rhein had met on an airplane. The two hit it off right away. They developed a plan to merge Gray's specialized auto insurance company with Rhein's Danielson Holding Corporation.

Along with two other men on the flight, they were looking for the investors to make the idea a reality. Godi Notes, twenty-seven, an Israeli-born American who was an up-and-coming executive of the investment banking firm assisting in the merger, Donaldson, Lufkin and Jenrette, sat across the aisle from Rhein. Forty-one-year-old William Story, president of a Danielson subsidiary in California, was in one of the eight first-class seats directly behind the cockpit on the upper deck, the domed section that gives the 747 its distinctive appearance.

In front of Story sat Jed Johnson, forty-seven, who ran a New York-based interior decorating business with his partner and companion, Alan Wanzenberg. The two had established a golden reputation for designs that were tasteful yet experimental and a world away from Johnson's Minnesota roots. The designer's boy-next-door good looks were straight out of the sixties and suited the nineties infatuation with retro chic. Johnson was very much in demand as a decorator with a roster of celebrity clients. His work was often featured in glossy shelter magazines and books.

Johnson was alone on this trip, shopping for a new textiles business he was starting. Wanzenberg, whom he'd know for fifteen years, stayed in New York taking care of the businesses in Manhattan and Southampton.

Jed Johnson had a twin brother, Jay. He was one of four people on the plane who had a twin. The others were Arlene Johnsen, a TWA flight attendant who had lived with her sister, Marlene, all her life, and Myriam Bellazoug, a New York architect whose twin was Jasmine. Passenger Katrina Rose had a twin brother, John. None of the four was traveling with his or her twin.

Judith Yee had only one misgiving about this trip, which she'd been planning for months. She worried that her beloved terrier, Max, was going to be miserable. Before leaving for the airport, she coaxed him into the small pet carrier. It was wedged securely underneath the seat in front of her, and occasionally she could see his small nose through the grate of the plastic carrier.

Judy Yee was fifty-three years old, but not a strand of gray could be found in her shiny, chin-length black hair, which she was in the habit of pushing off her wide forehead with her hand, stopping along the way to nudge large black glasses back up on her nose.

Her dog was her companion and more than a pet; he was a coworker. For the past two years she and Max spent nearly every Thursday morning at

P.S. 138, a public middle school in New York's Greenwich Village, providing severely disabled students with the opportunity to interact with the dog.

Judy and Max and another volunteer, Naomi Boak and her Labrador retriever, would arrive at the school first thing in the morning. Judy would place Max on a table where the children, some blind, some in wheelchairs, would gather around and pet or groom him.

Neither Judy nor Naomi had children of their own, so it wasn't surprising to either of them that they were developing an interest in the students at P.S. 138. Following their Thursday visits, they would walk together through the neighborhood, discussing the progress of the kids to whom they'd grown especially close.

As the 1996 school year drew to a close, the conversation also included Yee's plans to travel to France with a group of old friends. Yee had a take-charge personalty and organized practically every detail of the trip. She coordinated each traveler's itinerary and handwrote the details of their trips on the pink pages of pretty travel journals she'd bound by hand for each of them.

In Yee, the women had a generous friend and their own personal travel agent. She found and secured the house in France where they'd be staying, organized the car rental, and booked the airline tickets. With characteristic devotion to Max, Yee chose TWA because it was the only airline that would allow her to keep the dog with her in the passenger cabin, rather than a pressurized cargo hold.

Judy Yee sat close to the front of the plane with her cousin from New Jersey, Patricia Loo. The third woman traveling with them, fifty-three-year-old Angela Murta, a beautiful blond with a wide open face and dramatic green eyes, had been assigned to a seat far back behind the wing on the right-hand side of the 747.

Friends of the women found the relationship between Yee and Murta a delightful contradiction. Murta loved clothes and boyfriends and scrimped on some things to afford an elegant house in the Hamptons. Yee, on the other hand, was quite well off, not terribly interested in men, and she spent extravagantly on only two things: art and travel. She dressed in sloppy, comfortable clothes that mirrored the way she kept her Greenwich Village apartment. Despite their differences, the women had been dear friends since the 1970s. Since so many seats were empty on TWA Flight 800, Murta could have moved up to sit closer to the women she'd known half her life.

As the passengers waited for takeoff, air handling packs beneath the plane had been running for nearly three hours, keeping the passenger cabin comfortably cool. Outside it was 71 degrees, a cloudless, moonless, nearly windless summer evening. A perfect night for flying.

With the uncertainty about who would be flying the trip to Paris and the last-minute delays at the gate, it had been a brittle few hours for the men in the cockpit. Not that the unexpected is unusual. The people-moving business is always subject to the unpredictability of passengers, the vagaries of weather, and the inconsistent reliability of extremely complicated machinery.

Shortly after 8 P.M., the paperwork for Flight 800 was completed, the plane readied, the last-minute hassles with the gate agents and luggage handlers resolved. The doors were securely closed and the pilots cleared to bring their 747 into a line of colorful giants, a United Nations of airliners into which Kevorkian could steer the red-and-white jumbo jet bearing the logo of a company that had pioneered commercial aviation.

Even if TWA's domination of the skies was on the wane, from where he sat, three stories above the airfield, Captain Kevorkian was at the top of his game. He was in command of the biggest and most awe-inspiring passenger jet ever made, operating out of one of the biggest and most glamorous airports in the world. For most of the upcoming flight, he would fly the 747 on an isolated course, but for these moments he was part of a proud parade of airplanes, each moving with a slow grace along the taxiway, through waves of shimmering heat created by the exhaust of powerful jet engines.

Many airline pilots acknowledge with a laugh that the hardest part of flying is getting away from the gate. Approaching the moment of takeoff, Captain Kevorkian was like so many pilots, eager to go. Finally, the time had come to fly.

At 8:18 P.M., Captain Kevorkian pushed the throttles slightly forward and the plane began to race down the runway. In about forty-five seconds the jet reached 184 miles per hour. Kevorkian pulled back on the control yoke, the W-shaped wheel mounted in front of him, rotating the nose of the plane up, and the 747 was airborne.

Moments later, as the landing gear receded into the aircraft, the plane was over Jamaica Bay. Turning east, Captain Kevorkian increased air speed to 287 miles per hour.

It was a busy time in the air around Kennedy. Departure control notified the TWA crew to make a second left turn to keep clear of another flight.

"The traffic in the turn will be three o'clock and five miles northeast bound four thousand feet," came a voice from the FAA tower.

Captain Kevorkian had been hoping to turn back to the most direct course, to "Bette," the first of a series of navigational way points the pilots would pass on their way to Paris, but the controller's instruction made it clear a turn like that would put the jumbo jet too close to a smaller Saab plane that was also ascending.

"He's at three o'clock?" Kevorkian questioned Snyder.

"Yeah," Captain Snyder replied, "that's the problem."

As the plane ascended, Susan Hill, forty-five, a police detective from Portland, Oregon, might have strained forward against her seat belt to see New York City out the window two seats away. Sailing above New York's overwhelming cityscape, Susan was introspective. Three months had passed since her divorce and she was embarking on a new adventure, her first trip alone. Hill had never needed a reason to be bold. She was impulsive and energetic. The tattoo of a ladybug on her wrist was evidence of her willingness to try something new, especially if she could shock the people who thought they knew her.

For her five-week trip overseas, she'd opted for a new look to go with her new life. Her blond hair cut short, she dressed in tight, sexy jeans and comfortable sneakers. The career girl clothes were stashed in the closet. Who knew if she would ever go back to that restrained professional look. Her backpack held a dozen new CDs from salsa to country and western.

Her plan was to house-sit at the Paris home of the brother of a fellow Portland police officer, then head over to England and spend a few more weeks there. Susan was well traveled. When she was married she'd visited India, the South Pacific, Singapore, and Russia. She's never been to England or France.

This trip was Susan's second big adventure. Fifteen years earlier she had become a born-again Christian. She loved talking about it, so much so that she'd gotten herself in a little trouble. After she proselytized to suspects, her boss at the police bureau told her to keep her religious beliefs to herself.

This would not be a problem on Flight 800. Matthew Alexander, a twenty-year-old from Augusta, South Carolina, with a football player's build and a teddy bear personality, was seated next to Susan. He was en route to Dijon for a summer of Christian missionary work.

Seated directly behind them, fifteen-year-old Daniel Cremades was involved in his book. Cremades had spent three weeks in the United States, taking a college course for bright high school students at the Massachusetts Institute of Technology. Daniel was no egghead, though. He had an easy, self-confident manner that drew people to him, especially girls.

After his summer session at MIT, Daniel spent his final week in the states at the New Jersey home of his uncle and aunt, Dario and Jabina Cremades, and their eight-year-old son, David. Neither boy had a brother, so it was a thrill for both of them to be together. The two visited the museums in

New York, just over the George Washington Bridge from the Cremadeses' high-rise apartment building, and spent their last day together at the Jersey shore.

Languages were so important to Daniel's parents, Jose Cremades and Ana Vila, Spanish citizens living in France, that every summer they sent Daniel and his older sister, Tania, to countries where they would be totally immersed in another tongue. The parents' efforts paid off. Daniel spoke four languages. For his flight back home, Daniel was carrying a book in English, Orson Scott Card's *The Abyss.*

Seated behind the wings were the honeymooners, Monica and Mirco. They'd been to New York, Los Angeles, San Francisco, and Santo Domingo in the Dominican Republic. They'd become enchanted with two aspects of American culture: Walt Disney and Hollywood. The day after arriving in New York, Monica called home to speak with her sister-in-law, Katia Buttaroni.

Last night we found a store filled with Disney animals, and I've already stuffed my bag with Mickey and Donald Duck and Dalmatians. And I bought something special for the baby, she told Katia, who was expecting her second child.

Six days into their honeymoon, Monica and Mirco called home again and learned that his grandmother had died. It was a devastating blow. Mirco was unusually close to his maternal grandmother. Guests at his wedding remembered that he had broken down in tears explaining that she was too sick to attend. The couple's first response to the news was to plan an immediate return to Italy. It took a lot of talking to convince them not to end their honeymoon then and there. Ultimately, they decided to continue on their trip, winding up on the beaches of Santo Domingo for their last week.

Monica went tropical and had her long hair cornrowed with tiny white beads woven into each of the hundreds of thin braids, an exotic hairdo for the folks back home. Monica enjoyed the quiet clacking of the beads each time she moved her head.

The last day of their trip, Monica called her mother. We're tired and ready to be home, she told her. We'll arrive in Rome tomorrow morning and take the train from there. I can't wait to see you.

As she sat by the window on the left side of the plane, Monica's hair was still braided, her wedding ring still shiny and new.

Flight attendant Ray Lang, fifty-one, had noticed the honeymooners when they boarded the 747. He was planning to be married himself, to fellow flight attendant Melinda Torche, who was also working the flight.

The night before, Ray and Melinda had dinner at a favorite neighborhood Italian restaurant in Long Island and made plans for what they'd do during their brief layover in Paris. After dinner, Ray held court at a spontaneous slumber party at the house he shared with his niece, Wendy, also a TWA flight attendant; his brother; and their mother. As they gathered in the room Wendy shared with Melinda when she was visiting, Ray predicted better times ahead for TWA and employees like them. I see things definitely lookin' up, he said.

The airline was emerging from its second bankruptcy in four years. The company had just announced a $25 million profit for the second quarter of 1996 and a longer term plan to update its fleet of aircraft, the oldest fleet owned by a major U.S. carrier, by replacing dated planes like the L-1011 and B747 with the newer Boeing wide-body 767s. The airline was also adding twenty new long-range narrow-body 757s and fifteen McDonnell Douglas MD-83s.

The new jetliners were modern and sophisticated. The two-engine MD-83s, Boeing 767s and 757s consumed less fuel than the four-engine 747 and the three-engine L-1011, and a two-person cockpit crew saved the airline plenty in personnel costs.

Ray considered TWA's purchase a promising development. His faith in the reliability of Boeing was unshakable. "If it ain't Boeing, I ain't goin'" he'd told everyone gathered in the small bedroom. They all laughed in agreement.

When it came to enthusiasm for Boeing products, Lang had an ally in Captain Snyder, who loved the 747s he'd been flying for twenty-two years. In 1993 Snyder became a check captain on the wide-body, helping with the training of other 747 pilots.

On the night of July 17, 1996, Snyder was supervising Captain Kevorkian, a thirty-one-year veteran of TWA who had just become licensed by the FAA to fly the 747. As part of the airline's own training procedure, Kevorkian was completing twenty-five hours of actual flight time while the check captain, Snyder, reviewed and evaluated his performance.

Many pilots were intimidated by Snyder. His exhaustive interest in minimizing fuel consumption was just one example of his fastidious piloting. Snyder believed there was a good reason behind every routine flight procedure. Some pilots considered him a scold, while others attributed his "super pilot" persona to the breakup of his marriage in the seventies. Snyder's divorce was widely discussed because his wife, a TWA flight attendant, left him for another pilot. Since Snyder never remarried, his devotion to his job was noted and analyzed by everyone who knew his story.

As TWA 800 was pushing back from the gate, Snyder's attention to detail showed itself again.

"You got something else to do, Ralph," Snyder informed Kevorkian as the ground crew released the big jet's parking brakes.

"Number one ADP," Kevorkian replied, "and the electric," acknowledging that he knew the flight engineer needed to turn on the air-powered pump controlling the steering gear and ready the electric standby brake system.

Snyder wasn't content with the manner of Kevorkian's communication with the flight engineer.

"It's a command," he explained to Kevorkian. "That's a command," he repeated. It was a subtle adjustment, but Snyder's by-the-book correction left no room for a misinterpretation.

"Command," Kevorkian repeated. Changing his tone, he issued the order to the flight engineer, "Number one ADP on and the electric."

Before joining TWA in 1963, Snyder had spent four years in Cornell University's ROTC program and had flown for three years with the air force doing reconnaissance flights over Germany. His desire to establish a clear chain of command on the flight deck was less a function of his military background than of his often stated philosophy that good piloting required uncompromising clarity.

Kevorkian was not the sort of man who would have been stressed by a check ride with Snyder. The two had known each other for years, and Kevorkian knew what it was like to be in Snyder's seat as he'd supervised pilot performance himself when he was a captain on the wide-body L-1011, Lockheed's answer to the Boeing 747.

Sixty-three-year-old flight engineer Richard Campbell also had extensive experience with Snyder and 747s. He'd been a 747 captain until he turned sixty, the FAA's mandatory retirement age for pilots. After thirty years with TWA and a stint in the air force piloting the F-102 Interceptor, it was hard for Campbell to give up flying, so he began working as a fight engineer. At the airline, folks like Campbell are affectionately called "ropes," retired old pilot engineers.

Though Oliver Krick had been flying for TWA for only a few months, he was a member of the TWA family. His father, Ron Krick, was a DC-9 pilot for the airline. Oliver's brother, Chris, had also expressed an interest in flying, and someday the three hoped to fly together.

Days before the flight, when Krick learned that he'd be on a trip with Snyder, he asked his father if he should be worried. The Kricks had gone golfing to celebrate Oliver's twenty-fifth birthday, and were waiting out a downpour in the car, trying to decide whether to go home.

How am I going to get along with him? Ollie asked.

Ron Krick chuckled at the question from his fun-loving son and re-called his own experience.

Look, I flew with Snyder on my first international flight to London. It was an eight-hour flight, but buddy, it felt like two. He was constantly asking me questions and making me look up the answers in the book. It wasn't the kind of stuff I learned in ground school, either, Krick continued, so my advice to you is, don't take offense. Listen up, and you'll learn a lot.

Ollie Krick depended on his dad's experience as a pilot from the time when, barely six years old and seated in his father's lap, he took the controls of the small prop plane Ron Krick used to give flying lessons. Nineteen years later as they sat in the steamy car waiting out a summer storm, Oliver Krick felt reassured by his father once again.

Had he known about that conversation, Captain Kevorkian would have felt some envy. When his son turned twelve, Ralph Kevorkian encouraged him to fly by paying for lessons. When Doug Kevorkian turned sixteen and his dad told him he would have to start paying his own way, Doug opted out and saved his money for a car.

Kevorkian was not surprised that his son had chosen wheels over wings, but he held on to his dream that his only child would one day follow him into the skies. Kevorkian could see Krick at the flight engineer's desk by simply turning his head to the right. Looking at Ollie, he might have wondered what it would be like if Doug were there instead.

Krick's job as flight engineer included making sure the fuel tanks empty uniformly. Feeding engines on one side of the plane with fuel drawn from the wing tanks on the other, an operation called cross-feeding, lets the engineer distribute the weight of the fuel evenly between the wings.

As Krick began this process with the right wing tank, he notified Kevorkian, "I'll leave that on for just a little bit." Then turning to Campbell to confirm his judgment, he asked, "Is that right?" To which Campbell replied a second later, "Yes."

Pumps in the wing tank began feeding the fuel through a large aluminum pipe running along the back wall of the plane's center tank. It surged through the line at a rate of approximately eleven gallons a minute for the five minutes and eight seconds that remained of Flight 800.

The cockpit activity was routine, almost mundane. In the passenger cabin, even nervous flyers would have been comforted by that.

The beginning of a transatlantic flight means at least three hours of nonstop work for the flight attendants before they can switch off the cabin lights, leave passengers to the movie, and sit down to their own meal. On this particular trip, they were looking at more than 200 travelers inconvenienced by an hour delay. As soon as the plane cleared 10,000 feet, Lang, Torche, and the others were on their feet, though the pilot had not turned off the "Fasten Seat Belt" sign.

From her seat by the forward galley, Judith Yee watched the cabin attendants beginning the process; filling ice buckets, preparing the beverage carts, and catching up on the latest gossip.

On the flight deck, the pilots increased air speed to 368 miles per hour. Krick radioed an "off report" to TWA's flight control office, giving the final and official push back and takeoff times and fuel load for Flight 800.

"Estimating Charles de Gaulle at zero six two eight," Krick reported. Six twenty-eight Greenwich Mean Time, early morning in Paris, around 2 A.M. by the pilots' body clocks. They'd all be ready for bed when they arrived.

Air traffic controllers notified the crew of a Beech 1900, a small regional airplane, flying south of them. The pilots searched the sky off the right side of the jumbo jet with a casual interest. The cockpit was quiet.

FAA rules forbid extraneous cockpit conversation from the time a plane pushes back from the terminal at the airport until it clears an altitude of 10,000 feet. The rule is intended to reduce distractions during a critical time. Flight crews have been known to engage in racy banter, but there was not a hint of questionable conversation on the flight deck of TWA 800. Between routine radio transmissions and discussions among the crew about the performance of their tasks, there were long silences as the men concentrated on their jobs.

The disaster was less than two minutes away when Kevorkian broke the silence. A quick spike on one of four engine gauges caught his attention.

"Look at that crazy fuel flow indicator there on number four," Kevorkian said out loud. He quickly scanned the other engine performance monitors for any indication that something was amiss, but could see none and sensed by the steadiness of the engines that fuel was flowing normally despite the reading on the gauge. Eight seconds later the vertical indicator tape made another hop.

"See that?"

There was no response from the other men on the flight deck.

The flight crew was probably unaware that the fuel flow gauge had been a recurring problem on N93119. There had been nine instances of incorrect readings during the previous two years. In some cases, trips to the hangar resulted in repairs; other times, no cause could be found for the faulty readings. Crash investigators would find this history significant, noting that intermittent electrical malfunctions can be symptomatic of serious wiring problems.

Pilots familiar with the aircraft and the crew flying it on this night believe that the event was considered nothing more than a minor in-flight glitch, one of many that could be expected on a machine as complicated as the Boeing 747. The jumbo jet is made of six million parts, and experienced captains don't spend too much time thinking about every widget that goes awry.

The crew was equally dismissive about trouble the refuelers had trying to fill the plane's wing tanks before departure. An automatic shutoff device designed to prevent overfilling had activated. Maintenance records showed eight reports of similar difficulty in the four previous months. On the afternoon of July 17, the fuel technician simply overrode the shutoff by pulling the circuit breaker to the volumetric control system and proceeded to pump tens of thousands of gallons of Jet A fuel into tanks on both wings.

When the plane reached its assigned altitude of 13,000 feet, Kevorkian leveled off and reduced power to the engines.

"Somewhere in here I better trim this thing," he muttered, mostly for the benefit of the pilot supervising his performance, and he started making the subtle adjustments to the rudder and wings to keep the 747 poised in flight in perfect balance. He'd just completed it when air traffic control gave clearance for another climb, this time to 15,000 feet.

"Climb thrust," Kevorkian directed Krick. There was no response. Seconds later he called again to the flight engineer to adjust the throttles to climb thrust.

"Ollie," Kevorkian called again, this time getting the young engineer's attention.

"Huh?"

"Climb thrust, climb to one five thousand," Kevorkian repeated.

Krick pivoted his seat frontward so that he could reach up to the console between the two pilots and pushed the four throttle levers forward.

"Power's set," he notified the pilots, maneuvering his seat back into position facing the engineer's panel on the right-hand side of the cockpit.

The whirring noise of the electric seat moving along its track was the last discernible sound picked up by the microphones in the cockpit.

Susan Hill, her seatmate Matthew Alexander, Daniel Cremades, Judith Yee, and Patricia Loo sat about one third of the way back in the passenger cabin, in seats bolted to a track on the roof of the plane's 12,890-gallon center fuel tank. Though they could not feel it, the living room–sized tank beneath their seats was hot.

The center fuel tank was designed as an extended range fuel tank, but it also absorbed the heat being generated by equipment below it, three enormous air handling units that turn blistering 450-degree air from the engines into climate-controlled air for the pressurized areas of the plane.

On July 17, these units were like stovetop burners under a saucepan, baking the remnants of the kerosene inside the tank into a crisp fog; an already volatile mix of fuel vapor and air was becoming more easily combustible with each degree increase in temperature. Two minutes after Krick turned the cross-feed switch, thirteen minutes after Kevorkian took the 747 into the skies, thirty seconds after increasing thrust for another ascent, this brew in the tank exploded.

The immediate damage was to the two forward-most walls of the fuel tank. In a flash, a crucial structural beam for the plane cracked in two under a force estimated at 100 tons of pressure. It took less than seven seconds for the plane's entire forward support structure to disintegrate.

All fight systems were severed and the cockpit decapitated from the rest of the plane. TWA Flight 800 fell into the Atlantic in a shower of light and a cloud of mystery.

Flying miles above the earth in unsurvivably thin air, air travelers take it for granted that they will breathe as normally on an airplane as they would on the ground. Pressurization technology that keeps the cabin environment oxygen-rich has been around since the late 1930s.

At 13,700 feet, the altitude at which TWA Flight 800 exploded, the outside air had half as much oxygen as the air inside the cabin. It would have been difficult for passengers to breathe. The quick drop in pressure would have caused pain in their ears. The noise of the destruction, strong enough to cause plates to rattle on shelves twelve miles away, could puncture eardrums and was very likely deafening. The outside air temperature, estimated at 35 degrees Fahrenheit, quickly chilled the cabin.

Those remaining conscious through the explosion would have experienced a numbing of all senses and a steep increase in heart rate from fear-induced adrenaline poisoning. That would be just the beginning of the hellish last seconds of their lives.

There was a racing wind as the thick cabin air rushed to escape through the ruptures in the fuselage. Until the explosion, air pressure inside the plane had been building with increasing force as the plane climbed, pressing up against every inch of the passenger cabin. Now it was unleashed like air bursting free from a punctured balloon.

Below the passengers' seats, tremendous pressure from the explosion in the tank lifted the floor in the area between the wings, slightly forward of the halfway point in the plane. Seconds later, a ten-foot hole appeared near the feet of Deborah and Doug Dickey, chaperones for the high school students in the Montoursville French Club. Passengers in this area were sucked through an opening in the bottom of the plane. Dropping from two and a half miles in the sky, they smashed into the ocean at 120 miles per hour.

It wasn't just passengers falling. Overhead bins were popping open, contents ricocheting about. Even fixed interior components like the forward lavatory were ripped loose and pulled through the growing chasm in the floor. Chunks of the belly of the plane added to the heavy mist of debris.

At the same time, spidery fissures had raced up the walls at more than a mile a second, shredding ninety feet of fuselage into jigsaw puzzle-like pieces faster than the human eye could see it.

Monica Omiccioli was in a window seat, leaning against her husband when the tank exploded directly beneath them. In the subsequent breakup of the plane, this position somehow protected her from being torn apart and burned. Her new husband took the brunt of the assault. Susan Hill was torn to pieces. Daniel Cremades's face was damaged and his bones fractured. Only Judith Yee's bones were recovered, but her dog, Max, was not found. Mere fragments were all that remained of Matthew Alexander. Those who died from this severe and immediate trauma were the lucky ones.

With the area directly between the wings pulverized, the maelstrom was filled with pieces of the crumbling jumbo jet and the people onboard. High-velocity debris slammed into passengers. The medical examiner found pieces of the plane embedded in nearly all the victims. An upper-deck first-class passenger had been impaled through the abdomen by the components from an armrest. His body had been practically severed by it.

The destruction was so quick that much had happened before the event even registered with the cockpit crew. First there was the enormous blast of the center fuel tank rupturing toward them, followed so closely by the loss of electricity in the cockpit and the fog of decompression that it all seemed simultaneous.

Tearing metal; cables stretching, snapping, and whistling through the cabin; explosive thuds and shattering glass; screaming passengers—the dense cacophony was indecipherable. The crew was deafened by the noise and flying blind.

For moments, only a canopy of fuselage connected the cockpit and the first-class section to the rest of the jet. A giant crescent of lower fuselage was gone, leaving nothing to support the 18,000-pound nose. When it snapped off, it was propelled forward like a bullet until it lost momentum and began to arch down, picking up speed again as it headed toward the ocean.

Other airline pilots believe Captains Snyder and Kevorkian would have spent some of the last fifty seconds of their lives trying to fly the plane, instinct defying logic. Unaware of whether anyone could hear him, Snyder continued to talk into the microphone, documenting the chaos on the flight deck and his impressions of what was happening to the plane. Both Snyder and Kevorkian tried depressing the rudder pedals and pulling back on the control yokes in front of them, seeking a response from the plane, but it only continued its tumble through the air.

Braced in this way against the fall, four men with a cumulative century of piloting experience became passengers on their final flight.

The cockpit crew died of traumatic injuries when they hit the surface of the Atlantic. The pressure of impact on the right underside of the nose compressed it accordionlke all the way to the cockpit window line. Snyder, who very likely was not secured by all points of the shoulder, hip, and crotch belts of his safety harness, was blasted free of the plane.

Krick and Kevorkian went down with the ship, submerging slowly 120 feet to the smooth and sandy floor of the ocean. When they were found by Navy divers weeks later, Captain Kevorkian and Campbell were still strapped into their seats. Krick's brother Chris was told Oliver was intricately entangled in the aircraft wiring from the electronics bay under the floor of the flight deck.

"Embraced by his airplane," is how Krick's mother, Margret, thinks of it.

Once the front of the aircraft was gone, the center of gravity shifted, tilting the tail down. The engine fans, presumably still turning, drove the remainder of the 747 into a brief climb. This ascent was reversed when the outer ends of both wings snapped off.

As the plane began to fall, 24,000 gallons of fuel spun from the rupturing wing tanks, atomized, highly explosive kerosene clouds that quickly ignited, creating a huge fireball that was seen for miles. The right wing and a sizable piece of fuselage skin above it were burning when the wing folded up and snapped off. The left wing soon followed.

During all this, some passengers were shaken free of the plane entirely. Others were tossed out still strapped in seats that had been ripped off the mounting tracks. The pilots and passengers who were jettisoned with the front third of the aircraft had no way of knowing the plane had been severed, but the rear passenger cabin was still largely intact. Those passengers who were still conscious could see twilight where the front of the plane should have been and understood their situation with terrifying certainty.

These passengers were whipsawed back in their seats with the plane's ascent, then forced forward as it lost momentum and began to drop. All the while they were heaved from side to side with the uncoordinated tumbling of the jet in freefall.

The jumbo jet was generating enormous tongues of fire that were dropping from the sky along with eighteen four-foot tires and four two-ton engines. It continued to shed pieces and crumble from the gaping hole where the wing had been. A confetti of aluminum curlicues singed paths through the mild evening air.

The farther the tail section of the plane fell, the faster it went, so that when it hit the unforgiving surface of the Atlantic, it was moving about 400 miles per hour.

Through the narrow wraparound windows of the Eastwinds Airlines Boeing 737, Captain David McClaine watched the destruction of Flight 800 with his heart pounding.

Thirty seconds earlier, he estimated the plane headed directly toward him was a wide-body, probably a 747 or 767 starting a transatlantic flight. It was easy to see because its bright landing lights were still illuminated, even though the plane was probably above 10,000 feet, the altitude at which pilots usually turn out these lights. McClaine guessed the plane, ten miles in front of him, was TWA Flight 800, which he had just heard on the radio being cleared to ascend to 15,000 feet, still 1,000 feet below where he was flying.

Vinny, does that light look a little different to you, a little yellow? he asked his first officer.

Vincent Fuschetti looked up from the instrument panel and squinted into the sun, which was still shining off to his right.

Yeah, maybe. He shrugged. Fuschetti, who was piloting the plane, turned his attention back to adjusting the 737's course out of the path of Flight 800.

McClaine, however, continued to watch the plane, deciding, like a highway driver at night, to flash his own landing lights at Flight 800, as a reminder to the crew that their lights were still on.

His hand froze at the toggle switch. The 747 had exploded. He screamed at Fuschetti, "My God, Vinny, what the hell was that?"

The plane had become a blossom of flames, hovering briefly and then plunging, leaving dense black and orange trails above it. They watched the wings snap off, creating more flaming pillars as the wreckage spun toward the darkening sea.

McClaine's hand was trembling. He thumbed the button on the control yoke, cueing his radio mike to call to air traffic control using his airline designation Stinger Bee and his flight number 507.

"We just saw an explosion out here, Stinger Bee 507," the words tumbled out of him.

"Stinger Bee 507, I'm sorry I missed it . . . did you say something else?"

The voice of the controller sounded concerned.

"Ah, we just saw an explosion up ahead of us here, somewhere about sixteen thousand feet or something like that. It just went down"—McClaine paused—"into the water."

He could not take his eyes off the billowing trails of black smoke still suspended in the twilight. He was trying to understand what he'd seen. Are we seeing this? he asked Fuschetti. Then, why are we seeing this?

There had to be three hundred people on that plane and we saw them die! McClaine continued, though his quick guess of the passenger load was significantly less than what a Europe-bound jumbo would normally be carrying in the heart of summer.

McClaine and Fuschetti could hear the controller at the long-range control center in Boston trying to raise TWA 800 on the radio. For nearly three minutes, the controller pleaded for a response. Finally, one came from McClaine.

"I think that was him."

"I think so," the controller agreed.

McClaine's voice had calmed somewhat.

"God bless him."

At least nineteen passengers survived the explosions and the torrential hail of objects loosened by the deterioration of the aircraft. Autopsy reports showed both smoke and water in the lungs of some people, indicating that they lived through the fall, breathing the smoke-filled air, and even briefly survived the plunge into the Atlantic.

For a long time after the last of the wreckage had settled, 800 pounds of glitter that had been in the plane's cargo hold rained softly over the crash site, leaving the debris and the floating victims coated in a glistening veil.

About the Editor

Lamar Underwood is a former editor-in-chief of *Sports Afield* and *Outdoor Life* and is presently editorial director of the Outdoor Magazine Group of Harris Publications in New York.

Lamar edited *The Bass Almanac*, published by Nick Lyons and Doubleday in 1978, and is the author of the novel *On Dangerous Ground*, published by Doubleday in 1989 and later in paperback by Berkley. Lamar's novel draws considerably on his experiences as a magazine editor in New York, and his outdoor experiences in Alaska, where he was graduated from Fairbanks High School in 1954, when Alaska was still a territory. Born in Statesboro, Georgia, son of an Army officer who was stationed in Alaska during the Korean War, Lamar has maintained his affection for the Alaska outdoors, visiting there every chance he gets.

Lamar has edited several books for Amwell Press and twelve published by The Lyons Press. They were *The Quotable Soldier*, *The Greatest Hunting Stories Ever Told*, *The Greatest Fishing Stories Ever Told*, *Man-Eaters*, *The Greatest War Stories Ever Told*, *The Greatest Survival Stories Ever Told*, *Bowhunting Tactics of the Pros*, *Whitetail Tactics of the Pros*, the fly-fishing anthology *Into the Backing*, *The Greatest Adventure Stories Ever Told*, and *The Greatest Flying Stories Ever Told*.

Lamar is currently at work on four new books in the "Quotable" series. *The Quotable Army* and *The Quotable Navy* will be published in spring, 2003, to be followed by *The Quotable Marines* and *The Quotable Air Force* in the fall.

Permissions Acknowledgments